"'R.C. Sproul,' someone said to me in the 1970s, 'is the finest communicator in the Reformed world.' Now, four decades later, his skills honed by long practice, his understanding deepened by years of prayer, meditation, and testing (as Martin Luther counseled), R.C. shares the fruit of what became perhaps his greatest love: feeding and nourishing his own congregation at St. Andrew's from the Word of God and building them up in faith and fellowship and in Christian living and serving. Dr. Sproul's expositional commentaries have all R.C.'s hallmarks: clarity and liveliness, humor and pathos, always expressed in application to the mind, will, and affections. R.C.'s ability to focus on 'the big picture,' his genius of never saying too much, leaving his hearers satisfied yet wanting more, never making the Word dull, are all present in these expositions. They are his gift to the wider church. May they nourish God's people well and serve as models of the kind of ministry for which we continue to hunger."

—Dr. Sinclair B. Ferguson
Teaching Fellow
Ligonier Ministries

"Dr. R.C. Sproul, well known as a master theologian and extraordinary communicator, showed that he was a powerful, insightful, helpful expository preacher. This collection of sermons is of great value for churches and Christians everywhere."

—Dr. W. Robert Godfrey
President emeritus and professor of church history emeritus
Westminster Seminary California, Escondido, California

"I tell my students again and again, 'You need to buy good commentaries and do so with some discernment.' Among them there must be preacher's commentaries, for not all commentaries are the same. Some may tell you what the text means but provide little help in answering the question, 'How do I preach this text?' Dr. R.C. Sproul was a legend in our time. His preaching held us in awe for half a century, and these pages represent the fruit of his exposition at the very peak of his abilities and insights. Dr. Sproul's expositional commentary series represents Reformed theology on fire, delivered from a pastor's heart in a vibrant congregation. Essential reading."

—Dr. Derek W.H. Thomas
Senior minister
First Presbyterian Church, Columbia, South Carolina

"Dr. R.C. Sproul was the premier theologian of our day, an extraordinary instrument in the hand of the Lord. Possessed with penetrating insight into the text of Scripture, Dr. Sproul was a gifted expositor and world-class teacher, endowed with a strategic grasp and command of the inspired Word. When he stepped into the pulpit of St. Andrew's and committed himself to the weekly discipline of biblical exposition, this noted preacher demonstrated a rare ability to explicate and apply God's Word. I wholeheartedly recommend Dr. Sproul's expositional commentaries to all who long to know the truth better and experience it more deeply in a life-changing fashion. Here is an indispensable tool for digging deeper into God's Word. This is a must-read for every Christian."

—Dr. Steven J. Lawson
Founder and president
OnePassion Ministries, Dallas

"How exciting! Thousands of us have long been indebted to Dr. R.C. Sproul the teacher, and now, through Dr. Sproul's expositional commentaries, we are indebted to Sproul the preacher, whose sermons are thoroughly biblical, soundly doctrinal, warmly practical, and wonderfully readable. Sproul masterfully presents us with the 'big picture' of each pericope in a dignified yet conversational style that accentuates the glory of God and meets the real needs of sinful people like us. This series of volumes is an absolute must for every Reformed preacher and church member who yearns to grow in the grace and knowledge of Christ Jesus. I predict that Sproul's pulpit ministry in written form will do for Christians in the twenty-first century what Martyn Lloyd-Jones' sermonic commentaries did for us last century. Tolle lege, and buy these volumes for your friends."

—Dr. Joel R. Beeke
President and professor of systematic theology and homiletics
Puritan Reformed Theological Seminary, Grand Rapids, Michigan

MARK

AN EXPOSITIONAL COMMENTARY

MARK

AN EXPOSITIONAL COMMENTARY

R.C. SPROUL

 LigonierMinistries

Mark: An Expositional Commentary
© 2011 by R.C. Sproul

Published by Ligonier Ministries
421 Ligonier Court, Sanford, FL 32771
Ligonier.org

Printed in China
RR Donnelley
0000522
First edition, eleventh printing

ISBN 978-1-64289-179-9 (Hardcover)
ISBN 978-1-64289-180-5 (ePub)
ISBN 978-1-64289-181-2 (Kindle)

Cover design: Ligonier Creative
Interior typeset: Katherine Lloyd, The DESK

Unless otherwise noted, all Scripture taken from the New King James Version®. Copyright © 1982 by Thomas Nelson. Used by permission. All rights reserved.

Scripture quotations marked ESV are from the ESV® Bible (The Holy Bible, English Standard Version®), copyright © 2001 by Crossway, a publishing ministry of Good News Publishers. Used by permission. All rights reserved.

All emphases in Scripture quotations have been added by the author.

The Library of Congress has cataloged the Reformation Trust edition as follows:

Names: Sproul, R.C. (Robert Charles), 1939-2017, author.
Title: Mark : an expositional commentary / R.C. Sproul.
Description: Orlando : Reformation Trust, 2019. | Originally published: Orlando, Fla. : Reformation Trust Pub., c2011.
Identifiers: LCCN 2019000111 (print) | LCCN 2019022268 (ebook) | ISBN 9781642891799 (hardcover)
Subjects: LCSH: Bible. Mark--Commentaries. | Bible. Mark--Sermons.
Classification: LCC BS2585.53 .S67 2019 (print) | LCC BS2585.53 (ebook) | DDC 226.3/077--dc23
LC record available at https://lccn.loc.gov/2019000111
LC ebook record available at https://lccn.loc.gov/2019022268

For Guy and Penny Rizzo,
who love the Word of God

CONTENTS

SERIES PREFACE

When God called me into full-time Christian ministry, He called me to the academy. I was trained and ordained to a ministry of teaching, and the majority of my adult life has been devoted to preparing young men for the Christian ministry and to trying to bridge the gap between seminary and Sunday school through various means under the aegis of Ligonier Ministries.

Then, in 1997, God did something I never anticipated: He placed me in the position of preaching weekly as a leader of a congregation of His people—St. Andrew's in Sanford, Florida. Over the past twelve years, as I have opened the Word of God on a weekly basis for these dear saints, I have come to love the task of the local minister. Though my role as a teacher continues, I am eternally grateful to God that He saw fit to place me in this new ministry, the ministry of a preacher.

Very early in my tenure with St. Andrew's, I determined that I should adopt the ancient Christian practice of *lectio continua*, "continuous expositions," in my preaching. This method of preaching verse-by-verse through books of the Bible (rather than choosing a new topic each week) has been attested throughout church history as the one approach that ensures believers hear the full counsel of God. Therefore, I began preaching lengthy series of messages at St. Andrew's, eventually working my way through several biblical books in a practice that continues to the present day.

Previously, I had taught through books of the Bible in various settings, including Sunday school classes, Bible studies, and audio and video teaching series for Ligonier Ministries. But now I found myself appealing not so much to the minds of my hearers but to both their minds and their hearts. I knew that I was responsible as a preacher to clearly explain God's Word *and* to show how we ought to live in light of it. I sought to fulfill both tasks as I ascended the St. Andrew's pulpit each week.

What you hold in your hand, then, is a written record of my preaching labors amidst my beloved Sanford congregation. The dear saints who sit under my preaching encouraged me to give my sermons a broader hearing. To that end, the chapters that follow were adapted from a sermon series I preached at St. Andrew's.

Please be aware that this book is part of a broader series of books containing adaptations of my St. Andrew's sermons. This book, like all the others in the series, will *not* give you the fullest possible insight into each and every verse in this biblical book. Though I sought to at least touch on each verse, I focused on the key themes and ideas that comprised the "big picture" of each passage I covered. Therefore, I urge you to use this book as an overview and introduction.

I pray that you will be as blessed in reading this material as I was in preaching it.

—R.C. Sproul
Lake Mary, Florida
April 2009

PREFACE

The gospel of Mark, I believe, is both overlooked and underappreciated. Tucked away between the longer and more detailed Synoptic Gospels of Matthew and Luke, and lacking the rhetorical flair of John's account, Mark is rarely cited first when preachers and theologians look to bolster their arguments from the accounts of Jesus' life and ministry. If asked, few of us could readily say what makes Mark unique among the gospel accounts.

We need to get to know this little book. Above all, it was inspired by the Holy Spirit and included in the canon of Scripture for our edification. Moreover, it was composed for an audience of Gentiles, probably in the city of Rome itself, meaning it is highly relevant for Christians who lack a Jewish background today. Also, it is valuable for its succinct quality; the book moves quickly and emphasizes things that happened to Jesus in His ministry years.

Perhaps most important, however, Mark takes pains to show that Jesus was the Christ and the Son of God in the flesh. He opens by saying, "The beginning of the gospel of Jesus Christ, the Son of God" (1:1), and everything in the book leads up to Peter's great confession, "You are the Christ" (8:29). In a day and age when the world insists Jesus was at best a great teacher, we desperately need to see and be reminded of these truths. Mark actually seems to downplay Jesus' teaching in order to focus on the power and authority with which He carried out His ministry, demonstrating again and again that He was like no other man. This is a perspective we dare not neglect.

It is my prayer that as you read this collection of thoughts on Mark, your eyes will be opened to the identity of Jesus, and your faith in Him as the Christ and the Son of God will be strengthened.

1

THE COMING
OF THE CHRIST

Mark 1:1–8

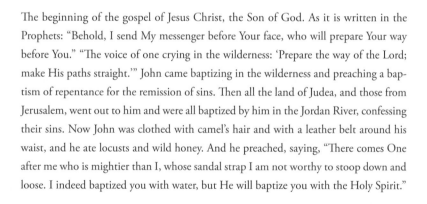

The beginning of the gospel of Jesus Christ, the Son of God. As it is written in the Prophets: "Behold, I send My messenger before Your face, who will prepare Your way before You." "The voice of one crying in the wilderness: 'Prepare the way of the Lord; make His paths straight.'" John came baptizing in the wilderness and preaching a baptism of repentance for the remission of sins. Then all the land of Judea, and those from Jerusalem, went out to him and were all baptized by him in the Jordan River, confessing their sins. Now John was clothed with camel's hair and with a leather belt around his waist, and he ate locusts and wild honey. And he preached, saying, "There comes One after me who is mightier than I, whose sandal strap I am not worthy to stoop down and loose. I indeed baptized you with water, but He will baptize you with the Holy Spirit."

Imagine for a moment that you are a Christian in first-century Rome. You are assembled with your congregation on the Lord's Day, but not in a church. The persecutions of the Emperor Nero are raging, and if the authorities discover that you are a believer, you will be arrested and subjected to the death penalty. So you and your fellow believers are gathered underneath the city in the catacombs, surrounded by skeletons and cadavers.

When Nero came to power, he reigned in calmness and with some ability for five years. However, in AD 59, he changed and began to engage in radically cruel and immoral actions. Then, in the year 64, a great fire devastated Rome. It is difficult for us to understand the extent of the destruction that took place as a result of that fire. When it broke out, it spread to seven wards of the city and raged for seven days. No sooner did it appear to be brought under control than it broke out again. Ultimately, it destroyed nearly 80 percent of the city. The devastation that Hurricane Katrina wrought on New Orleans is not worthy to be compared with the damage the fire caused in Rome.

When things like this happen, everyone looks for someone to blame. Many suspected Nero himself had set the fire. To deflect suspicion, Nero chose to blame it on Christians. Word swept through the city that the destruction had been caused by those antisocial, antireligious fanatics who bore the name of Jesus Christ. So Nero sent his military out to round up every Christian he could find. When he arrested the Christians, he clothed them in the skins of wild animals; then, in a public display of cruelty, he let feral dogs loose against them. Thinking they were assaulting wild animals, the dogs attacked the Christians garbed in skins and killed them. Other Christians Nero dipped in pitch or tar and ignited their bodies, using them to illuminate his private gardens. If that was not enough, other Christians were brought into the Colosseum and fed to the lions for entertainment.

In all probability, it was around the year 65, in the immediate aftermath of the great fire, that the first written record of the life and ministry of Jesus Christ appeared—the gospel according to Mark. It is basically a settled matter of historical investigation that the initial audience for this gospel was the Christians suffering persecution in Rome. This gospel reminded them of their salvation in Christ, taught them about the suffering that Jesus Himself experienced, and even revealed that Jesus was driven into the wilderness and was under the threat of wild beasts.

So, imagine yourself in the catacombs, worshiping with a little band of believers. On this Lord's Day, however, the pastor of your congregation comes with a new document. It is the newly written gospel of Mark. You are about to hear the Word of God in the first reading of this gospel.

Authorship and Themes

Though he is not named in the text itself, the author of this gospel is without question John Mark, who was a companion of Paul with Barnabas early in their missionary journeys. Mark was fired by the Apostle Paul and then went on with Barnabas, as Paul went with Silas (Acts 13:5, 13; 15:36–41). Later, Mark was reconciled to Paul and became a valuable comrade to him in the later days of Paul's apostolic ministry (2 Tim. 4:11). However, men of great importance in the second-century church, such as Papias, Eusebius, and Irenaeus, give a consistent testimony that the work on this gospel was directed largely by the Apostle Peter, for whom Mark served as a secretary. There is some doubt as to whether the gospel was written before or after Peter's death, but it is virtually certain that Peter gave his stamp of approval to the content.

One of the most marked characteristics of Mark's gospel is its brevity, the breathtaking pace with which it moves from beginning to end. For instance, there are no details about the birth of Jesus (we find those in Matthew and Luke). Thus, the gospel of Mark is not a biography. It does not give us a chronological account about Jesus, such as we find in Matthew's gospel. Rather, it might be called a "witness document," something like a tract that someone would hand out to give a summary of the significant work of Jesus.

One of the most important Greek words in the gospel of Mark is *euthus*, which is translated "immediately" or "straightway." It is used forty-two times in Mark's gospel and only twelve times in the rest of the New Testament. My best friend in college and seminary grew up on the mission field in Ethiopia, and he later ministered to people deep in the jungle there. Their principal transportation was a powerboat that was christened *Euthus*. I asked him why they called the boat *Euthus*. He explained: "My Dad was familiar with the Greek New Testament, and he was reading the gospel of Mark one day in the Greek where it said, '*Euthus* the boat,' or, 'Straightway the boat left the shores of Galilee.' There it was, *euthus* the boat, so I named my boat *Euthus*." *Euthus* is certainly a good word to describe Mark's gospel, for he dives right into his account and moves along swiftly. It seems Mark is in a hurry to give us the major facts about Jesus and His life and ministry.

The facts Mark gives us are included to demonstrate two things: Jesus is the promised Messiah and the Son of God. Mark makes this affirmation at the beginning of his work, saying, **The beginning of the gospel of Jesus Christ, the Son of God** (v. 1). That is the thematic statement for the entire gospel.

By organizing his material as he did and writing in this style, Mark introduced a new literary genre to the ancient world, the genre that came to be known as "the gospel." We have the gospel of Mark, the gospel of Matthew, the gospel of Luke, and the gospel of John, and there are other "gospels" that are not canonical, such as the gospel of Peter. The Greek New Testament does not state the title as, for instance, "the gospel of John." It simply says, *kata Iohannan*, which means "according to John." Then we have "according to Matthew," "according to Mark," and "according to Luke." We have understood this to mean "*the gospel* according to Matthew," "*the gospel* according to Mark," and so on. The word *gospel,* or "good news," is added because this literary genre is designed to focus attention on the person and work of Christ. Thus, Mark writes, "The beginning of the gospel [the good news] of Jesus Christ."

Notice that Mark does not simply say he is presenting "the gospel of *Jesus.*" This book drives us relentlessly to the Caesarea Philippi confession (8:27–30), when Jesus said to His disciples, "Who do men say that I am?" They replied, "John the Baptist; but some say, Elijah; and others, one of the prophets." Jesus then said, "But who do you say that I am?" At that point, Peter, the champion of Mark, gave the great confession: "You are the Christ." Mark foreshadows this great confession when he affirms that this is the gospel of Jesus *Christ,* which means it is the good news of Jesus, the Messiah, who is also the Son of God.

The Messiah's Forerunner

Mark then takes us quickly to the Old Testament, which was such an important part of the preaching of the early church. Paul does that constantly when he affirms the character of Jesus and teaches that He was the One of whom the Old Testament authors wrote as the coming Messiah. In the same way, Mark immediately locates the appearance of Jesus in the context of the promised Messiah of the Old Testament by saying, **As it is written in the Prophets** (v. 2a).

He then gives us a summary of three distinct Old Testament texts. One comes from Exodus, one from Malachi, and one from Isaiah. Mark merges them together and writes: **"Behold, I send My messenger before Your face, who will prepare Your way before You. The voice of one crying in the wilderness: Prepare the way of the LORD; make His paths straight"** (vv. 2b–3). These prophecies all foretold that before the Messiah would come, God would send a herald, and that herald's responsibility would be to prepare the way for the coming Messiah. The herald would not be the Messiah, but he would be sent by God to announce the coming of the Messiah.

When John the Baptist appeared, there was much discussion about his identity. Many believed he was Elijah come again. Even today, whenever Jews gather for the Passover Seder, there is an empty chair at the table. If you are a guest in the home when they are celebrating the Passover, you might ask: "Did someone who was expected not show up? Why do you have the empty chair?" They will explain to you that the empty chair is there for Elijah. They remember the last prophecy at the close of the Old Testament canon, on the last page of the book of Malachi—the promise that before the Messiah would come, God would bring Elijah back (Mal. 4:5). Elijah, who was caught up into heaven, did not die. God said he would come once more before the Messiah would appear. The Jews are still waiting for him.

So, when John the Baptist appeared on the scene of Israel, when he came out of the desert and began to preach after hundreds of years of silence since the last Old Testament prophet, his appearance stirred more national interest than Jesus' initial appearance. In fact, in some of the literature of the early first century, more attention is given to John the Baptist than is given to Jesus. The people had thought God was finished with prophets, but suddenly a prophet emerged out of the wilderness.

The first question the authorities asked John was, "Who are you? . . . Are you Elijah?" He answered, "I am not" (John 1:19–21). Yet when they asked Jesus who John was, Jesus said he *was* Elijah (Matt. 17:12–13). How do we reconcile these statements? If we look at the whole picture, that conundrum is explained. We are told that John came in the spirit and the power of Elijah (Luke 1:17), and Jesus affirmed that the ministry of Elijah was fulfilled in the work of John the Baptist. It was not that Elijah himself came back, so John was speaking the truth by saying, "No, I am not Elijah." However, Jesus explained that John ministered in the spirit and power of Elijah.

Notice that one of the prophecies Mark quotes refers to "the wilderness." In the Old Testament, the traditional meeting place between God and His prophets was always the wilderness. Moses saw the burning bush in the Midianite wilderness. God called a nation to Himself when He brought them out of Egypt into the wilderness. Elijah was ministered to by ravens in the wilderness. That motif goes through the Old Testament, and now Mark begins his New Testament gospel with this strange figure coming out of the desert, out of the wilderness, looking for all the world like Elijah.

The other gospels give us much more information about John the Baptist. For instance, Luke tells us the story of the conception of John the Baptist and of the announcement of the angel Gabriel to John the Baptist's father, Zacharias. John gives great detail to explain John the Baptist's mission. But Mark goes right to the heart of the matter. He links the Old Testament promise of the forerunner, who was coming to make the path straight for the Messiah, to John the Baptist.

The Message John Proclaimed

Mark writes: **John came baptizing in the wilderness and preaching a baptism of repentance for the remission of sins. Then all the land of Judea, and those from Jerusalem, went out to him and were all baptized by him in the Jordan River, confessing their sins** (vv. 4–5). When John appeared, he came out of the wilderness and addressed the people. Soon, all Judea flocked around him. He was an instant celebrity.

What did John proclaim? He called the people to get ready for the Messiah's coming. He told them they needed to be cleansed from their sins. In other words, they needed to be baptized.

When John began baptizing Israelites, the Pharisees, the conservative religious leaders, objected. They declared that the Israelites, the children of Abraham, the chosen people of God, had no need for cleansing. Baptism was for Gentiles, the unclean ones. That sparked a major controversy. It also set the stage for John's baptism of Jesus, which we will consider in the next chapter.

Mark then adds a brief description of John: **Now John was clothed with camel's hair and with a leather belt around his waist, and he ate locusts and wild honey** (v. 6). In his rough clothing and with his somewhat wild appearance, John met the classic image of the prophet.

Finally, Mark relates one of the key truths John taught: **And he preached, saying, "There comes One after me who is mightier than I, whose sandal strap I am not worthy to stoop down and loose. I indeed baptized you with water, but He will baptize you with the Holy Spirit"** (vv. 7–8). In Israel at that time, everyone wore sandals, even aristocrats, and their feet got filthy on the dusty roads. However, it was beneath the dignity of the aristocrats to take off their own sandals and thus get their hands dirty, so they had their slaves do it. But John said he was not even worthy to untie the shoes of the One who was coming after him. He was saying, basically: "Do not get excited about me. Get excited about the One I'm pointing you to, the One who is the Messiah, the One who is the Son of God. Yes, I'm baptizing you with water, but the One who comes after me will baptize you with the Holy Spirit of power. Your Messiah is coming."

Matthew quotes John as saying, "Even now the ax is laid to the root of the trees" (3:10a). In other words, John was saying the Messiah was not just coming sometime in the future, but He was right around the corner. His coming was about to happen. The kingdom was going to break through very shortly.

As those huddled in the catacombs heard anew the message of the preparation for the Messiah, they rejoiced in their certain knowledge that the Messiah had come. Because of their faith in Him, they were willing to gather in secret and, if necessary, to be eaten by dogs, burned as torches in the gardens of Nero, or thrown to the lions. How they loved to hear the story of the coming of the Messiah, the Son of God.

2

EMPOWERMENT
AND TESTING

Mark 1:9–13

It came to pass in those days that Jesus came from Nazareth of Galilee, and was baptized by John in the Jordan. And immediately, coming up from the water, He saw the heavens parting and the Spirit descending upon Him like a dove. Then a voice came from heaven, "You are My beloved Son, in whom I am well pleased." Immediately the Spirit drove Him into the wilderness. And He was there in the wilderness forty days, tempted by Satan, and was with the wild beasts; and the angels ministered to Him.

Picture yourself outside the city of Jerusalem, on the banks of the Jordan River, surrounded by a huge throng of people. These people are pushing and shoving as everyone tries to get a glimpse of the man known as the Baptizer. It seems that all of Jerusalem has come out to be baptized by John. You have joined the throng and are waiting your turn to be baptized.

The previous week, you were just an observer here, and you heard John mention that there was One coming after him whose sandals he was not worthy to loose, One who would baptize with the Holy Spirit instead of water (Mark 1:7–8). Today, as you wait your turn to be baptized in the Jordan River, you see John divert his attention from his task of baptizing. He looks into the throng and fixes his eyes on one person. When John sees Him, he begins to sing the *Agnus Dei*: "Behold! The Lamb of God who takes away the sin of the world!" (John 1:29). John fulfills his vocation by pointing the multitudes to their Messiah as He approaches.

You turn and see a man you have never seen before. His name is Jesus, and He comes forward and asks John to baptize Him. John says, "I need to be baptized by You, and are You coming to me?" (Matt. 3:14). He is saying, in essence: "I cannot do what You ask. I told everyone that this is a baptism of repentance from sin, and I have announced You as the Lamb of God, the Lamb without blemish, who takes away the sin of the world. You have no need to be baptized. You should be baptizing me."

Fulfilling All Righteousness

John was certainly right in hesitating to baptize Jesus. Why did Jesus, who was sinless, want to submit to a rite symbolizing repentance from sin? I think we get a hint of the reason He did so in Matthew's account of this event. Matthew tells us that Jesus spoke somewhat cryptically when He responded to John's question, saying, "Permit it to be so now, for thus it is fitting for us to fulfill all righteousness" (3:15). It was as though He was saying to John: "Let it be. I do not have time for a theological lecture right now. Trust Me on this. It must be done to fulfill all righteousness."

Jesus' work as the Messiah, in His life as well as His death, was vicarious. It was substitutionary. He was, as Paul would say, the new Adam or the second Adam (1 Cor. 15:45). Just as the first Adam represented the whole human race, and by his sin plunged the whole of humanity into corruption and death, the new Adam also was a representative, and by His obedience He redeemed His people for eternity.

However, for Jesus to qualify as our Redeemer, it was not enough for Him simply to go to the cross and be crucified. If you ask a six-year-old child, "What did Jesus do for you?" that child, if he or she has been to Sunday school, will answer, "Jesus died on the cross for my sins." That's true, but that is only half of the matter. If all that was necessary to redeem us was for a substitute to bear the punishment that we deserve, Jesus did not have to be born to Mary. He could have descended from heaven as a man, gone straight to Golgotha, died on the cross, risen, and left again, and our sin problem would be fixed.

But if Jesus had only paid for our sins, He would have succeeded only in taking us back to square one. We would no longer be guilty, but we still would have absolutely no positive righteousness to bring before God. So, our Redeemer not only needed to die, He had to live a life of perfect obedience. The righteousness that He manifested could then be transferred to all who put their trust in

Him. Just as my sin is transferred to Him on the cross when I put my trust in Him, His righteousness is transferred to my account in the sight of God. So, when I stand before God on the judgment day, God is going to see Jesus and His righteousness, which will be my cover. That is the gospel.

John did not understand all of that, so Jesus explained, in essence, that His task as Messiah was to submit Himself to every word that proceeds from the mouth of God, to obey every dimension of the law in full, to keep every requirement that God had given to His people. So, even though He was not a sinner, He sought to submit to baptism to identify with John the Baptist and the rest of sinful humanity, in order to fulfill all righteousness.

Thus, as Mark writes, **It came to pass in those days that Jesus came from Nazareth of Galilee, and was baptized by John in the Jordan** (v. 9). The Son of God went down into the water, and John dutifully baptized Him.

A Trinitarian Moment

The baptism of Jesus was a Trinitarian event. Mark writes, **And immediately, coming up from the water, He saw the heavens parting and the Spirit descending upon Him like a dove** (v. 10). God the Father sent Jesus into the world and into the water. The Father's Son, the second person of the Trinity, united to the humanity of Jesus, submitted to baptism. Then came the third person of the Trinity, the Holy Spirit, who descended on Jesus at His baptism.

Does this mean that Jesus finally got His deity, that He was only human at birth and He became God incarnate because the Holy Spirit came on Him at His baptism at age thirty? No, Jesus had His divine nature from eternity past, He had it at the moment of His conception, and He will have it on to eternity.

What, then, was the significance of the Holy Spirit's descent on Him? The Spirit anointed the human nature of Jesus. We tend to think that Jesus performed His miracles in His divine nature. Actually, He performed them in His human nature through the power of the Holy Spirit given to Him at His baptism. It was there that God empowered Jesus to fulfill the mission He had been given.

God the Father then capped this anointing by publicly commending His Son: **"You are My beloved Son, in whom I am well pleased"** (v. 11b). The gospel records note three occasions when God the Father was heard to speak audibly. This is the first of the three. He also spoke at Jesus' transfiguration (9:2–7). John also reports that, in answer to Jesus' prayer that the Father would glorify His name, the Father said, "I have both glorified it and will glorify it again" (12:28).

It is interesting to note the first thing the Holy Spirit did after descending on Jesus. Rather than moving Him to preach or to begin healing people on the spot, **Immediately the Spirit drove Him into the wilderness** (v. 12). The Holy Spirit did not whisper in Jesus' ear and say, "I want you to go out to the Judean wilderness." The force of this passage is that Christ was compelled by the Holy Spirit, driven urgently into a desolate, God-forsaken place.

When He was baptized, Jesus' ministry was inaugurated, but before it went public, He had to undergo a time of testing. The second Adam, just like the first Adam, was put in a place of testing, where He was exposed to Satan's assaults. Mark writes, **He was there in the wilderness forty days, tempted by Satan, and was with the wild beasts** (v. 13a).

Jesus Tempted and Tried

There were great differences between the circumstances of the temptation of Adam and Eve and the temptation of Jesus. During Adam and Eve's temptation by the Serpent, they were in the midst of a lush garden where they had every imaginable food at their disposal. Their bellies were filled. Furthermore, they were enjoying intimate companionship, a woman and a man together without sin in any way marring or disfiguring their relationship, or the fellowship they had with God.

The second Adam's test took place not in a garden paradise but in a desolate wilderness, and He was absolutely alone, with no human companionship or fellowship. Not only that, His test took place in the midst of a fast, forty days with nothing to eat. He had a human nature, and that human nature was ravaged by hunger. It was only after He had sunk into this lonely, supremely weakened condition that the prince of hell came to Him.

Here is where the dissimilarity between the two temptations ends and the similarity begins. The point of both tests was exactly the same. When Satan came to Adam and Eve, he came with a question and a deception: "Has God indeed said, 'You shall not eat of every tree of the garden'? . . . You will not surely die [if you eat of the tree of the knowledge of good and evil]. For God knows that in the day you eat of it your eyes will be opened, and you will be like God, knowing good and evil" (Gen. 3:1–5). That was the temptation. Eve went for it, and Adam with her. So the issue that was presented to God's first humans was, "Are you going to believe and obey God's Word?"

In the Judean wilderness, when Satan came to Jesus in His loneliness and weakness, He did not say: "I want to see how much power You have. Turn these stones into bread." Instead, he said something much more subtle: "If you are the Son of God, command that these stones become bread" (Matt. 4:3). He was saying, in essence: "This is no place for the Son of God. I cannot understand how the Son of God could suffer such humiliation, such deprivation, such hunger, such loneliness. If You're the Son of God, You should be in a palace. Make it easy on Yourself, Jesus. If You're really the Son of God, turn these stones into bread."

What were the last words, according to Scripture, that were ringing in Jesus' ears before He came to the wilderness? They were the audible words spoken by God the Father: "You are My beloved Son" (v. 11). Satan basically said: "Are You *really* His Son? Well, if You are, turn the stones into bread."

Jesus replied, "It is written, 'Man shall not live by bread alone, but by every word that proceeds from the mouth of God'" (Matt. 4:4). Jesus said, in essence: "I'm sorry, Satan, I'm afraid you do not understand the Word of God. I know that there is no sin in having breakfast when you are hungry, but right now, I am committed to this fast, and I cannot break it to have breakfast until My Father says so."

Then the temptation continued. Satan took Jesus to the top of the temple and said, "If You are the Son of God, throw yourself down" (Matt. 4:6a). Here he was saying, "If You're really the Son of God, jump off the temple, because the Bible says He will give His angels charge over You lest You dash Your foot against a stone." Jesus told Satan the Bible does say that, but it also says that we must not put God to the test. Jesus made it clear to Satan that He did not need to jump off the temple to know that God would take care of Him.

Satan still did not give up. He took Jesus to a high mountain vista and showed Him the kingdoms of the world. He said, "All these things I will give You if You will fall down and worship me" (Matt. 4:9). It was as if the Devil was saying: "What a wasted life You have, Jesus. Why can't we be partners? I'm the prince of this world and the power of the air. All You have to do is bow down to me here in private when no one is watching. You're completely anonymous. You do not have to grovel in the dirt, just give one slight genuflection, and I will give You all of the kingdoms of this world."

I can picture the thrust of Jesus' counter to Satan's offer: "God says that we are not to have any other gods before Him, and Him only may we serve. You see, if I bow down to you, that would be an act of idolatry, and I would lose My Father's house. Satan, it profits a man nothing if he gains the whole world and loses his soul. As lonely as I am, as hungry as I am, as humiliated as I am, none of those things are worth My soul."

I do not think we understand a fraction of the stress that hell imposed on Jesus in this situation. He withstood everything that Satan had to throw at Him. In his frustration, Satan left, but let us note two things. First, he departed from Jesus "until an opportune time" (Luke 4:13). This would not be the last time in Jesus' life or ministry that Satan would throw everything he had against the

Son of God. Second, no sooner had Satan left than the angels came. As Mark writes, **the angels ministered to Him** (v. 13b).

The people who were hearing Mark's gospel being read in the catacombs realized that very soon they might find themselves in a wilderness of suffering on the floor of the Colosseum for the sake of the gospel. But they knew that if they were led in chains to the arena, they had these gospel words, that their Savior had been here and done this—and He said He would never leave them or forsake them, because He was their Champion who had resisted all things with which Satan had tempted Him and stayed the course.

3

"FOLLOW ME"

Mark 1:14–20

Now after John was put in prison, Jesus came to Galilee, preaching the gospel of the kingdom of God, and saying, "The time is fulfilled, and the kingdom of God is at hand. Repent, and believe in the gospel." And as He walked by the Sea of Galilee, He saw Simon and Andrew his brother casting a net into the sea; for they were fishermen. Then Jesus said to them, "Follow Me, and I will make you become fishers of men." They immediately left their nets and followed Him. When He had gone a little farther from there, He saw James the son of Zebedee, and John his brother, who also were in the boat mending their nets. And immediately He called them, and they left their father Zebedee in the boat with the hired servants, and went after Him.

As I was reading the newspaper one morning, I noticed an article about a course being offered at a school in Kansas. The title of the course, as the paper reported, was "Intelligent Design, Creation, and other Religious Mythologies." That course title relegated the biblical account of God and His creation to the category of myth.

Myths have a place in cultural histories. They can be very effective for communicating moral truths or spiritual insights. However, the Old Testament categorically rejects myth as the context for divine revelation. Rather, biblical religion finds its context for religious truth in real space and time. In other words, Christianity is married to history. If it is not historical in its foundational assertions, it is worth less than any myth. As Mark begins to give us the history of Jesus' public ministry, it is important for us to note that the context for it is not mythological but historical.

Scholars have pointed out that the gospel record comes to us clothed not in the forms of ordinary history but in a particular form that scholars call redemptive history. Because it is redemptive history, some have claimed that it is not really historical. But even though it is *redemptive* history, it is redemptive *history*. The sphere in which God reveals His work of redemption is real space and time, real history. That truth is at the heart of the announcement Jesus made as He began His public ministry.

The Gospel of the Kingdom

Mark introduces the beginning of Jesus' Galilean ministry with this statement: **After John was put in prison, Jesus came to Galilee, preaching the gospel of the kingdom of God** (v. 14). This is a very brief statement, but these words are worthy of far more exposition than I can possibly provide in a single chapter. They are packed with theological significance.

Let me begin by calling attention to Mark's statement that when Jesus came to Galilee, He was preaching the gospel of the kingdom of God. Your Bible may have a different reading there. Instead of saying, "preaching the gospel of the kingdom of God," it may say, "preaching the gospel of God." Why are there such differences among English translations?

We do not have the original gospel that Mark wrote, but we do have many copies of it. These were very carefully copied down in many places through the ages; today, there may be some two thousand extant copies of the gospel of Mark. Unfortunately, they do not always read in perfect agreement with one another. There are, however, various schools of copies, and those who seek to reconstruct the original text, which is a science in and of itself, consider many technical points to determine which wording in all probability was in the original manuscript.

Verse 14 represents one of those rare instances where the textual evidence provides no clear-cut preferred wording. The phrasings "the gospel of the kingdom of God" and "the gospel of God" are found in almost equal numbers of copies.

However, we should not be concerned. There is no significant difference in the meaning of the text, regardless of which of the two wordings we settle on. Both wordings communicate the truth that Jesus came preaching the gospel of God, which was the gospel of the kingdom of God. There is no difference theologically in the two readings.

Let us explore this further. First, think about the option that Jesus came

preaching "the gospel of God." I like that wording, for it is the same wording the Apostle Paul uses at the beginning of his letter to the Romans, where
he declares that he sees himself as set apart to the gospel of God (1:1). It is
significant that Paul is not speaking of the good news *about* God. Rather, the
grammar he uses is possessive; Paul means that the gospel *belongs* to God. God
is its Author. We might say that God owns it. He is the One who gave this
message, not John the Baptist, and not even Jesus. It was not Jesus' gospel, as
such. It was the Father's gospel that the Son declared.

We have seen that Mark developed a new literary genre called the gospel.
Now we see that the term *gospel* also refers to the coming of the kingdom of
God. In the epistles of the New Testament, the term *gospel* refers to the person
and work of Jesus. It then becomes the gospel of Jesus Christ.

Second, consider "the gospel of the kingdom of God." At the beginning of
Jesus' ministry, when He came preaching the gospel of God, the content of that
good news was the coming of the kingdom of God. That which He preached
was the gospel of the kingdom. One key motif that runs through all the Old
Testament and is fulfilled perfectly in the New Testament is the idea of the
coming kingdom of God.

What do we mean when we say "the kingdom of God"? Hasn't the kingdom
of God always existed? Hasn't God been the omnipotent Lord from all eternity?
Yes, but when the Old Testament speaks of the coming kingdom of God, it
refers to God's personal visitation to this fallen world to manifest redemption.
The people of Israel in the Old Testament looked forward to the day when
God's rule would be manifest here on earth in the coming of His Anointed One.

So, following in the footsteps of John the Baptist, who had announced the
coming of the kingdom, Jesus declared the gospel of the kingdom of God.

A Lesson in Time

Mark also tells us that He preached, saying: **"The time is fulfilled, and the
kingdom of God is at hand. Repent, and believe in the gospel"** (v. 15).
When Mark records Jesus' statement, "The time is fulfilled," he uses a very
interesting Greek word: *kairos*. There are two words in the Greek language that
are translated by the English word *time*. One is *chronos*, which refers to the
moment-by-moment passing of time. The other word is *kairos*, which refers
to a particular moment in time that is so significant, it defines everything that
comes after it.

We do not have corresponding distinctions in the English language for
chronos and *kairos*. The closest English words are these: *historical* and *historic*.
Everything that takes place in space and time is historical, but not everything

that takes place is historic. We reserve the word *historic* for events of great significance. For something to be considered historic, it has to be so important, so momentous, that it shapes history.

Of course, the most "kairotic" event in all of history was the birth of Jesus. In fact, all of history is defined by that moment. We use the designations BC (before Christ) and AD (*anno Domine*, or "year of our Lord") to date events before or after His birth. Christ's birth is the dividing line of history in the Western world. His death on the cross was another major kairotic moment. Likewise, His resurrection was a kairotic moment. In the Old Testament, the exodus of Israel was a kairotic event.

Thus, when Jesus said "the time is fulfilled," He was saying that a very significant time in human history had arrived. The arrival of the kingdom of God was surely a kairotic moment.

The Greek word that is translated as "fulfilled" is *pleroma*, which means "super fullness." Usually, when we fill a cup with water or a mug with coffee, we do not fill it to the brim because, if we do, the water or the coffee is likely to spill over. We leave a little room at the top so that we can move the cup or mug without spilling the contents. But when we fill something in the sense of *pleroma*, it is spilling over the edge. Thus, Jesus was announcing that the time for the arrival of the kingdom of God was "super full."

In effect, Jesus was saying, "The *kairos* and the *pleroma* have come together." Time and all of history up until that moment had been prepared by the Lord God omnipotent, the Creator of the universe, who stands over all time and space. The time of waiting for the manifestation of the kingdom of God was over; it was about to happen.

In just the same way, the term "at hand" means "near," but Jesus was not saying that the kingdom of God was near simply in terms of the clock. Rather, He meant that it was "at hand" physically. The kingdom of God was at hand because the King was there. The people could reach out and touch Him. The long-awaited Messiah had come. The kairotic moment was unfolding in the person of Jesus.

Why did Jesus call the people to repent? The moment when the King came was a moment of profound crisis. The English word *crisis* is a transliteration of the Greek *krisis*, which means "judgment." When the kingdom broke through and the Messiah appeared, it brought the most profound crisis humanity had ever faced. That crisis was this: those who received Him would receive eternal life; those who did not would pass into God's judgment. Jesus was saying to the Jews, "Your crisis is right now." He says the same to everyone in the world today who hears His name. No one can hear the gospel and walk away indifferent.

When someone receives the gospel, it is the greatest moment of his life. But if he rejects the gospel, he brings the greatest judgment on himself. The gospel is a two-edged sword. Jesus was saying, in essence, "You are not ready for the coming of the kingdom; therefore, repent and believe." Those two actions are absolutely necessary to receive the Savior. The coming of Christ requires repentance and faith by all who hear of Him.

Much of what passes for evangelism today concerns me. People say, "If you want to have a personal relationship with Jesus, then come forward to the altar, raise your hand, sign a card, or pray the sinner's prayer." All those techniques together add up to cheap grace, because what is noticeably absent from these attempts to evangelize is any serious call to repentance. No one can enter the kingdom of God without repentance, without fleeing from sin and putting his trust in Christ alone. This is how our Lord Himself did evangelism. He announced the gospel, then He said, in essence, "Your response must be to repent and believe."

Calling Four Disciples

Mark quickly moves on to the calling of the first disciples of Jesus: **As He walked by the Sea of Galilee, He saw Simon and Andrew his brother casting a net into the sea; for they were fishermen. Then Jesus said to them, "Follow Me, and I will make you become fishers of men"** (vv. 16–17). The Sea of Galilee is an inland lake about thirteen miles long and about seven miles wide. It is fed by the Jordan River in the north and emptied by the Jordan on the south. The first-century Jewish historian Josephus writes about the great beauty surrounding the sea, noting that the land watered by the lake was highly fertile. In his judgment, the sea was "the pride of nature." It features prominently in numerous events recorded in the Gospels, as we will see as we proceed through Mark.

The Sea of Galilee was one of the most productive bodies of water in the ancient world for the fishing industry. According to Josephus, when the Romans invaded Palestine in the year 68, they commandeered some 250 fishing boats from the Sea of Galilee, which gives an indication of how many fishermen were working the sea in those days. There were many varieties of fish in the Sea of Galilee that were not found elsewhere, and these fish were caught and exported to other countries. We think of the disciples as poverty-stricken fisherman trying to eke out a living, but these men actually had lucrative businesses.

Many fishermen on the Sea of Galilee practiced their trade with nets. These nets were about fifteen feet in diameter, and there were weights on the edges that caused them to sink. The fisherman would throw his net so that it would land flat on the surface of the water. The weights would sink to the bottom and close the net, encircling several fish. In most cases, a rope was attached to the middle of the net, and the fisherman would pull the rope, causing the hems of the net to close, trapping the fish. Then the fisherman would pull the net to the surface, remove his catch, and sell it in the marketplace.

On one occasion, as Jesus walked along the shore, He saw two of these fishermen, Simon and Andrew, casting a net into the sea. Jesus called them to follow Him, promising to make them "fishers of men." Although they were in the midst of practicing their trade, **They immediately left their nets and followed Him** (v. 18).

Mark goes on to say: **When he had gone a little farther from there, He saw James the Son of Zebedee, and John his brother, who also were in the boat mending their nets. And immediately He called them, and they left their father Zebedee in the boat with the hired servants, and went after Him** (vv. 19–20).

Jesus was calling disciples. We hear about the twelve disciples and the twelve Apostles, so many people think that *disciple* is just another word for *apostle*. That is not the case. Jesus had at least seventy disciples (Luke 10:1), and many of them were never included in the apostolic band. The word *disciple* refers to someone who is under the discipline of a tutor or a rabbi. A disciple is simply a student, a learner. When Jesus called Peter, Andrew, James, and John, He was enrolling them as disciples in His rabbinic school. (By contrast, an Apostle was a "sent one," commissioned and empowered by Jesus to preach the gospel, as we will see later in Mark.)

What Jesus was doing was very unusual. In the ancient Jewish world, rabbis never recruited students. Students applied to study with certain rabbis, just as students apply to study at colleges today. They had to pass examinations to demonstrate that they were qualified to study under Hillel, Gamaliel, or another rabbi. But Jesus was different from every other rabbi in Israel; He went out and handpicked His students.

Jesus' words "follow Me" are interesting because there is a literal sense to them. In ancient Greece, Plato established his academy in the great cultural center of Athens. His most brilliant and famous student was Aristotle. Later, Aristotle started his own school in Athens called the Lyceum, but Aristotle was what we call a "peripatetic philosopher." The word *peripatetic* means "given to walking." Aristotle would walk while he lectured. His students would follow along behind him, listening and trying to remember what he said.

Jesus was a peripatetic rabbi. He went from town to town, and on the way, He lectured. His disciples walked behind Him and memorized the terse, pithy aphorisms and parables that He taught. So much of Jesus' teaching survived in the oral tradition after His incarnation, before His words were written down, because His disciples were skilled in memorizing His teaching. That was their task.

A disciple of a rabbi was also a servant. He took care of the shoes of the professor and prepared the evening meals for him. Wherever the professor went, the disciple would go and serve his master. That is why Jesus said, "A servant is not greater than his master" (John 13:16). So, enrolling in a rabbinical school was a rigorous pursuit.

When Jesus approached Simon and Andrew and said, "Follow me," He was inviting them to come into His school, to be His students and His servants. Without any further discussion, they put down their nets and left to follow Jesus. They went down the road a little farther and encountered James and John sitting in a boat with their father, Zebedee, and their father's servants. Jesus called James and John to follow Him. Can you imagine Zebedee's astonishment when his sons, for whom he had built a lucrative fishing business, got out of the boat? They likely left their father scratching his head. All he had left were the servants. He watched them walk away with a strange young rabbi and two other fishermen.

In 1955, a movie titled *A Man Called Peter* was released. It was about the Senate Chaplain Peter Marshall, who was a famous preacher in the middle of the twentieth century. His sermons were so lyrical that people called him "Twittering Birds Marshall." When he died young, his widow, Catherine Marshall, had a book of his sermons published under the title *Mr. Jones, Meet the Master*. It was one of the first books I read after my conversion in 1957.

I vividly remember how, in one of those sermons, Marshall told the story of a fishmonger in Baltimore named Joe Botts. Joe loved his business and it was very lucrative. However, one morning, just after he had opened his shop for the day, the bell rang over the door. Joe looked up and saw a man in a blue serge suit walk in the door. The man looked at Joe and said, "Joe, close the shop and come with me." Joe could see there was an indefinable "something" about this man. He couldn't ask any questions. He couldn't proffer any arguments. Instead, he took off his apron, set it down on a chair, and went over and flipped the sign in the window from "Open" to "Closed." Then he followed the man in the blue serge suit out the door.

This was Marshall's modern parable of what happened by the Sea of Galilee when Jesus said to four men, in essence: "From this day forward, you are Mine. You are My students and My servants." Every Christian who has followed Jesus since that day has had to make that same choice—to leave everything and follow Him.

4

AUTHORITY
LIKE NO OTHER

Mark 1:21–28

⁓

Then they went into Capernaum, and immediately on the Sabbath He entered the synagogue and taught. And they were astonished at His teaching, for He taught them as one having authority, and not as the scribes. Now there was a man in their synagogue with an unclean spirit. And he cried out, saying, "Let us alone! What have we to do with You, Jesus of Nazareth? Did You come to destroy us? I know who You are—the Holy One of God!" But Jesus rebuked him, saying, "Be quiet, and come out of him!" And when the unclean spirit had convulsed him and cried out with a loud voice, he came out of him. Then they were all amazed, so that they questioned among themselves, saying, "What is this? What new doctrine is this? For with authority He commands even the unclean spirits, and they obey Him." And immediately His fame spread throughout all the region around Galilee.

After Jesus called His first four disciples, He began His Galilean ministry in Capernaum. Mark writes, **they went into Capernaum, and immediately on the Sabbath He entered the synagogue and taught** (v. 21). Capernaum was one of many towns and villages along the shore of the Sea of Galilee. The name of the town comes from the Hebrew *Kfar Nahum*, meaning "the village of Nahum," indicating that it may date back to the days of

21

the Old Testament prophet by that name. The town was on the northwest side of the lake, and it was probably the most upscale town in the region at that time. Quite a bit of evidence indicates that after Jesus moved away from His childhood home of Nazareth, He made Capernaum His home. There is even evidence that later He possibly lived in the home of Peter, which is mentioned in verse 29.

Capernaum had a seawall of eight feet that extended for half a mile in front of the village and several piers that extended a hundred feet out into the water. There was a tremendous fishing industry in Capernaum, as well as a busy community of merchants, artisans, and scribes. There was also a Roman colony that was friendly to the Jews in Capernaum.

Without any doubt, there was a synagogue in Capernaum. In antiquity, all that was required for the establishment of a synagogue in a village was a quorum of at least ten Jewish men older than thirteen. The synagogue was not equal to the temple in Jerusalem, where people went for worship. The synagogue was a place of assembly where the Scriptures were taught, though not by the leader of the synagogue, who was basically an administrator. Rather, various teachers and visiting rabbis would read and comment on the Scriptures. It was as a visiting rabbi that Jesus went into the Capernaum synagogue.

The significance of this event, which Mark wants us to observe very early in his gospel, had to do with the character of Jesus' ministry. Three elements distinguished His ministry: teaching, healing, and the casting out of demons. So Mark begins by calling attention to Jesus' teaching, and especially to the people's response to it.

Teaching with Authority

Mark tells us, **they were astonished at His teaching, for He taught them as one having authority, and not as the scribes** (v. 22). The people of Capernaum who were in the synagogue reacted to Jesus' teaching with sheer amazement. Even the word *amazement* (let alone the word *astonishment*) does not do full justice to the import of the term in the text. The idea is that not only were they surprised, they were terrified, because they had never heard anyone talk like Jesus. He exhibited an authority on a whole new plane.

Of course, the scribes were not without their own authority. They were the most learned expositors of the Old Testament law. Scribes were like PhDs in theology, and their opinions were accorded great weight by those who heard them. But when Jesus spoke, He evoked an authority far beyond anything the people had experienced with the scribes. The scribes could cite other scholars and rabbinic traditions. They could try to marshal arguments to support what they were teaching, just as we try to do today in the academic world. But Jesus did not do that—He provided no footnotes, no citations, no marshaling of other people's arguments. His teaching might have inspired bumper stickers on the chariots in those days: "Jesus said it, that settles it." When God says something, the argument is over.

The Greek word *exousia* is translated as "authority." It is made up of a prefix and a root. The prefix *ex-* means "out of" or "away from"; an "exit" is a way out. The root, *ousia*, is the present participle of the verb *to be*, so its literal translation is "being." Ancient Greek philosophers were very much concerned with that word because *ousia* represented the ultimate reality the philosophers were seeking, the ultimate, transcendent, supreme being. But the word is also important in Christian history. In the fourth century, the church went through a great crisis with respect to its understanding of the person of Christ. That controversy reached its culmination at the Council of Nicaea, which declared that Christ was *homoousios*, of the same being, essence, or substance as the Father. So the word *ousia* is not just a participle of the verb *to be* but is loaded with implications in the history of Greek and Christian thought.

Ousia could also be translated as "substance." Jesus spoke *exousia*, out of substance. His teaching was supremely substantive; there was nothing superficial or light about it. This was the utterance of the One who was of the same essence as the Father, so Jesus' authority was rooted and grounded in God Himself. That is what terrified the people. They said, "Never have we heard anyone speak like this."

The authority in Jesus' teaching was reminiscent of that of the Old Testament prophets, who prefaced their oracles not by saying, "In my studied opinion. . . ." Rather, the prophets prefaced their announcements by saying, "Thus says the Lord. . . ." But in the synagogue of Capernaum, the Lord Himself, the Word of God incarnate, rose to speak on matters theological. When He opened His holy mouth, all present were stopped in their tracks, filled with amazement, and pierced by a sense of dread to hear the truth proclaimed with such transcendent finality. That is how we should respond every time we hear the Word of God. We are not listening to the word of scribes, preachers, or theologians, so our hearts should be filled with a holy dread and awe when the Bible is proclaimed.

Confronting a Demon-Possessed Man

Mark goes on to write: **Now there was a man in their synagogue with an unclean spirit. And he cried out, saying, "Let us alone! What have we to do with You, Jesus of Nazareth? Did You come to destroy us? I know who You are—the Holy One of God!"** (vv. 23–24).

In the Old Testament, there are very few references to the demonic world, and instances of demonic possession are extremely rare. Likewise, there are few references to it in later church history. However, while Jesus was on the earth, it is safe to say, "all hell broke loose." Demonic representatives and Satan himself seemed to oppress people everywhere. Jesus Himself announced the significance of His work of demon exorcism by saying to His hearers, "If I cast out demons by the Spirit of God, surely the kingdom of God has come upon you" (Matt. 12:28).

Interestingly, it seems that the first ones to fully recognize the identity of Christ hidden in His incarnation were the demons. While many people failed to recognize Him in His fullness, these ambassadors of hell instantly recognized Him.

There was a demon-possessed man in the synagogue, and when Jesus turned His attention to him, the man began to scream, saying, "Did You come to destroy us?" (v. 24). Why did he use the plural? Was it because the man was filled with many demons, or was one demon speaking on behalf of himself and the man he possessed? I suspect that he was representing the whole kingdom under the domination of the prince of the power of the air, the prince of this world, Satan himself (Eph. 2:2).

On behalf of Satan and his legions of demons, this man—this demon—screamed against Jesus, basically saying: "What do You have to do with us? What do we have to do with You?" The answer to these questions was, in one sense, absolutely nothing. The demons had nothing in common with Christ—they represented two different realms, the realm of Satan and the realm of God. The only relationship the demons had with Christ was one of conflict, and now they were faced with defeat and judgment. The demons recognized that they were under God's sentence. They knew that when the Son of God appeared on the earth, their doom would be certain, for Christ was coming to bind the strong man, Satan, with all of his hellish powers (3:27).

The demon in the man then uttered a strange statement: "I know who You are—the Holy One of God!" What was happening here? We gain a clue from the Old Testament account of Jacob's wrestling with an angel (Gen. 32:24–29). After they had wrestled all night, Jacob demanded a blessing, which prompted the angel to ask his name. When the angel blessed him, Jacob asked the angel's name, but he would not give it. Revealing one's name to an adversary was seen as an act of submission. When Jacob asked the angel for his name, he was asking him to submit. That is why the demon revealed Jesus' name. It was one last attempt to get rid of Him. The demon unveiled His identity, thinking that if he named Him properly, he could defeat Him.

Manifesting the Holy

Of course, the demon also was terrified. He realized he was in the presence of the holy God, and nothing strikes more terror into the heart of creatures than to be in the presence of the holy. We will see this motif throughout the gospel of Mark; when the holiness of Christ was made manifest, the immediate response was fear and dread. We fear the holy because we are not holy. When we are brought into the presence of the unveiled holiness of God, as Peter was (Luke 5:8), we say, "Depart from us, for we are sinful people." That is why the demon screamed when the Holy One of God came into his presence.

Jesus refused to tolerate this screaming and protesting. He rebuked the unclean spirit, saying, **"Be quiet, and come out of him!"** (v. 25). What Jesus said would not be considered polite conversation today. A more accurate translation of what He said to the demon would be: "Shut up. I do not want to hear any more from you. Come out of him." The result, according to Mark, was that **when the unclean spirit had convulsed him and cried out with a loud voice, he came out of him** (v. 26). When Jesus commanded, the demon obeyed.

Mark continues: **Then they were all amazed, so that they questioned among themselves, saying, "What is this? What new doctrine is this? For with authority He commands even the unclean spirits, and they obey Him"** (v. 27). Jesus was not behaving like a shaman, rattling a bunch of beads or playing games of healing. He did none of the tricks that are employed by charlatans. Jesus just spoke, and the demon obeyed because he knew Christ had authority even over him. Not surprisingly, as Mark tells us, **immediately His fame spread throughout all the region around Galilee** (v. 28).

5

THE HEART
OF JESUS' MISSION

Mark 1:29–45

Now as soon as they had come out of the synagogue, they entered the house of Simon and Andrew, with James and John. But Simon's wife's mother lay sick with a fever, and they told Him about her at once. So He came and took her by the hand and lifted her up, and immediately the fever left her. And she served them. At evening, when the sun had set, they brought to Him all who were sick and those who were demon-possessed. And the whole city was gathered together at the door. Then He healed many who were sick with various diseases, and cast out many demons; and He did not allow the demons to speak, because they knew Him. Now in the morning, having risen a long while before daylight, He went out and departed to a solitary place; and there He prayed. And Simon and those who were with Him searched for Him. When they found Him, they said to Him, "Everyone is looking for You." But He said to them, "Let us go into the next towns, that I may preach there also, because for this purpose I have come forth." And He was preaching in their synagogues throughout all Galilee, and casting out demons. Now a leper came to Him, imploring Him, kneeling down to Him and saying to Him, "If You are willing, You can make me clean." Then Jesus, moved with compassion, stretched out His hand and touched him, and said to him, "I am willing; be cleansed." As soon as He had spoken, immediately the leprosy left him, and he was cleansed. And He strictly warned him and sent him away at once, and said to him, "See that you say nothing to anyone; but go your way, show yourself to the priest, and offer for your cleansing those things which Moses commanded, as a testimony to them." However, he went out and began to proclaim it freely, and to spread the matter, so that Jesus could no longer openly enter the city, but was outside in deserted places; and they came to Him from every direction.

Excavations of a synagogue in Capernaum have shown that it was a magnificent limestone edifice that was built in the first century on the foundation of an earlier synagogue. That earlier synagogue was obviously the one in which Jesus preached and where He exorcized a demon-possessed man, as described in the passage we studied in the previous chapter.

Further excavations have revealed a building that stood very close to the synagogue and dated to the latter part of the first century and into the second century. Religious graffiti appear on the walls of this structure. It was a home, but it was built with the unusual feature of doors opening into a large area where people could gather. Historians and archaeologists believe, based on their excavations, that this home served as a church in early Christian times. The conclusion of the historians, with almost complete certainty, is that this excavated building was the home of Peter.

That conclusion seems to square with descriptions in the first chapter of Mark's gospel. He tells us that **as soon as they had come out of the synagogue, they entered the house of Simon and Andrew, with James and John** (v. 29). This verse clearly shows that Peter's home was close to the synagogue.

As we saw in the previous chapter, Mark highlights several aspects of Jesus' ministry: teaching, healing, and casting out demons. We saw how both His teaching and His power over demons aroused astonishment in those who observed Him. In the passage we are considering in this chapter, Mark focuses immediately on Jesus' power to heal, a power that brought multitudes to Him for help.

When Jesus entered the home, **Simon's wife's mother lay sick with a fever, and they told Him about her at once. So He came and took her by the hand and lifted her up, and immediately the fever left her. And she served them** (vv. 30–31). Mark's account of Jesus' healing of Peter's mother-in-law is not exceedingly dramatic. Jesus performed many more striking acts of healing in the biblical record; His healing of the leper that we will consider later in this chapter is one of these. Obviously, however, Mark's record of this particular event was supplied by his mentor, Peter himself.

I find it interesting that there is no mention of the presence of Peter's wife. She may have been dead at this time, or perhaps Mark simply did not see a need to mention her. In any case, the Roman Catholic view is that Peter became the first pope of the Christian church and that the papacy was established on Peter.

The irony is that the first pope, as they view Peter, was married. This raises some embarrassing questions for those who hold a view of imposed celibacy for clergy. I am happy that I can stand in the tradition of Peter by being married as well.

After recounting the healing of Peter's mother-in-law, Mark writes: **At evening, when the sun had set, they brought to Him all who were sick and those who were demon-possessed. And the whole city was gathered together at the door** (vv. 32–33). Obviously, Mark's statement that "the whole city" came to the door of Peter's home is hyperbole, a way of saying that there was a huge throng. The news about the healing of Peter's mother-in-law had spread quickly. So, **He healed many who were sick with various diseases, and cast out many demons; and He did not allow the demons to speak, because they knew Him** (v. 34). It appears Jesus spent some time ministering to these people into the late hours of the evening, healing many and casting out more demons in a great display of His power and authority. But He would not let the demons speak, lest they try to gain power over Him by naming Him. As we will see time and again, Jesus did not want His fame to spread needlessly at this time.

Praying in a Solitary Place

Then Mark tells us, **in the morning, having risen a long while before daylight, He went out and departed to a solitary place; and there He prayed** (v. 35). Our Lord had labored long the previous day, but He nevertheless awoke well before sunrise. He did this so He could distance Himself from the pressing crowd and go to a solitary place to refresh Himself by prayer. This is one of three specific instances Mark mentions when Jesus went out at night to seek a place to be alone with His Father. The others occurred on the night He walked on the water (6:46) and in Gethsemane on the night He was betrayed (14:32–35).

Mark writes that when they awoke and found Jesus missing, **Simon and those who were with him searched for Him** (v. 36). The force of the verb here is that they went on a hunt, searching high and low. It was not easy for them to discover where Jesus had isolated Himself for prayer, but **when they found Him, they said to Him, "Everyone is looking for You"** (v. 37). This was a thinly veiled rebuke. They were saying, in essence: "Where have You been, Jesus? You do not have time to seclude Yourself in prayer. You have ministry to perform. Your fame is spreading everywhere, and the place is filled with seekers."

How did Jesus respond to that? He did not say: "That's fantastic. We should plant a church here. We have a wonderful core of people who are excited that I'm healing their diseases." In fact, Jesus was saddened by this news. He knew the multitudes were pressing to the door looking for healing, not for truth. They were not coming to Him to hear the announcement of the breakthrough of the kingdom of God. They were not flocking to Him so that they could listen to Him preach the gospel or expound the Word of God. They were coming to look for improvement to their health or relief of their suffering. Of course, there was nothing wrong with people coming to Jesus out of their needs of the flesh. Yet that was not the chief end for which He had come. He had not come to this earth to heal everyone's diseases or perform miracles for everyone in need. He had come to preach the truth that His Father had sent Him to declare. Jesus could tell that people were not coming out of faith to receive Him and His kingdom, but for relief from their physical pain.

Sometimes we are like that. We come to God in prayer when we are sick, when our bodies hurt, but we neglect to come to Him in times of health and peace. We go to Him quickly when we have needs, but we do not pursue Him so eagerly to hear and understand His Word.

So, Jesus said to His disciples, **"Let us go into the next towns, that I may preach there also, because for this purpose I have come forth"** (v. 38). He said, in effect: "These people are so caught up now in My power, they do not want to hear My Word. So let's go to the other cities of Galilee, where I can resume My ministry of preaching, because that's why I came." Jesus was not going to be diverted from His mission because everyone was clamoring for His power. Mark tells us that **He was preaching in their synagogues throughout all Galilee, and casting out demons** (v. 39).

Healing a Leprous Man

We now come to what I find to be one of the most moving accounts in Mark's gospel. He writes, **Now a leper came to Him, imploring Him, kneeling down to Him and saying to Him, "If You are willing, You can make me clean"** (v. 40). In the ancient world, there were seventy-two distinct diseases of the skin under the broad heading of leprosy. Mark does not explain which variety of leprosy this poor man had. It may have been Hansen's disease, the worst form of leprosy, but any form of leprosy was tragic and disastrous for people in those days.

By way of background, Leviticus 13 and 14 describe in detail the woeful status of lepers and the law concerning leprosy. If you were a Jew in the ancient world and you woke up one morning with a strange appearance on your skin, it would strike terror into your heart. First, you were required to go to the priest, who, using the guidance of God's Word, determined whether this outbreak in your flesh was a harmless skin affliction or whether it was leprosy. If it was leprosy, that not only meant that you had a dreadful physical malady that probably would be with you for the rest of your life, it was the worst possible announcement you could hear with respect to your fellowship in your home, the community, and the assembly. If you were found to have leprosy, you were deemed to be not just unwell but unclean. Leprosy could not be healed in the ancient world, so lepers were cast out of the covenant community. You were not allowed near the temple and could not enter the gates of Jerusalem. You had to live alone, without the fellowship of family members and friends. You wore tattered clothes and had unkempt hair. It was necessary to cover the lower portion of your mouth so you could be noticed from a distance as a leper. You were not allowed to come within fifty paces of another human being. If you saw anyone else approaching, you had to cry out, "Unclean, unclean," lest you spread your contamination. To be a leper was to be the ultimate pariah in the household of Israel.

This man in Mark's gospel had been examined by the priest. The sore had turned white, and the verdict was leprosy. So, he had left his family, his wife, his children, and his home, and he lived as a homeless person isolated from human contact. However, somehow he heard that Jesus was in the neighborhood, and he ran up to Him, breaking the law of Moses. He cried out to Jesus in faith, begging for mercy: "If You are willing, You can make me clean."

Mark writes, **Then Jesus, moved with compassion, stretched out His hand and touched him, and said to him, "I am willing; be cleansed"** (v. 41). The Lord Jesus Christ, the sinless one, whose food was to do the will of the Father to fulfill all righteousness (John 4:34; Matt. 3:15), violated the ceremonial law. Not only was the leper not allowed to touch a non-leper, the non-leper was not allowed to touch a leper. But Jesus touched him, notwithstanding any controversies with the Jewish religious leaders that would come after that. Mark shows us that Jesus was the Lord of the ceremonial law, with the authority to set it aside for His own redemptive processes.

Sometimes you find yourself in a traffic jam. Maybe there has been a minor accident, and a police officer shows up to direct traffic. You come to the street corner and the traffic light is red, but the officer waves you through. His presence supersedes the written law, so you must obey the embodiment of the law in the traffic officer rather than the red light. Jesus is the embodiment of the law and the enforcer of the law. Just as God brought the world into existence by His word, by the divine imperative, so Christ exercised that divine imperative in the case of this leper.

Mark's note that Jesus was "moved with compassion" could be translated as "angry." Jesus was not angry because the man had violated the ceremonial law in coming to Him; rather, He was filled with a righteous indignation against the ravages of the fallen world, such as disease. He hated disease, but He cared for the person afflicted by the disease.

Mark tells us, **As soon as He had spoken, immediately the leprosy left him, and he was cleansed** (v. 42). Do not miss the power of the word of Jesus. By the word of His power, He healed a disease for which there was no known cure, one of the most dreaded afflictions of the ancient world.

Then Jesus **strictly warned him and sent him away at once** (v. 43). That warning consisted of several instructions: **"See that you say nothing to anyone; but go your way, show yourself to the priest, and offer for your cleansing those things which Moses commanded, as a testimony to them"** (v. 44). Jesus was not throwing away the law of Moses. He was basically telling the man to obey the law as it applied to his disease.

Why did Jesus tell the man to keep quiet about his healing? Much has been said about the so-called messianic secret of Jesus. He frequently told those to whom He ministered, "Tell no one." We can only guess why that was, but I think the context of Mark's gospel gives us a good insight. Everywhere Jesus went, people completely misunderstood His mission and what the Messiah was to do. They were waiting for the champion who would deliver them from Rome, not for the Suffering Servant of God who would deliver them from their sins. So, Jesus was loath to make public His true identity, particularly early on in His ministry. Not only that, if this leper went out and told everyone in the countryside that he had just been cleansed by Jesus of Nazareth, every leper within hearing would rush to Jesus, and He would not have time to do the mission that He had been called to do.

However, Mark tells us the healed leper **went out and began to proclaim it freely, and to spread the matter** (v. 45a). Here was an evangelist in disobedience. Jesus told him not to do it, but he went and did it anyway, to such an extent **that Jesus could no longer openly enter the city, but was outside in deserted places; and they came to Him from every direction** (v. 45b).

Now that Jesus has been to the cross, died and risen again, and been raised to the right hand of the Father, the messianic secret is no longer in effect. The church is charged with telling one and all about Jesus. I pray that people today will come to Him from everywhere, not simply to be released from their pain, but also to hear His message, the message that God has come into the world and is born to us as a Savior, who is Christ, our Lord.

6

POWER TO HEAL
BODY AND SOUL

Mark 2:1–12

~⧝~

And again He entered Capernaum after some days, and it was heard that He was in the house. Immediately many gathered together, so that there was no longer room to receive them, not even near the door. And He preached the word to them. Then they came to Him, bringing a paralytic who was carried by four men. And when they could not come near Him because of the crowd, they uncovered the roof where He was. So when they had broken through, they let down the bed on which the paralytic was lying. When Jesus saw their faith, He said to the paralytic, "Son, your sins are forgiven you." And some of the scribes were sitting there and reasoning in their hearts, "Why does this Man speak blasphemies like this? Who can forgive sins but God alone?" But immediately, when Jesus perceived in His spirit that they reasoned thus within themselves, He said to them, "Why do you reason about these things in your hearts? Which is easier, to say to the paralytic, 'Your sins are forgiven you,' or to say, 'Arise, take up your bed and walk'? But that you may know that the Son of Man has power on earth to forgive sins"—He said to the paralytic, "I say to you, arise, take up your bed, and go to your house." Immediately he arose, took up the bed, and went out in the presence of them all, so that all were amazed and glorified God, saying, "We never saw anything like this!"

Perhaps, at some time in your life, you have received drop-in visitors. How you felt about that experience probably depended on how prepared you were for the visitors and, of course, on the visitors themselves. Jesus, who had been besieged by throngs of people wanting to see Him, encountered a drop-in visitor like no other—yet He was more than prepared to receive him.

After a tour of preaching in various synagogues throughout Galilee (1:39), Jesus came back to Capernaum, where He had been based until the crowds mobbed Him there. They had so pressed against Him that it had become impossible to continue the mission on which the Father had sent Him—to preach the coming kingdom of God. So, Jesus had withdrawn from Capernaum and taken His ministry to other villages.

Mark tells us, **again He entered Capernaum after some days, and it was heard that He was in the house** (v. 1). Another way of translating this verse is "He was at home," which adds credibility to the notion that Jesus made His home in Capernaum, His family having moved away from Nazareth. It is also possible that the home in view was Peter's, and that Peter was sharing it with Jesus.

In any case, no sooner did Jesus come into the house than once again a huge multitude pressed together to hear Him teach and to watch Him perform His powerful works. Mark tells us: **Immediately many gathered together, so that there was no longer room to receive them**, **not even near the door. And He preached the word to them** (v. 2).

Company on the Roof

Mark tells us that while Jesus was teaching, four men carrying a stretcher or a pallet **came to Him, bringing a paralytic** (v. 3). They were obviously seeking healing for this afflicted man. **And when they could not come near Him because of the crowd, they uncovered the roof where He was** (v. 4a). The entrance to the house was blocked by the crowd, so to get this suffering man to Jesus, they carried him up the stairs to the roof, and they began breaking through the roof to make a hole through which they could let this man down so that Jesus could touch him.

In Palestine during Jesus' time, houses normally had one story with a flat roof. Roofs were constructed of beams laid across and resting on the walls of the house. Between the beams were interlaced sticks and reeds, and within these was woven a kind of thatch. On top of the thatch lay several inches of mud. This mud was packed down hard against the thatch, because builders in the ancient world used rollers to pack and smooth this mud until it was very hard and stable. Stairs outside the building led up to the roof, which was the place where people would go for fresh air. They would often eat their meals on the roof and receive company there. So the roof served as something like a deck, as we would have on our houses today.

Luke tells us that the four friends of the paralytic had to remove tiles from the roof (5:19). Some critical scholars say Luke made a mistake here because homes in Palestine did not have tiled roofs like those we find throughout Europe even to this day. But the Greek word that is translated as "tile" in Luke can simply refer to any kind of hard, baked clay or ceramic. Also, we know that Capernaum was an upscale village along the shores of the Sea of Galilee, and in such places, actual tiles were used. So, this home had either real tiles or hard, sun-baked mud that had the effect of ceramic tile, which must have made the task of the rooftop visitors even more challenging.

Eventually they succeeded, however. As Mark writes, **So when they had broken through, they let down the bed on which the paralytic was lying** (v. 4b). It is amazing to me how determined these men were to bring relief to their friend. They did not let the crowds defeat them, and they damaged, at least temporarily, someone's roof and interrupted Jesus' teaching.

Only God Can Forgive Sins

Mark tells us, **When Jesus saw their faith, He said to the paralytic, "Son, your sins are forgiven you"** (v. 5). There is nothing in the text that suggests the paralyzed man was looking for forgiveness. He was looking for healing. But Jesus did not say, "Sir, your sins are forgiven." He addressed him as an adult would a child, as a superior would a subordinate. He called the man "son" and told him his sins were forgiven. He looked past the terrible paralysis of the man's body and saw the even deeper need—relief from guilt.

That statement was so radical that it occasioned a reaction from the scribes, those theologians of the day who were part of that crowd paying attention to Jesus' every word. Already they were trying to trap Jesus if they could. Mark tells us: **And some of the scribes were sitting there and reasoning in their hearts, "Why does this Man speak blasphemies like this? Who can forgive sins but God alone?"** (vv. 6–7). Why did they think of blasphemy when Jesus declared the man's sins forgiven? It was because every scribe knew the principle in Old Testament Judaism that no man, not even the Messiah, would have the authority to forgive people's sins. They tenaciously held the position that God and God alone has the authority to forgive sins. It seemed to them that Jesus was acting as though He had the authority of God Himself.

Some groups today, such as the Jehovah's Witnesses, argue that the New Testament does not really teach the deity of Christ. Somehow they overlook the explicit teachings of the New Testament in the epistles and in narratives such as this one, where we see a clear implication of Jesus' claim to deity. What the Jehovah's Witnesses and likeminded groups fail to see, the Jews of Jesus' day saw. They understood that Jesus was claiming divinity. That is why they were so exercised.

Jesus knew what they were thinking. Mark writes: **But immediately, when Jesus perceived in His spirit that they reasoned thus within themselves, He said to them, "Why do you reason about these things in your hearts? Which is easier, to say to the paralytic, 'Your sins are forgiven you,' or to say, 'Arise, take up your bed and walk'?"** (vv. 8–9).

This is a difficult passage. From our perspective, it seems that the easier of the two options would have been to say, "Your sins are forgiven," because no one could test whether the sins were forgiven. There was no way to verify or disprove the truth of what Jesus pronounced. But if He said, "Get up, take your bed, and go home," He would put Himself on the spot, and people would know whether He had the power to heal the man or not. However, I do not think Jesus Himself thought that it was easier to say, "Your sins are forgiven." In that culture, in the presence of His enemies, it would have been far easier for Jesus to say, "Get up and walk." Jesus knew that if He said, "Your sins are forgiven," He was throwing down the gauntlet, because He was claiming to be divine. So Jesus was not taking the easy way out.

The plot thickened. Jesus explained what He was about to do and why He was going to do it: **"But that you may know that the Son of Man has power on earth to forgive sins"—He said to the paralytic, "I say to you, arise, take up your bed, and go to your house"** (vv. 10–11). Jesus wanted to show that the Son of Man had the authority to forgive sins. What happened to the man made that authority clear, as Mark describes: **Immediately he arose, took up the bed, and went out in the presence of them all, so that all were amazed and glorified God, saying, "We never saw anything like this!"** (v. 12).

The Forgiveness of Sins

The New Testament frequently uses two titles for Jesus: Son of God and Son of Man. Mark has already introduced the title Son of God (1:1); in this healing, Jesus introduced the title Son of Man for Himself. The most frequent title for Jesus in the New Testament is Christ. The second is Lord. Number three is Son of Man. However, it is far and away Jesus' favorite self-designation. The title Son of Man occurs more than eighty times in the New Testament, and in every case except two, Jesus used the title of Himself.

Who is the Son of Man? The book of Daniel describes the appearance and character of the Son of Man. He is a heavenly being appointed by the Ancient of Days (7:9) to be the Lord of the earth and to receive the kingdom forever (vv. 13–14). The Son of Man, having descended from heaven, returns there and is enthroned in glory. So, when Jesus called Himself the Son of Man, He was not practicing humility. He was saying: "I have descended from heaven. I am heavenly, not from this earth." That title was pregnant with theological significance concerning Jesus' deity and office. That was why Jesus used it here; He wanted to show His divine authority to forgive sin.

The Roman Catholic Church teaches that one of the sacraments of the church is penance. Part of the sacrament of penance is confession and priestly absolution. The penitent man goes into the confessional and says, "Father, I have sinned." He recites his sins, then the priest says, "*Te absolvo*," or, "I absolve you."

Some Protestants are upset when they learn about this practice. They say, "What right does an ordinary priest have to say, 'I absolve you'?" The church was very careful for centuries to point out that no priest has the inherent authority to forgive sins. Only God can forgive sins. By saying "*Te absolvo*," the priest is simply saying, "By your repentance I declare you absolved in the name of Jesus Christ, who has the authority to forgive your sins." Although the Reformers disliked many aspects of the Roman Catholic understanding of penance, Martin Luther actually kept the confessional because he felt that people need a word of assurance that they are forgiven.

Twenty-five years ago, a psychiatrist who had a very prosperous practice in South Florida asked me to come on his staff. He offered me what at that time would have been a princely salary to join his team. I said: "I do not have a degree in psychiatry. Why do you want me?" He said, "R.C., 95 percent of my clients do not need a psychiatrist. They need a priest, because their lives are being destroyed by unresolved guilt."

Do you ever wish that Jesus would put His hand on your head and say, "Your sins are forgiven"? Well, He says that to us in His Word, and that should be enough. By the power of His blood, through the work of His cross, our sins are forgiven.

7

ASSOCIATING WITH "SINNERS"

Mark 2:13–22

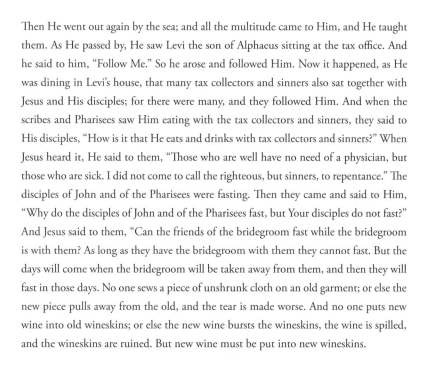

Then He went out again by the sea; and all the multitude came to Him, and He taught them. As He passed by, He saw Levi the son of Alphaeus sitting at the tax office. And he said to him, "Follow Me." So he arose and followed Him. Now it happened, as He was dining in Levi's house, that many tax collectors and sinners also sat together with Jesus and His disciples; for there were many, and they followed Him. And when the scribes and Pharisees saw Him eating with the tax collectors and sinners, they said to His disciples, "How is it that He eats and drinks with tax collectors and sinners?" When Jesus heard it, He said to them, "Those who are well have no need of a physician, but those who are sick. I did not come to call the righteous, but sinners, to repentance." The disciples of John and of the Pharisees were fasting. Then they came and said to Him, "Why do the disciples of John and of the Pharisees fast, but Your disciples do not fast?" And Jesus said to them, "Can the friends of the bridegroom fast while the bridegroom is with them? As long as they have the bridegroom with them they cannot fast. But the days will come when the bridegroom will be taken away from them, and then they will fast in those days. No one sews a piece of unshrunk cloth on an old garment; or else the new piece pulls away from the old, and the tear is made worse. And no one puts new wine into old wineskins; or else the new wine bursts the wineskins, the wine is spilled, and the wineskins are ruined. But new wine must be put into new wineskins.

W hen Jesus began spending time with despised tax collectors and others, He did not endear Himself to the scribes and Pharisees. His behavior was consistent with His calling, but they did not understand that. In the end, Jesus' willingness to associate with these individuals sparked yet another clash between our Lord and the religious leaders of His day.

Continuing to minister in Capernaum, Jesus **went out again by the sea; and all the multitude came to Him, and He taught them** (v. 13). Jesus had left Capernaum for a time because the people were more interested in benefitting from His healing power than in hearing His teaching and preaching on the kingdom of God, which was His mission (1:39). At this point, however, it seems the people were more willing to listen, and Jesus was able to teach a large multitude.

A Tax Collector's New Calling

Mark writes: **As He passed by, He saw Levi the son of Alphaeus sitting at the tax office. And He said to him, "Follow Me." So he arose and followed Him** (v. 14). Jesus recruited another disciple for His band of followers, just as He recruited Peter, Andrew, James, and John earlier (1:16–20). This man was named Levi, Mark says, but later he lists him as Matthew (3:18). Likewise, the parallel account of this event in Matthew's gospel names him Matthew, and he is widely seen as the author of the gospel that bears that name.

The "tax office" where Levi was sitting was not a building but a small booth or shanty erected beside one of the busy byways of Capernaum, probably near a commercial district. As we have seen, Capernaum was very important as a center for the fishing industry. It was a strategic and lucrative place for a tax collector to set up shop.

The Jewish people were subjected to oppressive taxes by the Roman Empire. The tax collectors were Jews who placed bids for the available jobs by submitting estimates of how much tax revenue they could collect. If the government liked a person's bid, he would be selected as a tax collector and given a quota. Once the tax collector met his quota, everything else he collected was his. So, tax collectors worked on a commission basis.

While competition for tax collector jobs was fierce because the position was so lucrative, the job came with heavy social costs. Jews who became tax collectors were regarded as traitors. They had to give up their Jewish identity, their social status, and their membership in the synagogue, and they were seen as disgraced in the eyes of their families. Furthermore, anyone who dealt with a tax collector as a friend was considered unclean.

Thus, it was scandalous when Jesus walked up to Levi's tax shanty and said to him, "Follow Me." It was unthinkable that He would select a tax collector to be part of His band of disciples. However, Mark earlier showed Jesus willingly healing and even touching a leper. Here he shows Jesus reaching out to a social outcast. As scandalous as it was for Jesus to touch a leper, it was even more scandalous that He would invite a tax collector to follow Him, yet Jesus showed no hesitation in either instance.

Self-Righteous Snobbery

To make matters worse, after He called Levi into His entourage, and Levi arose and followed Him, Jesus went to dinner in Levi's house. Mark sets the scene: **Now it happened, as He was dining in Levi's house, that many tax collectors and sinners also sat together with Jesus and His disciples; for there were many, and they followed Him** (v. 15). The original language tells us that these dinner guests were not just sitting, they were reclining. This was no average dinner. It was a feast, and perhaps a celebration. Levi was the host and Jesus was the guest of honor, but other guests included the whole company of hated tax collectors associated with him and others whom the religious authorities branded as "sinners."

When the scribes and Pharisees saw this, they were dismayed, and **they said to His disciples, "How is it that He eats and drinks with tax collectors and sinners?"** (v. 16b). When the scribes and Pharisees called people "sinners," they were thinking of the rank-and-file Jews who were not committed to in-depth study of the things of God, especially the law of God. These people went the way of the culture and followed the customs of the day rather than the details of the law. The Pharisees were just the opposite. The word *Pharisee* is derived from a Hebrew word meaning "separated one," for the Pharisees were strongly committed to keeping the law of God, and they believed that salvation came from distancing themselves from anyone who was morally loose. So it was important for them, in order to maintain their holiness and their sanctity, to have no dealings with people whom they regarded as sinners.

There are Christians like that, who actually believe that there is some sanctity in avoiding any contact with unbelievers or pagans. Several years ago, a woman called me to say her husband wanted to play golf with me. She said she would pay for the round as a birthday gift for her husband, and I agreed to play golf with him. We played eighteen holes of golf, and then after the round we went into the Men's Grill. As he was leaving, he saw me then go to sit with my friends at the club, many of whom were not believers at the time but who are now members of my congregation. This man was so upset that I was friendly with these people that he took it on himself to call the board of directors of Ligonier Ministries and complain that I was mixing with the wrong kind of people.

Jesus did not spend His life in a monastery. He was where people were, where there was pain and suffering, because He cared about people. But the religious establishment of His day could not stomach that Jesus, who was supposed to be a rabbi, was willing to dine with despised tax collectors and ordinary Jews. So they came to Jesus' disciples and asked, "Why is He doing it?"

When Jesus heard about their complaint, He said to them: **"Those who are well have no need of a physician, but those who are sick. I did not come to call the righteous, but sinners, to repentance"** (v. 17). What good is a doctor who associates only with well people? It is a good thing for doctors to be involved in preventive medicine, but we need doctors even more when we are sick. Of course, not everyone who is sick and needs a physician realizes it—such were the scribes and Pharisees.

There was some irony in Jesus' words when He said to the scribes and Pharisees, "I did not come to call the righteous, but sinners, to repentance." The implication was that these religious leaders themselves needed to repent of their sin. They were the sickest of the sick, all the while thinking they had no need of a physician.

A Question on Fasting

That answer did not satisfy Jesus' enemies. Mark tells us: **The disciples of John and of the Pharisees were fasting. Then they came and said to Him, "Why do the disciples of John and of the Pharisees fast, but Your disciples do not fast?"** (v. 18). The law of Moses required fasting only during the period leading up to the Day of Atonement. Over the centuries, however, it had become customary for the Jews to fast on occasions of national import, of mourning, and so on. Fasting also had become associated with repentance. If someone was guilty of a severe sin and came to repentance, he would manifest his repentance by fasting. John fasted even more frequently because he was an ascetic; he was given to self-denial, and his disciples emulated him in that. The Pharisees, however, made it a duty to fast twice a week and saw it as a badge of their personal piety. Thus, when they saw that Jesus' disciples were not fasting, they questioned Him about it.

In His reply, Jesus essentially told them that there is a time and a place for everything, and this was not the time to fast. Why? He used the metaphor of the bridegroom and reminded them of what happened at weddings in their own culture: **"Can the friends of the bridegroom fast while the bridegroom is with them? As long as they have the bridegroom with them they cannot**

fast" (v. 19). Weddings in Israel did not last twenty or thirty minutes, followed by a reception that went on for a couple of hours, after which everyone went home. A wedding feast lasted for a week. It was a time of eating and drinking. No one wanted to be involved in a fast when a wedding feast was on the calendar. That was a time to celebrate and revel.

The Old Testament never refers to the Messiah as the bridegroom. The bridegroom in the Old Testament is God and the bride is Israel. But in the New Testament, the bridegroom is the Son of God and the bride is His church. Given the Old Testament context of the metaphor, it is clear Jesus was claiming even more than messiahship when He referred to Himself as the bridegroom.

He also let them know they would not always have the bridegroom with them: **"But the days will come when the bridegroom will be taken away from them, and then they will fast in those days"** (v. 20). He was referring to His own coming execution and departure from this planet. After that, He said, would be the time for His disciples to fast.

Cloth Patches and Wineskins

Then Jesus switched His metaphors and said, **"No one sews a piece of unshrunk cloth on an old garment; or else the new piece pulls away from the old, and the tear is made worse"** (v. 21). Jesus here used a metaphor every homemaker would understand. If a garment has been washed several times and has shrunk, if it is then ripped, it cannot be patched with new cloth. If it is, the new cloth will then shrink, and the patch will tear loose and the original tear will be exacerbated.

He followed with an illustration of a wineskin: **"And no one puts new wine into old wineskins; or else the new wine bursts the wineskins, the wine is spilled, and the wineskins are ruined. But new wine must be put into new wineskins"** (v. 22). In the ancient world, the standard wineskin was a goatskin. When new wine was put in a new goatskin, the wine would ferment, emitting gasses that would expand and stretch the wineskin. New wine went into new wineskins because the new wineskins could stretch and handle the expansion. But every Jew in Israel understood that new wine could not be put into old wineskins because the old wineskins had already been stretched to the max. New wine would ferment and expand an old wineskin to the point of bursting. Then both the wineskin and the wine would be lost.

With these metaphors, Jesus was saying, in essence, "You cannot take the new and force it into the old structures because the old structures cannot bear it." He was not condemning the Old Testament law of God. He was condemning the traditions that had developed among the scribes and Pharisees. He was warning them that their King had come, and they would not be able to deal with this King unless they got rid of the structures that made it impossible for them to receive Him. Something so transcendentally new had happened that they could not receive Christ into their lives without being made new themselves. It would be impossible to be a Christian and keep to the old ways.

In short, He was warning the Pharisees that, when the heavenly feast came, they were not going to be ready because they were rejecting their King. They were rejecting the Son of God.

The message for us is that if we indeed have embraced Christ in all of His newness, we may look eagerly to the future, when people from all over creation will sit down with Him in His Father's house, celebrating the marriage feast of the Lamb.

8

LORD
OF THE SABBATH

Mark 2:23–3:6

Now it happened that He went through the grainfields on the Sabbath; and as they went His disciples began to pluck the heads of grain. And the Pharisees said to Him, "Look, why do they do what is not lawful on the Sabbath?" But He said to them, "Have you never read what David did when he was in need and hungry, he and those with him: how he went into the house of God in the days of Abiathar the high priest, and ate the showbread, which is not lawful to eat except for the priests, and also gave some to those who were with him?" And He said to them, "The Sabbath was made for man, and not man for the Sabbath. Therefore the Son of Man is also Lord of the Sabbath." And He entered the synagogue again, and a man was there who had a withered hand. So they watched Him closely, whether He would heal him on the Sabbath, so that they might accuse Him. And He said to the man who had the withered hand, "Step forward." Then He said to them, "Is it lawful on the Sabbath to do good or to do evil, to save life or to kill?" But they kept silent. And when He had looked around at them with anger, being grieved by the hardness of their hearts, He said to the man, "Stretch out your hand." And he stretched it out, and his hand was restored as whole as the other. Then the Pharisees went out and immediately plotted with the Herodians against Him, how they might destroy Him.

We have been witnessing a rising tide of conflict between Jesus and the religious authorities of His day. Though it was still early in Christ's public ministry, the hatred and antagonism of those who opposed Him already had grown intense.

The next chapter in this conflict began innocently enough. Mark tells us: **Now it happened that He went through the grainfields on the Sabbath; and as they went His disciples began to pluck the heads of grain. And the Pharisees said to Him, "Look, why do they do what is not lawful on the Sabbath?"** (vv. 23–24). When the disciples picked a few heads of grain on the Sabbath, the Pharisees accused them of violating Sabbath law. Actually, they did not violate the Sabbath command, but they did violate at least one rabbinic tradition and probably two.

God gave the laws governing behavior on the Sabbath day to the Jewish people at Sinai. These laws were contained in the Ten Commandments (Exodus 20) and in other guidelines for holy living (Exodus 16, 20, 23, 31, 35; Leviticus 16, 19, 23). Over the centuries, as they did with so many God-given laws, the rabbis devoted themselves to fine-tuning the Sabbath laws and adding specific prohibitions to guard the observation of the Sabbath day. Their prohibitions included many details found nowhere in sacred Scripture, but their traditions eventually became as binding on the people's consciences as Scripture itself.

One of those prohibitions had to do with what the rabbis called a "Sabbath-day journey," the maximum distance Jewish people were allowed to travel on the Sabbath. The rabbis defined the Sabbath-day journey as 1,999 paces, a little over half a mile. If a person took one step beyond 1,999, he was considered a Sabbath breaker. Presumably that rabbinic prohibition was in view in this incident recorded by Mark, because the disciples walked quite a while through the grain fields searching for something to eat, and in all likelihood they went over the limit of 1,999 steps.

The rabbis also had determined that since any commerce was prohibited on the Sabbath day, any unnecessary labor on the Sabbath also violated God's law. So, there was a prohibition against reaping crops on the Sabbath day. The Pharisees considered that when the disciples went through the fields plucking grain, they were guilty of harvesting on the Sabbath day—a terrible infraction in their view.

A Precedent from Jewish History

When Jesus responded to this question from the religious leaders, He first directed their attention to the Bible. As any good attorney would do, He cited a precedent to justify the behavior of His clients, in this case, the disciples.

Jesus reminded them of an incident from the life of David: He said to them, **"Have you never read what David did when he was in need and hungry, he and those with him: how he went into the house of God in the days of Abiathar the high priest, and ate the showbread, which is not lawful to eat except for the priests, and also gave some to those who were with him?"** (vv. 25–26). Jesus began by asking, basically, "Have you read your Bibles?" The Pharisees probably found this question insulting. After all, they were supposed to be experts on the Hebrew Scriptures. But it seems they had not considered this incident, which is recorded in 1 Samuel 21:1–6.

When David was a fugitive from Saul, he gathered a "band of brothers" who went with him throughout the land. On one occasion, when they were without food, David remembered there were loaves of bread within reach in the tabernacle, sitting on the table of showbread. So, he went there and asked the priest for that holy bread, then gave it to his men.

Jesus used this illustration because He knew that, in the minds of the Pharisees, the great hero of ancient Israel was David. He was their idea of the ideal king. But Jesus had been preaching the breakthrough of a new kingdom that would fulfill the kingship of David. Jesus, the son of David, appealed to something that David did in order to silence His critics.

Those who believe there are discrepancies in Scripture like to point out that 1 Samuel 21 tells us that Ahimelech was the high priest at that time. Yet Jesus said that this incident took place in the days of Abiathar the high priest. Did our Lord make a mistake? In the Old Testament period, there were two Ahimelechs, but Abiathar was the main high priest at the time, and that period of Jewish history was marked as the era of Abiathar. Jesus did not say Abiathar actually was the high priest when David took the showbread from the tabernacle, but the incident took place in that era. So, I think we can exonerate Jesus from those critics who want to doubt Him for what He said on this occasion.

The Authority to Regulate the Sabbath

Jesus then drew a lesson from the story of David and the showbread: **"The Sabbath was made for man, and not man for the Sabbath"** (v. 27). Jesus was not downplaying the Old Testament law, but rather the rabbinic tradition that had been added to the law. Where God had left people free, the rabbis had put them in chains. They had multiplied prohibitions for the Sabbath to an astonishing degree. For example, in trying to define what it meant to go beyond necessary labor on the Sabbath, they decreed that it was a sin to untie a knot on the Sabbath. If someone accidentally knotted his sandal laces, he had to leave them knotted until the Sabbath was over because untying them would be unnecessary work. In another example, they said that if a person tore a garment, he was allowed to sew one stitch, but no more. This is where legalism leads—to absurdity.

Unfortunately, this sort of legalism is all too common within the Christian community, where all kinds of rules are established that have nothing to do with God's laws. When I began work as a professor at a Christian college, I went to a picnic at the campus lake before classes started. I saw some students playing cards and asked what game they were playing. "Rook," they said. "Don't you know that's the Christian card game? We're not allowed to play any other game of cards." It seems that other card games used the joker, the symbol of the Devil, so the students were prohibited from playing those games. There were many other rules in that campus environment—no movies, no dancing, all that sort of thing. Of course, that college was not unique in its establishment of nonbiblical rules. Like the Pharisees, we create rules that we can keep instead of obeying the rules God gives us, which are much more difficult to follow.

Jesus' point in saying the Sabbath was "made for man" was that it is a gift from God to His people, a gift to keep them from wearing out their bodies, their animals, their servants, and their fields. However, the rabbinic tradition had turned the Sabbath from a great gift to a laborious burden. People had to take great care not to overstep the boundaries the rabbis had set.

Then came the bombshell: Jesus said, **"Therefore the Son of Man is also Lord of the Sabbath"** (v. 28). With this assertion, Jesus once again declared His authority. He wanted the religious leaders to know that He not only had the authority to forgive sins (2:5–12), but also that He was (and is) Lord of the Sabbath.

There are many ongoing debates about the Sabbath day. One of them concerns when the Sabbath was instituted. Some scholars say the Sabbath was not really instituted until God gave the fourth commandment at Sinai and delivered it by Moses. Others believe the Sabbath was instituted long before, at creation. God Himself followed the pattern of working for six days and resting on the seventh day. Not only did He rest on the Sabbath day, He hallowed it (Gen. 2:1–3). He made it a holy day, a holiday, all the way back at creation. I am with the group that believes the Sabbath was instituted at creation, long before Moses ever walked this earth.

What does it mean for Jesus to be the Lord of the Sabbath? He was saying that He made the Sabbath and is therefore sovereign over it. We are told that all things were made through the Word of God, the second person of the Trinity (John 1:3). In effect, then, He was claiming to be the Creator. It is little wonder the religious leaders could not wait to put their heads together and figure out a way to kill Jesus.

A Display of Authority

Jesus not only declared His authority over the Sabbath and creation, He displayed it. Mark tells us: **He entered the synagogue again, and a man was there who had a withered hand. So they watched Him closely, whether He would heal him on the Sabbath, so that they might accuse him** (3:1–2). In other words, the Pharisees and scribes were watching to see whether He would break the law again, or at least the law as they defined it. **And He said to the man who had the withered hand, "Step forward"** (v. 3). Of course a withered hand was not a life-threatening malady. So, according to the rabbis, Jesus should have said, "If you want Me to fix your hand, you'll have to wait until tomorrow." But Jesus saw no need to wait to show compassion, and told the man to step forward. Probably the last thing that poor man wanted was to be used as exhibit A in a dispute against Jesus, but surely the first thing he wanted was to get back the use of his hand, so he came forward as Jesus asked.

Again Jesus put a question to His enemies: **He said to them, "Is it lawful on the Sabbath to do good or to do evil, to save life or to kill?" But they kept silent** (v. 4). Jesus was not asking, "Is it lawful on the Sabbath to do what the rabbis permit?" but, "Is it okay to do good?" His point was that good things may be done not just six days a week but seven days a week. Is it lawful for a nurse or a doctor to treat people who are sick on the Sabbath day? Is it lawful for a farmer to feed his cattle? Is it lawful for ordinary Christians to travel about to visit shut-ins? Of course it is. All these things are good things.

I believe Jesus was speaking with irony because He knew what was going on in the minds of the religious leaders. They were ready to bring charges against Him for doing good on the Sabbath day even while they were plotting on that same Sabbath day to kill Him. Could there have been a worse way of violating the sanctity of the day God set apart for the well-being of His people than to plot to kill the Lord of the Sabbath on the Sabbath day?

Mark tells us that Jesus was very upset by the stance of the Pharisees: **He . . . looked around at them with anger, being grieved by the hardness of their hearts** (v. 5a). The hypocritical religious authorities provoked Him to anger. The Greek word Mark uses here is not the word used for simple annoyance or even righteous indignation. It is the word for fury. Jesus was outraged that the religious leaders cared more about their traditions than the welfare of a suffering human being. But His anger was mixed with pain. Mark tells us that Jesus was grieved in His soul at the hardness of their hearts. In other words, He had compassion for them, too.

Nevertheless, the Lord was undeterred in His purpose to do good for the man with the withered hand on the Sabbath. Mark writes: **He said to the** man, "Stretch out your hand." And he stretched it out, and his hand was restored as whole as the other. Then the Pharisees went out and immediately plotted with the Herodians against Him, how they might destroy Him (vv. 5b–6). The Pharisees refused to hear Jesus' teaching and immediately began plotting against Him with the Herodians, who were part of a political group that supported the dynasty of Herod the Great and his sons.

It saddens me deeply to see how the Pharisees' hardness of heart grieved Jesus. The Bible warns us about grieving the Holy Spirit (Eph. 4:30). Before He brought the flood on the earth, God looked at the evil in this world and said, "My Spirit shall not strive with man forever" (Gen. 6:3). It is clear that God was becoming grieved with man at that point. The fact that the flood followed soon after shows that there is a point when His compassion ends, where His mercy stops, and His anger erupts.

Until that time, the Holy Spirit uses God's Word to quicken our consciences, to make us aware of our rebellion against God. But all of us have some degree of callousness of heart, some stiffness of neck. We know that nothing exposes us like God's Word, so we want nothing to do with it. Is that true of you? Do you have some kind of shield you use to keep God's truth from piercing your heart? I urge you, do not harden your heart when you hear the Word of God.

We must guard against reading a story like this, where we see our Lord angry and grief-stricken over human sin, and simply say to ourselves, "Oh, those bad Pharisees." When we do that, we are just like them. Rather, we should go to God in prayer and say: "O God, do not be angry with me. Do not let me give You cause to be furious with me. Do not let me grieve You because my heart is hardened. Instead, tell me what You want from me. Give me ears to hear, and a heart open to embrace everything that You say."

9

TWELVE FOLLOWERS
CALLED TO JESUS

Mark 3:7–19

$\sim$

But Jesus withdrew with His disciples to the sea. And a great multitude from Galilee followed Him, and from Judea and Jerusalem and Idumea and beyond the Jordan; and those from Tyre and Sidon, a great multitude, when they heard how many things He was doing, came to Him. So He told His disciples that a small boat should be kept ready for Him because of the multitude, lest they should crush Him. For He healed many, so that as many as had afflictions pressed about Him to touch Him. And the unclean spirits, whenever they saw Him, fell down before Him and cried out, saying, "You are the Son of God." But He sternly warned them that they should not make Him known. And He went up on the mountain and called to Him those He Himself wanted. And they came to Him. Then He appointed twelve, that they might be with Him and that He might send them out to preach, and to have power to heal sicknesses and to cast out demons: Simon, to whom He gave the name Peter; James the son of Zebedee and John the brother of James, to whom He gave the name Boanerges, that is, "Sons of Thunder"; Andrew, Philip, Bartholomew, Matthew, Thomas, James the son of Alphaeus, Thaddaeus, Simon the Cananite; and Judas Iscariot, who also betrayed Him. And they went into a house.

T he early days of Jesus' public ministry in Galilee produced a rising tide of public acclaim. This popularity was not entirely a good thing; the crowds became so large that Jesus could not enter a city but had to stay out in deserted places (1:45), and He could not receive and minister to all the people who wanted His help (2:2).

Sadly, it is clear that the overwhelming desire of the crowds was not for Jesus' message but for His healing touch; they were seeking to be relieved of their pain and suffering. In other words, they were more concerned with their bodies than their souls.

We are like those people of Galilee. Our prayer requests tend to focus mostly on our physical problems and those of others we love. Of course, God made us physical beings, and we see throughout Scripture that God is deeply concerned with the well-being of our bodies. The body is not a mere prison for the soul; it is not something to be despised. As Christians, we believe that our bodies will be resurrected and reunited to our souls someday. So, it is good for us to be concerned about the welfare of our bodies and of other people's bodies.

However, we are not merely bodies, for God made us body and soul, and Jesus made the care of our souls a top priority in His teaching. He set forth His value system when He said: "What will it profit a man if he gains the whole world, and loses his own soul? Or what will a man give in exchange for his soul?" (8:36–37). We need to be much in prayer for the well-being of our souls as well as our bodies.

Jesus said, "Where your treasure is, there your heart will be also" (Matt. 6:21). It always amazes me that polls consistently show that the lowest-paid vocation in the United States of America is the clergy. By contrast, one of the highest-paid vocations is that of physicians. This tells us what we value. We value our bodies highly, but we value our souls very little. In the Old Testament, God established the principle of the tithe for a specific purpose—to support the ministry of the church, the preaching, teaching, and other priestly functions; in other words, the care of souls. That was the only function that God ordained to be supported by divine taxation. God did not let the market determine the support for the ministry because He knew that in a fallen world, if people were left to themselves, they would never put a premium on the care of their souls.

The people's great concern for physical well-being was definitely an issue for Jesus. But even as His popularity was going through the roof, He faced a rising tide of opposition from the Jewish religious authorities. After His healing of a man's withered hand on the Sabbath, the Pharisees and Herodians were angry enough to discuss ways of killing Him, as we saw in the previous chapter. It seems likely that these two factors were the reason why **Jesus withdrew with**

His disciples to the sea (v. 7a). Perhaps He was looking for a respite from the crowds and some distance from the Pharisees and their allies.

Healing and Silencing Demons

If Jesus' withdrawal to the sea was an attempt to escape the crowds, it did not work out: **And a great multitude from Galilee followed Him, and from Judea and Jerusalem and Idumea and beyond the Jordan; and those from Tyre and Sidon, a great multitude, when they heard how many things He was doing, came to Him** (vv. 7b–8). Indeed, this may have been the largest crowd He had yet seen. It included Galileans, of course, but some had come from Judea, Jerusalem, and Idumea well to the south, and from the region beyond the Jordan to the east. Plus, there were people from the largely Gentile region around Tyre and Sidon to the northwest; it is unclear whether Jews, Gentiles, or both were in this group, but they themselves constituted a large multitude, for Jesus' fame had spread even there.

It is clear that the size of this crowd was a concern to Jesus. Mark tells us: **He told His disciples that a small boat should be kept ready for Him because of the multitude, lest they should crush Him. For He healed many, so that as many as had afflictions pressed about Him to touch Him** (vv. 9–10). In His compassion, Jesus began to heal the many people coming to Him with diseases and other maladies, but that only caused the people to press against Him even more eagerly, hoping to touch Him and be healed. In self-defense, Jesus instructed His disciples that they should keep a small boat ready on the shore of the Sea of Galilee should He need to withdraw from them.

Mark adds: **And the unclean spirits, whenever they saw Him, fell down before Him and cried out, saying, "You are the Son of God." But He sternly warned them that they should not make Him known** (vv. 11–12). Mark earlier noted Jesus' ability to command evil spirits as a sign of His authority (1:27). In that incident, an evil spirit identified Him as "Jesus of Nazareth" and "the Holy One of God" (v. 24). Here, again, Mark goes out of His way to show how the spirits behaved and what they said when Jesus cast them out. They fell down before Him in a posture of obeisance and they confessed that He was the Son of God. It is interesting to note that this is the first confession of Jesus' Sonship that Mark records. As he seeks to set forth Jesus as the Jewish Messiah for His Gentile audience, the confession of these evil spirits carries great weight.

As we saw when we studied the earlier incident of demonic possession, the demons hoped that naming Jesus and revealing His identity would somehow give them power over Him. The concept of naming is very significant in the Bible. One of the first tasks that God gave to Adam in the garden was to name the animals, for naming them manifested the dominion of the human over the beast. Of course, in God's economy, no fallen spirit could possibly have power over the second person of the Trinity, so the demons' shouting of Jesus' identity was pointless.

When Jesus heard what the spirits said, He sternly warned them not to make Him known. It was not yet time for His divine identity to be proclaimed abroad, so Jesus silenced them with a word of command. In this incident, we see a foreshadowing of the final conflict between Christ and the forces of hell. Whenever hell collides with heaven, the inevitable result is silence. Whenever evil appears before God, its mouth is shut. Scripture tells us repeatedly that people appearing before God at the last judgment will place their hands over their mouths in His presence and will keep silent. No sinner has anything to say in the presence of the holy God.

Calling the Disciples

Finally, somehow, Jesus escaped the crowds: **And He went up on the mountain and called to Him those He Himself wanted. And they came to Him. Then He appointed twelve, that they might be with Him and that He might send them out to preach, and to have power to heal sicknesses and to cast out demons** (vv. 13–15). Jesus went to a mountain, apparently with no more than a small contingent of followers, and called certain of His disciples to Himself, not for the purpose of ministering to them but so that they might be set apart to minister. His goal was that they should be students in His rabbinical school, to be trained to be sent out to do the same things He was doing—preaching and healing.

Mark has already shown us the initial calling of at least some of the disciples. In chapter 1, he recounted the calling of four fishermen, Peter and his brother Andrew, and James and his brother John (vv. 16–20). In chapter 2, he told of the call of Levi, or Matthew (v. 14). As we saw when we studied those passages, Jesus' selection of disciples was a radical departure from the custom of the time. Normally, when someone wanted to study with a particular rabbi, he would make application, just as students today apply for admission to colleges. Jesus, however, recruited those He wanted to tutor.

On the mountain, Jesus "called to Him those He Himself wanted." Presumably there were more people following Jesus than the five handpicked men Mark has mentioned. Out of that group, He called Peter, Andrew, James, John, Matthew, and others. He called them not to a study of the law, of science, or of a trade; rather, He called them to Himself. Jesus called the ones He wanted, and His call was a sovereign one, because everyone He called to that office came to that office, and they came willingly to join that band of men who were to be a part of whom He was.

In a sense, this is a microcosmic look at what Jesus does for the whole kingdom of God—He calls those whom He wants. The Greek word that is translated as "church" in the Bible is *ekklesia*. This word is made up of a prefix and a root. The prefix is *ek* or *ex*, which means "out of" or "from." The root word is a form of the verb *kaleo*, which means "to call." Thus, *ekklesia* means "those who are the called-out ones." Simply put, the invisible church, the true church, is composed of those who are called by God not only outwardly but inwardly by the Holy Spirit. When Jesus calls someone to discipleship, He is calling that person to Himself, to belong to Him, to follow Him, and to learn from Him and of Him.

It is true that the only faith by which a person can be justified is his own faith. No one can be justified by his spouse's faith, his parents' faith, his children's faith, or anyone else's faith. At the final judgment, everyone will stand before God alone, and judgment will be rendered based on what is in his heart alone.

However, every time Christ saves an individual, He places him in a group. There is a corporate dimension to the kingdom of God that we must not overlook. I spoke recently with a woman whose church has called a new pastor. She is not happy with the new pastor, so she has left the church. When I asked her what she is doing for worship, she replied that she watches religious programming on television on Sunday morning. The obvious problem with this is that she is not *in* church on Sunday morning. She is not with the people of God in corporate worship, in solemn assembly. The Christian life is a corporate thing, for Christ places His redeemed people in the church to learn together, grow together, serve together, and worship together.

Called to Come and to Go

Mark writes that Jesus "appointed twelve, that they might be with Him and that He might send them out to preach, and to have power to heal sicknesses and to cast out demons." The Greek word that the New King James Version translates as "appointed" is a form of a verb that can also mean "to make something" or "to create something," and that is its primary meaning in the Bible. It is exactly the word that the Septuagint (the Greek Old Testament) uses in Genesis 1:1: "In the beginning God created the heavens and the earth." God did not appoint the heavens and the earth. He did not select them. No, He created them. In the same way, Jesus did not simply appoint twelve men to a task or a body. Rather, He made them into something. He made them His intimate group. In a sense, He made them the church.

It is fascinating to me that Jesus did not choose ten, or eight, or twenty. He chose twelve, certainly calling to mind the Old Testament structure of the twelve tribes of Israel. Twelve is not a common number in Hebrew numerology, but by choosing twelve disciples to become the twelve Apostles, Jesus established a symmetry between the church of the Old Testament and the church of the New Testament.

Jesus chose them, in the first analysis, that they might be with Him. One of the most important doctrines that we find in the writings of the Apostle Paul is the doctrine of the mystical union of the believer with Christ. When we come to faith in Christ for the first time, in New Testament terms, we do not simply believe in Jesus, we believe *into* Jesus. When Paul told the Philippian jailor, "Believe on the Lord Jesus Christ, and you will be saved" (Acts 16:31a), the Greek word translated as "on" is *eis*, which means "into." Faith moves us from outside Christ, from a state of separation from Christ, to union with Him. We embrace Him, and so we move *into* Christ. Once we believe *into* Christ, we experience "Christ in you, the hope of glory" (Col. 1:27). The Greek word translated as "in" here is a different word that literally means "inside of." So, every Christian who is called by Jesus enters into Jesus, into this profound mystical union. We are in Christ and Christ is in us. This is the origin of the communion of saints; we are in this together. We have a spiritual bond that will last for eternity, for we have been called by Jesus to be with Him.

On the night of His betrayal, in the upper room, Jesus said: "Let not your heart be troubled; you believe in God, believe also in Me. In My Father's house are many mansions; if it were not so, I would have told you. I go to prepare a place for you. And if I go and prepare a place for you, I will come again and receive you to Myself; *that where I am, there you may be also*" (John 14:1–3). Jesus wants us to be with Him. Is there any greater blessing than to be in the presence of Christ, to be with Him, to have Him with us?

Of course, Jesus had a further purpose for the disciples—to send them out to preach and minister. Any time Jesus says, "Come to Me," as soon as we come, the "come" becomes "go." When we come to Him, He gives us a mission. We are to go into the world and make disciples. As we carry out that mission, He is with us.

Finally, Mark names the twelve disciples Jesus called to Himself: **Simon, to whom He gave the name Peter; James the son of Zebedee and John the brother of James, to whom He gave the name Boanerges, that is, "Sons of Thunder"; Andrew, Philip, Bartholomew, Matthew, Thomas, James the son of Alphaeus, Thaddaeus, Simon the Cananite; and Judas Iscariot, who also betrayed Him** (vv. 16–19). These men would be with Him for three years, undergoing preparation to be His Apostles. In time, He would also send them out, and they would turn the world upside down (Acts 17:6).

10

BLASPHEMY AGAINST THE SPIRIT

Mark 3:20–35

∼≈∼

Then the multitude came together again, so that they could not so much as eat bread. But when His own people heard about this, they went out to lay hold of Him, for they said, "He is out of His mind." And the scribes who came down from Jerusalem said, "He has Beelzebub," and, "By the ruler of the demons He casts out demons." So He called them to Himself and said to them in parables: "How can Satan cast out Satan? If a kingdom is divided against itself, that kingdom cannot stand. And if a house is divided against itself, that house cannot stand. And if Satan has risen up against himself, and is divided, he cannot stand, but has an end. No one can enter a strong man's house and plunder his goods, unless he first binds the strong man. And then he will plunder his house. Assuredly, I say to you, all sins will be forgiven the sons of men, and whatever blasphemies they may utter; but he who blasphemes against the Holy Spirit never has forgiveness, but is subject to eternal condemnation"—because they said, "He has an unclean spirit." Then His brothers and His mother came, and standing outside they sent to Him, calling Him. And a multitude was sitting around Him; and they said to Him, "Look, Your mother and Your brothers are outside seeking You." But He answered them, saying, "Who is My mother, or My brothers?" And He looked around in a circle at those who sat about Him, and said, "Here are My mother and My brothers! For whoever does the will of God is My brother and My sister and mother."

As soon as Jesus came down from the mountain, Mark tells us, **the multitude came together again, so that they could not so much as eat bread** (v. 20). It seems that the crowd was, if anything, larger and more passionate than before, with the people packing themselves in so tightly that Jesus and His disciples could not even eat.

Something about this public frenzy raised concerns among some people close to Jesus: **But when His own people heard about this, they went out to lay hold of Him, for they said, "He is out of His mind"** (v. 21). It is not clear precisely who these people were. Some scholars believe they were friends or associates, but in all probability they were family members. The incident that Mark records later in this passage, when Jesus' mother and brothers sought to speak with Him, seems to confirm this. Whoever they were, they decided to forcefully bring Jesus home, for they had concluded that He was out of His mind. It appears that this was an attempt at a family intervention against one who had stirred up a great deal of controversy and hostility.

This is reminiscent of that occasion when Paul the Apostle stood before King Agrippa and Festus, the Roman governor of Judea. As Paul was telling of his conversion, Festus cried out: "Paul, you are beside yourself! Much learning is driving you mad!" (Acts 26:24b). Jesus certainly was not the first to be considered insane for the positions that He took, and by no means was He the last. What happened to Jesus here has happened again and again throughout church history, and it is no less common today.

Has anyone ever called you a religious fanatic? If you answer that question in the negative, my next question is, "Why not?" Anyone who takes his faith seriously and speaks on behalf of Christ and His kingdom will be accused of fanaticism at some point. It is interesting to me that people who excitedly follow their favorite teams and show their allegiance plainly are called "fans," a word that usually has positive or at least neutral connotations. However, people who follow Christ and show their allegiance to Him are likely to be called "fanatics," a word with clear negative connotations. I once read that a fanatic is someone who, having lost sight of his goal, doubles his efforts to get there. In other words, a fanatic is a person who has no idea where he is going or even why he is going there, but he is going there with all of his might. However, if that is a proper definition of a fanatic, it certainly does not fit the Christian. If the definition of a fanatic is someone who is zealous for the faith, I would be proud to be called a fanatic.

Why did this happen to Jesus? Why did people close to Him object to His activities? It was because He seemed to be calling down on Himself and everyone around Him the wrath of the Jewish religious leaders. They were concerned that when the authorities decided to crack down on Jesus, they also would crack down on everyone close to Him. They saw Him as being out of His mind because He was willing to stand up to the Pharisees, the scribes, and the rabbis. Of course, at the root of this attitude was sheer unbelief in who Jesus was.

Mark breaks away from this narrative in verse 22 to report another theory about Jesus and His response to it, but before we consider that, it would be good to close the loop on the attitude of "His own people," which closure seems to come in verses 31–35. Mark tells us first: **His brothers and His mother came, and standing outside they sent to Him, calling Him. And a multitude was sitting around Him; and they said to Him, "Look, Your mother and Your brothers are outside seeking You"** (vv. 31–32). Jesus' brothers and His mother arrived as He was teaching and sent in a message in which they asked to see Him. It is interesting that the term "brothers" here is used throughout Mark to mean siblings from the same parents, which makes a strong argument against the Roman Catholic teaching that Mary remained a virgin after Jesus' birth (Rome teaches that the term can refer to other relatives). In any case, Scripture refers numerous times to Jesus' four brothers or half-brothers, and here they accompanied their mother to speak with Jesus.

What did Jesus do? **He answered them, saying, "Who is My mother, or My brothers?" And He looked around in a circle at those who sat about Him, and said, "Here are My mother and My brothers! For whoever does the will of God is My brother and My sister and mother"** (vv. 33–35). These words, which seem slightly rude on the surface, were not a denial or repudiation by Jesus of His mother and brothers. Instead, they are a profound teaching about union with Christ. Jesus declared that those who believe in Him and do God's will have a relationship with Him that is closer than the blood relationships between parents, children, and siblings. We must never lose sight of the fact that we are bound to Jesus by mighty mystical cords that cannot be broken.

The Source of His Power

Jesus' "own people" considered Him insane, but the religious leaders had another theory. Mark tells us, **the scribes who came down from Jerusalem said, "He has Beelzebub,"** and, **"By the ruler of the demons He casts out demons"** (v. 22). This was the most vicious charge leveled against Jesus up to this point and perhaps in His whole life. Basically, the scribes theorized that Jesus was acting insane (challenging the status quo) because He was possessed by an evil spirit, which also explained where He got the power to cast out demons.

The scribes specifically suggested Jesus was possessed by Beelzebub. In antiquity, Beelzebub was seen as a demigod, a lesser deity, who ruled over filth, carrion, and flies. He was called "the Lord of the Dunghill." The title of the classic novel *The Lord of the Flies* is a takeoff on this title for Beelzebub. Some of the manuscripts indicate that the word used by the scribes was not "Beelzebub" but "Beelzebul," a reference to the god Baal, who was considered the lord of all the demonic realm. In that case, this was a title for Satan himself. That interpretation is supported by the fact that the scribes also theorized that "By the ruler of the demons He casts out demons." Their charge, in short, was that Jesus was in league with the Devil. They could not deny that He had power and that he was using it to perform miracles, to heal the sick, and to cast out demons. However, it made no sense to them that God would empower an uneducated carpenter to do such things, especially since He seemed to have so little regard for their traditions. Their conclusion was that Christ was working through the power of Satan.

I believe the scribes committed a serious theological error with these comments. Contrary to their theory—and, I might add, to the widespread belief in the evangelical Christian world today—I do not believe Satan has ever performed a bona fide miracle. Satan does not have divine power because he is a creature. He is stronger than we are, but he cannot do the things that only God can do. Scripture says his works are lying signs and wonders (2 Thess. 2:9). That is, they are counterfeits. However, the scribes were not saying that Jesus' miracles were counterfeit. They were granting that they were real, but they mistakenly attributed them to Satan.

Of course, Mark has clearly showed that Jesus was anointed and endowed for His ministry by the power not of Satan but of the Holy Spirit. Furthermore, the consistent biblical testimony is that the power by which Jesus cast out demons, healed people who were afflicted with various diseases, and did other miracles was of the Spirit. But His enemies were flatly denying the role of the Spirit in Jesus' work. "It is not the power of God," they said. "It is the power of the Devil. This man is with the Devil."

Jesus got wind of what the scribes were saying. He took this charge seriously and responded to it forcefully: **So He called them to Himself and said to them in parables: "How can Satan cast out Satan? If a kingdom is divided against itself, that kingdom cannot stand. And if a house is divided against itself, that house cannot stand. And if Satan has risen up against himself, and is divided, he cannot stand, but has an end** (vv. 23–26). Jesus called the scribes to Himself and spoke to them in parables. These were not long, elaborate parables such as the parable of the sower, which we will consider in the next chapter. Rather, these were short, figurative statements. But like most parables, they packed a punch.

Jesus first showed the scribes the logical absurdity of their theory. "How can Satan cast out Satan?" He asked. Clearly, Satan would never allow his power to be used to defeat his own minions. Furthermore, it was a well-known truism that a kingdom or a house divided against itself could not stand. If a country or a family split into bickering factions, its very existence was threatened. Simply put, if Satan was allowing Jesus to drive out his own demons, he was fighting against himself—another illogical move that would be uncharacteristic of the shrewd Devil.

Then Jesus gave another mini-parable, saying: **"No one can enter a strong man's house and plunder his goods, unless he first binds the strong man. And then he will plunder his house"** (v. 27). If a burglar wants to break into the home of a man who is stronger than he is, the burglar must think of a way to subdue the strong man. He has to render him ineffective. He might choose to point a gun at him, he might drug him, or he might have accomplices tie his hands. If he cannot counter the man's strength, he cannot plunder his home. In saying these things, Jesus was alluding to His own ministry, for He had broken into the domain of Satan and bound him, rendering him impotent to prevent the plundering of his house. Jesus' power over evil spirits was evidence that He was not working by the power of Satan but was working *against* Satan.

The Unpardonable Sin

With those words, Jesus concluded His defense against the ridiculous charge that He was in league with Satan. But He did not stop there. He went on to give the scribes and the others listening in a very severe warning. He said: **"Assuredly, I say to you, all sins will be forgiven the sons of men, and whatever blasphemies they may utter; but he who blasphemes against the Holy Spirit never has forgiveness, but is subject to eternal condemnation"** (vv. 28–29).

I cannot tell you how many times in my teaching career very distraught Christians have come to me to ask about the unpardonable sin and whether they might have committed it. I suspect most believers have asked themselves whether they have done something unforgivable. It is not surprising that many people struggle with this issue because the precise nature of "the unpardonable sin" is difficult to discern and many theories about it have been set forth through church history. For instance, some people have argued that the unpardonable sin is murder and others have said that it is adultery, because they see the serious consequences that those sins wreak on the sanctity of life and the sanctity of marriage. But I can speak with full assurance that neither of those sins is unpardonable. There are two reasons for my assurance. First, Scripture shows us examples of people who committed these sins and were forgiven. Exhibit A is David, who was guilty of both adultery and murder, and yet, after his confession and repentance, he was restored fully to his state of grace. Second, and more important, when Jesus taught on the unpardonable sin, He said nothing about murder or adultery.

What, then, did Jesus say? He began in a radical way by saying, "Assuredly, I say to you." Sometimes evangelical Christians who want to express agreement with something they have heard from a preacher or a teacher will say "Amen." The word *amen* is transliterated from the Hebrew *amein*, which means "truth" or "it is true," so those saying "Amen" are agreeing with what they have heard. But instead of giving His teaching and waiting for His hearers to say "Amen," Jesus *Himself* said "Amen" *before* He gave His teaching. The word translated as "assuredly" here is the Greek equivalent of the word *amein*. In other words, Jesus announced that He was about to say something true. This was a way of saying, "Now hear this." He was giving great emphasis to the teaching He was about to utter.

Jesus then stated that "all sins" can be forgiven, including "whatever blasphemies"—except for the specific blasphemy of the Spirit. Luke's account of this teaching is even more specific: "Anyone who speaks a word against the Son of Man, it will be forgiven him; but to him who blasphemes against the Holy Spirit, it will not be forgiven" (12:10).

At this point, we need to define blasphemy, and this verse from Luke gives us a clue as to what it is. The two phrases "who speaks a word against" and "who blasphemes" are parallel. Blasphemy, then, involves speaking a word against God. It is a verbal sin, one that is committed with the mouth or the pen. It is desecration of the holy character of God. It can involve insulting Him, mocking Him, or dishonoring Him. In a sense, it is the opposite of praise. Even casually using the name of God by saying, "Oh, my God," as so many do, constitutes blasphemy. We can be very thankful that the unpardonable sin is not just any kind of blasphemy, because if it were, none of us would have any hope of escaping damnation. All of us have, at many times and in many ways, routinely blasphemed the name of God.

Jesus' statement that "Anyone who speaks a word against the Son of Man, it will be forgiven him" seems shocking in light of the abuse and mistreatment He later went through, culminating in His execution on a Roman cross. But we must remember how, as He hung on the cross, Jesus looked at those who had delivered Him to the Romans and mocked Him as He was dying, and said, "Father, forgive them, for they do not know what they do" (Luke 23:34). Even though these men opposed Christ to the point of executing Him, there was still hope of forgiveness for them. Likewise, in the book of Acts, Peter told the people of Jerusalem that they had delivered Jesus to the Romans and denied Him, but he added, "I know that you did it in ignorance, as did also your rulers" (Acts 3:17), and he called on them to repent. So, on at least two occasions, the New Testament makes it clear that forgiveness was possible for those who despised Christ so much that they killed Him. These accounts verify Jesus' assertion that any sin against the Son of Man could be forgiven.

But what of blasphemy against the Spirit? To understand this difficult saying, we need to see that it came in the context of Jesus' opponents charging Him with doing His work by the power of the Devil rather than by the power of the Holy Spirit. However, they were not slandering the Spirit—not quite. Their statements were directed against Jesus. So, He said to them: "You can blaspheme Me and be forgiven, but when you question the work of the Spirit, you are coming perilously close to the unforgivable sin. You are right at the line. You are looking down into the abyss of hell. One more step and there will be no hope for you." He was warning them to be very careful not to insult or mock the Spirit.

Humanly speaking, everyone who is a Christian is capable of committing the unforgivable sin. However, I believe that the Lord of glory who has saved us and sealed us in the Holy Spirit will never let us commit that sin. I do not believe that any Christians in the history of the church have blasphemed the Spirit. As for those who are not sure they are saved and are worried they may have committed the unpardonable sin, I would say that worrying about it is one of the clearest evidences that they have not committed this sin, for those who commit it are so hardened in their hearts they do not care that they commit it. Thanks be to God that the sin that is unpardonable is not a sin He allows His people to commit.

11

THE PARABLE
OF THE SOWER

Mark 4:1–20

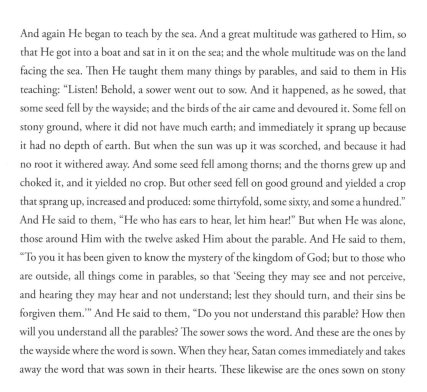

And again He began to teach by the sea. And a great multitude was gathered to Him, so that He got into a boat and sat in it on the sea; and the whole multitude was on the land facing the sea. Then He taught them many things by parables, and said to them in His teaching: "Listen! Behold, a sower went out to sow. And it happened, as he sowed, that some seed fell by the wayside; and the birds of the air came and devoured it. Some fell on stony ground, where it did not have much earth; and immediately it sprang up because it had no depth of earth. But when the sun was up it was scorched, and because it had no root it withered away. And some seed fell among thorns; and the thorns grew up and choked it, and it yielded no crop. But other seed fell on good ground and yielded a crop that sprang up, increased and produced: some thirtyfold, some sixty, and some a hundred." And He said to them, "He who has ears to hear, let him hear!" But when He was alone, those around Him with the twelve asked Him about the parable. And He said to them, "To you it has been given to know the mystery of the kingdom of God; but to those who are outside, all things come in parables, so that 'Seeing they may see and not perceive, and hearing they may hear and not understand; lest they should turn, and their sins be forgiven them.'" And He said to them, "Do you not understand this parable? How then will you understand all the parables? The sower sows the word. And these are the ones by the wayside where the word is sown. When they hear, Satan comes immediately and takes away the word that was sown in their hearts. These likewise are the ones sown on stony ground who, when they hear the word, immediately receive it with gladness; and they have no root in themselves, and so endure only for a time. Afterward, when tribulation or persecution arises for the word's sake, immediately they stumble. Now these are the ones sown among thorns; they are the ones who hear the word, and the cares of this world, the deceitfulness of riches, and the desires for other things entering in choke the word, and it becomes unfruitful. But these are the ones sown on good ground, those who hear the word, accept it, and bear fruit: some thirtyfold, some sixty, and some a hundred."

The story recorded in this passage is found in all three Synoptic Gospels (Matt. 13:1–23; Luke 8:4–15). Some call it the parable of the sower. Others refer to it as the parable of the seed. Still others call it the parable of the soils. All of these titles are acceptable, because any one of these three things—the sower, the seed, the soils—can be seen as the point of major importance and emphasis in the parable.

This parable differs from most of Jesus' parables because, as a general rule, His parables have one central point or meaning. We generally do not interpret parables as allegories, finding significance in each part of the story. However, in this parable, an allegorical interpretation is acceptable. Why? Because in this passage we also have Jesus' own interpretation of the parable, and His interpretation is basically allegorical.

Still, despite the fact that we have Jesus' interpretation in this case, there has been disagreement about the meaning of the parable even among those who have contemplated its significance for many years.

Jesus began the parable with a very strong word. In the Greek, it is the word *akouete*. In the Latin, it is *audite*. In both cases, the form of the word is an imperative, a command. It is translated into English as **"Listen!"** (v. 3a). Jesus chose to begin with this strong exhortation; He was saying, "I want you to listen carefully to what I have to say."

There's an unusual twist in the Greek language. The verb "to hear" is *akouein*, and the verb "to obey" is *hupakouein*, which simply adds the prefix *hup*, which we would translate as "hyper." So in biblical terms, obedience is "hyper-hearing." There's hearing and then there's hyper-hearing. That's what Jesus was calling for here—the kind of hearing that goes beyond the eardrum and affects the heart, prompting obedience.

God and His Word

Jesus said: **"Behold, a sower went out to sow"** (v. 3b). Although Jesus did not say so explicitly in His interpretation, the sower here is God. Jesus did explain the meaning of the seed: **"The sower sows the word"** (v. 14). It is God who, in the final analysis, distributes His Word into the world.

This parable might cause us to wonder about God's efficiency as a sower, as it seems that He distributes the seed haphazardly, so that some of it falls on the pathway, some on rocks, some among thorns, and some on good soil. We might be tempted to ask why God is so inaccurate in the planting of His seed. What farmer would go out and waste his seed by throwing it on the road, on the rocks, or among the thorns? Farmers are very careful how they use their seed. They plow their ground and till it well, then very carefully plant their seed in the kind of soil that at least seems suitable to bring forth a harvest. But the sower in this parable seems to throw his seed carelessly, casting it on the pathway, in the rocks, and in the thorns. What kind of farming is this?

Simply put, it is the kind of farming the Israelites practiced in the ancient world. At that time and place, the land was not cleared of stones and plowed before the seed was planted. The common way of planting was to go out and scatter the seed, then plow. In fact, the term *plow* has little relation to what we think of as plowing today. In ancient Israel, a plow was little more than a pointed stick with which one broke up the soil a little so that some seed would sink in.

One scholar tells of going to Galilee, where this parable originally was given, and seeing a place where the soil was packed down because people had walked back and forth, ridden donkeys, and so on. Alongside this pathway were thorns and bushes, and then there was a section where it was very stony. But just beyond the stony section, this scholar reported, there was a lush, verdant field where a fine crop was growing. He said to himself: "I have just lived the parable of the sower. I have walked on the very kind of ground Jesus described."

The point, of course, is that when God sows His seed, which is His Word, it is spread about, in a sense, indiscriminately. God *does* display His pearls before swine (Matt. 7:6). He does give His Word to people who have no interest in it whatsoever, who are basically so hostile to it that it seems as though God's Word, His seed, is being wasted.

But is it? In the ancient world, a harvest was considered successful if it produced a tenfold increase over the amount of seed that was planted. But when God sows His seed, the harvest that He brings in is **"thirtyfold, some sixty, and some a hundred"** (v. 8b). So we simply cannot conclude that the sower is operating in a willy-nilly fashion and that his planting is thwarted by the poor quality of the soils on which his seed falls. We must remember that it is God's choice to use His Word as the means to save His people. He has empowered that Word so that it carries salvation with it. God, the sower, has promised that

His Word will not return to Him void (Isa. 55:11). He is sovereign, so when He sends His Word forth, it accomplishes what He designs.

Three Bad Soil Types

In the parable, Jesus told of seed falling on four different types of soil, each producing a different result. Three of those outcomes are negative. He said: **"Some seed fell by the wayside; and the birds of the air came and devoured it. Some fell on stony ground, where it did not have much earth; and immediately it sprang up because it had no depth of earth. But when the sun was up it was scorched, and because it had no root it withered away. And some seed fell among thorns; and the thorns grew up and choked it, and it yielded no crop. But other seed fell on good ground and yielded a crop that sprang up, increased and produced: some thirtyfold, some sixty, and some a hundred"** (vv. 4b–8).

When Jesus explained the parable, He first spoke about the seed that fell on the pathway. He noted that birds came and ate it, for it was exposed on the hard-packed soil. All farmers have to deal with birds when they plant seed. When we started the Ligonier Valley Study Center in western Pennsylvania, I was the landscaper. In that role, I planted a vast expanse of a lawn. I raked the ground, I removed the stones, I turned over the soil, I scattered the seed, I covered it with straw, and I watered it meticulously. Of course, I had to deal with the birds that came to eat my precious seed, and I thought I would go crazy because I knew that every one of the seeds that the birds ate was one less blade of grass I was going to get from my labor. In such a scenario, birds can seem positively evil. That is appropriate, because when Jesus interpreted His parable, He likened the birds to Satan, **who "comes immediately and takes away the word that was sown"** (v. 15b). Indeed, Satan always wants to interfere with the progress of God's Word. Remember, however, that God's Word does not return to Him void, and Satan can do only what the sovereign God allows him to do.

What of the seed that fell on stony ground? Jesus said that the stony ground has reference to those who, when they hear the word, **"immediately receive it with gladness; and they have no root in themselves, and so endure only for a time. Afterward, when tribulation or persecution arises for the word's sake, immediately they stumble"** (vv. 16b–17). This is a theologically vivid description of a spurious conversion. We see it often. The evangelist gives his altar call and the people rush to the front of the church, where they sign the commitment card. Or they raise a hand or pray a "sinner's prayer." They are excited. They are filled with joy. But the next day, they are confronted by life as usual, with all its trials and difficulties, and they do not continue on in the faith. We all know people who have been through experiences like that.

On the night I was converted, my best friend also made a profession of faith. Before we went to bed that night, we both sat down and wrote to our girlfriends about our conversions. However, when we woke up in the morning, my friend had completely repudiated what he had embraced with joy the night before, whereas my life was changed forever. Since then, it has always haunted me to see people responding to the gospel; I find myself hoping and praying that the Word will take root in those making professions.

Jesus also explained the meaning of the thorny soil: **"they are the ones who hear the word, and the cares of this world, the deceitfulness of riches, and the desires for other things entering in choke the word, and it becomes unfruitful"** (vv. 18b–19). The thorns grew up and choked the seed that fell in this soil, and it yielded no crop. Here again we see an example of a spurious conversion, of someone who makes a profession of faith, but in this case the person cannot let go of the enticements of this world, the quest for money, fame, and other fleeting pleasures. What he professes is choked out, and the Word never takes root.

The Good Soil Bears Fruit

Only one of the four types of soil brings forth a harvest that is **"thirtyfold, some sixty, and some a hundred"** (v. 20b). It is the good soil, **"those who hear the word, accept it, and bear fruit"** (v. 20a).

As I have said many times, no one is justified by a profession of faith. We must possess the faith we profess if we are to be justified. The seed of God's Word has to take root in our hearts if we are to enter the kingdom of God. A superficial profession of faith is no sign of true redemption.

Moreover, when the seed of the Word takes root, there will be fruit. One of the most ghastly doctrines that has made inroads in the evangelical church today is the idea of the carnal Christian. The carnal Christian is described as a person who is truly redeemed but whose life never brings forth fruit. Even though he is saved, he remains altogether carnal. We must not confuse this idea with the New Testament teaching that the truly converted person has to fight against his flesh all of his life. The difference is that the New Testament promises that the Christian *will* see progress in his fight; he will not remain carnal (Rom. 12:1–2; 2 Cor. 3:18). There is simply no such thing as a Christian who is totally carnal. It is a contradiction in terms.

Perhaps this idea comes from evangelists who do not like to admit that they are dealing with false professions. They see people who make professions and then give no evidence of change in their lives, so they say, "We'll count them as converts, they're just carnal Christians." Tragically, this gives people who are not converted the false assurance that they are, in fact, converted.

What, then, makes the good soil "good"? We have to be careful here. We can say: "Jesus must mean that the seed cannot take root unless the person who hears the Word is a good person. I'm a Christian because I believed the Word, and the reason why I believed the Word is because I'm a good person." If we think that, we have never received the Word at all. That is not the point of this parable.

This question drives us back to one of the basic questions with which we wrestle in theology: Why does one person receive the Word of God in his heart while another person rejects it? The majority view is that it is because there is something more righteous in the person who receives it. Some people think they are Christians because, of their own will, they made the right decision; they embraced Christ, whereas their friends hardened their hearts and did not use their wills to accept the gospel. Those people therefore have something of which to boast eternally; they said "yes" to the gospel offer of salvation.

However, Jesus clearly said: "Unless one is born again, he cannot see the kingdom of God. . . . Unless one is born of water and the Spirit, he cannot enter the kingdom of God" (John 3:3, 5). He also told His disciples, "No one can come to Me unless the Father who sent Me draws him" (John 6:44a). The Apostle Paul also says, "You He made alive, who were dead in trespasses and sins. . . . By grace you have been saved through faith, and that not of yourselves; it is the gift of God" (Eph. 2:1, 8).

The good soil is good because of the supernatural work on the soul by God the Holy Spirit. The only people who embrace the Word of God are those who have first been changed by the Holy Spirit, making them able to receive the Word of God. In short, regeneration comes before faith. The Holy Spirit has to change a person's heart before he will ever say "yes" to Jesus.

That's the power of the Sower. He prepares the soil to receive the seed of His Word. For this reason, we say salvation is of the Lord, and to Him alone belongs the glory.

12

PARABLES
OF THE KINGDOM

Mark 4:21–34

⁓

Also He said to them, "Is a lamp brought to be put under a basket or under a bed? Is it not to be set on a lampstand? For there is nothing hidden which will not be revealed, nor has anything been kept secret but that it should come to light. If anyone has ears to hear, let him hear." Then He said to them, "Take heed what you hear. With the same measure you use, it will be measured to you; and to you who hear, more will be given. For whoever has, to him more will be given; but whoever does not have, even what he has will be taken away from him." And He said, "The kingdom of God is as if a man should scatter seed on the ground, and should sleep by night and rise by day, and the seed should sprout and grow, he himself does not know how. For the earth yields crops by itself: first the blade, then the head, after that the full grain in the head. But when the grain ripens, immediately he puts in the sickle, because the harvest has come." Then He said, "To what shall we liken the kingdom of God? Or with what parable shall we picture it? It is like a mustard seed which, when it is sown on the ground, is smaller than all the seeds on earth; but when it is sown, it grows up and becomes greater than all herbs, and shoots out large branches, so that the birds of the air may nest under its shade." And with many such parables He spoke the word to them as they were able to hear it. But without a parable He did not speak to them. And when they were alone, He explained all things to His disciples.

Not one but three parables are contained in the passage that is before us. Unlike the long and detailed parable of the sower in the opening verses of this chapter of Mark, these parables are short and pithy, clearly communicating one central idea, as do most parables. All three of these parables teach us something about the kingdom of God.

I have to take issue with one part of the English translation in the first of these brief parables. The New King James translation (printed above) and, indeed, most other English translations, render verse 21 with an indefinite article rather than a definite article before the word *lamp*. Quoting Jesus, it says, **"Is a lamp brought to be put under a basket or under a bed?"** (v. 21a). The concept of the lamp is left in a generic sense, even though the Greek New Testament clearly uses the definite article and makes the lamp the subject of the sentence. There is only one proper way to translate what is in the original Greek: "Does *the* lamp come in order to be put under a basket or under a bed?"

If the article in the Greek New Testament is clearly definite, why is it so often rendered as indefinite in translations of Mark? I can only speculate, but one possible reason has to do with the fact that this parable about the lamp is found in all three of the Synoptic Gospels, but both Matthew and Luke use an indefinite article. I suspect that our translators use the indefinite article in Mark because that is what is found in Matthew and Luke.

However, I think that not only does the Greek text call for the definite article, the context does, too. Without the definite article, we miss the significance of what Jesus said here. He was not talking about any lamp. He was talking about *the* lamp. What is that lamp? More properly we should ask, who is that lamp? In biblical categories, God Himself (and particularly His law) is referred to as the lamp. But Jesus is speaking here about the light that has come into the world with the breakthrough of the kingdom of God, and the lamp is Jesus Himself. He is saying: "I did not come here to be concealed forever. I came here as a lamp that is to be set on a lampstand, so that the light that I bring may burst forth and manifest itself clearly to all who dwell in darkness. I did not come to be covered with a basket or hidden under a bed. I came to shine forth."

The metaphor of the lamp that Jesus used here was drawn from the common experience of the people of that day, whose homes were illumined at night by oil lamps. Such a lamp was a piece of pottery that was something like a bowl with a couple of the edges pinched together. Oil was poured into the bowl, and a floating wick came up through the point where the edges were pinched together. That wick was drenched in the oil from the lamp, so it could be lit and would keep burning. This tiny lamp was expected to give light to the room. Naturally, no one lit a lamp and then put it under a basket or a bed. Doing so shut out the light; it defeated the purpose of the lamp. For that reason, Jesus asked an obvious rhetorical question: **"Is it not to be set on a lampstand?"** (v. 21b). Manifestly, a lamp is put wherever its light will provide the most illumination.

I recently was asked to deliver the keynote address to the National Religious Broadcasters convention, and I chose to speak on "The Eclipse of God." I believe we are seeing an eclipse of God in our day, not only in the secular culture around us, but inside the church. In an eclipse of the sun, the moon passes between the earth and the sun. The moon does not destroy the sun, it merely hides it. I believe that is what is happening today—God is being hidden or obscured rather than revealed.

It seemed to me that God was obscured during the service when I spoke to the religious broadcasters. I was sitting on the front row during the two-hour worship service, waiting to preach. The room was prepared as a stage, and the various parts of the service were announced as performances. Just before I spoke, there was a twenty-minute segment of music, which was introduced as the worship portion of the gathering—as if listening to the Word of God is not a part of worship. As I sat waiting to go up on the platform, my spirit kept going down and down. I felt uncomfortable preaching on a stage in the context of entertainment, particularly when my message was a plea to the leaders of evangelicalism to stop the eclipse of the character of God. It appalls me that we can allow that to happen when Jesus said: "I did not come to be hidden. I came to be the light of the world." Yet we are allowing God to be eclipsed by vignettes of pop psychology from the pulpit or by ministers communicating their private opinions on social and political issues of the day.

It is the duty of the church in every generation, of every pastor, and of every Christian to take up that lamp, cast the basket aside, and put the light in a prominent place where people can behold the truth of God and of His Son.

Letting Jesus Shine Forth

Jesus added, **"There is nothing hidden which will not be revealed, nor has anything been kept secret but that it should come to light"** (v. 22). We live in a world that prefers darkness to light, a world of people who like to dwell in secret, so their evil deeds will not be revealed. When Adam and Eve committed the first sin, they immediately went into hiding (Gen. 3:8). Like them, we fear the light, lest we be exposed by it. It is our nature, as corrupt people, to try to put some kind of barrier between us and the pure light of the gospel. But John wrote, "The light shines in the darkness, and the darkness did not comprehend [or "overcome"] it" (John 1:5). Here in Mark, Jesus said, in essence: "It is impossible to quench this light. Nothing that is in secret now will stay in secrecy. Everything that is hidden, everything that is concealed, will be revealed." Jesus was talking about the full manifestation of His nature and of His kingdom at the last day.

He went on to say, **"If anyone has ears to hear, let him hear"** (v. 23). He was saying: "Are you listening? Are you paying attention to what I'm saying? I am the lamp of God, and I am going to be made manifest. Do you grasp My teaching?"

Why did Jesus put so much emphasis on proper hearing? He explained: **"Take heed what you hear. With the same measure you use, it will be measured to you; and to you who hear, more will be given"** (v. 24). There's a play on words here. The basket Jesus spoke about was a basket that was used for measurement. So it is as if Jesus was saying that the same size basket we put over the lamp will be put over us. If we hide His light completely, whatever light we have had will be taken away. Conversely, by the same measure we manifest Jesus, He will manifest His glory in us.

We are called to be children of the light, to set forth the light of Christ to this dying world around us. He promises that however much we listen and heed, however much we are involved now, whatever we possess of the light in this earthly sojourn, when the kingdom comes in its fullness, all the more will be given to us. There is an echo here of the parable of the talents (Matt. 25:14–30; Luke 19:12–27). If we take our talents and bury them in the ground, they eventually will be taken away. It is the same with the light if we cover it with a basket.

The Power of a Simple Word

Turning to another parable, Jesus said, **"The kingdom of God is as if a man should scatter seed on the ground, and should sleep by night and rise by day, and the seed should sprout and grow, he himself does not know how"** (vv. 26–27). Here again Jesus chose to tap the metaphor of sowing and seed, just as He did in the parable of the sower, which we considered in the previous chapter. Here, however, Jesus did not talk about the different soils into which seed is sown, but about one of the most remarkable dimensions of nature. We plant seeds and go to bed. Overnight, rain falls on the seeds. The next day, sunlight warms them. Soon, **"the earth yields crops by itself: first the blade, then the head, after that the full grain in the head. But when the grain ripens, immediately he puts in the sickle, because the harvest has come"** (v. 28). Jesus said the spread of the kingdom of God is much like this process. It begins small, but while our attention is elsewhere, so to speak, the kingdom grows. Like the growth of a seed, it is a mysterious process.

When I was in seminary, we often read and discussed the ideas of the higher critical scholars, who attacked every page of the Bible with their cynicism and skepticism. One of my professors constantly expressed amazement at "the arrogance of these men." When I asked what he meant, he said, "They think that they can watch the grass growing from two thousand years away." I instantly understood his point. We cannot see grass growing in the here and now; it is not a process we can observe with the naked eye. In the same way, the higher critical scholars are not able to make actual observations to support their conclusions about the biblical texts.

I find it very comforting to know that this is how God's kingdom works. This parable teaches me that the things I say and do, though they seem infinitely insignificant to me, may have eternal significance as God uses me in the building of His kingdom.

Once, when I was standing at the church door after a service, a young man came up to me and began to tell me that he had heard me speak fifteen years before at a small church in Pennsylvania. He told me that following that service, he had asked me a question, and he was able to repeat my answer to him verbatim all those years later. He said, "When I went home, I could not get your words out of my head, and God used that comment that you made that day to convict me to go into the ministry." As I reflected on his story, I wondered how many other words I had spoken to people that had helped them—or, perhaps, wounded them, leaving scars on their souls that they carry to this day. We have no idea how powerful a simple word can be, for good or ill.

Every year in the United States, thousands of pastors leave the ministry. Some leave for moral reasons, but most leave because they feel unappreciated by their congregations. They feel like they're spinning their wheels, that they're preaching their hearts out but nothing is happening. They need to hear this parable. Or they need to listen to Paul when he says, "Neither he who plants is anything, nor he who waters, but God who gives the increase" (1 Cor. 3:7). God can and does use their faithful preaching of His Word, though the preachers themselves may never see the effect their words have.

I have been blessed to have some glimpses into how God has used my words. Some time ago, I had a conversation with Joni Eareckson Tada. At the time, she was dealing with chronic pain, and it was so bad she could not even sit in her wheelchair. To my surprise, she said, "I've been watching your videos and listening to your tapes every single day for hours, and I'm getting strength from those." Similarly, I received a letter recently from a man telling me how he first heard one of my lectures twenty years ago, then read some of my books, and he simply wanted to thank me for Ligonier Ministries. The letter was written by a man who is on national radio every day; he's one of the great leaders of the church today. I had no idea that anything I had said or written had had any impact on him.

That's the way the kingdom is. We often do not know what God does with our service. We plant the seed, go to bed, and, while we sleep, God germinates the seed so that life grows and eventually produces a full harvest. Then God Himself reaps for His own glory. We simply need to forget about trying to see the fruit of our service immediately. It does not matter if we ever see it. We are called to take the light and let it shine, then let God do with it whatever He pleases.

Growth from a Tiny Beginning

Jesus continued His string of short parables with another drawn from agriculture. He said: **"To what shall we liken the kingdom of God? Or with what parable shall we picture it? It is like a mustard seed which, when it is sown on the ground, is smaller than all the seeds on earth; but when it is sown, it grows up and becomes greater than all herbs, and shoots out large branches, so that the birds of the air may nest under its shade"** (vv. 30–32).

In the 1980s, I was involved with the International Council on Biblical Inerrancy, which sought to call the church and the church's scholars back to a firm defense of the inspiration and infallibility of Holy Writ. There was a New Testament professor at one of the largest seminaries in America who had abandoned the doctrine and was teaching his students that no one could believe in the inerrancy of sacred Scripture because there is a clear mistake in this passage. He would tell his students, "Jesus said that the mustard seed was the smallest of all seeds, but botanists have discovered seeds that are more minute than the mustard seed." This man had rejected the inerrancy of Scripture based on that issue.

When I heard about this professor's teaching, I thought, "Is there no room for hyperbole in the teachings of Jesus?" Consider this statement by Luke: "Early in the morning all the people came to Him in the temple to hear Him" (21:38). Must we understand this to mean that every man, woman, and child in Jerusalem, including invalids, came to the temple that day? No. What we see here is hyperbole, a literary device that is used for emphasis. Furthermore, in Hebrew idiom, it was common for the Jews to refer to the mustard seed as the smallest seed because it was superlatively small. There is small, smaller, and smallest, and the mustard seed was in the category of the superlatively small. For this reason, accusing Jesus of falsehood in this passage is astonishing to me.

Those who make such arguments completely miss the point of this parable. A mustard seed is tiny, but if it is put into the earth, from it erupts a bush that grows into a tree so big that birds may build their nests in its branches. The kingdom of God is similar. God can use the smallest words that we speak, the smallest service that we give, and bring a kingdom out of it. This points not to the greatness of the mustard seed but the greatness of God, who works everyday to bring about His plan for the ages.

God is at work even now, building His kingdom, not with entertainment, not with flash, not with all of the pizzazz that we try to conjure up, but by obedience to His Word, which is attended by His Spirit, so that the kingdom grows and grows until the day when the Lord of the harvest comes for His fruit.

13

STILLING THE
WIND AND WAVES

Mark 4:35–41

⟨≈⟩

On the same day, when evening had come, He said to them, "Let us cross over to the other side." Now when they had left the multitude, they took Him along in the boat as He was. And other little boats were also with Him. And a great windstorm arose, and the waves beat into the boat, so that it was already filling. But He was in the stern, asleep on a pillow. And they awoke Him and said to Him, "Teacher, do You not care that we are perishing?" Then He arose and rebuked the wind, and said to the sea, "Peace, be still!" And the wind ceased and there was a great calm. But He said to them, "Why are you so fearful? How is it that you have no faith?" And they feared exceedingly, and said to one another, "Who can this be, that even the wind and the sea obey Him!"

When we compare the descriptive narratives of the Synoptic Gospels, we frequently find that those from Mark's pen are more brief than those from Matthew's and Luke's. Mark tends to give just the bare facts, while we get longer and more detailed versions of events from Matthew and Luke. But in the case of this narrative, we get more details from Mark, leading many scholars to conclude that Mark got this account directly from his mentor, Peter, who, of course, was an eyewitness of the things recorded here, having been one of those terrified disciples in the boat during the storm that night.

Jesus had been sitting in a boat while He taught the multitude on the beach (4:1). It was from that boat that He taught them the parables we have studied in the two previous chapters. Finally, **when evening had come, He said to them, "Let us cross over to the other side"** (v. 35). It is clear from the context that Jesus made this suggestion to His disciples, and they obeyed His command: **When they had left the multitude, they took Him along in the boat as He was. And other little boats were also with Him** (v. 36). It seems the disciples were all in the boat with Him, and there was no need to go back to shore. Jesus and His disciples simply set out for the far shore, accompanied for at least a while by other boats.

Several years ago, archaeologists made an interesting discovery along the shores of the Sea of Galilee. In one of the many archaeological digs there, they found an intact fishing boat. When carbon-14 dating was applied to this discovery, it indicated that the boat dated from right around the beginning of the first century AD, the very time of the narrative we are exploring. The boat that was found was twenty-seven feet long, so it is safe to assume this was the size of a normal fishing boat and was most likely the size of the boat Jesus and His disciples were in. So, it was not a mere rowboat in which these men set off across the Sea of Galilee, but it was not an extremely large craft either.

If you ever go to Israel and have the opportunity to go out in a boat on the Sea of Galilee, you will certainly be warned by those who man the boat that there is always a profound danger of storms arising there without warning. There are climatic and geographic reasons for that. The surface of the Sea of Galilee is seven hundred feet below sea level, making it the lowest freshwater lake on the earth. Because it sits at the bottom of the Jordan River Valley, it is surrounded by steep hills and mountains. Valleys and gorges between those mountains can funnel wind from the west off the Mediterranean Sea or from the east off the desert. These winds can stir up violent storms, and just such a storm arose as Jesus and His disciples were crossing the sea: **And a great windstorm arose, and the waves beat into the boat, so that it was already filling** (v. 37).

This storm struck in the evening. That was unusual. The Sea of Galilee was a rich source for fish, and most of the fishing was done at night because the worst winds usually occurred during the day. The fact that this storm arose at night gives us some insight into the exceedingly great fear that the seasoned fishermen among Jesus' disciples experienced on that occasion.

Jesus, however, was not alarmed in the slightest. In fact, **He was in the stern, asleep on a pillow** (v. 38a). Every time I read this verse, I think of Dr. James Montgomery Boice, the late pastor of Tenth Presbyterian Church in

Philadelphia. Many years ago, we had done a conference together in San Francisco and we were flying back east. Shortly after takeoff, our plane encountered heavy turbulence. I grabbed the armrest and began praying. When I looked over at Jim, I was amazed to see that he was half asleep. When I expressed my astonishment that he could sleep through such buffeting, he said: "Isn't it wonderful? I love to be up in the air when it's like this." Like Jesus, he was calm in the midst of the storm.

A Series of Rebukes

The reaction of the disciples, by contrast, was more like mine. They were terrified by the storm rocking their boat. To their credit, they turned to Jesus in their fear. They found Him in the back of the boat, sleeping. To their discredit, they took His ability to sleep through such a maelstrom as a lack of concern not just for His own safety but for theirs. We see from Mark's description that the disciples were both afraid and angry. They not only woke Jesus, they rebuked Him, saying, **"Teacher, do You not care that we are perishing?"** (v. 38b).

How typical of the creature to rebuke the Creator. How like the servant to sass the master. The disciples rebuked their Lord for taking a nap. This is the only time in Scripture where we read of Jesus sleeping. Certainly He slept every night (except for those occasions when He stayed up all night praying), but this is the only time the gospel writers specifically tell us about it. Jesus was trying to get a nap after a heavy day of teaching, but His disciples rebuked Him.

When Jesus awoke and heard the disciples' rebuke, He delivered not one but two rebukes of His own. The first was to the wind: **He arose and rebuked the wind, and said to the sea, "Peace, be still!" And the wind ceased and there was a great calm** (v. 39). The Lord of glory, who created heaven and earth, who was master over nature, who could curse a fig tree and make it wither (11:12–14, 20), gave a command to the elements and was instantly obeyed. Just as the Father had commanded the light to appear in creation, the Son said to the wind and sea, "Peace, be still!" and as soon as the command came from His lips, the sea was like glass. There was not the slightest zephyr to be felt in the air. Everything was calm.

Everything, that is, except the disciples. They remained agitated, not by the wind and the waves outside the boat, but by the man inside the boat. Jesus turned to them and delivered His second rebuke: **"Why are you so fearful? How is it that you have no faith?"** (v. 40). What followed? Mark does not tell us that the disciples calmed down. Instead, he writes, **They feared exceedingly, and said to one another, "Who can this be, that even the wind and the sea obey Him!"** (v. 41).

Notice that in this passage Mark three times uses the descriptive term *great* or *enormous*. The Latin translation uses the word *magna* and the Greek employs the term *mega*. Both of these terms clearly have reference to things that are large.

Mark first uses this term to describe the tempest that struck the boat carrying Jesus and His disciples (v. 37). It was not just a storm, it was a mega-storm, an enormous tempest that surpassed the usual maelstroms that came down on the Sea of Galilee. It threatened the lives of the disciples, for it raised waves that both beat on the boat and sloshed over its gunwales, so that it took on large amounts of water. It was at that point that the disciples went to their Master, woke Him, and said, "Please do something or we're going to perish."

When Jesus rebuked the wind and the sea, Mark tells us, the mega-storm turned into a mega-calm (v. 39). Great violence was instantly transformed into great peace.

However, it is Mark's third use of the term *mega* in this passage that interests me most. Mark uses it to describe the fear of the disciples (v. 41). He says that they "feared exceedingly."

Notice the progress of the disciples' fear. When the storm came up, they were intimidated. But when the storm was calmed, their fear intensified. Their greatest fear came after the threatening storm had been removed. We dare not miss the significance of this in the lives of the disciples, for the intensification of their fear is their response to a new depth of understanding about the person of Christ.

Recently, I saw a list of the top ten phobias that assault people's comfort zones in the United States of America. The number one phobia among people in the United States is the fear of public speaking, which is called glossophobia. People are also afraid of open spaces (agoraphobia), of water (aquaphobia), and small, cramped spaces (claustrophobia). Another of the major phobias is the fear of strangers, of aliens, of people who are different; this is the fear one ethnic group feels for another (xenophobia). People suffer from this phobia when they are not familiar with the customs and behaviors of others, because they are not sure how to respond. In Mark Twain's short story "The Mysterious Stranger," people do not know how to respond to an unknown man who comes into their community. As a result, they're frightened. In much the same way, Hollywood uses the ultimate strangers, extraterrestrial beings, to scare us. These are examples of xenophobia.

In a sense, what the disciples experienced that night on the sea was ultimate xenophobia—the fear of the ultimate Stranger, of One who was unlike every other man.

Religion: A Crutch against Fear?

Years ago, when I was teaching at a seminary in Philadelphia, I taught a course on the history of atheism, and I required my students to read primary sources. I did not want them to just read about atheism, I wanted them to read atheists. I made them read Friedrich Nietzsche, Jean-Paul Sartre, Albert Camus, Karl Marx, and Ludwig Feuerbach, and I had them read Sigmund Freud's *The Future of an Illusion* and *Civilization and Its Discontents*. These were some of the most brilliant atheists of the past two centuries. After my students read these men's works, we discussed their arguments against the existence of God.

There was a common thread that ran through the thought of all these men, particularly nineteenth-century atheists. During the Enlightenment, many leading thinkers said: "We no longer have to look to the idea of God to account for the beginning of the universe or the origin of human beings. Now we know that the universe came to pass through spontaneous generation." The question that was left for the followers of the Enlightenment was this: Since there is no God, how is it that everywhere we go on this planet, we find people who practice religion? No one could deny that mankind seems to be *homo religiosus*. If there is no God, why is that the case? Why is there so much religion? The same answer is given over and over again in the atheistic philosophers—religion was invented as a crutch. They all agree that religion is nothing more than a psychological bromide to help us cope with the scary things that surround us.

Freud had an interesting theory about this. He said that as human beings, we are frail. We are always in imminent danger of having our lives terminated. We can succumb to fatal illnesses. We can be killed by wild animals. We can be killed in hurricanes, earthquakes, fires, or other natural disasters. So, Freud said, nature is hostile to us and is a threat to our survival. We understand that clearly. We see a clear picture of that in Mark's account of the great storm on the Sea of Galilee. The disciples were afraid when they were threatened by the force of nature, the great wind, the great turbulence in the sea, the beating of the waves against their boat. They knew the storm threatened their very lives.

Freud also observed that we have learned how to cope to some degree with hostile people. If someone is angry at me and is expressing that anger, and I want to calm that anger, I can do a few things. I can beg for mercy from the other person. I can apologize to him; maybe that will turn away his anger. Or I can offer him a gift, hoping it will assuage his anger. Freud said that these techniques, which occasionally work to placate human anger, are adopted by religions as techniques that we hope will remove the malevolence of nonhuman entities. We personalize the impersonal forces of nature and then sacralize them. In other words, we invent personal gods who live in the hurricane, the earthquake, the sea, and so forth. Then we have sea gods, wind gods, and all the rest, and we can talk to them, pray to them, and offer sacrifices to them. Freud believed that was how religion arose. He said that monotheism, the belief in one God, was simply an economical approach—having one God permits a person to pray to one deity to cope with any threat.

I think it is true that people throughout history have tended to sacralize non-sacred objects and to personalize things that have no personality. However, I think Freud's theory breaks down completely when it tries to account for Christianity. Why? Because in all of their inventive creativity, the one thing human beings have never done is to invent a god who is more terrifying than the force they want to tame. Above all, human beings do not want a personal god who is holy, for nothing threatens sinful humanity more than the presence of the holy. Thus, no one would have invented the God of Christianity.

Glimpses of the Holy

Luke records a different incident that happened on the Sea of Galilee:

> So it was, as the multitude pressed about Him to hear the word of God, that He stood by the Lake of Gennesaret, and saw two boats standing by the lake; but the fishermen had gone from them and were washing their nets. Then He got into one of the boats, which was Simon's, and asked him to put out a little from the land. And He sat down and taught the multitudes from the boat. When He had stopped speaking, He said to Simon, "Launch out into the deep and let down your nets for a catch." But Simon answered and said to Him, "Master, we have toiled all night and caught nothing; nevertheless at Your word I will let down the net." And when they had done this, they caught a great number of fish, and their net was breaking. So they signaled to their partners in the other boat to come and help them. And they came and filled both the boats, so that they began to sink. When Simon Peter saw it, he fell down at Jesus' knees, saying, "Depart from me, for I am a sinful man, O Lord!" For he and all who were with him were astonished at the catch of fish which they had taken. (Luke 5:1–9)

Peter's reaction to this miraculous catch of fish is very interesting. He was a businessman, an entrepreneur. He might have said: "Jesus, fifty percent of my business is Yours. You do not have to go out on the boat with us every night. You do not have to labor on the docks and repair the nets. All You need to do is to come down here once a month and do the trick You just did, filling my nets." But that's not what Peter did. When he saw the nets filled to overflowing, he turned to Jesus and said, "Depart from me, for I am a sinful man, O

Lord." Essentially, he reacted in the same way as when he and the other disciples witnessed Jesus calming the sea—he became exceedingly afraid. He had seen something he could not explain in human terms. He knew he was in the presence of deity. He might very well have asked the same question the disciples asked: "Who can this be?"

We meet all kinds of people, and as we meet them, we unconsciously sort them. We do this every time we walk down a street, instantly pigeonholing every person we see. Is that person smiling? He seems safe. Is there a look of fury in that person's eyes? We give him a little extra space because we know what unbridled anger can be like in human beings. We separate everyone into categories: safe, dangerous, nice, cantankerous, whatever. But we do not have a category for someone who can speak to the waves and cause them to obey Him. Such a One is in a class by Himself. This One is so alien, so other, that there is no compartment for Him.

In a word, what the disciples experienced on the Sea of Galilee that night was the holiness of Christ. They liked His power when they were in trouble, so they were quick to wake Him when the boat seemed endangered. But when He showed them His power, they said: "This is not common power. This is holy power. This man is different from every other person on the face of the earth." And finding themselves in the presence of the Holy One of Israel, they were consumed by fear.

Freud never understood that the thing all people in the world fear most—the thing Freud himself feared most—is the holiness of God. That's why people run from God and from Jesus Christ. As soon as God manifests His transcendent majesty, men are reduced to terror.

If Christ in His majesty were to knock on your door this morning, you would not say to Him, "Hi, buddy, come on in." Rather, you would fall on your face. When the resurrected Christ in His glory and the manifestation of His holiness appears, all creatures will fall at His feet because He is other. He is holy. That means that not only do people tremble at His voice, but seas that have no ears listen to His command, and winds that have no knowledge know enough to stop blowing when He says, "Be still." That is our Lord.

14

STILLING THE
CHAOS OF HELL

Mark 5:1–20

Then they came to the other side of the sea, to the country of the Gadarenes. And when
He had come out of the boat, immediately there met Him out of the tombs a man with
an unclean spirit, who had his dwelling among the tombs; and no one could bind him,
not even with chains, because he had often been bound with shackles and chains. And
the chains had been pulled apart by him, and the shackles broken in pieces; neither
could anyone tame him. And always, night and day, he was in the mountains and in
the tombs, crying out and cutting himself with stones. When he saw Jesus from afar,
he ran and worshiped Him. And he cried out with a loud voice and said, "What have I
to do with You, Jesus, Son of the Most High God? I implore You by God that You do
not torment me." For He said to him, "Come out of the man, unclean spirit!" Then
He asked him, "What is your name?" And he answered, saying, "My name is Legion;
for we are many." Also he begged Him earnestly that He would not send them out of
the country. Now a large herd of swine was feeding there near the mountains. So all
the demons begged Him, saying, "Send us to the swine, that we may enter them." And
at once Jesus gave them permission. Then the unclean spirits went out and entered the
swine (there were about two thousand); and the herd ran violently down the steep place
into the sea, and drowned in the sea. So those who fed the swine fled, and they told it
in the city and in the country. And they went out to see what it was that had happened.
Then they came to Jesus, and saw the one who had been demon-possessed and had the

legion, sitting and clothed and in his right mind. And they were afraid. And those who saw it told them how it happened to him who had been demon-possessed, and about the swine. Then they began to plead with Him to depart from their region. And when He got into the boat, he who had been demon-possessed begged Him that he might be with Him. However, Jesus did not permit him, but said to him, "Go home to your friends, and tell them what great things the Lord has done for you, and how He has had compassion on you." And he departed and began to proclaim in Decapolis all that Jesus had done for him; and all marveled.

Mark 5 contains the account of Jesus' restoration of a demon-possessed man; His healing of a woman who had suffered with a hemorrhage for twelve years; and His resurrection of Jairus' daughter from the dead. These three narratives have led some commentators to refer felicitously to this portion of Mark as "the Saint Jude chapter" of the New Testament. In Roman Catholicism, Saint Jude is the patron saint of hopeless causes. That's why, when Danny Thomas decided to found a hospital in Memphis devoted to treating supposedly incurable children's diseases, he named it after Saint Jude. As we will see, however, the supposedly hopeless causes in Mark 5 proved to be not so hopeless when Jesus came on the scene.

In this chapter, I want to consider Mark's narrative of the man who was possessed by a legion of demons. When I read this account in the gospel of Mark and the parallel accounts in Matthew and Luke, I cannot help but ask a speculative question: Why did the Holy Spirit choose to inspire the gospel records of this event? In other words, what value is there in this text for us?

I'm sure you have heard sermons on this text, and most of them probably dealt with the psychological benefits that come to Christians who put their faith in Jesus, when Christ comes to us and frees us from the violent forces that torture our souls inwardly. Again, I do not know why the Spirit inspired the record of this incident in the life of Jesus, but I am convinced that the purpose of this narrative is not to give us psychological tranquility. It is not about us.

I think this text, which follows right on the heels of the narrative about Christ's calming of the tempest on the Sea of Galilee, is intended to reveal to us the character of Jesus. John writes, "these [accounts] are written that you may believe that Jesus is the Christ, the Son of God, and that believing you may have life in His name" (John 20:31), and that applies to every word in the gospel narratives. Therefore, our study of this passage ought to increase our understanding of the deity, majesty, and power of Christ.

One commentator I read on this passage pointed out that the common theme between Christ's stilling of the storm on the Sea of Galilee and His redemption of this demon-possessed man is Christ's power over chaos. The wind and the waves of the sea threatened to destroy Jesus and His disciples, and the demons from hell threatened to destroy the man whose body they were inhabiting. Both of these are examples of chaos, which Christ overcame.

This picture of Christ as the One who brings salvation from chaos is appropriate, for the Bible makes clear that He was the acting agent of creation, bringing order out of the primordial chaos. Genesis tells us, "The earth was without form, and void; and darkness was on the face of the deep" (1:2a). Against this picture of chaos, Genesis tells us, "God said, 'Let there be light'; and there was light" (1:3). The eternal, omniscient One triumphed over chaos at the very beginning of the work of creation. When we come to the New Testament, we find that Christ was intimately involved in this creative work. John writes: "In the beginning was the Word, and the Word was with God, and the Word was God. He was in the beginning with God. All things were made through Him, and without Him nothing was made that was made" (1:1–3). Likewise, Paul says, "Of Him and through Him and to Him are all things" (Rom. 11:36a). So, Scripture gives us a portrait of the cosmic Christ, the One who, along with the Father and the Spirit, was responsible for the creation of the universe, and who possesses the power to calm chaos wherever He encounters it.

In the book *Cosmos*, Dr. Carl Sagan, the late astrophysicist from Cornell University, made the statement that as science seeks to understand the universe, it proceeds on the assumption that the world is cosmos, not chaos. He was saying that if the external universe were ultimately chaos, it would be impossible to know anything about it, because ultimate chaos is irrational and therefore unintelligible. So, the metaphysical assumption of all scientific inquiry is that the universe is inherently knowable and intelligible, and for it to be knowable and intelligible, it must ultimately be ordered. It must be cosmos, not chaos.

That is why I am somewhat surprised and amused by the contemporary debate over intelligent design as a notion that has nothing to do with science. Without pleading a religious interpretation, previous scientists have understood that design is a prerequisite for science, so "unintelligent design" is an oxymoron. It is like postulating accidental order. If it is accidental, it is not orderly. It is chaos.

So, in both the previous passage and this one, we see Christ manifesting His authority over chaos—first the chaos of nature, then the chaos of hell.

A Man of Great Uncleanness

As we saw in the previous chapter, Jesus and His disciples had set out by boat to go to the other side of the Sea of Galilee, but their journey was briefly interrupted by a violent storm. However, Jesus commanded the wind and waves to be still, so that a great calm ensued, and they completed their journey without further incident, arriving at **the country of the Gadarenes** (v. 1b).

There is disagreement as to where "the country of the Gadarenes" actually was. Matthew even identifies the site as "the country of the Gergesenes" (8:28). Simply put, there are textual variations about the location of this place, leaving scholars unsure as to where this encounter happened. Likewise, archaeology provides little help. We know there was a town called Gadara southeast of the Sea of Galilee and a town called Gerasa even farther southeast, but the actual site may have been a village called Khersa that was right on the eastern shore of the lake. It was in Decapolis, a largely Gentile area where there were several Roman garrisons. Our text seems to argue for Khersa when it says that Jesus encountered a man **immediately** (v. 2) after getting out of the boat. It seems that Jesus had no time to walk inland to Gadara or Gerasa.

Mark describes the person who met Jesus as **a man with an unclean spirit, who had his dwelling among the tombs** (vv. 2b–3a). To a Jew, the worst thing that could happen to a person was to be declared unclean in the sight of God. The Old Testament books of Leviticus, Numbers, and Deuteronomy are packed with laws, rules, and procedures for dealing with ceremonial uncleanness. Later, rabbinic traditions greatly expanded these rules for the Jewish community. For instance, the Old Testament declared that a person who touched a dead body was to be considered unclean for seven days and had to go through purification rites (Num. 19:11–12). But the Jews expanded on that principle to require cleansing if a person merely touched any of the accouterments of death. If he touched the bier on which a body was transported or if he went into a cemetery and touched a gravestone, seven more days of purification were required. So the Israelites were deeply concerned about ceremonial cleanness before God, and by New Testament times, possession by an unclean (evil) spirit had come to be one of the chief horrors among them.

Mark shows that this miserable person was unclean in four ways. First, he tells us that the man had an unclean spirit, which actually turned out to be not just one spirit but a legion of them; he was inhabited by demons. Second, he lived among the tombs, among the dead, the worst of all possible circumstances of uncleanness from the Jewish perspective. Third, his dwelling was in the Decapolis, which, as I mentioned, was a largely Gentile region. The Jews regarded the Gentiles as unclean people. Fourth, he lived near people who raised pigs. Pigs were unclean animals and Jews could not eat them (Lev. 11:7).

In all of Scripture, I can think of only one person whose misery rivals that of this man—Job. This narrative in Mark is brief; the book of Job gives us forty-two chapters about the misery of Job as he lost his wealth, his family, and his health, and then had to deal with the ungodly counsel of his wife and his friends. Even today we speak of the suffering of Job in our day-to-day speech. Yet, I wonder whether Job's misery, as terrible as it was, really approached the misery of this poor soul, who was tormented every moment by the focused power of hell.

Consider Mark's descriptions of this man. He "had his dwelling among the tombs" (v. 3a). Apparently he was exiled from human contact, either voluntarily or forcibly, and he lived in a graveyard, among the dead. Furthermore, **no one could bind him, not even with chains, because he had often been bound with shackles and chains. And the chains had been pulled apart by him, and the shackles broken in pieces** (vv. 3b–4a). It seems the people of that region had tried to bind him, but he had burst the chains and shackles they put on him with superhuman strength. Simply put, **neither could anyone tame him** (v. 4b). The Greek word rendered as "tame" here was used in reference to the taming of wild and vicious beasts of nature. This was a wild man, and no techniques could subdue him. Mark adds, **And always, night and day, he was in the mountains and in the tombs, crying out and cutting himself with stones** (v. 5). In his unbridled torment, he wandered through the mountains, continually screaming and injuring himself with stones, adding misery to misery.

Demons Address the Son of God

Life went on this way for this wretch until, one day, he saw a man getting out of a boat, and he knew it was Jesus. Mark tells us: **When he saw Jesus from afar, he ran and worshiped Him. And he cried out with a loud voice and said, "What have I to do with You, Jesus, Son of the Most High God? I implore You by God that You do not torment me." For He said to him, "Come out of the man, unclean spirit!"** (vv. 6–8).

Let me point out two crucial aspects of this statement; one of them has to do with the speaker and one has to do with the One he addressed.

It is not clear whether these words came from the man or from the demons inside him. However, Matthew attributes the voice that cried out to Jesus to the devils (Matt. 8:29). Matthew also adds one small variation to the man's statement that I believe provides further evidence that these are the words of the demons. Whereas Mark reports that the man said, "I implore You by God that You do not torment me," Matthew tells us that he said, "Have You come here to torment us *before the time?*" (8:29). I think those three words "before the time" are critical to understanding everything that unfolds in this text. Why do I say that?

In chapter 3, I noted that the New Testament makes a distinction between two types of time. One is *chronos*, the normal, moment-by-moment passage of time that we can measure by chronometers or watches. Then there is *kairos*, which refers to a specific moment in time. All *kairos* takes place in *chronos*, but not all *chronos* is *kairos*. Similarly, in English, everything that happens is historical, but not everything that happens is historic. We save the word *historic* for something that is of lasting significance. So, the Bible talks about history not only in terms of the moment-by-moment changing of the hour, the day, the week, and the year, but in terms of specific moments in time that are pregnant with meaning. The exodus was Israel's greatest *kairos*, its greatest kairotic moment. It was the time of their deliverance. Likewise, the birth of Jesus was the long-awaited moment or hour of the Messiah's advent.

The comments made by this man of the tombs show us that the demons of hell understand that, in His plan of redemption, God has appointed a day when Satan will be bound and all of the forces of hell will be crushed once and for all. Every last demon knows what Satan knows—that their days are numbered. When the Lord comes to draw history to a close, the demonic world will not be able to match His power. It will be no contest. The demons live in mortal fear of that moment in history when all of their diabolical activity will be over once and for all.

However, on this day in the tombs of Gadara, the demons knew that the time had not yet come. It was not time for their demonic activity to end. Not only did they know it, Jesus knew it. Even though Jesus had power over them and He could liberate this poor wretch, He knew that all things must happen in His Father's time, and the time for the final conquest of the Satanic world was not yet. So, the demons' words were a sort of protest; they were reminding Jesus that it was not yet time for Him to finish them off. When Jesus ordered them to come out of the man, He could have sent them into the pit forever; He certainly had the power to do so. But it was not time for that yet. However, it *was* time for the redemption of this poor possessed human being. Therefore, Jesus ordered the demons to come out of the man without sending them to their destruction, as we will see.

The second aspect of this statement that I want to point out has to do with the One to whom the demons spoke—Jesus. Specifically, I want you to see how they addressed Him. They cried out, "What have I to do with You, Jesus, Son of the Most High God?"

I love this address, for not only was Jesus acknowledged to be the Son of God, but that acknowledgment came from the pagan Gentile world. One of the great discoveries of nineteenth- and twentieth-century studies of world religions was that even in cultures that believed there was a god in every tree, every rock, and every river, there was a hazy understanding of a mighty god who lived on the other side of the mountain. When sociologists of religion began to explore this, they discovered that there was an ineradicable idea in every tribe, despite their polytheism and animism, of one god who was most high. Thus, the idea of monotheism is implicit in every world religion, even polytheistic ones. All of them have the idea of one God who transcends all other gods, who is the Most High God.

As I said earlier, I am convinced that the purpose of this text is not to tell us how to have tranquility when we're bothered by tempests in this world, but to let us know who Jesus is, that He is the Son of the Most High God. I do not think it was by accident that Mark arranged his book so that the event that preceded this incident was Christ's demonstration of His power over nature when He stilled the tempest. He followed that expression of His power by stilling the violence of this man who was assaulted by hell.

Just as the winds and the ocean waves obey Him, demons from hell tremble before Him. The Son of the Most High God transcends all other gods in His power and authority.

Gentiles Fear the Son of God

Seeing this man in his misery, Jesus asked: **"What is your name?" And he answered, saying, "My name is Legion; for we are many"** (v. 9). In the Roman armies, a legion was composed of fifty-six hundred men. That does not mean there were exactly fifty-six hundred demons within this man; in the popular parlance of the day, the term *legion* was used for any large host. Clearly, there were very many demons in this man, a further indication of his wretchedness.

The demons had already acknowledged Jesus' power and authority to "torment" them, even to send them into the pit of destruction at the God-ordained time. We see again here that they recognized Jesus was their superior: **Also he begged Him earnestly that He would not send them out of the country** (v. 10). Begging was certainly the right approach for the demons in this situation, but because both they and Jesus knew the time for their final destruction was not at hand, there was room for negotiation. Thus, Mark tells us: **Now a large herd of swine was feeding there near the mountains. So all the demons begged Him, saying, "Send us to the swine, that we may enter them"** (vv. 11–12). Jesus had already commanded them to come out of the man, but they wanted a new host for their parasitic existence. A herd of pigs was nearby, and the demons asked Jesus to send them there. Mark notes: **And at once Jesus gave them permission. Then the unclean spirits went out and entered the**

swine (there were about two thousand); and the herd ran violently down
the steep place into the sea, and drowned in the sea (v. 13).

This incident has struck some biblical commentators as a wanton waste.
Some even charge Jesus with a lack of compassion for the pigs, and others go
so far as to charge Him with sin for allowing the destruction of the pigs at a
huge cost to their owners. A herd of two thousand pigs was extremely valuable
in the economy of that day. How are we to respond to these serious charges?

We have to keep in mind that Jesus had the authority to do this in His
divine nature. As the Lord God omnipotent, He was free to do with the swine
whatever He pleased, according to His own sovereignty. However, there is
another element that we often overlook, particularly in this day and age. Jesus
had authority to do this even in His human nature. As the second Adam, He
has dominion over the earth. Man was created in the image of God and was
given dominion over all created things; human beings are to rule over all things
(Gen. 1:26). The incident with the pigs was a dramatic manifestation of that
human dominion. Furthermore, Jesus was not displaying a lack of compassion;
He was exercising proper compassion. He was willing to sacrifice two thousand
pigs, as valuable as they were, to rescue the demon-possessed man. It is as if
Jesus was saying, "This is a human being, a creature made in the image of God,
who is being destroyed day and night by these demons; whatever it takes, I'm
going to redeem this human being." So, before we charge Jesus with a lack
of compassion, we need to see that it was His compassion that drove Him to
destroy the pigs for the sake of one human life. That is how valuable human
life is. Only in a culture of death, where human life is denigrated, do people
value animals more than people.

Of course, it is not every day that a herd of two thousand pigs plunges into
the sea and drowns. This was a terrible event, and those who were in charge of
feeding the pigs, having witnessed what happened, **fled, and they told it in
the city and in the country. And they went out to see what it was that had
happened** (v. 14). Apparently the herders spread their news far and wide, so
that a large crowd assembled to see for themselves what had occurred: **Then
they came to Jesus, and saw the one who had been demon-possessed and
had the legion, sitting and clothed and in his right mind** (v. 15a). Remember, attempts had been made to bind this man with chains, to control his wild
behavior, but no one had been able to tame him (vv. 3–4). Now, however, he
was manifestly calm and rational. The people saw the fruit of the redemptive
touch of Christ. They saw that He had done what no one else could do—He
had rescued a man from the ravages of hell. They saw something that they never
in their wildest dreams expected to see.

What was their response? **They were afraid. And those who saw it told them how it happened to him who had been demon-possessed, and about the swine. Then they began to plead with Him to depart from their region** (vv. 15b–17). Here is yet another parallel to the previous narrative of the storm on the Sea of Galilee. The disciples were frightened by the storm, but they were even more afraid when Jesus calmed the storm. Likewise, when these people of Decapolis recognized this man who haunted the mountains and the tombs in his madness seated, clothed, and in his right mind, they were afraid. Like the disciples in the boat, these people were confronted by the presence of the holy. When the Holy One is manifest in the midst of unholy people, the only appropriate human response is dread. So, they began to beg Jesus to leave. They simply could not stand to be in His presence.

In great contrast, the man who had been demon-possessed, changed as he was, did not want to be separated from the presence of Christ. Just as the demons had begged Jesus not to torment them, just as the people had begged Him to leave, this man begged to be allowed to go with Him: **And when He got into the boat, he who had been demon-possessed begged Him that he might be with Him** (v. 18).

However, whereas Jesus gave the demons permission to go into the swine and granted the request of the people that He depart, He denied the request of this man who had been restored. He said, **"Go home to your friends, and tell them what great things the Lord has done for you, and how He has had compassion on you"** (v. 19b). The man obeyed and took Jesus' command to heart: **He departed and began to proclaim in Decapolis all that Jesus had done for him; and all marveled** (v. 20). Thus, the message of Jesus' power and authority to still the very chaos of hell was spread abroad throughout that Gentile region.

15

POWER OVER
DISEASE AND DEATH

Mark 5:21–43

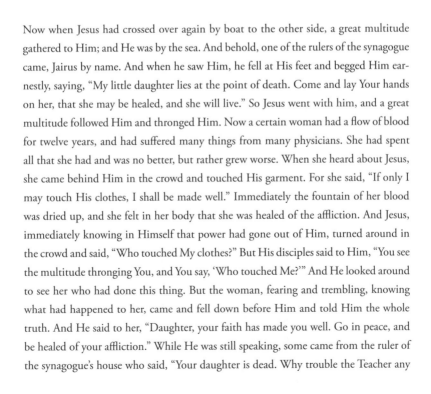

Now when Jesus had crossed over again by boat to the other side, a great multitude
gathered to Him; and He was by the sea. And behold, one of the rulers of the synagogue
came, Jairus by name. And when he saw Him, he fell at His feet and begged Him earnestly, saying, "My little daughter lies at the point of death. Come and lay Your hands
on her, that she may be healed, and she will live." So Jesus went with him, and a great
multitude followed Him and thronged Him. Now a certain woman had a flow of blood
for twelve years, and had suffered many things from many physicians. She had spent
all that she had and was no better, but rather grew worse. When she heard about Jesus,
she came behind Him in the crowd and touched His garment. For she said, "If only I
may touch His clothes, I shall be made well." Immediately the fountain of her blood
was dried up, and she felt in her body that she was healed of the affliction. And Jesus,
immediately knowing in Himself that power had gone out of Him, turned around in
the crowd and said, "Who touched My clothes?" But His disciples said to Him, "You see
the multitude thronging You, and You say, 'Who touched Me?'" And He looked around
to see her who had done this thing. But the woman, fearing and trembling, knowing
what had happened to her, came and fell down before Him and told Him the whole
truth. And He said to her, "Daughter, your faith has made you well. Go in peace, and
be healed of your affliction." While He was still speaking, some came from the ruler of
the synagogue's house who said, "Your daughter is dead. Why trouble the Teacher any

further?" As soon as Jesus heard the word that was spoken, He said to the ruler of the synagogue, "Do not be afraid; only believe." And He permitted no one to follow Him except Peter, James, and John the brother of James. Then He came to the house of the ruler of the synagogue, and saw a tumult and those who wept and wailed loudly. When He came in, He said to them, "Why make this commotion and weep? The child is not dead, but sleeping." And they ridiculed Him. But when He had put them all outside, He took the father and the mother of the child, and those who were with Him, and entered where the child was lying. Then He took the child by the hand, and said to her, "Talitha, cumi," which is translated, "Little girl, I say to you, arise." Immediately the girl arose and walked, for she was twelve years of age. And they were overcome with great amazement. But He commanded them strictly that no one should know it, and said that something should be given her to eat.

I noted in the previous chapter that Mark 5 has been called "the Saint Jude chapter" of the New Testament because in it Jesus deals with several seemingly hopeless causes. As we saw, however, the cause of the demon-possessed man proved anything but hopeless when Jesus exercised His power. We will see the same as we study the second half of Mark 5 in this chapter. Just as we have seen Jesus' power over nature in the calming of the storm (Mark 4:35–41) and His power over the realm of the demonic (5:1–20), we now see His power over disease and even death itself.

Mark begins, **When Jesus had crossed over again by boat to the other side, a great multitude gathered to Him; and He was by the sea** (v. 21). Jesus came back from the far side of the Sea of Galilee, from the region of the Gadarenes, where He had restored a demon-possessed man, only to be invited to leave by the terrified inhabitants of the area. Returning, He was once more surrounded by multitudes of people who wanted to gain something from close proximity to Him.

One of these was a man of significant status: **And behold, one of the rulers of the synagogue came, Jairus by name. And when he saw Him, he fell at His feet and begged Him earnestly** (vv. 22–23a). Jairus was a layman, not a rabbi. Synagogue rulers were in charge of taking care of the building and ordering all of the services that took place within it. Thus, he was a man of some expertise and some importance in the community, yet he came and fell at the feet of Jesus. Here was another person who was facing a hopeless crisis, someone who came begging with all earnestness that Jesus would intercede in his crisis and resolve his problem.

This was his cry: **"My little daughter lies at the point of death"** (v. 23b). I am sure that the translators struggled with the Greek word that is rendered as "at the point of death." There is a branch of theology that deals with the last things. It is called eschatology, which term is derived from the Greek word *eschatos*, which means "last, utmost, extreme." In the Greek text of Mark 5, that is the word that is used. When Jairus said, "My little girl is at the point of death," he was saying she was at her utmost extremity. She was at the very end. She was at death's door. She was breathing her last. It was not just that she was very sick and in intensive care; she was at the end of hospice care. Jairus was saying that if Jesus did not act immediately, the girl would surely die. But even at such a point, he had faith that Jesus could help. He said, **"Come and lay Your hands on her, that she may be healed, and she will live"** (v. 23c). In the midst of the throng, with many people competing for His attention, Jesus heard this desperate plea: **So Jesus went with him, and a great multitude followed Him and thronged Him** (v. 24).

A Woman with a Flow of Blood

At this point, Mark breaks away from his account of Jairus' crisis to tell how Jesus resolved another crisis on the way to Jairus' home. He writes: **Now a certain woman had a flow of blood for twelve years** (v. 25). An unceasing hemorrhage was bad enough, but the Old Testament law declared that someone with the condition described here was ceremonially unclean. That meant this woman could not be a part of the worshiping community of Israel (Lev. 15:25–33). She was as unclean as a leper. No one was allowed to touch her or her clothes lest he or she, too, become unclean. So this woman was suffering not just physical misery, but social and religious misery, because she had been banished from the presence of the people of God. Just by being in the multitude that was thronging around Jesus she was actively disobeying the Old Testament ritual law.

Not only was she miserable in these various ways, she was destitute. She **had suffered many things from many physicians. She had spent all that she had and was no better, but rather grew worse** (v. 26). She had gone to doctor after doctor, spending her last cent, but the doctors only made her condition worse. I doubt that the doctors in the ancient world *wanted* to make her condition worse; they simply did not have the medicine, the knowledge, and the tools at their disposal to give her relief. According to the medicine of the first century, her condition was incurable.

It is rather amazing to me that this poor woman had any hope left. Yet, we know that she did, for Mark tells us: **When she heard about Jesus, she came behind Him in the crowd and touched His garment. For she said, "If only I may touch His clothes, I shall be made well"** (vv. 27–28). Like Jairus, she had faith for healing, and that faith was rewarded: **Immediately the fountain**

of her blood was dried up, and she felt in her body that she was healed of the affliction (v. 29).

In one sense, what the woman did was commendable. Her action was certainly a demonstration of faith in the testimonies she had heard about Jesus. In another sense, however, it was not commendable at all. One of the widespread beliefs of that day was that if one could get close to a great man or to a healer and touch his clothing, that would be all it would take. So her hope was based at least partly on superstition. Surprisingly, people still accept such ideas. Ministers on television offer to send handkerchiefs they have blessed in return for a donation, and the dollars pour in. The idea, basically, is that physically touching someone (or something he has touched) who has a hotline to God will prove beneficial. Of course, there is no biblical support for such an idea.

Whatever her reasoning, this woman said to herself: "This is my last chance, my last resort. I've heard so many things about this Jesus. He doesn't have to stop. I won't bother Him. He doesn't have to lay His hands on me. If I can just get close to Him and touch His clothes, maybe that will do it." So, she made her way through the crowd, and even though the law of God forbade her from touching anyone in her uncleanness, she stretched forth her hand and touched Jesus. When she did so, the hemorrhage instantly stopped, and she knew it. She could tell that she had been healed.

Likewise, Jesus knew right away that something had happened. Mark writes, **And Jesus immediately knowing in Himself that power had gone out of Him, turned around in the crowd and said, "Who touched My clothes?"** (v. 30).

We believe that Jesus is *vere homo, vere Deus*, "truly man and truly God," but this doctrine causes much confusion and has been the flashpoint for many heresies in church history. Simply put, in the incarnation, Jesus' divine nature lost none of its attributes. His divine nature stayed divine. Likewise, the human nature stayed human. The human nature was not deified and the divine nature was not humanized. That means that, touching His human nature, Jesus was not omniscient. He did not know everything. As we will see, Jesus Himself acknowledged that He did not know the day or hour that the Father had appointed for the destruction of Jerusalem (13:32). Here in Mark 5, we see another example of Jesus' lack of omniscience. He knew someone had touched Him and that power had gone out from Him to heal. However, He did not know who had touched Him.

So, He stopped. Remember, He was on His way to minister to a young girl who was at the point of death, and every minute was precious. He did not have time to delay—at least from a human perspective—but He stopped and asked, "Who touched My clothes?"

If ever Jesus' disciples were irritated by their Master, it was here. His question seemed ludicrous. They said, **"You see the multitude thronging You, and You say, 'Who touched Me?'"** (v. 31b). The disciples were surely correct that there was a great deal of incidental contact with Jesus in the bustling crowd. However, Jesus knew that something extraordinary had happened. So, He simply ignored the disciples' exasperation and **looked around to see her who had done this thing** (v. 32). Besides, He was not expecting an answer from the disciples; when He asked, "Who touched My clothes?" He was calling on the person who had touched Him to confess.

When the woman heard Jesus' question, she knew her deed was known, so she came forward: **The woman, fearing and trembling, knowing what had happened to her, came and fell down before Him and told Him the whole truth** (v. 33). She was fearful, but grateful, as well, and in her gratitude she told him everything: "Jesus, I touched You. I'm unclean. I've just made You unclean according to the law, because I touched You. I hope You'll forgive me, but I was desperate because I've had this condition for twelve years. I went to every doctor I knew of, and they took my money, but they only made me worse. I'm sorry, Jesus, but I just knew that if I could touch You, I would finally be healed." She told Him the whole truth.

Notice that Jesus did not rebuke her for touching Him. Later, in a discussion with the Pharisees, Jesus said:

> "Have you not read what David did when he was hungry, he and those who were with him: how he entered the house of God and ate the showbread which was not lawful for him to eat, nor for those who were with him, but only for the priests? Or have you not read in the law that on the Sabbath the priests in the temple profane the Sabbath, and are blameless? Yet I say to you that in this place there is One greater than the temple. But if you had known what this means, 'I desire mercy and not sacrifice,' you would not have condemned the guiltless." (Matt. 12:3–7)

Jesus' point was that the needs of God's people are a higher priority for Him than ceremonial observances. Therefore, He did not make an issue of the woman's technical violation of the law. He was very gentle in dealing with this woman who had suffered so long.

What did Jesus say to her? He did not say, "Daughter, *your touch* has made you well." Neither did He say, "Daughter, *My garments* have made you well." No. He said, **"Daughter,** your faith **has made you well"** (v. 34a). What did He mean? There was no intrinsic power in her faith. Her faith was not the efficient cause of her healing; Jesus was. But her faith was the instrumental cause of her healing.

Just as in our justification, God does not declare us righteous because there is any inherent righteousness in our faith, prompting God to say, "Because you have faith, I will save you." No, faith is the instrumental cause of justification because it is the tool or instrument by which we take hold of Christ. Christ is the efficient cause of our justification. In the same way, it was Jesus who healed the woman.

Finally, Jesus said, **"Go in peace, and be healed of your affliction"** (v. 34b). The words "go in peace" could be seen as nothing more than a standard, customary valediction, something like "goodbye." But I think they meant much more to this woman who had not had a moment's peace in twelve years. Jesus spoke tenderly to her and said, "Go now, not in fear, not in trembling, not in misery, but in peace, and be healed." The verb tense Jesus used told the woman, "You are healed permanently."

A Girl in the Grip of Death

As soon as this happened, while Jesus was still speaking to the woman, **some came from the ruler of the synagogue's house who said, "Your daughter is dead. Why trouble the Teacher any further?"** (v. 35). From a human perspective, all hope for the girl was lost. We can reach that point, the point where we say to ourselves: "Why should I trouble God anymore? Everything I feared would happen has happened. Why should I bother praying now? My husband died. My child died. I'm dying. Why trouble God now?" At such times, we must remember that we should never stop "troubling" the Lord, because it is never any trouble for Him to hear us cry and to wipe away our tears. So, Jesus immediately said to Jairus, **"Do not be afraid; only believe"** (v. 36b). It was as if Jesus was saying to him: "Jairus, I know what they said. I know you are devastated. But it is not too late, despite what they say. Do not be afraid, Jairus. Do not give in to your terror. Just trust Me. This is not over." With that, **He permitted no one to follow Him except Peter, James, and John the brother of James** (v. 37). He sent the crowd and most of His disciples away, and went on only with Peter, James, and John, His inner circle.

Arriving at Jairus' house, Jesus saw a scene of confusion: **Then He came to the house of the ruler of the synagogue, and saw a tumult and those who wept and wailed loudly** (v. 38). Most likely, these were not family members and friends. It was the Jewish custom that when there was a death, the family hired professional mourners to rend their garments, weep, and wail to signify the great calamity that had befallen the household. The size of the professional mourning committee was determined by economics. The rabbis said that, at minimum, a family must hire two flute players and one female wailer when there was a death. But Jairus was a ruler of the synagogue, so his family likely had a whole team of these professionals. We can only imagine the noise. As Jesus approached the house, they were wailing, crying out, and weeping.

Jesus quickly put a stop to the ruckus: **When He came in, He said to them, "Why make this commotion and weep? The child is not dead, but sleeping"** (v. 39). He was not saying the girl was only comatose; He was using *sleeping* as a euphemism for death. This is a common euphemism in the Scriptures. But the professional mourners had been at many deathbeds. They knew death when they saw it, and they had no doubt that they had seen its heavy hand on Jairus' daughter. Therefore, **they ridiculed Him** (v. 40a). The mourners became mockers. They laughed at Jesus.

Jesus was not deterred in the slightest. He took full command of the situation: **But when He had put them all outside, He took the father and the mother of the child, and those who were with Him, and entered where the child was lying. Then He took the child by the hand** (v. 40b–41a). Just as Jesus was ritually defiled by the touch of the woman with the flow of blood, here He was defiled by touching a corpse; but again, Jesus saw that the need of one of God's people outweighed that ceremonial law.

Then, He **said to her, "Talitha, cumi," which is translated, "Little girl, I say to you, arise"** (v. 41b). God brought the whole world into creation by the sound of His voice, by fiat, by imperative. Christ brought Lazarus out of the tomb by His oral command. In the same way, He spoke in Aramaic to this little girl in her state of death and commanded her to rise, and again His almighty word was effective: **Immediately the girl arose and walked** (v. 42a). All of her strength returned immediately. She was returned not only to life but to full health.

As we might expect, **they were overcome with great amazement** (v. 42b). Perhaps their faith had been large enough to encompass a healing (v. 23), but they had never expected to see a resurrection; indeed, who in this world of sin and death would expect to see such a thing?

In such a situation, overcome by their joy, the girl's parents must have been ready to run through the town crying out what Jesus had done for them. That was not what Jesus wanted: **He commanded them strictly that no one should know it, and said that something should be given her to eat** (v. 43). Jesus often commanded those He helped miraculously to keep quiet about Him so that His mission would not be troubled by excessive popular acclaim. Thus, He gave Jairus and his wife a simple task—get the child a meal—and directed them to keep the miracle secret.

The power over disease, the power over death, the power over lost causes—all of these converged in the touch of Jesus. This is the Lord in whom we place our trust for all things for all time.

16

A PROPHET IN HIS
OWN COUNTRY

Mark 6:1–6

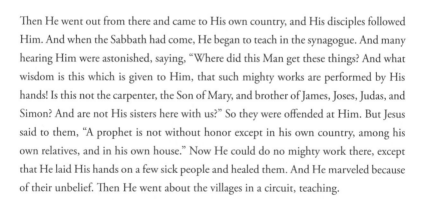

Then He went out from there and came to His own country, and His disciples followed Him. And when the Sabbath had come, He began to teach in the synagogue. And many hearing Him were astonished, saying, "Where did this Man get these things? And what wisdom is this which is given to Him, that such mighty works are performed by His hands! Is this not the carpenter, the Son of Mary, and brother of James, Joses, Judas, and Simon? And are not His sisters here with us?" So they were offended at Him. But Jesus said to them, "A prophet is not without honor except in his own country, among his own relatives, and in his own house." Now He could do no mighty work there, except that He laid His hands on a few sick people and healed them. And He marveled because of their unbelief. Then He went about the villages in a circuit, teaching.

To this point in the gospel of Mark, the public ministry of Jesus has been focused on the region around Capernaum and the Sea of Galilee. In Mark 6, the scene shifts; Jesus, Mark says, **went out from there and came to His own country, and His disciples followed Him** (v. 1). Jesus moved away from Capernaum and from Galilee, and went home to Nazareth, along with His disciples. We are not told why Jesus chose to go back to Nazareth at this time; possibly He simply wanted to spend time with and minister to people He knew and loved.

Nazareth, of course, was not the place of Jesus' birth (He was born in Bethlehem), but it was the village where He grew up. It lies about twenty-five miles southwest of the Sea of Galilee and Capernaum. In Jesus' time, Nazareth was a small, obscure village. Built on a rocky hillside, it covered a mere sixty acres, and fewer than five hundred people lived there. Having grown up in this tiny place, Jesus probably knew almost everyone in the town.

Jesus was in Nazareth when the weekly Sabbath occurred. Mark tells us, **And when the Sabbath had come, He began to teach in the synagogue** (v. 2a). We know from Luke that Sabbath attendance was Jesus' custom. But on this occasion, He did more than sit in the congregation; He taught the people. It may seem odd to our Protestant understanding that the local rabbi did not teach, but any adult male was free to speak in the gathering. We saw earlier in Mark that Jesus taught in the Capernaum synagogue (1:21), and there are several other references in the Gospels to the same practice.

Jesus' teaching left a distinct impression: **And many hearing Him were astonished, saying, "Where did this Man get these things? And what wisdom is this which is given to Him, that such mighty works are performed by His hands!"** (v. 2b). The Greek word that is translated here as "astonished" appears regularly in the gospel accounts as Jesus' teaching, His authority, and His miracles provoked amazement. People were often powerfully struck by the things Jesus said and did. Such was the case in Nazareth. The people freely acknowledged that Jesus' teaching was amazing and that the miracles they had heard about manifested great wisdom.

However, there was a unique element to the astonishment of the people of Nazareth. They were amazed that it was coming from Jesus, of all people. The people were surprised to hear Jesus teaching like a rabbi (and obviously training disciples like a rabbi) when He was not, in fact, a rabbi.

The problem was that these people knew Jesus. They knew He had not studied under any of the great rabbis of the day. Thus, for all intents and purposes, He was not qualified to be a teacher. They were simply shocked that He entered the synagogue and began teaching there without having the proper credentials. They did not understand that it was the Word of God incarnate who was teaching them, so He had no need for a degree from the great rabbi Gamaliel to be an expert in theology.

The Source of the People's Astonishment

Mark tells us that, in their astonishment, they said to one another: **"Is this not the carpenter, the Son of Mary, and brother of James, Joses, Judas, and Simon? And are not His sisters here with us?" So they were offended at Him** (v. 3).

Let us think about that first question: "Is this not the carpenter?" The people did not ask, "Is this not the son of the carpenter Joseph?" They knew Jesus Himself as a carpenter. However, the Greek word here, *tekton*, can mean "carpenter," "stone mason," or anyone who is involved in the craft of building; it is the word from which we get our word *architect*, which simply means "chief builder." It is very possible that instead of being a carpenter who worked with wood, Jesus was a stone mason; that would explain the strength that He obviously developed as a young man. In all probability, however, He worked with both wood and stone, as builders in His day produced all sorts of things, from houses to cabinets to yokes for oxen.

When Jesus was a young man, Herod Antipas inherited a portion of the kingdom of his father, Herod the Great, and became the tetrarch of Galilee. He set out to build a city to serve as the regional capital of Galilee and to construct a palace for himself just a few miles north of Nazareth. Historians tell us that he hired craftsmen and laborers from all around the district to help him build his city. It is possible that those he hired included Joseph and Jesus. It is interesting to speculate that Jesus may have worked on this project for a man who would question Him and mock Him during His passion (Luke 23:6–12).

In any case, Jesus was known as a lad who had grown up in Nazareth and worked as a builder. But in that time and place, builders did not have a lot of prestige. They were not high on the ladder of status. They were considered menial laborers. So the people looked at Jesus and said, "What is this carpenter doing here, teaching in the synagogue?"

It is also curious that the people asked, "Is this not the carpenter, the Son of Mary?" Why did they do this? It surely was not because they were enamored of the virgin mother. This was not a thinly veiled testimony to the virgin birth or an expression of honor for Jesus' mother. In almost every case, the Jews identified men according to their relationships to their fathers, not to their mothers. Legally speaking, among the Jews, Jesus was the Son of Joseph. Even if Joseph was dead by this time, it still would have been customary to call Jesus the Son of Joseph, but instead they called Him the Son of Mary. The best guess as to the reason for this is that they still believed Jesus was an illegitimate son, that Mary had conceived Him out of wedlock. Perhaps they were saying: "Isn't He that carpenter who was the son of that woman? We know *that* family." If so, this comment is nothing short of ridicule.

Notice that the people knew Jesus' siblings: "Is this not the . . . brother of James, Joses, Judas, and Simon? And are not His sisters here with us?" Some people jump through a whole lot of hoops to support the perpetual virginity of Mary. When they are confronted by biblical passages such as this one, they argue that these brothers and sisters must have been children of Joseph by a previous marriage, but there is nothing in the Bible or in extrabiblical sources to support that argument. Sometimes they suggest that these were cousins, arguing that the Greek word for "brothers" and "sisters" can be translated as "cousins." But it is not normally translated that way; there is a specific word for "cousin" in the Greek language. The text is clear—Jesus had brothers and sisters, and only a person with a theological bias tries to deny it.

We do not know much about Jesus' siblings, but one of the things we do know is shocking—during His public ministry, they were not believers. Luke reports that His brothers were with the small band of believers after His resurrection (Acts 1:14), and His brother James became the leader of the church in Jerusalem and wrote the New Testament book of James. But at this time, when Jesus came back to Nazareth, His own brothers and sisters did not understand or support Him; as we saw earlier in Mark, it is possible that they thought He was insane (3:21). Probably Joseph had died by this time, and the only believer in Jesus' household was His mother.

So, the people of Nazareth were "offended" by Jesus. The Greek word used here is *skandalizamei*. The noun form of this word is *skandalon*, which comes over into the English language as the word *scandal*. These people were scandalized by Jesus. They were profoundly offended. They did not want to have any identification with Him because He embarrassed them and shamed them.

The word *skandalon* was also used of a building stone that was rejected. When builders selected stones to be used in the construction of buildings, they examined the quality and strength of the available stones, just as Michelangelo would go to the quarries in Italy to choose the very best marble for his statues. Sometimes he would find flaws, even in Carrara marble, so he would reject it. In both cases, the goal was to find the best materials, and some stones had to be rejected.

Jesus, of course, is seen as the rejected stone in Scripture. Psalm 118:22 says, "The stone which the builders rejected has become the chief cornerstone." Jesus quoted this verse in reference to Himself in His debates with the Jewish religious leaders (Matt. 21:42; Mark 12:10; Luke 20:17), and Peter quoted it before the Sanhedrin and in his first epistle (Acts 4:11; 1 Peter 2:7). Remember, the prophets and the Apostles are called the foundation for the church (Eph. 2:20), but Jesus Himself is the cornerstone. Yet, He was "despised and rejected by men" (Isa. 53:3). He was rejected by His own people, by His family, by the townsmen, by the nation of Israel. The One whom God appointed to be the cornerstone of His building was considered flawed and repulsive by His contemporaries.

Is Christ a *skandalon* for you? Are you embarrassed by Him? Are you "a secret service Christian," not wanting anyone to know your real identity, because you find that being identified with Him is an embarrassment, a source of shame? If so, I urge you to pray that He will change your heart and cause you to love and adore Him, for adoration is the only proper response to the One the Father has placed as the cornerstone.

The Source of Jesus' Astonishment

Jesus knew what was going on, so He said to them, borrowing an ancient Semitic adage, **"A prophet is not without honor except in his own country, among his own relatives, and in his own house"** (v. 4). I think I have some slight idea of what it must have been like for Jesus to go home. When I go back to my hometown and run into people I grew up with, they cannot believe I am a minister. It almost seems they cannot wait to say: "How in the world did you ever become a minister? If the board that ordained you had talked to us, you wouldn't have stood a chance of being ordained to the ministry." Those people remember my ungodly ways as I was growing up. Of course, Jesus never engaged in ungodliness, but the people of Nazareth knew His family and His background, and that was enough for them to question His call.

Mark adds a curious detail: **Now He could do no mighty work there, except that He laid His hands on a few sick people and healed them** (v. 5). What does this mean? It was not that Jesus suddenly lost His power when He went to Nazareth, that He became incapable of manifesting the miraculous signs that had already begun to mark His ministry. Rather, the circumstances by which God the Holy Spirit unleashed that power were not available there, because there was a judgment of God on the town of Nazareth. In other words, God mostly withheld His power from the stiff-necked people who held Jesus in contempt.

Just as the people were astonished at Jesus, Jesus was astonished at them: **And He marveled because of their unbelief** (v. 6a). It seems odd to me that Jesus was surprised to encounter unbelief in Nazareth; after all, He had to deal with it every day of His life. I believe Mark is saying that He was surprised not that they were not believers, but at the depth of their callousness. With unbelief comes hostility. Those who did not believe in Christ soon grew to hate Him.

Why did they not believe in Him? Was it because they had seen Him working with His hands? Because they knew His mother? Because they knew His brothers and sisters? Because they knew He had not studied under a well-known rabbi? No. They did not believe in Jesus for the same reason your next-door neighbor does not believe in Jesus. God the Holy Spirit had not invaded their hearts and regenerated their souls. Unless the Spirit renews the hearts of sinful human beings, none can truly come to Him. Before the Spirit invaded your heart and opened your eyes, Jesus was a stumbling block to you. You rejected Him as strongly as these people from Nazareth.

We are surrounded in this world by people who want nothing whatsoever to do with Jesus. I do not know how many times I have heard people say, "I don't need Jesus." I cannot think of any more foolish statement a human being could ever make. Perhaps some of you reading this book have said that, and perhaps you are still saying it. Your spouse or a friend gave you this book and suggested you read it, and out of respect for that person you decided to glance over it, but your heart is far from Him. I say to you, there is nothing on this earth you need more desperately than Jesus, because if you do not have Jesus, you have no hope in this life or in the world to come. Let me say it again. If you do not have Jesus, you have no hope. You do not want to be among those people who are embarrassed by the name of Jesus.

There's a great danger here. The people of Nazareth had the Lord of glory in their midst for more than three decades, and all they saw was the offense. In the end, He could do no mighty works among them, and **He went about the villages in a circuit, teaching** (v. 6b). Being rejected in His hometown, He took His ministry elsewhere.

What is it about Jesus that offends you? The great danger is that Christ will be offended by you. All who trip over the *skandalon*, the scandalous Christ, will have His offense in return. Let us learn from the people of Nazareth.

17

A TRIAL MISSION
FOR THE TWELVE

Mark 6:7–13

~~~

And He called the twelve to Himself, and began to send them out two by two, and gave them power over unclean spirits. He commanded them to take nothing for the journey except a staff—no bag, no bread, no copper in their money belts—but to wear sandals, and not to put on two tunics. Also He said to them, "In whatever place you enter a house, stay there till you depart from that place. And whoever will not receive you nor hear you, when you depart from there, shake off the dust under your feet as a testimony against them. Assuredly, I say to you, it will be more tolerable for Sodom and Gomorrah in the day of judgment than for that city!" So they went out and preached that people should repent. And they cast out many demons, and anointed with oil many who were sick, and healed them.

Jesus was a peripatetic teacher; that is, He taught as He walked about. In the first few chapters of Mark, we have seen Jesus on the go almost constantly; at the end of the previous chapter, we saw Him going about the villages "in a circuit" (6:6). As He went, He taught not only the people in the places He visited, He taught His closest disciples as He walked along. Jesus had a goal in His training of these men, and, as we see in the passage before us in this chapter, at a certain point He intensified their training by sending them on a trial mission.

Mark writes, **And He called the twelve to Himself** (v. 7a). We need to remember who these twelve were. Earlier in Mark, we saw that Jesus "appointed twelve, that they might be with Him and that He might send them out to preach, and to have power to heal sicknesses and to cast out demons" (3:14–15). He told them, "To you it has been given to know the mystery of the kingdom of God" (4:11a). Since that time, they had been with Jesus, traveling about with Him and observing Him as He taught and performed wondrous signs. The twelve included Peter, James, John, and nine others (3:16–19).

One day, Mark writes, Jesus called the twelve to Him. It seems they were not all with Him, some perhaps having returned to their homes or their businesses temporarily, but Jesus summoned them to assemble for a purpose. He called them in order to send them out to preach, just as He intended when He chose them (3:14). But it is important that we not miss that the calling came before the sending. We like to hear Jesus say, "Come to Me, all you who labor and are heavy laden, and I will give you rest" (Matt. 11:28). But when we do come to Jesus, what does He then say? "Go therefore and make disciples of all the nations" (Matt. 28:19a). That pattern of coming and going, of being summoned and then sent out, appears here in Mark's gospel account.

Sent in Jesus' Name

Jesus, Mark says, **began to send them out two by two** (v. 7b). When Mark writes that He "began to send them," he uses the verb form of the Greek noun *apostolos* ("one sent forth"), from which we get our word *apostle*. We read in the New Testament about disciples and apostles, and we tend to think that the two words are synonyms. They are not. A disciple is a learner, a student. An apostle is one who is commissioned by his master with the master's own authority, then sent out in the master's name. That distinction is critically important for us because the New Testament tells us that the prophets and the Apostles are the foundation of the church (Eph. 2:20). That means the Apostles had what we call "apostolic authority" over the church of all ages, which authority they were given by the One who sent them.

The first Apostle in the New Testament, the Apostle par excellence, was Jesus. He said, "I have not spoken on My own authority; but the Father who sent Me gave Me a command, what I should say and what I should speak" (John 12:49). Our Lord Himself is the supreme Apostle of the Father, for He carries in His ministry nothing less than the authority of the Father. The twelve, however, were Jesus' Apostles, having been chosen from the much larger group of disciples who followed Jesus (see Luke 6:13). Thus, Jesus gave to them His own authority.

This is very important in this day and age, when people are trying to tear the Bible into various parts. I hear it all the time: "I like Jesus, but I cannot stand Paul—he's a chauvinist who denigrates women." We have to see that Paul said nothing to the church except by the authority of Jesus Christ. Therefore, if you do not like Paul, you do not like Jesus. Jesus Himself said to the Apostles, "He who receives you receives Me, and he who receives Me receives Him who sent Me" (Matt. 10:40). We know nothing about Jesus except what comes to us through the testimony of the Apostles. So it is a false dichotomy to separate apostolic authority from the authority of Christ. The church has to fight that battle in every generation.

Why did Jesus send the twelve out in pairs? It seems to me that they could have covered more ground if He had sent them out one by one, with each one going to a separate village. That would have doubled their missionary outreach. But sending them two by two provided companionship. It also hearkened back to the Old Testament principle that something is established as true if testimony is given to it by two witnesses (Deut. 19:15; Matt. 18:16). What one proclaimed, the other could verify.

Given Power over Demons

Mark tells us that Jesus also **gave them power over unclean spirits** (v. 7c). The word translated here as "power" is one we already have encountered in Mark. It is *exousia*, which sometimes is translated as "power" and other times as "authority." The Greek word that normally indicates sheer power or force is *dunamis*, from which we get the word *dynamite*. But *exousia* has to do with the power that is contained within authority. In this case, the Apostles specifically had power or authority over unclean spirits, to order them to come out of people they possessed.

Why did Jesus do this? His reason had to do with the true purpose of miracles, which is one of the things that Christians seem to misunderstand more than anything else in the Bible. The fundamental purpose of miracles, both in the Old Testament and the New Testament, was to authenticate agents of revelation. The Pharisee Nicodemus came to Jesus at night and said, "Rabbi, we know that You are a teacher come from God; for no one can do these signs that You do unless God is with him" (John 3:2). You see, God does not empower demons to perform authentic miracles. They do lying and counterfeit works. Bona fide miracles are restricted in the Bible to those on whom God places His seal of approval.

In Exodus 3–4, we read of the struggle Moses went through to accept his call to go to Egypt and lead the people of Israel out of bondage. God commanded him to go to Pharaoh and order him to let his Israelite slaves go. Moses was hesitant, protesting that the Israelites would not believe that he had been sent by God. So God gave him a series of signs—his staff would become a serpent when cast to the ground, his hand would be covered by leprosy when slipped into his cloak, and water from the Nile would turn to blood when he poured it out. God said He was giving these signs "that [the Israelites] may believe that the LORD God of their fathers, the God of Abraham, the God of Isaac, and the God of Jacob, has appeared to you" (Ex. 4:5). When the Israelites expressed doubt about his call, Moses could demonstrate God's power in such a way that no one would be able to gainsay his authority.

Jesus gave the twelve power over demons for the same reason. As He Himself said elsewhere, "If I cast out demons with the finger of God, surely the kingdom of God has come upon you" (Luke 11:20). Successfully commanding demons to come out of possessed people would reveal the authority that had been given to the twelve.

Commended to Providence

Then **He commanded them to take nothing for the journey except a staff—no bag, no bread, no copper in their money belts—but to wear sandals, and not to put on two tunics** (vv. 8–9). Jesus was telling them to travel light. This brings to mind Exodus and the Passover, the night when the children of Israel were to leave Egypt. They were commanded to be ready at a moment's notice to leave their homes at the summons of God. They were to be dressed to move quickly and travel light. Jesus gave His Apostles the same orders.

It is interesting that the other gospel accounts of this incident report that Jesus said the Apostles should take no staff (Matt. 10:10; Luke 9:3). There is a distinction here. As we know, Psalm 23:4 says, "Your rod and Your staff, they comfort me." The rod and staff were the traditional implements of a shepherd. The staff was the shepherd's crook, by which he could guide his sheep, and which also served him as a walking stick. That is what Mark is speaking about. Matthew and Luke, by contrast, have the rod in view. This was a shepherd's weapon against animals such as bears or lions, or against thieves. So there is no conflict between Mark and the rest of the Gospels. Jesus was saying, "You're not allowed to take powerful rods with you, but you can take a walking stick."

Jesus further forbade them from taking bags, food, or money. When He spoke of a "bag," He was referring not to a satchel but to a beggar's bag. He was forbidding them from begging for their needs. They were going to have needs, for He also denied them food and money by which to buy food. Last but not least, they were not to take extra clothing. (According to Mark, Jesus permitted them to take light sandals, but Matthew notes that He prohibited heavier shoes; Matt. 10:10.) It was as if He was saying: "You're going to have to depend on My Father at every point of this mission. You are not to take anything with you, not even the slightest bit of change in your purse." He wanted them to leave everything burdensome behind and rely totally on divine providence.

Their provision was to come from people they met along the way. Jesus said, **"In whatever place you enter a house, stay there till you depart from that place"** (v. 10). Clearly, Jesus meant that the Apostles would receive unexpected hospitality as they traveled about. With their physical needs provided, they would be able to focus on their mission. Incidentally, the provision of housing on their way was another reason Jesus instructed the men not to take two tunics. In the ancient world, travelers often had to sleep outdoors, and the purpose of the second tunic was to serve as a covering against the elements. Jesus was saying His Apostles would not need to worry about that; they would be indoors at night.

It is possible Jesus had another reason for giving this pointed command. He may have been saying that if a poor person offered his humble abode for their use during their stay in his town, they were to accept it gladly. But once they had entered the poor man's home, they were not to leave, not even if a wealthy man later invited them to move to his home. In other words, they were not to be open to better offers at the risk of offending a humble homeowner.

I see this kind of thing in the ministry all the time. A small church invites a preacher to speak. He accepts the invitation. He puts it on his calendar. But then the organizers of a big national event come along, promising an audience of thousands and a large honorarium. Most preachers in that situation ask the small church to reschedule. Tradesmen also do this; they promise to be at your home for a small repair job at a specific time, but they do not show up. Why? They landed a bigger, more lucrative job. Jesus gave us the bottom line: "Let your 'Yes' be 'Yes,' and your 'No,' 'No.' For whatever is more than these is from the evil one" (Matt. 5:37).

Prepared for Rejection

Jesus added, **"Whoever will not receive you nor hear you, when you depart from there, shake off the dust under your feet as a testimony against them"** (v. 11a). The practice of shaking the dust off one's feet goes back to antiquity. When Jews who had traveled in Gentile regions came home, they were required to shake the dust off their feet at the border lest they bring the contamination of the pagan world into Israel. That action symbolized God's judgment on paganism. It is interesting that Paul and Barnabas actually did this at least once during their first missionary journey, when the Jews interfered with a promising work among the Gentiles in Antioch of Pisidia (Acts 13:51).

There is no such thing as indifference to Christ. You are for Him or against Him. In the kingdom of God, there is no neutral ground. In the church today, when we do mass evangelism, the standard technique is to offer an invitation after the sermon. We say, "As many as would like to respond to Christ, come now." However, we do not usually add, "As many as would not like to respond to Christ, go to hell." But the gospel is a two-edged sword. If we receive it, the benefit is eternal life. If we reject it fully and finally, we do so to our everlasting peril.

Jesus provided a horrifying comparison to illustrate that peril: **"Assuredly, I say to you, it will be more tolerable for Sodom and Gomorrah in the day of judgment than for that city!"** (v. 11b). Not all the manuscripts of antiquity include this extension of verse 11. However, the same comparison from the lips of Jesus is recorded in the other Synoptic Gospels in other contexts, so it is worth considering. Simply put, Jesus was saying that anyone who rejected the good news of the gospel from the lips of His representatives would incur a more severe judgment than the evil Old Testament cities of Sodom and Gomorrah—which God destroyed by fire (Gen. 19:24–25).

There are at least a couple of lessons for us in this chilling statement from our Lord. First, Jesus was not hesitant to talk about a final judgment. In fact, He talked about it quite a lot. There *will* be a last judgment, and every one of us will have to appear. Second, the last judgment will be a matter of degrees. There are degrees of sin. There are degrees of obedience. Though our works carry no intrinsic merit, Jesus often said that our reward in heaven will be according to the measure of obedience that we give in this life. In the same way, there will be levels of punishment in hell. Paul warns the impenitent Romans against "treasuring up for yourself wrath in the day of wrath" (Rom. 2:5). One of my seminary professors once said, "The sinner in hell would give everything that he had and do anything that he could to make the number of his sins during his lifetime one less." It should chill us to the bone to hear Jesus say that there will be a greater judgment given to those people who rejected the Apostles than even the cities of Sodom and Gomorrah, which symbolized the nadir of human decadence in the Old Testament.

Few people believe this truth today. Many do not believe there will be a judgment. Even those who concede there will be a judgment often conclude that a person is either saved or condemned, and there is no distinction between the best and worst saints and sinners. People sometimes say, "Well, I've lusted, I might as well go ahead and do it again," or, "One little sin won't hurt anything." The bottom line is that we do not believe in a God who is deeply offended by each violation of His holy standards. We need to see that every sin will be brought into the judgment, and God's justice will be perfect. Some will be visited with many stripes, some with few (Luke 12:47–48).

Mark concludes: **So they went out and preached that people should repent. And they cast out many demons, and anointed with oil many who were sick, and healed them** (vv. 12–13). The Apostles did as Jesus commanded. They preached and they exercised their authority over demons and disease. It was a successful trial run, a micro-picture of the mighty and ongoing mission of the church.

18

THE DEATH OF
JOHN THE BAPTIST

Mark 6:14–29

Now King Herod heard of Him, for His name had become well known. And he said, "John the Baptist is risen from the dead, and therefore these powers are at work in him." Others said, "It is Elijah." And others said, "It is the Prophet, or like one of the prophets." But when Herod heard, he said, "This is John, whom I beheaded; he has been raised from the dead!" For Herod himself had sent and laid hold of John, and bound him in prison for the sake of Herodias, his brother Philip's wife; for he had married her. Because John had said to Herod, "It is not lawful for you to have your brother's wife." Therefore Herodias held it against him and wanted to kill him, but she could not; for Herod feared John, knowing that he was a just and holy man, and he protected him. And when he heard him, he did many things, and heard him gladly. Then an opportune day came when Herod on his birthday gave a feast for his nobles, the high officers, and the chief men of Galilee. And when Herodias' daughter herself came in and danced, and pleased Herod and those who sat with him, the king said to the girl, "Ask me whatever you want, and I will give it to you." He also swore to her, "Whatever you ask me, I will give you, up to half my kingdom." So she went out and said to her mother, "What shall I ask?" And she said, "The head of John the Baptist!" Immediately she came in with haste to the king and asked, saying, "I want you to give me at once the head of John the Baptist on a platter." And the king was exceedingly sorry; yet, because of the oaths and because of those who sat with him, he did not want to refuse her. Immediately the king sent an executioner and commanded his head to be brought. And he went and beheaded him in prison, brought his head on a platter, and gave it to the girl; and the girl gave it to her mother. When his disciples heard of it, they came and took away his corpse and laid it in a tomb.

Herod the Great, who ruled over Palestine as a vassal king of the Roman Empire from 37 to 4 BC, was the "Herod" who is mentioned in the gospel accounts of Jesus' birth. Upon his death, his kingdom was divided into four parts and given to his four sons, each of whom became the "tetrarch" ("ruler of a fourth") of one of the four pieces. Herod Antipas, who became tetrarch of Galilee and Perea, was the "Herod" who is mentioned in Luke's account of Jesus' passion (23:6–12). Thus, members of the Herod family appear in Scripture at both the beginning and end of Jesus' life, but Herod Antipas is also mentioned in Mark 6, as Mark breaks away from His narrative of Jesus' work to recount the fate of John the Baptist.

When Herod Antipas was nearly thirty years into his forty-three-year reign as tetrarch, he began to hear rumors of a man who could work miracles. He could come to only one conclusion as to who this man might be and how He came by His powers. Mark writes: **Now King Herod heard of Him, for His name had become well known. And he said, "John the Baptist is risen from the dead, and therefore these powers are at work in him"** (v. 14).

Until this point in Jesus' public ministry, His fame was overshadowed by that of John the Baptist, because the Jews were absolutely astonished at the renewal of the office of prophet. The prophets had been supremely important in Old Testament days, but the prophetic word had ceased for hundreds of years until John came out of the wilderness in the spirit and the power of Elijah. Such was John's fame that even Herod Antipas was well acquainted with him. But Herod had been more than a casual admirer of John; their relationship had become very personal.

Herod's first thought was that John the Baptist had come back from the dead, for John was dead by this time, as Mark soon explains. Herod was haunted by the idea that John had returned to life because, in the ancient world, there was a popular idea that resurrections were signs of impending judgment. If John had been raised, Herod reasoned, he must be bringing the judgment of God on his enemies, number one of whom was Herod, who had been responsible for John's death.

Others proposed alternative theories about Jesus, perhaps to soothe Herod's guilty conscience: **Others said, "It is Elijah." And others said, "It is the**

Prophet, or like one of the prophets" (v. 15). Actually, these theories probably were of little comfort to Herod. Elijah was a formidable figure. "The Prophet" was perhaps a reference to the prophet Moses foretold (Deut. 18:15). Someone "like one of the prophets" would bring a message from God that could not help but confront the decadent Herod.

In any case, Herod would not be swayed from his opinion: **But when Herod heard, he said, "This is John, whom I beheaded; he has been raised from the dead!"** (v. 16). Here, for the first time, we learn the fate of John the Baptist—Herod had executed him by beheading. Mark then goes on to tell the whole grisly story.

An Unrestrained Monarch

It is sometimes said that power corrupts and that absolute power corrupts absolutely. I think that axiom, in the literal sense, is flawed, because the only being who possesses absolute power is God Himself, and He is absolutely without corruption. Still, we cannot deny that on the human plane, the more power one has, the more corrupt one tends to be. Heading almost every list of the great criminal minds and evil personages of world history are men such as the Pharaohs of ancient Egypt, the Emperor Nero, Adolf Hitler, and Joseph Stalin. These men had one thing in common—they were rulers who wielded virtually unlimited power. That is, no one (at least within their own nations) exercised restraints on them. Herod did not possess the same power as a Hitler or a Stalin, but in his little realm, his evil impulses were unrestrained. And yet, John the Baptist was brave enough to try to restrain him.

It all began when John confronted Herod about a sin in his life and Herod reacted vengefully: **For Herod himself had sent and laid hold of John, and bound him in prison for the sake of Herodias, his brother Philip's wife; for he had married her. Because John had said to Herod, "It is not lawful for you to have your brother's wife." Therefore Herodias held it against him and wanted to kill him, but she could not; for Herod feared John, knowing that he was a just and holy man, and he protected him. And when he heard him, he did many things, and heard him gladly** (vv. 17–20). Let me provide some background and then try to break down this terrible incident.

We saw earlier that when John appeared out of the wilderness, he came as the herald of the Messiah. He was God's anointed witness to declare to Israel the coming of the kingdom of God and the appearance of God's anointed King. John was the first human witness to Jesus; he leaped in the womb of his mother, Elizabeth, when Mary, pregnant with Jesus, came to visit her (Luke 1:41). Later, of course, he bore witness to Jesus as "The Lamb of God who takes away the sin of the world!" (John 1:29). His main function was to call the people of Israel to prepare themselves for the coming of their King, but in at least one instance, he got much more specific in denouncing sin—he thundered against Herod Antipas for his adulterous lifestyle.

Herod had been married to the daughter of Aretas, who was king of Nabatea, a nation adjacent to the region Herod Antipas ruled. However, he began an adulterous affair with Herodias, his half-brother's wife, and eventually married her. According to Jewish law, this arrangement was unlawful on two grounds. On the one hand, there was the problem of adultery. On the other hand, Jewish law prohibited sexual relations with one's brother's wife (Lev. 20:21). John, with the fearlessness so typical of many of the prophets, had confronted Herod about this sin.

It seems that Herodias was more irked about John's denunciations of Herod than was Herod himself, and that she prompted Herod to respond to John; Mark writes that Herod had John imprisoned "for the sake of Herodias." But Herod would not give in to Herodias' demands that John be executed. Mark tells us why: "Herod feared John, knowing that he was a just and holy man, and he protected him." Furthermore, he "heard him gladly." It seems that Herod had a certain admiration or respect for John.

The single greatest restraint on evil that God has placed in this world is conscience. The most wicked people, sociopaths and psychopaths, are sometimes described as being without conscience; nevertheless, they have not been able to annihilate altogether that voice of right and wrong that God has implanted in every human creature. Paul speaks of the law written on the heart, so that one's conscience bears witness to God's standards and one's thoughts therefore accuse or excuse (Rom. 2:12–16).

Of course, we cannot fall into the trap of "Jiminy Cricket theology"; we cannot always let our consciences be our guides. If we follow our consciences at every point, they will guide us into disaster. Even though God plants a conscience in the mind of every human being, our repeated transgressions put calluses on our consciences, and we learn how to silence the voice of conscience and almost completely eradicate it. In other words, our consciences can be distorted. They can be twisted. Thus, if we let conscience alone be our guide, we will probably live in unrestrained wickedness.

However, no matter how far we may go in our wickedness and no matter how much we seek to stifle our consciences, we cannot finally do so. The people in this world who are hostile to the things of God, who have no qualms about the godless behavior in which they are involved every day, nevertheless do not always sleep easily at night. When they put their heads on the pillow, they know that the way they are living is not good. I think that, to some degree, explains Herod's fascination with John the Baptist.

At the beginning of the twentieth century, a German theologian and sociologist studied human beings' reactions to whatever they deemed to be holy, and he found that holiness is both terrifying and fascinating to the sinner. We know that we are not holy. We know that our lives are not right. However, we do not want to hear judgments against us. Therefore, we fear that which is holy. That is why Mark tells us that Herod "feared John." His fear was not the result of any power John had to harm Herod. Rather, it was because he knew John was "a just and holy man." And yet, when the holy comes near, as fearful as it is, we have a certain attraction to it. Thus, even in his fear, Herod wanted to hear John talk. He was both fearful of John and drawn to him.

I have a friend who played on the Professional Golfers' Association tour years ago. He once told me about an acquaintance of his who had been voted the golfer of the year. On one occasion, this top-level golfer played a round with Billy Graham. Afterward, the golfer stormed off the eighteenth green, went over to the practice tee, and began hitting drives in a state of fury. My friend observed his evident agitation and asked why he was upset. He replied, "I don't need to have Billy Graham forcing religion down my throat." Then he went back to pounding drives down the range. When he finished, my friend walked over to him and said, "Billy really came on strong to you, did he?" At that, the golfer hung his head and said: "No, actually Billy didn't say a word about religion. I just had a bad round." Isn't that fascinating? Dr. Graham said not one word about religion to this man, but he did not have to. Dr. Graham's mere presence and what he represented to this golfer was enough to make him supremely uncomfortable.

This golfer was like Herod Antipas in front of John the Baptist. He could not deny that John was a just man, a holy man. He was both fearful and fascinated. He agreed to put John in jail to make his wife happy, but he would not go any further. He did not want to put John to death.

An Unwise Oath

But Herodias found a way to achieve her desired end by trickery. Mark writes, **Then an opportune day came when Herod on his birthday gave a feast for his nobles, the high officers, and the chief men of Galilee** (v. 21). Herod threw a party in his own honor, and the guest list was a who's who of Galilean society—leaders, noblemen, bureaucrats, tradesmen, and so on. The entertainment was provided by his stepdaughter: **Herodias' daughter herself came in and danced** (v. 22a). The Bible doesn't give her name, but Josephus, the

Jewish historian, writes that her name was Salome. The kinds of dances that were performed in these situations were erotic and sensuous, and given Herod's character, Salome's dancing was well-received: she **pleased Herod and those who sat with him** (v. 22b).

In his happiness and desire to appear gallant and generous in front of his guests, Herod said to Salome: **"Ask me whatever you want, and I will give it to you. . . . Whatever you ask me, I will give you, up to half my kingdom"** (vv. 22c–23). Of course, the expression "up to half my kingdom" is not to be taken literally. It was a common expression of rulers in antiquity, an idiom designed to say, "I am prepared to reward you generously."

Hearing this, Salome sought her mother's advice: **So she went out and said to her mother, "What shall I ask?" And she said, "The head of John the Baptist!"** (v. 24). At last, Herodias saw her chance. She ordered her daughter to ask the king to execute John. There is no indication in the text that the girl was disappointed not to get something for herself; perhaps she was as opposed to John as was Herodias, or perhaps she just did not dare disagree with her strong-willed mother. In any case, Mark writes, **Immediately she came in with haste to the king and asked, saying, "I want you to give me at once the head of John the Baptist on a platter"** (v. 25).

What was Herod's response? He **was exceedingly sorry** (v. 26a). He had never dreamed that Salome would ask for such a thing. However, **because of the oaths and because of those who sat with him, he did not want to refuse her** (v. 26b). Having promised the girl whatever she requested in the hearing of his guests, the king did not want to back down. He considered himself bound by the oath he had sworn.

Taking an oath or a vow is a very serious act. The Westminster Confession of Faith, one of the greatest doctrinal statements of church history, devotes an entire chapter to lawful oaths and vows. But today, we have lost our understanding of the sanctity of oaths. We make promises before God, before witnesses, before family members, and before the church, and then as soon as the service is over, we forget them. We have to learn to guard the oaths that we take with our very lives. The Bible warns us, "Better not to vow than to vow and not pay" (Eccl. 5:5).

At the same time, the Bible shows us that some vows are unlawful and should not be fulfilled. In the book of Judges, Jephthah, preparing for battle, vowed to God that if his army triumphed, he would sacrifice the first thing that came out of the door of his house when he returned home. He did win his battle, but when he came home, it was his daughter who walked out the door. Jephthah should have repudiated his foolish vow on the spot, for it was apparent that he had bound himself to do something God forbids. Instead, he followed through and sacrificed his daughter.

Herod's vow was unlawful in just this way. It bound him to do something evil in God's eyes. But in his pride, he would not back down—as if keeping promises was something sacred to this man. The problem, of course, was that his guests, the upper crust of Galilean society, had heard him promise, and in his twisted thinking, he believed he would somehow be diminished if he did not keep his word.

Mark writes: **Immediately the king sent an executioner and commanded his head to be brought. And he went and beheaded him in prison, brought his head on a platter, and gave it to the girl; and the girl gave it to her mother** (vv. 27–28). What a ghastly narrative this is. What a birthday party, where a man's severed head was brought in on a tray in full view of the guests.

Several decades ago, a leading theologian said that American culture was no longer a Christian culture; rather, it had become neo-pagan. Today, *neo-pagan* may be too mild a term. Perhaps the best way to describe American culture today is with the word *barbaric*. Yes, our culture is highly literate and educated. Yet, we slaughter a million and a half babies in the womb each year. That is barbaric. But since it is legal, we think it must be okay. Perhaps a party like Herod's would not seem so horrific in America today.

Mark gives us the sad postscript to this narrative: **When his disciples heard of it, they came and took away his corpse and laid it in a tomb** (v. 29). John's followers lost their master because of a foolish whim of an evil ruler. Not only had Herod killed him, he had mutilated him. All the disciples could do in their sadness was give him a proper burial.

John's death was a chilling precursor of the vicious torture, mutilation, and death Jesus Himself would endure in the not-so-distant future. Herod would be there to mock Christ as He suffered under another uncaring ruler, Pontius Pilate.

19

THE SHEPHERD
FEEDS HIS FLOCK

Mark 6:30–44

Then the apostles gathered to Jesus and told Him all things, both what they had done and what they had taught. And He said to them, "Come aside by yourselves to a deserted place and rest a while." For there were many coming and going, and they did not even have time to eat. So they departed to a deserted place in the boat by themselves. But the multitudes saw them departing, and many knew Him and ran there on foot from all the cities. They arrived before them and came together to Him. And Jesus, when He came out, saw a great multitude and was moved with compassion for them, because they were like sheep not having a shepherd. So He began to teach them many things. When the day was now far spent, His disciples came to Him and said, "This is a deserted place, and already the hour is late. Send them away, that they may go into the surrounding country and villages and buy themselves bread; for they have nothing to eat." But He answered and said to them, "You give them something to eat." And they said to Him, "Shall we go and buy two hundred denarii worth of bread and give them something to eat?" But He said to them, "How many loaves do you have? Go and see." And when they found out they said, "Five, and two fish." Then He commanded them to make them all sit down in groups on the green grass. So they sat down in ranks, in hundreds and in fifties. And when He had taken the five loaves and the two fish, He looked up to heaven, blessed and broke the loaves, and gave them to His disciples to set before them; and the two fish He divided among them all. So they all ate and were filled. And they took up twelve baskets full of fragments and of the fish. Now those who had eaten the loaves were about five thousand men.

I n the nineteenth century, there developed a school of theology known as the religious-historical school, which sometimes is described as historical liberalism. It was a definite movement that was anti-supernatural from beginning to end. Its impact spilled over to the twentieth century with neo-liberalism and, later, the Jesus Seminar. This school attacked every narrative found in Scripture, particularly in the New Testament, that involved miracles or the supernatural, because the tacit assumption of the critics was that there is no such thing as divine, supernatural intervention in history. When they came to the narrative of Jesus' feeding of the five thousand, they took it upon themselves to explain how natural interpretations could be given that would not ask us to stretch our imaginations to believe in miracles. Some of these explanations ranged from the bizarre to the ridiculous.

When I was growing up in Pittsburgh, my minister taught that there were two possible explanations of what happened at the feeding of the five thousand, both of which he received from the religious-historical school. The worst explanation was that Jesus carefully prepared for this event by deviously filling a cave near the Sea of Galilee with a large supply of loaves and fishes. Jesus had a flowing robe with loose sleeves, much as you might see on a magician. When it came time to feed the people, the disciples formed a bucket brigade, passing loaves and fishes to Him through the back of His robe, which He then distributed to this mass of humanity that was gathered in front of Him. So, the feeding of the five thousand was merely a hoax perpetrated by a fraudulent preacher.

The other explanation was that when Jesus finished His teaching that day, the people were tired and hungry, but very few of them had thought ahead and brought food for their nourishment. Jesus asked His disciples to go around and find out who had brought food, and it turned out that some had brought loaves and some fish. So, Jesus addressed the multitude and said, "Share what you have one with another." Thus, everyone was able to eat because those who had brought food shared with those who had not. The true miracle that took place was an ethical miracle. It was the miracle of human beings sharing their provisions one with another.

One commentator in the twentieth century said it well when he declared that these explanations manifest nothing short of unbelief. They do not reflect the straightforward testimony of the text Mark sets before us.

The Compassionate Shepherd

In chapter 17, we saw Jesus sending twelve of His disciples on a trial mission (Mark 6:7–13). Mark did not conclude that narrative right away; rather, he related the story of the death of John the Baptist, which we studied in the previous chapter. As a result, Mark presents two consecutive narratives that revolve around dramatic feasts. The first was hosted by Herod Antipas. The second was hosted by Jesus. At the first feast, only the nobles and the elite of Galilee were invited. At the second feast, the people of the land, the commoners, gathered to be fed by the provisions set forth by Jesus. At the first feast, the food was prepared by gourmet chefs. At the second feast, it was prepared by the hand of the Messiah. At the first feast, the entertainment was exotic dancing. At the second feast, the first item on the agenda was the exposition of the truth of God by the Son of God. Finally, the climax of the first feast was the heartless execution of a man of God. At the second feast, the dominant theme was the compassion of the Son of God for people who were like sheep without a shepherd.

Returning to his account of the twelve and their trial mission, Mark writes: **Then the apostles gathered to Jesus and told Him all things, both what they had done and what they had taught. And He said to them, "Come aside by yourselves to a deserted place and rest a while." For there were many coming and going, and they did not even have time to eat** (vv. 30–31). The disciples came back to Jesus and told Him all about their various journeys in pairs, the things they had taught and done. Jesus' response was compassionate: He urged them to come with Him to a place of solitude and to rest for a while, for there was much activity around Him, and the disciples were kept so busy they could not even find time to eat. We have noted before that the traditional meeting place between God and His people is the wilderness. Therefore, it is not surprising that Jesus said, "Let's get away from the cities, the villages, and the crowds; let's go out and be alone, just ourselves with God." **So they departed to a deserted place in the boat by themselves** (v. 32).

Jesus' plan to leave the crowds was not successful: **But the multitudes saw them departing, and many knew Him and ran there on foot from all the cities. They arrived before them and came together to Him** (v. 33). Jesus and His disciples did not go far; clearly they did not cross the Sea of Galilee, which would have been a trip of fifteen to twenty miles, and the crowds would not have been able to keep up and arrive before them. It seems that the group simply sailed along the shore for a short distance, looking for a quiet, uninhabited place. However, the huge crowd that had been gathered around Jesus, a crowd that perhaps had grown since the Apostles' teaching mission, simply followed along on the shore, keeping the boat in sight, and was waiting for Him when the boat put in once more.

What was Jesus' reaction to this interruption of His plan? **And Jesus, when He came out, saw a great multitude and was moved with compassion for them, because they were like sheep not having a shepherd. So He began to teach them many things** (v. 34). He was not frustrated that He could not find some peace and quiet. He was not annoyed that the people would not give Him and His tired disciples a respite. He could have said: "Sorry, you need to make an appointment. I have to spend time with My disciples today, and you folks are not invited." Instead, Mark tells us, Jesus was moved by compassion. The Greek word that is translated here as "compassion" is used to describe only Jesus in all of the New Testament. This was a compassion that reached a level that was far deeper than human concern and empathy for people in pain.

Jesus looked at the great multitude that was waiting for Him so eagerly and saw them as "sheep not having a shepherd." Once, when I was playing a round of golf, a flock of sheep somehow got out of a nearby field and began running around on the fairway, interrupting my golf game. Their movements seemed completely random. They ran one way, then turned in another direction. They ran aimlessly, as if they were blind. That was how Jesus saw the people on the shore. Thus, He was not angry at them. He felt sorry for them.

I love the Old Testament image that is found in so many of the prophecies of the Messiah. It was said that the Messiah would be a Shepherd King, that He would be the Good Shepherd, that He would lay down His life for His sheep (Pss. 23:1; 78:72; Isa. 40:11; Ezek. 34:11). Jesus here demonstrated that He was the fulfillment of these prophecies. In His compassion, the Good Shepherd looked on His sheep and determined to meet their need.

Notice what Jesus did: He began to teach the people. In the New Testament church, Jesus is the Shepherd of the sheep, but the pastor is the undershepherd, and his primary responsibility is to feed the sheep. We live in a time when churches are weak, and one of the main reasons is that the people demand that the pastor do everything but preach and teach. I believe about 95 percent of the labor of the pastor in the church should be preaching and teaching. The congregation belongs to the Lord; they are His sheep. He has given them pastors as shepherds to keep them fed, giving them food that will not make them sick but will nurture them—the very Word of God. When Jesus set out to feed His sheep, He taught them.

The Feeding of the Sheep

Either Jesus began teaching late in the day or He taught for a very long time, for the hour grew late and the disciples grew concerned: **When the day was** now far spent, His disciples came to Him and said, "This is a deserted place, and already the hour is late. Send them away, that they may go into the surrounding country and villages and buy themselves bread; for they have nothing to eat" (vv. 35–36). Perhaps we see a bit of compassion from the disciples here; they were wondering how the people would be able to find food if Jesus did not cease teaching soon and send the people off to find food in the countryside and the villages. Because they were in a deserted place, the people would have to travel some distance.

In reply, Jesus made a suggestion that the disciples had never considered: "You give them something to eat" (v. 37a). He had been feeding them spiritual food; now He suggested that the disciples give the people physical food. They were flabbergasted: And they said to Him, "Shall we go and buy two hundred denarii worth of bread and give them something to eat?" (v. 37b). The main problem the disciples saw was the cost of providing for all the people who had gathered to hear Jesus. They estimated they would need to spend two hundred denarii. A denarius was the equivalent of a day's wage for a laborer; two hundred was an appreciable portion of a yearly salary. So, the disciples focused on the obstacles.

Jesus told them to take inventory: He said to them, "How many loaves do you have? Go and see." And when they found out they said, "Five, and two fish" (v. 38). It was not nothing, but it was next to nothing given the size of the crowd. Certainly there was nothing in this inventory that bolstered the disciples' faith that the people could be fed on the spot.

But the small amount of food was no obstacle for Jesus: Then He commanded them to make them all sit down in groups on the green grass. So they sat down in ranks, in hundreds and in fifties. And when He had taken the five loaves and the two fish, He looked up to heaven, blessed and broke the loaves, and gave them to His disciples to set before them; and the two fish He divided among them all. So they all ate and were filled. And they took up twelve baskets full of fragments and of the fish. Now those who had eaten the loaves were about five thousand men (vv. 39–44).

This text has rather obvious parallels with a similar miracle in the Old Testament, which happened when the people of Israel were in the wilderness and became so discontent they wanted to go back to Egypt. God had supernaturally given them bread every day in the form of manna, but they were tired of it; they wanted variety (Num. 11:4–6). They forgot about the yoke that had been on their necks in Egypt. They forgot about the oppression of Pharaoh. They were ready to sell their citizenship in the kingdom of God for leeks, onions, and garlic. Moses appealed to God for help, and God promised that on the very next day He would give the people meat to eat, enough for a whole month, so much meat it would come out of their nostrils and become loathsome to them (vv. 19–20). God did as He promised; He brought massive flocks of quail down on the Israelite camp, so that the Israelites had more meat than they could consume (vv. 31–32). When God works, feeding a multitude is a simple thing.

So, the disciples obeyed Jesus. They gave Him the loaves and fish, then had the people sit down on the grass. Then Jesus looked to heaven and prayed a simple prayer. Mark does not tell us the words that He prayed, but in all probability He prayed the common Jewish prayer for meals at that time: "Praise be to You, O Lord, our God, King of the world, who makes bread to come forth from the earth and who provides for all that You have created." It was a prayer praising the providence of God. Then Jesus blessed and broke the loaves, and gave the pieces to His disciples with the fish. By His supernatural power, the meager bits of food were multiplied. Everyone ate and was satisfied, then twelve baskets of leftovers were gathered.

Finally, Mark gives the astounding figure with the even more astounding implication: the number of those who ate was five thousand *men*. The Greek word Mark uses here clearly means "men," not human beings in general, indicating that there were additional people, women and children, who ate. The crowd may have been as large as fifteen or even twenty thousand people.

We cannot and should not read this account without thinking of that night in which our Lord was betrayed. In the midst of celebrating the Passover once more with His disciples, He took the bread, and when He had blessed it, He broke it, and said, "Take, eat; this is My body" (14:22). In the same way, He took the cup and said, "This is My blood of the new covenant, which is shed for many" (v. 24). Today, when the sacrament of the Lord's Supper is celebrated, the undershepherds of Christ invite all who trust in Christ by faith to come to His table to be fed and nourished by their compassionate Shepherd. In this way, we see His ongoing care for His sheep.

20

MANIFESTING THE GLORY OF GOD

Mark 6:45–56

Immediately He made His disciples get into the boat and go before Him to the other side, to Bethsaida, while He sent the multitude away. And when He had sent them away, He departed to the mountain to pray. Now when evening came, the boat was in the middle of the sea; and He was alone on the land. Then He saw them straining at rowing, for the wind was against them. Now about the fourth watch of the night He came to them, walking on the sea, and would have passed them by. And when they saw Him walking on the sea, they supposed it was a ghost, and cried out; for they all saw Him and were troubled. But immediately He talked with them and said to them, "Be of good cheer! It is I; do not be afraid." Then He went up into the boat to them, and the wind ceased. And they were greatly amazed in themselves beyond measure, and marveled. For they had not understood about the loaves, because their heart was hardened. When they had crossed over, they came to the land of Gennesaret and anchored there. And when they came out of the boat, immediately the people recognized Him, ran through that whole surrounding region, and began to carry about on beds those who were sick to wherever they heard He was. Wherever He entered, into villages, cities, or the country, they laid the sick in the marketplaces, and begged Him that they might just touch the hem of His garment. And as many as touched Him were made well.

H aving studied Jesus' feeding of the five thousand in the previous
chapter, we now come to Mark's account of Jesus walking on the
waters of the Sea of Galilee. These are two of the better-known
incidents from the life of Jesus. Between these two accounts, however, there is
an interesting segue, a small account that we should not overlook as we focus
on the major events.

Mark writes, **Immediately He made His disciples get into the boat and
go before Him to the other side, to Bethsaida, while He sent the multitude
away** (v. 45). Mark does not tell us why Jesus abruptly sent His disciples away to
Bethsaida while He remained behind to dismiss the people. We know, however,
that occasionally, when He performed a significant miracle, particularly when
large crowds were present, the people would begin to press on Him, wanting to
anoint Him as their King, looking to Him to deliver them from the oppression
of Rome. I am speculating here, but I cannot help but wonder whether this same
desire surfaced once again on this occasion, and whether the crowd response
was so strong that the disciples themselves were caught up in it. Perhaps He
saw that they were as excited as the crowd, that they were looking to Him with
the hope that He might be the One to drive the Romans out of the land. If so,
it is hardly surprising that Jesus bustled the disciples off to Bethsaida. In this
way, He headed off any spontaneous moves to make Him King.

But Jesus had business of His own: **And when He had sent them away,
He departed to the mountain to pray** (v. 46). There was nothing particularly
unique about this. Obviously, Jesus was a man of prayer. Still, there are only
three occasions when the Bible specifically describes Jesus in prayer. When He
went apart like this, as He did on the night before He called His Apostles and
on the night before His crucifixion, a crisis usually was pressing in on Him that
had something to do with His vocation, His mission. The first time it was the
choosing of the disciples who would accompany Him in this mission. The third
time (Gethsemane), the climax of His mission was directly in front of Him,
with that cup that the Father had filled with His own wrath. The reason for
Jesus' withdrawal in this instance is less clear, but He is at a point of growing
fame and is soon to meet greater opposition from the Pharisees. Perhaps these
matters were on His mind.

An Encounter with the Glory of God

Jesus did not pray all night on this occasion. Mark writes: **Now when evening
came, the boat was in the middle of the sea; and He was alone on the land.
Then He saw them straining at rowing, for the wind was against them. Now
about the fourth watch of the night He came to them, walking on the sea,**

and would have passed them by (vv. 47–48). While Jesus was coming down from the mountain of prayer, He looked out into the Sea of Galilee, and in the distance He could see that His disciples were making very little progress in getting to the other side. There was a fierce wind blowing against them, so they could not sail across the sea. Thus, they had resorted to their oars, and Jesus observed that they are straining as they rowed. Elsewhere in the Bible, the word here translated as "straining" is rendered as "torment"; evidently the disciples were experiencing great pain and frustration in their attempt to obey Jesus' command.

Seeing His disciples in torment, Jesus set out to go to them about the fourth watch of the night, which was between three and six o'clock in the morning. Jesus went to them by walking on the surface of the sea. The language Mark uses in the text leaves no doubt about what he is saying; the words mean that Jesus walked literally "on top of" the water. He was doing something no mortal is able to do.

In the previous chapter, we saw how scholars of the religious-historical school in the nineteenth century mounted an assault against those biblical passages that touch on the supernatural. We discussed some of the rather pathetic attempts of these scholars to explain away Jesus' miraculous feeding of the five thousand. These same scholars explained Jesus' walk on the water by saying that the disciples saw an optical illusion in the darkness and mist. Others theorized that Jesus walked out on a sandbar to meet His disciples in a lake that at least some of them knew as well as the backs of their hands. These critics simply could not tolerate the possibility that what Mark describes here actually took place.

There is a strange detail in Mark's narrative. He writes, "He came to them, walking on the sea, *and would have passed them by.*" Jesus saw that His disciples were in trouble, straining so hard at their oars that they were in physical torment, so He walked out onto the sea to the place where the boat was. But then He was about to pass them by. Why would He have done this?

One of the basic principles of biblical interpretation is that Scripture interprets Scripture. To gain a good understanding of what this text is about, we have to go back to the Old Testament. When God manifested Himself in the Old Testament, He often did so by means of a theophany. This word comes from the Greek words *theos*, which means "God," and *phano*, which means "to manifest, show, demonstrate, or display." Thus, a theophany is a manifestation of God in some visible form. In Genesis, when God promised Abraham that he would inherit the land of Canaan, he asked, "Lord God, how shall I know that I will inherit it?" (15:8). So God appeared to him as a smoking oven and a burning torch as part of a covenant-making ceremony (v. 17). That was a theophany. Likewise, when God appeared to Moses as a burning bush (Exodus 3), that, too, was a theophany.

Perhaps the two most famous theophanies of the Old Testament are found in the books of Exodus and 1 Kings. In the first example, found in Exodus 33, Moses asked God, "Please, show me Your glory" (33:18). God said:

> "I will make all My goodness pass before you, and I will proclaim the name of the LORD before you. I will be gracious to whom I will be gracious, and I will have compassion on whom I will have compassion." But He said, "You cannot see My face; for no man shall see Me, and live." And the LORD said, "Here is a place by Me, and you shall stand on the rock. So it shall be, while My glory passes by, that I will put you in the cleft of the rock, and will cover you with My hand while I pass by. Then I will take away My hand, and you shall see My back; but My face shall not be seen." (vv. 19–23)

Three times in this passage, God spoke of passing by Moses, of causing His goodness or His glory to pass by. In this account of a theophany, even as in the Genesis 15 passage, when God showed Himself to a man, His glory passed by.

In the second example, which is in 1 Kings 19, Elijah fled from the wicked Queen Jezebel and hid in a cave at Mount Sinai. God appeared to him and asked, "What are you doing here, Elijah?" (v. 9). Elijah replied, "I have been very zealous for the LORD God of hosts; for the children of Israel have forsaken Your covenant, torn down Your altars, and killed Your prophets with the sword. I alone am left; and they seek to take my life" (v. 10). I call this "the Elijah syndrome," that feeling of hopelessness many of us experience from time to time when we think we are the only ones who are faithful. God said to Elijah, "Go out, and stand on the mountain before the LORD" (v. 11a). Then we are told: "And behold, the LORD passed by, and a great and strong wind tore into the mountains and broke the rocks in pieces before the LORD, but the LORD was not in the wind; and after the wind an earthquake, but the LORD was not in the earthquake; and after the earthquake a fire, but the LORD was not in the fire; and after the fire a still small voice" (vv. 11b–12). In that crisis encounter, Elijah, like Moses before him, experienced a theophany as the glory of the Lord passed by.

That is what happened on the Sea of Galilee. Jesus self-consciously made Himself a theophany. The glory of God, bursting through the shroud of the humanity of Jesus, was made manifest to the disciples. In the middle of their distress, they looked up and saw the glory of God passing by, the glory of the Lord shining out of the Son of God.

A Manifestation to Soften Hearts

The disciples were not immediately aware that they were seeing the glory of God. Mark tells us, **And when they saw Him walking on the sea, they supposed it was a ghost, and cried out; for they all saw Him and were troubled** (vv. 49–50a). They knew they must be seeing something supernatural. They thought He was a ghost, but the same word can be translated "demon," and that would fit with a popular idea that the churning of the sea was the result of the visitation of demonic beings. Naturally, they were troubled, and some cried out in fear. **But immediately He talked with them and said to them, "Be of good cheer! It is I; do not be afraid"** (v. 50b). Jesus reassured them by identifying Himself.

One of the key features of the gospel of John is Jesus' repeated use of the phrase "I am." He gave Himself various titles: "I am the bread of life" (6:48); "I am the light of the world" (8:12); "I am the door" (10:7); "I am the good shepherd" (10:14); and so on. When a person says "I am" in Greek, he can do it in two ways. He can say *"Eimi"* or *"Ego eimi."* Both of these terms mean "I am." But in John's gospel, when Jesus made His "I am" statements, He chose to say, *"Ego eimi."* This is an intensive form of "I am." However, it is also an expression that translates the ineffable name of God that God gave to Moses from the burning bush: "I AM WHO I AM" (Ex. 3:14), which name is usually rendered as *Yahweh* in the Hebrew. When *Yahweh* is translated into Greek, it is by *"Ego eimi."*

Mark's gospel also has an "I am" statement. As Jesus passed by the disciples' boat, walking on the sea, He said to them: "Be of good cheer! It is I; do not be afraid." When Jesus said "It is I," He said *"Ego eimi,"* or "I AM." If there was any doubt that this was a theophany, Jesus' use of the sacred name of God to identify Himself as He walked on the water made it virtually certain.

But why did He do this? Why did He feel it necessary to give His disciples a theophany at this place and time? We do not need to speculate, for Mark explains.

First he notes: **Then He went up into the boat to them, and the wind ceased. And they were greatly amazed in themselves beyond measure, and marveled** (v. 51). Jesus got into the boat, and when He did, the wind suddenly stopped. Just as He had done earlier (4:35–41), Jesus calmed the sea. However, despite having seen the same miracle before, and others besides, the disciples were dumbfounded.

Then Mark writes, **For they had not understood about the loaves, because their heart was hardened** (v. 52). What had they not understood? Simply put, they should have understood that the One with whom they had to do was God incarnate. Who else could feed thousands and thousands of people with a few loaves and some fish? But instead of seeing the presence of God, they saw the presence of a liberator from the military oppression of Rome. They did not understand.

Mark even tells us *why* they did not get it. Their hearts were hard. When people fail to understand the identity of Christ, it is not because they are unintelligent, it is because their hearts are recalcitrant. Their hearts are made out of stone, for sin has caused great calluses to grow on their hearts, so that Christ Himself could walk in front of them on the water and they still would not believe.

The disciples did not get it when Jesus fed the five thousand. They did not get it when He walked on the water. They did not get it when He called Himself *"Ego eimi."* They did not get it when He stepped into the boat and the wind died. Their hearts were hardened.

Thankfully, Jesus was not finished with them yet. Soon there was more evidence for them to see: **When they had crossed over, they came to the land of Gennesaret and anchored there. And when they came out of the boat, immediately the people recognized Him, ran through that whole surrounding region, and began to carry about on beds those who were sick to wherever they heard He was. Wherever He entered, into villages, cities, or the country, they laid the sick in the marketplaces, and begged Him that they might just touch the hem of His garment. And as many as touched Him were made well** (vv. 53–56). Reaching the other side of the sea, Jesus was mobbed again, and the people brought all their sick friends and relatives, that they might touch His garment. Those who touched it were healed. Surely the Lord was in that place.

21

GOD'S LAW AND MAN'S TRADITION

Mark 7:1–8

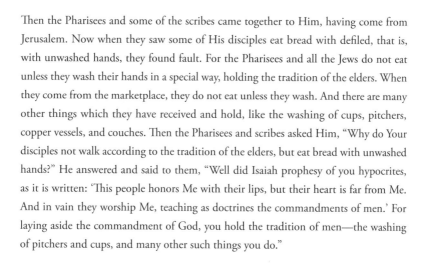

Then the Pharisees and some of the scribes came together to Him, having come from Jerusalem. Now when they saw some of His disciples eat bread with defiled, that is, with unwashed hands, they found fault. For the Pharisees and all the Jews do not eat unless they wash their hands in a special way, holding the tradition of the elders. When they come from the marketplace, they do not eat unless they wash. And there are many other things which they have received and hold, like the washing of cups, pitchers, copper vessels, and couches. Then the Pharisees and scribes asked Him, "Why do Your disciples not walk according to the tradition of the elders, but eat bread with unwashed hands?" He answered and said to them, "Well did Isaiah prophesy of you hypocrites, as it is written: 'This people honors Me with their lips, but their heart is far from Me. And in vain they worship Me, teaching as doctrines the commandments of men.' For laying aside the commandment of God, you hold the tradition of men—the washing of pitchers and cups, and many other such things you do."

There seems to be a shift in the tone of Mark's gospel when we come to chapter 7. So far, he mostly has recorded Jesus' marvelous supernatural works as he makes his case that Jesus is the Son of God. However, he has put very little accent on the content of Jesus' teaching to this point, with the exception of the parables recorded in chapters 3 and 4. In the other Synoptic Gospels, by contrast, large sections of teaching are interspersed with the narratives. Finally, here in Mark 7, we begin to find some additional teaching from Jesus, but even here the teaching is provoked by an incident.

Mark writes, **Then the Pharisees and some of the scribes came together to Him, having come from Jerusalem** (v. 1). It is about ninety miles from Jerusalem to Capernaum on the shore of the Sea of Galilee. The fact that these religious leaders made this journey strongly suggests they were highly motivated to observe and confront Jesus, perhaps having heard of His growing popularity in Galilee. He had already had at least one interaction with Pharisees and with scribes from Jerusalem (3:22); now they found another occasion to question Him.

Mark writes, **Now when they saw some of His disciples eat bread with defiled, that is, with unwashed hands, they found fault** (v. 2). On the surface, it might appear that the Pharisees and scribes were concerned about hygiene, so they got in Jesus' face to ask: "Aren't You concerned about the health of Your disciples? Why are You letting them eat food without washing their hands properly?" However, hygiene had nothing to do with their complaint. They were addressing ritual defilement and cleansing. The washing in question here was merely symbolic. In fact, the amount of water that the Pharisees and scribes used to wash their hands before eating was so slight it would not have done much to promote good hygiene. They did it only to fulfill a ritual that had been prescribed by Jewish leaders in former times.

For the benefit of his Gentile audience in Rome, Mark explains: **For the Pharisees and all the Jews do not eat unless they wash their hands in a special way, holding the tradition of the elders. When they come from the marketplace, they do not eat unless they wash. And there are many other things which they have received and hold, like the washing of cups, pitchers, copper vessels, and couches. Then the Pharisees and scribes asked Him, "Why do Your disciples not walk according to the tradition of the elders, but eat bread with unwashed hands?"** (vv. 3–5).

Before we dig into this background material, it is important to note that while the Pharisees and scribes came with a complaint about the behavior of Jesus' disciples, the obvious target of their hostility was not the disciples but Jesus Himself. Notice that when they came to Him, they did not say, "Why do those people do what they do?" Rather, they asked pointedly, "Why do *Your disciples* behave in this manner?" It is clear that the authorities from Jerusalem were holding Jesus responsible for the behavior of His followers.

Also, this was not the first time Jesus had found Himself in a dispute with the Pharisees over matters of law. They had raised concerns about those with whom Jesus was meeting for table fellowship (2:15–17). Also, they had taken issue with His healing on the Sabbath day, a practice that so angered them they began to plot His death (3:1–6). So this incident was merely part of an ongoing dispute.

The Tradition of the Elders

What was the cause of this new flareup in the dispute? There are principles of ritual cleanliness set forth by God in the Old Testament, but they are few and are easy to follow. For instance, the Old Testament law required the priests of Israel to wash their hands before they entered the Holy Place and offered sacrifices. However, there was no law that required ordinary people to go through a ritual cleansing before they ate bread. But over the centuries, as we have seen, the rabbis who interpreted the law of God had added to the law's ritual requirements, so that their regulations far exceeded the regulations that the law of God imposed on the people.

Where did these man-made laws come from? The Jews had the *Halakhah*, which included the oral teachings of the rabbis. This is what the Pharisees had in view when they spoke of "the tradition of the elders." All of the principles and regulations that the rabbis added to the law of God were passed on from generation to generation orally as part of the *Halakhah* until they were finally compiled in the third century AD as the *Mishnah*, which comprised the bulk of the Jewish *Talmud* at that time.

When we read the Sermon on the Mount in Matthew's gospel (chaps. 5–7), it sometimes seems that Jesus is setting Himself against the law of God. For instance, He says: "You have heard that it was said, 'You shall love your neighbor and hate your enemy.' But I say to you, love your enemies, bless those who curse you, do good to those who hate you, and pray for those who spitefully use you and persecute you" (5:43–44). What was going on there?

There are two phrases that we have to be familiar with when we read the Bible, idiomatic expressions that had a clear meaning to any Jew. One is, "It is written." When a Jew said, "It is written," he did not mean simply that someone had written some words on papyrus. Among pious Jews, "It is written" meant "The Bible says." The writing that was in view when "It is written" was uttered was the sacred writing of Scripture. In clear distinction from the written Scriptures were the oral traditions that were passed down, being added to the written Scriptures. So, in the Sermon on the Mount, when Jesus said, "You have heard that it was said," He was making reference not to the Bible, not to the inscribed law of God, but to what was said orally by the rabbis. Never in the New Testament do we find the Lord Jesus Christ criticizing or disobeying the written law of God. But it seems as if every day, everywhere He went, He violated the oral tradition.

The Rites of the Pharisees

It is important to note that 25 percent of the *Mishnah* was devoted to ritual cleanliness and purity. The Pharisees believed that salvation came from ethnic separation, that they were saved by keeping themselves clean from any contamination from unbelievers or sinners. So they established all kinds of rites.

The oral traditions prescribed rituals for achieving different levels of cleanliness. The first level of cleanliness was reached by following such practices as washing one's hands before eating bread. The second level of purification was much more difficult to achieve. Mark makes mention of it: when a person came back from the marketplace, he had to be ritually cleansed, and that cleansing was accomplished by immersion. In the market, Jews had to deal with Gentiles, so they became ritually contaminated. Thus, they had to take a full bath after shopping. As Mark notes, there were "many other things which they have received and hold, like the washing of cups, pitchers, copper vessels, and couches."

One commentator has called this practice of the Jews "regulation madness." This is what happens when people who have a disposition to control others' lives begin to chip away at their freedoms and accumulate power for themselves. This has happened in every society in every culture in the history of the world, but the Pharisees did it with a vengeance. First, they would comment on the law. Then they would write a policy about the law. After some time, the policy would be elevated to a regulation, and shortly thereafter the regulation would become as conscience-binding as the written law of God. That process can happen in a society. It can happen in a church. It can happen in any subgroup where people meet.

When I was doing my doctoral work in Holland, one of the first idiomatic expressions I heard was, *U hebt de wet overtreden*, which means, "You have trespassed the law." The Dutch people were governed to death. They had laws for this and laws for that. If I broke a pane of glass in my house, I had to get written permission to repair it from the federal government. That is the kind of culture the Pharisees created in ancient Israel.

The Dangers of Legalism

This kind of thing is known as legalism. Legalism raises its ugly head in the lives of the people of God in many ways, but when religious authorities bind people's consciences where God has left them free, adding human regulations to the law of God, that is the worst and most devastating form of legalism.

Here is the irony: every time we add to the law of God, we inevitably subtract from it, because instead of putting our attention on the things that God is concerned about, human regulations cause us to *lose sight* of what concerns Him. We begin to major in minors. We begin to give our devotion to our own traditions, our own human regulations.

We have seen this in the Christian community again and again. In some groups, Christian piety is defined as refraining from wearing lipstick, dancing, going to movies, playing cards, and so forth, as if these activities had anything to do with the kingdom of God. In one sense, when these kinds of regulations are established, authentic righteousness is not simply obscured, it is discounted. After all, it is easier to refrain from wearing lipstick than from displaying pride. It is easier to stop going to movies than to start loving one's enemies. We have all we can do to seek the righteousness that God's law sets forth for us without worrying about petty issues. But that is what had happened in Israel. The Pharisees were absolutely majoring in minors. They had turned the supreme law of God into petty regulations, which obscured the majesty of the law of God.

I am an ordained minister of the gospel, but I have no right or authority to bind anyone's conscience absolutely. Only God has the power and the authority to do that. You might not like the traditions that I like. You are not going to be judged for that. However, there is an apostolic tradition. This is the tradition that has been passed down in the church from God Himself. That is where our focus is to be, and we must not let anyone or anything divert us from that to something of human invention.

No person in the history of our planet has come close to obeying the whole law of God—except Jesus, who kept it perfectly. Only Jesus could dare to say to His contemporaries, "Which of you convicts Me of sin?" (John 8:46a). In other words, "Show Me where I have ever broken the law of God." His food was to do the will of His Father (John 4:34). As the new Adam, it was His obligation to keep every jot and tittle of the law of God, and He did just that. However, He could not have cared less for human conventions. When Jesus saw a person suffering with leprosy, He touched Him. When He saw a man who could not walk, He healed him, even though it was the Sabbath day. When He saw a man in the throes of demonic possession, screaming in a graveyard, He went into that place and cast out that evil spirit.

The major problem with legalism is that it is a subtle form of idolatry; it elevates that which is human above that which is divine. It substitutes human traditions, human policies, and human regulations for the very Word of God. Whenever we serve the creature rather than the Creator, we are involved in idolatry. The Pharisees and scribes thought they were the most righteous people on the face of the earth, but they were idolaters.

The Hypocrisy of Men

Because of this, Jesus spoke sharply to them: **"Well did Isaiah prophesy of you hypocrites, as it is written: 'This people honors Me with their lips, but their heart is far from Me. And in vain they worship Me, teaching as doctrines the commandments of men.' For laying aside the commandment of God, you hold the tradition of men—the washing of pitchers and cups, and many other such things you do"** (vv. 6–8).

Quoting Isaiah, Jesus called attention to two parts of the human body—the lips and the heart. The lips are on the surface. The heart is the very core of a person's being. Jesus told the Pharisees and scribes: "Your lips move. You sing praises. You say prayers. You say that you love God, but it is no deeper than your lips. It doesn't come from the center of your being. My Father wants people to worship Him in spirit and in truth, not just with their lips, because lip service is the very essence of hypocrisy."

We are prone to look on outward appearances, but God looks on the heart. Thus, outward cleansing is of little ultimate value compared with inward cleansing. We need to ask God to cleanse us in our inward parts, to make our hearts right, that our words would not be evidence of hypocrisy.

A few years ago, I was invited to speak at a conference on the Westminster Confession of Faith, where I was asked to address this question: "How does the doctrine of God affect our understanding of Christianity?" The basic thrust of my message was that the doctrine of God defines and controls every other doctrine in the Christian faith. When I finished showing the many ways in which the doctrine of God affects our theology and our lives, I came down to this: "If you really want to get a feel for your doctrine of God, look at your worship." Far more than what we confess with our lips, how we worship God shows what we really believe about His character. If we worship the God of the Bible, we can never worship Him in a cavalier manner. Worship can never be an exercise in entertainment. When we walk through the sanctuary doors, we understand that we are coming into the presence of the God of the universe who is searching for people to worship Him in spirit and in truth. If that's how we understand God, our worship will have an element of *gravitas*, of holiness, of reverence, of adoration. The fun and games will end in the parking lot.

What did Jesus mean when He quoted Isaiah's words, "In vain they worship Me"? He meant that the Pharisees' worship was futile because it did not come from the heart. They paid more attention to human regulations and human traditions than to His law. They taught commandments made by men as if they were the very words of God. They were not concerned to discover and teach that which God had said.

Basically, then, when the Pharisees asked Jesus, "Why do Your disciples not walk according to the tradition of the elders?" He answered by asserting that the tradition of the elders was not equal to the law of God. It was mere human tradition, a replacement of the law of God by the law of men.

The temptation to add to God's law is not unique to the Pharisees. We have to deal with it every day in the Christian life. That is why, when people say, "You ought to do this but you ought not to do that," our best course is to take the Word of God to our bosoms, search the Scriptures, and say, "O God, I want to please You, not according to the traditions of men, but according to Your law."

22

DEFILEMENT
IN THE HEART

Mark 7:9–23

He said to them, "All too well you reject the commandment of God, that you may keep your tradition. For Moses said, 'Honor your father and your mother'; and, 'He who curses father or mother, let him be put to death.' But you say, 'If a man says to his father or mother, "Whatever profit you might have received from me is Corban"—' (that is, a gift to God), then you no longer let him do anything for his father or his mother, making the word of God of no effect through your tradition which you have handed down. And many such things you do." When He had called all the multitude to Himself, He said to them, "Hear Me, everyone, and understand: There is nothing that enters a man from outside which can defile him; but the things which come out of him, those are the things that defile a man. If anyone has ears to hear, let him hear!" When He had entered a house away from the crowd, His disciples asked Him concerning the parable. So He said to them, "Are you thus without understanding also? Do you not perceive that whatever enters a man from outside cannot defile him, because it does not enter his heart but his stomach, and is eliminated, thus purifying all foods?" And He said, "What comes out of a man, that defiles a man. For from within, out of the heart of men, proceed evil thoughts, adulteries, fornications, murders, thefts, covetousness, wickedness, deceit, lewdness, an evil eye, blasphemy, pride, foolishness. All these evil things come from within and defile a man."

I n a discussion sparked by His disciples' failure to wash their hands according to the oral traditions of the Jews, as we saw in the previous chapter, Jesus rightly accused the Pharisees and scribes of legalism. The word *legalism* is often bandied about quite loosely in the Christian community. This can lead to confusion, because there is more than one type of legalism by which the truth of God's Word is distorted.

Perhaps the most basic type of legalism is also the most devastating. It is the belief that we can be justified in the sight of God by obedience to the law. This dependence on our good works is diametrically opposed to the way of salvation that God declares so plainly in Scripture—justification by faith alone in Christ alone, who provides the only righteousness that can possibly avail for us. If we are trusting any other righteousness than the righteousness of Jesus, we are caught in the snare of legalism.

Another type of legalism is the one Jesus exposed in the Pharisees and scribes in the opening verses of Mark 7—the elevation of the traditions of men to the point where they are allowed to bind the consciences of God's people where God has left them free. This type involves adding to the law of God commandments and prohibitions that God has not spoken. As we saw, Jesus thoroughly condemned this practice.

A third kind of legalism drew Jesus' ire as He continued His critique of the Pharisees and scribes in Mark 7. I call this type of legalism "loophole-ism." It happens when people try to discern ways to get around the law of God. They try to adhere to the letter of the law even while they trample the whole point and spirit of it underfoot. One well-known example involved the prohibitions in Israel about limiting one's travel on the Sabbath to what was called a "Sabbath-day journey," which was a very short distance. The rabbis allowed a person to get around this law by stashing personal objects at various points along the route he planned to travel on the Sabbath. The rabbinic reasoning was that placing a personal item on a piece of real estate established residency. Thus, the person could go from "domicile" to "domicile" on the Sabbath until he reached his destination, never having traveled more than a Sabbath-day journey between stops. This was clearly "loophole-ism," an attempt to get around the law of God regarding the keeping of the Sabbath.

Looking for Loopholes

Jesus shrewdly exposed the Pharisees' and scribes' "loophole-ism" when He said: **"All too well you reject the commandment of God, that you may keep your tradition. For Moses said, 'Honor your father and your mother'; and, 'He who curses father or mother, let him be put to death.' But you say, 'If a** man says to his father or mother, "Whatever profit you might have received from me is Corban"—' (that is, a gift to God), then you no longer let him do anything for his father or his mother, making the word of God of no effect through your tradition which you have handed down. And many such things you do" (vv. 9–13).

The key to grasping what Jesus is saying here is understanding this strange term *Corban*. It had to do with giving or setting aside one's private property or personal wealth to God. In itself, that was a good principle. But it had been twisted by the rabbis as a way to get around one of the most important laws of God, the commandment that required people to honor their fathers and mothers.

Jesus said to them, "All too well you reject the commandment of God, that you may keep your tradition." Notice that Jesus did not say, "The problem with you is that you keep the law *and* the tradition." Rather, He said: "You reject the law of God and replace it with your tradition. In fact, you are using your tradition as an excuse to keep from obeying the law of God."

He then specifically referred to the fifth commandment: "For Moses said, 'Honor your father and your mother,' and, 'He who curses father or mother, let him be put to death.'" Then He added, "But you say. . . ." Notice the contrast. First Jesus noted what Moses said. Moses was the spokesman for God; he delivered divine revelation. Then Jesus prepared to contrast Moses' words with what the Pharisees and scribes said. These religious experts were delivering their opinions, which fell far short of divine revelation. The Pharisees and the scribes were not agents of divine revelation, but Moses was. The contrast was utterly stark.

What precisely did the Pharisees and scribes say? Jesus said, "But you say, 'If a man says to his father or mother, "Whatever profit you might have received from me is Corban"—' (that is, a gift to God), then you no longer let him do anything for his father or his mother."

The Jews had developed a method of deferred giving, whereby a person could promise that at his death he would give all of his worldly goods to the work of God. That meant that during his lifetime he would not be able to use his personal wealth for any other purpose, because it had been committed to God. So, in the name of piety, a person could escape the obligation of caring for his parents in times of illness or in their old age, when they might be too frail to support themselves. He could simply say: "Mother, Father, I am very sorry. I would like to help you, but my wealth is Corban. Everything I have is committed to the Lord, and I cannot give the Lord's money to you."

Strangely, the regulations for Corban permitted a person to use wealth that had been committed to God for himself during his lifetime. He just could not spend it on anyone else. This tradition sought to sanctify a way for a person to get out from under the responsibility that God puts on His people to give honor to their parents.

I think it needs to be said that among all the ethnic groups in the world, there well may be none that does more for the care of its aged members than the Jewish community. Despite all of this rabbinic nonsense, the law that God gave through Moses in the Old Testament has been honored even to this day as families care for their own without depending on other institutions, such as the government, in times of crisis. But no ethnic group is perfect, of course. Thus, even among the Jews, there were those who tried to use this rabbinic tradition to avoid their responsibility. Yes, there was a legitimate place for Corban, but this practice should never have been used to cancel out a commandment set forth by God.

Following the Law of Faith

Herein is a lesson for us. There is a science in theology and in biblical studies that we call hermeneutics. It is the science of biblical interpretation. It teaches objective principles and rules that govern our treatment of the text, lest we turn the Bible into a piece of clay that we can shape and form for our own desires, as the Pharisees did. At the heart of the science of hermeneutics in Reformed theology is the *regula fidei*, or "the law of faith," which says that no portion of Scripture must ever be set against another portion of Scripture. The first assumption here is that all of Scripture is the Word of God. The second assumption is that God does not speak with a forked tongue, that what He reveals in His Word is always consistent. It is sometimes said consistency is the hobgoblin of little minds. If that adage is true, we have to say that the tiniest mind to be found is the mind of God. However, I believe consistency is the sign of clarity of truth, and God's Word is consistent with itself.

For a glaring example of pitting one portion of Scripture against another, we need look no farther than Jesus' temptation in the wilderness. When Satan tried to seduce Jesus, he quoted Scripture to Him. He took Jesus to the pinnacle of the temple in Jerusalem and dared Him to leap off, saying, "He shall give His angels charge over you," a quotation from Psalm 91:11 (Matt. 4:6). He was saying to Jesus: "Throw Yourself down. Nothing bad will happen because God has promised that His angels will catch You." But Jesus replied, "It is written again, 'You shall not tempt the Lord your God'" (Matt. 4:7; Deut. 6:16). Jesus said: "Satan, you're violating the rule of faith. You're operating with a poor hermeneutic. You're setting Scripture against Scripture. The Bible says I am not to tempt God. If I am to be obedient to that dictum, I cannot acquiesce to your suggestion." He did not allow Satan to tempt Him to act on one verse of Scripture ripped from the context of the entire Word of God.

That is the kind of thing Jesus was dealing with in His dispute with the Pharisees and scribes. Their traditions were opening all kinds of loopholes to permit people to get out from under the clear teaching of the truth of God. For this reason, He said, they were "making the word of God of no effect through [their] tradition" (Mark 7:13).

The biggest theological controversy in church history was the Protestant Reformation of the sixteenth century. On the surface, it seemed as if the whole controversy was about one doctrine—justification by faith alone, which is the gospel itself. When Martin Luther was brought into disputes with the princes of the church, they reminded him that his understanding of justification was not the traditional understanding, that the church long had explained justification in different categories. But Luther simply said: "Here is what the Bible says. My conscience is held captive by the Word of God. I must submit to Scripture, not to man-made traditions." So, the secondary issue was the question of authority.

Where does ultimate authority lie? Is it in the Scriptures alone or is it in the Scriptures and tradition? If it is in both Scripture and tradition, tradition trumps everything by giving the binding interpretation of Scripture. So, for all practical purposes, there are not really two sources of authority, Scripture and tradition, but one, tradition, which becomes more important than the Word itself.

I do not understand how any sentient creature could read the New Testament teaching, particularly Paul's words in his letter to the Romans about justification, and draw from it anything that resembles the Roman Catholic doctrine, which is based on tradition. But it is not only Roman Catholics who fall prey to this problem. We all do. We all tend to give our traditions more weight than Scripture. It is easy for us to look back and say, "Shame on the Pharisees," "Shame on the rabbis," or "Shame on the medieval theologians of Rome." But we need to look no farther than our own hearts. The final arbiter of all theological and moral debates *must* be the Word of God.

Jesus completed His rebuke of the Pharisees and scribes by noting that their use of the Corban vow was not the only method by which they sought to get around the law of God. He said, "Many such things you do." The religious leaders of Jesus' day were systematically minimizing the impact of the Word of God on the lives and hearts of the people of Israel.

Pinpointing the Source of Defilement

Jesus then turned to the assembled crowd and said, **"Hear Me, everyone, and understand . . ."** (v. 14b). He was calling the people to attention to hear an authoritative pronouncement. Jesus was about to give an oracle from God. He said: **"There is nothing that enters a man from outside which can defile him; but the things which come out of him, those are the things that defile a man. If anyone has ears to hear, let him hear!"** (vv. 15–16). With these words, Jesus took on the whole rabbinical system of ritual purification, especially the elaborate food and cleansing regulations. He declared, "It's not what you eat and it's not what you drink; nothing from the outside defiles you or contaminates you." He pinpointed man's problem not as something outside himself but as something inside, something internal that produces defilement.

Later, when Jesus had retired from the crowds to a house, the disciples asked Him to elaborate, and He said: **"Are you thus without understanding also? Do you not perceive that whatever enters a man from outside cannot defile him, because it does not enter his heart but his stomach, and is eliminated, thus purifying all foods?"** And He said, **"What comes out of a man, that defiles a man"** (vv. 18–20). Could Jesus have been any clearer? No foods cause spiritual impurity in a man, for the simple reason that whatever is consumed is digested or eliminated. It has no spiritual effect on his heart. The obvious implication was that no avoidance of particular foods could bring righteousness. Simply put, the whole dietary system of Israel was worthless in terms of producing righteousness.

Finally, Jesus said: **"For from within, out of the heart of men, proceed evil thoughts, adulteries, fornications, murders, thefts, covetousness, wickedness, deceit, lewdness, an evil eye, blasphemy, pride, foolishness. All these evil things come from within and defile a man"** (vv. 21–23). With this catalog of sins, Jesus made His meaning perfectly clear. The sins a man conceives in his heart and commits bring him into defilement, that is, into debt to God. Food does not stain the heart, and refraining from various foods does not prevent it from being stained. Therefore, it is the heart that needs attention, not the diet.

We need to understand this because we all admit that we are sinners. Oh, we blithely say, "To err is human, to forgive is divine" and "Nobody's perfect." When we say such things, we demonstrate that we see sin as something on the edge, something tangential, something peripheral to our existence. Jesus said: "No, defilement comes from the very core of your being."

The book of Proverbs says, "As he thinks in his heart, so is he" (23:7a). We usually think of the brain as being the organ of thought, but here it is the heart that is said to think. We have all kinds of conflicting thoughts in our minds, but what we really believe is that which drives our behavior. Ideas may go in and out of our ears, and we may entertain them for a while in our thinking, but that which pierces the heart determines how we live. In short, a man is defined by that which he holds in his heart. If the heart is evil, there will be evil thoughts, adulteries, fornications, murders, thefts, covetousness, and all the other sins Jesus lists here. Eating or refraining from certain foods will not change this list one iota, nor will washing one's hands. It is the heart that must be cleansed.

23

CRUMBS FOR "DOGS"

Mark 7:24–30

From there He arose and went to the region of Tyre and Sidon. And He entered a house and wanted no one to know it, but He could not be hidden. For a woman whose young daughter had an unclean spirit heard about Him, and she came and fell at His feet. The woman was a Greek, a Syro-Phoenician by birth, and she kept asking Him to cast the demon out of her daughter. But Jesus said to her, "Let the children be filled first, for it is not good to take the children's bread and throw it to the little dogs." And she answered and said to Him, "Yes, Lord, yet even the little dogs under the table eat from the children's crumbs." Then He said to her, "For this saying go your way; the demon has gone out of your daughter." And when she had come to her house, she found the demon gone out, and her daughter lying on the bed.

Having forcefully confronted the Pharisees and scribes about issues of ritual purity, showing that defilement comes out from the heart rather than from that which enters the body, Jesus withdrew into a region that the Jews considered notoriously unclean. This is the only time in the record of our Lord's public ministry that He is seen leaving the ancient borders of Israel and going into a pagan land. As we will see, Jesus' venture into this region was not a missionary journey to the Gentiles. He saw it as His vocation to proclaim the kingdom of God to the Jews, with outreach to the Gentiles to be carried out later by His Apostles.

155

Mark writes: **From there He arose and went to the region of Tyre and Sidon** (v. 24a). Tyre was twenty miles to the northwest of Capernaum, where Jesus had been laboring. Sidon was farther north. Both were situated on the Mediterranean coast and had been part of the Phoenician culture. It was from that region that Jezebel had come and tormented the prophet Elijah. By the first century, like all of Israel, Tyre and Sidon were under Roman administration. The Jewish rabbis said that the region of Tyre and Sidon was committed to gross paganism and idolatry. Today, both cities are part of Lebanon.

Why did Jesus go into this region of rank paganism? Mark notes, **He entered a house and wanted no one to know it, but He could not be hidden** (v. 24b). It appears that Jesus went outside the borders of Israel to seek a place where He could rest from the pressing multitudes and from the debates that He had been going through. It is not clear why Jesus chose this particular region as a place of retreat; perhaps it simply seemed to be the place where He would have the lowest profile.

In any case, as Mark says, "He could not be hidden." Although Mark was speaking in a literal sense, that observation remains true in an ultimate sense. No matter how people try to hide Jesus, He cannot be hidden even in the darkest places of this world.

A Desperate Plea

It seems Jesus had only just arrived when He was sought out by a person with a need: **For a woman whose young daughter had an unclean spirit heard about Him, and she came and fell at His feet. The woman was a Greek, a Syro-Phoenician by birth, and she kept asking Him to cast the demon out of her daughter** (vv. 25–26). Somehow word about Jesus spread, at least in a limited way, and a woman came to seek his help.

Notice the background information Mark provides about this woman: she "was a Greek, a Syro-Phoenician by birth." When Mark calls her a Greek, he simply means that she was from an area that had been conquered by Alexander the Great and afterward hellenized, so that she spoke the Greek language. He does not mean she was a native of Greece. Indeed, her nationality was "Syro-Phoenician," which simply tells us that the area of her birth previously had been part of the Syrian and Phoenician cultures. She was manifestly not a Jew. Indeed, Matthew calls her "a woman of Canaan" (15:22).

Mark says the woman came to Jesus and "fell at His feet." This posture indicates two things. First, she was paying homage to Jesus, showing profound respect to Him even though she knew Him only by reputation. But not only was this a sign of homage, it was a sign of abject pleading. She fell to the ground in front of Jesus because, from her perspective, her last hope for the redemption of her little girl, who was possessed by a demon, was a touch from the man in front of her.

It is interesting that this event follows so closely on the heels of Jesus' denunciation of the Jewish regulations for ritual cleanliness. The religious authorities of the Jews, who considered themselves clean, had manifested their unbelief and their unwillingness to pay homage to Jesus, but this pagan woman, who was manifestly unclean according to rabbinical categories, prostrated herself before the Lord Jesus Christ and begged Him for His mercy.

Mark tells us that this woman "kept asking Him to cast the demon out of her daughter." She did not simply come and say, "Jesus, please heal my daughter." She was persistent. She begged him over and over again. She was a living embodiment of the widow who pleaded with the unjust judge in Jesus' parable until he relented and gave her relief (Luke 18:1–5). Simply put, she was so committed to the rescue of her daughter that she simply would not take "no" for an answer.

A Strange Reaction

The strange thing about this narrative is Jesus' reaction: **But Jesus said to her, "Let the children be filled first, for it is not good to take the children's bread and throw it to the little dogs"** (v. 27). First, it seems that He was not quick to answer her petition. He allowed her to repeat it over and over. Then, when He did reply, He gave an answer that, at least on the surface, seems harsh and insensitive, for He spoke of certain people eating before the dogs were fed—and the implication was that the woman and her people were the dogs. This does not seem to have been a compassionate response to this woman who was beseeching Him for relief for her little girl.

In order to grasp how offensive this comment might have seemed, we need to understand that one of the worst insults one person could hurl at another in that region in antiquity was to call him or her a dog. In most cases at this time, dogs were not pleasant, companionable creatures such as we enjoy as house pets; rather, they were half-wild scavengers. They would eat garbage and carrion, and would even devour corpses. They were the filthiest animals in the towns. Jesus Himself said in the Sermon on the Mount, "Do not give what is holy to the dogs; nor cast your pearls before swine" (Matt. 7:6a), using "dogs" as a euphemism for those who reject the gospel.

Several years ago, a feminist scholar wrote an essay giving a scathing critique of Jesus' response to the Syro-Phoenician woman, saying that His insensitivity and harshness were so severe on this occasion, that He so demeaned this woman in typical chauvinistic fashion, that He transgressed all boundaries of courtesy and crossed the line even into slander. This text, she charged, is Exhibit A that Jesus was not sinless, because He wronged this innocent woman by calling her a dog.

Sometime later, I heard a Christian professor give an academic address in which he rebutted the charges of the feminist scholar. He went over her attack against Jesus in great detail, but as he did, he referred to her repeatedly as "a renowned evangelical scholar." After his address, I told him that I appreciated his effort to rebut the charges the feminist scholar had made against Jesus, but I also shared with him that I felt his use of the word *evangelical* to describe her was out of place. It is simply unthinkable that a person could deny the sinlessness of Jesus and still be considered an evangelical. An evangelical, in the first instance, is one who embraces the evangel, which is the gospel, the good news of the saving work of Christ in His atoning death. If Jesus committed a sin in His treatment of this woman, He was not sinless. And if Jesus had a single sin, He did not have what was necessary to atone for His own sin, let alone to atone for ours. So, as you can see, there is a great deal at stake when it comes to our understanding of how Jesus treated that woman. If He sinned against her, then He is no Savior of her, you, or me.

Did He actually sin against her? We need to touch on a couple of additional details in the text. First, notice that in the New King James translation, the word *dogs* is qualified by the adjective *little*. That is because, in the Greek, the word for *dog* is rendered in the diminutive sense. This is an important detail. Although most of the dogs in Jesus' day were half-wild scavengers, small, domesticated dogs were kept as house pets, and these dogs tended to gather under the family table at mealtimes. They typically were fed the table scraps, but only after the family had eaten.

In my family, we try to follow that principle with our dogs. We have three rules. First, we do not feed our dogs human food. They eat carefully prepared, nutritious dog food. I have to admit, we do not always obey that rule, so we have a second rule: if we give the dogs human food, it must never, ever be given to them from the table, because we understand that if we start giving our dogs food from the table, they will anticipate it and become a nuisance as we are having our family meals. However, there are times when our dogs look at me so longingly that I cannot resist giving them food from the table. Therefore, we have a third rule: if I feed the dogs from the table, it must be after dinner is ended and everyone else has left the table. So, my dogs know very well that they are not allowed to take anything from the table and they have to wait patiently until everyone is finished.

However, in addition to these three rules, we have a corollary: if some food falls inadvertently from the table, the dogs are allowed to eat those scraps or crumbs. That corollary seems to have been in effect in homes in Jesus' day.

Jesus addressed this Gentile woman with an arrangement something like this in mind. He asserted, "The children eat first," referring to the children of Israel. He was saying: "My ministry has a priority. My ministry is to take care of the children of Israel, not to give the food that is meant for the children to the little dogs." That was simply another way of saying that His ministry was to the people of Israel and that the outreach to the Gentiles would come later, just as a family eats at the table and the family dogs, the beloved pets, are fed afterward.

An Accepting Response

Just how much of the pejorative idea of "dog" was incorporated into Jesus' statement we must leave for further debate. If there actually was any pejorative connotation, it seems that it did not bother the woman. She registered no feminist complaint; she did not say, "How dare you compare me to a dog." That was not her response. Instead, she simply said, **"Yes, Lord, yet even the little dogs under the table eat from the children's crumbs"** (v. 28).

In essence, she said: "Yes, Lord, I understand. I have no prior claim to Your mercy. I am not numbered among the children. I have no right to sit at the table and feast on the food that You set before Your children. I do not want that. I'm satisfied, Lord, with the crumbs. All I'm asking is that You will let me have one crumb from Your table. Then I'll be satisfied. Heal my daughter, please. I know she's not in Your family. I know she's not numbered among the children. We are the dogs who wait for the crumbs, but one crumb is all I'm asking for."

Do you see the difference between this woman and the Pharisees? She was not interested in fighting for her rights or for her dignity. She knew who she was. Very often in the Bible, when people come before the living God, they identify themselves with the lowest forms of life. David said, "I am a worm, and no man" (Ps. 22:6a). He was saying: "I have no claim on the sweetness of Your grace. Every crumb that You bestow on me is given to an unworthy servant." The Syro-Phoenician woman was adopting the same posture, which is the only proper posture for anyone coming to the almighty God.

Yet, the true believer savors every crumb that comes from the hand of God. The good news is that in the overflow of mercy and grace that comes to us from the hands of God, though we should be satisfied with crumbs, He is not satisfied with giving us crumbs. He has lavished His grace on us.

Mark writes: **Then He said to her, "For this saying go your way; the demon has gone out of your daughter." And when she had come to her house, she**

found the demon gone out, and her daughter lying on the bed (v. 29–30). Matthew tells us that He said, "O woman, great is your faith!" (15:28). He had not found faith like hers among the Pharisees, the rabbis, or the people of Israel. But here, in a pagan place, He found a woman to whom faith in the Savior had been given, and He permitted her to eat.

I am convinced that this woman, for the rest of her life, never complained about a single word that Jesus spoke to her. It was not in her heart to describe our Lord as harsh, insensitive, demeaning, or sinful. She was forever grateful to God that she met the living Christ, who, by His spoken word, drove the demon out of her daughter. He did not even have to go with her. He simply said: "You can go home. It's okay. Your daughter is healed."

Those of us who are of non-Jewish descent need to remember that we are wild olive branches that have been grafted into the tree of Israel (Rom. 11:17–18). In terms of redemptive history, we are the dogs. But because the children refused the gift of the Father to them, the Father gave that gift to us who had no claim on it originally. Would any of us trade in the crumb of our salvation for anything in this world? That crumb is the pearl of great price. Jesus gave it to the Syro-Phoenician woman. He gives it to us, as well.

24

HEALING A DEAF AND MUTE MAN

Mark 7:31–37

⁓

Again, departing from the region of Tyre and Sidon, He came through the midst of the region of Decapolis to the Sea of Galilee. Then they brought to Him one who was deaf and had an impediment in his speech, and they begged Him to put His hand on him. And He took him aside from the multitude, and put His fingers in his ears, and He spat and touched his tongue. Then, looking up to heaven, He sighed, and said to him, "Ephphatha," that is, "Be opened." Immediately his ears were opened, and the impediment of his tongue was loosed, and he spoke plainly. Then He commanded them that they should tell no one; but the more He commanded them, the more widely they proclaimed it. And they were astonished beyond measure, saying, "He has done all things well. He makes both the deaf to hear and the mute to speak."

Jesus, as we have seen throughout Mark, had a peripatetic teaching ministry. He was constantly on the go, even journeying outside the Jewish homelands to the region of Tyre and Sidon, as we saw in the previous chapter. It seems He did not stay there long, but soon returned to the area around the Sea of Galilee. However, Mark's description of Jesus' itinerary in this passage has baffled biblical scholars for centuries.

Mark tells us, **departing from the region of Tyre and Sidon, He came**

through the midst of the region of Decapolis to the Sea of Galilee (v. 31). From this description, it seems that Jesus left Tyre and went north to Sidon, then turned east and eventually south, moving in a huge arc to the eastern shore of the Sea of Galilee, a journey of about 120 miles. This roundabout way of getting back to His normal area of ministry seems reminiscent of the wilderness wandering of the people of Israel in the Old Testament.

Mark, however, never gives a reason for this itinerary and tells us nothing of what happened as Jesus and His disciples traveled. As with so many things from the life and ministry of Jesus, these details are among those that would fill more books than the world could contain (John 21:25). We must remember that Mark is writing with a specific purpose—to convince Gentile readers, probably in Rome, that Jesus is the Son of God. Therefore, he sees it as much more helpful to report what happened when Jesus and His disciples were back in the region of the Sea of Galilee.

The Gift of Hearing and Speech

He writes, **Then they brought to Him one who was deaf and had an impediment in his speech, and they begged Him to put His hand on him** (v. 32). Mark's description of the malady that afflicted this man does not come across as powerfully in English as it does in the original language. When Mark tells us that the man had a speech impediment, he uses a Greek word, *mogilalos*, that means he had a severe difficulty in speaking, such that people could not discern the words that he was saying.

There has been considerable speculation as to the cause of his problem. Some say that he must have been born deaf, for those born without the ability to hear, unless they receive extensive training by professional speech pathologists, are usually doomed to muteness as well. This man, however, was able to speak to some degree, so other scholars say he probably was not born deaf, but that deafness afflicted him early in his life, with the result that the speech patterns he was able to develop were primitive. But beyond that speculation, all we know for sure is that the man could not hear or speak clearly.

Let me come back to the possible reasons Mark included this episode in his gospel. Jesus healed people of many different diseases and disabilities, but Mark alone among the gospel writers provides a report of this particular healing. Why did it seem so important to Mark? I believe that the Greek word translated as "speech impediment," *mogilalos*, is the key to answering this question.

This word is found only twice in all of the Bible, here and in Isaiah 35, where it appears in the Greek translation of the Old Testament, the Septuagint. When we turn to Isaiah 35, we observe that in the preceding chapters, Isaiah delivered oracles of doom that God had commissioned him to pronounce on Israel and her neighbors. He told the Israelites that the judgment of God was going to lay their land waste and that they were going to go through a period of severe desolation. We get a sense of the severity of that judgment when we read: "For it is the day of the LORD's vengeance, the year of recompense for the cause of Zion. Its streams shall be turned into pitch [tar], and its dust into brimstone; its land shall become burning pitch. It shall not be quenched night or day; its smoke shall ascend forever. From generation to generation it shall lie waste; no one shall pass through it forever and ever" (Isa. 34:8–10).

Who will own this land? Isaiah says:

> But the pelican and the porcupine shall possess it, also the owl and the raven shall dwell in it. And He shall stretch out over it the line of confusion and the stones of emptiness. They shall call its nobles to the kingdom, but none shall be there, and all its princes shall be nothing. And thorns shall come up in its palaces, nettles and brambles in its fortresses; it shall be a habitation of jackals, a courtyard for ostriches. The wild beasts of the desert shall also meet with the jackals, and the wild goat shall bleat to its companion; also the night creature shall rest there, and find for herself a place of rest. There the arrow snake shall make her nest and lay eggs and hatch, and gather them under her shadow; there also shall the hawks be gathered, every one with her mate. (Isa. 34:11–15)

Do you get the picture? This is a graphic description of divine judgment on a land. Could anything be more severe than for God to take the land away from the prince and deliver it to the jackals, the snakes, and the birds of the air? This is the crescendo of a rising litany of judgment that goes on for several chapters as God lays out the destruction that He has planned for this part of the world.

But when God gives an announcement of judgment for His people, He almost always gives a word of future hope, because God never abandons His remnant to desolation. Sure enough, we hear such a word immediately after Isaiah announces the day of the Lord, the day of the Lord's visitation, the day of His destruction that was to come on the land.

The prophet writes in chapter 35: "The wilderness and the wasteland shall be glad for them, and the desert shall rejoice and blossom as the rose; it shall blossom abundantly and rejoice, even with joy and singing. The glory of Lebanon shall be given to it, the excellence of Carmel and Sharon. They shall see the glory of the LORD, the excellency of our God" (vv. 1–2). Do you see the contrast? Isaiah moves from desolation to glory, from destruction to the excellence of the manifestation of the Lord. He says: "Strengthen the weak hands, and make firm the feeble knees. Say to those who are fearful-hearted, 'Be strong, do not fear! Behold, your God will come with vengeance, with the recompense of God; He will come and save you'" (vv. 3–4).

This text reiterates a principle that is repeated over and over again in the Old Testament—salvation is of the Jews, for God is working through this stiff-necked people to bring His redemption to the whole world.

Here is the climax: "Then the eyes of the blind shall be opened, and the ears of the deaf shall be unstopped. Then the lame shall leap like a deer, and the tongue of the dumb sing. For waters shall burst forth in the wilderness, and streams in the desert. The parched ground shall become a pool, and the thirsty land springs of water; in the habitation of jackals, where each lay, there shall be grass with reeds and rushes. A highway shall be there, and a road, and it shall be called the Highway of Holiness" (vv. 5–8a).

Here in this climactic passage, when Isaiah rejoices that "the tongue of the dumb [shall] sing," we find the other appearance of *mogilalos*. Centuries before Jesus was born in Bethlehem, God gave this message of hope to His people, looking past the destruction and desolation to the messianic age, when the kingdom of God would break through and the Messiah would come. He promised that the Messiah would give sight to the blind and hearing to the deaf, and He would loosen the tongues of the mute. Surely Mark has this marvelous promise in mind as he pens the narrative of Jesus' encounter with the deaf and mute man, for the healing powerfully connected Jesus to this messianic prophesy.

A Touch and a Command

Mark continues, **And He took him aside from the multitude, and put His fingers in his ears, and He spat and touched his tongue** (v. 33). Remember, this man, like the Syro-Phoenician woman, was not a Jew. He was from the region of the Decapolis, an area dominated by Gentiles, those whom the Jewish religious leaders deemed to be unclean. Yet, the first thing Jesus did was to take him aside and touch him. First, He put His fingers in the man's ears. Then He spat, probably on His own hands, after which He dabbed the spittle on the man's tongue.

Spittle was classified as an unclean emission in the Jewish purification laws. However, there was a tradition in the ancient world that those who were endowed with healing powers would often use spittle as a medium to communicate that power to the people to whom they ministered. Jesus certainly did not need to use spittle to heal this man, but perhaps He did so to give the man confidence that He knew how to heal people. Some, however, see a far deeper symbolic significance to Jesus' use of spittle to bring relief to a suffering human being;

they say it foreshadows the outpouring of His blood, which not only heals the bodies of His people but saves them altogether.

So, Jesus touched the man's ears and tongue, **Then, looking up to heaven, He sighed, and said to him, "Ephphatha," that is, "Be opened." Immediately his ears were opened, and the impediment of his tongue was loosed, and he spoke plainly** (vv. 34–35). When Mark tells us that Jesus "sighed," he means that He groaned inwardly, indicating a passionate appeal to the Father to intervene. He then spoke an Aramaic word that Mark translates for his Greek-speaking readers: "Be opened." At the command of Jesus, those ears that had heard no sound for many years, if ever, and that tongue that had been in chains, making it impossible for the man to speak clearly, were set free. He could hear and speak.

It would be remarkable enough if Mark said, "Immediately his speech impediment was cured." But Mark says more than that. Immediately, instantly, after Jesus touched his tongue and made the commandment, the man not only could speak, he could speak "plainly." Any pathology that was there was removed, and he was articulate in what he said.

In a very real sense, this is what happens to every Christian. Before the Holy Spirit opens us to the things of God, we are as deaf to the Word of God as this poor man was deaf to all verbal communication. Until the Holy Spirit cleanses our hearts and regenerates our souls, our tongues practice deceit and "the poison of asps is under [our] lips" (Rom. 3:13), so that our tongues can only blaspheme. God sets us free from these afflictions by the regenerating power of His Holy Spirit.

He Does All Things Well

Finally, **He commanded them that they should tell no one; but the more He commanded them, the more widely they proclaimed it. And they were astonished beyond measure, saying, "He has done all things well. He makes both the deaf to hear and the mute to speak"** (vv. 36–37). Jesus, as He often did, commanded the man and the multitude not to speak about the miracle, but they simply would not listen, for they were utterly astonished and could not stop talking about what they had seen.

The people also gave a stirring assessment of Jesus and His work: "He has done all things well." Jesus never did anything poorly in His life. When He set His face toward Jerusalem and determined that obedience to the will of His Father would be His food (John 4:34), He did it well. There was no failure. There was no blemish to His work. The Father Himself agreed with the people when He spoke from heaven and said, "This is my beloved Son, in whom I am well pleased" (Matt. 3:17).

I remember when my friend James Montgomery Boice was diagnosed with terminal cancer. There were only six weeks from the time of the diagnosis to the time of his death. As you might expect, many of us were upset and distraught, but he said to us: "Be at peace about this. God does all things well." That's the heart of a Christian.

The God who took Jim Boice home to glory was the same God who was manifest in Jesus as He healed the man on the shore of the Sea of Galilee. It was the same God who created the heavens and the earth, and who, when He was finished with His creative work, saw that it was "very good" (Gen. 1:31). What He did in creation, He did well. It is this same God who redeems us. When Christ carried out His work of redemption for our souls, He did it well, and in all His dealings with us, He does all things well. That's why we can sing, even in the midst of tribulation, "Though great distress my soul befell, the Lord, my God, did all things well."[1] These Gentiles noticed this about Jesus. "Look at Him," they said to one another. "Everything He does, He does it well, because He's God incarnate." The One who creates, the One who redeems, the One who opens deaf ears and loosens tongues does all things well.

Someone recently told me about seeing a televised interview with the actor Robert De Niro. The interviewer asked De Niro, "At the end of your days, if you come before God, what will you say to Him?" De Niro, in his trademark cocky manner, said, "What I'm going to say to God is, 'You have some explaining to do.'" Actually, De Niro will be the one doing the explaining. God does not have to explain anything He is pleased to bring to pass in this world. He did not have to explain to Israel why jackals were inhabiting the land and its streams had become like rivers of tar. He did not have to explain why He chose to afflict a Gentile man with deafness and muteness. He is the sovereign Lord of all things, who is free to do as He pleases. And the testimony of Scripture and of those whose hearts love Him is that He does all things well.

---

[1] From the hymn "All Praise to God Who Reigns Above" by Johann J. Schutz, 1675.

25

THE LEAVEN
OF THE PHARISEES

Mark 8:1–21

In those days, the multitude being very great and having nothing to eat, Jesus called His disciples to Him and said to them, "I have compassion on the multitude, because they have now continued with Me three days and have nothing to eat. And if I send them away hungry to their own houses, they will faint on the way; for some of them have come from afar." Then His disciples answered Him, "How can one satisfy these people with bread here in the wilderness?" He asked them, "How many loaves do you have?" And they said, "Seven." So He commanded the multitude to sit down on the ground. And He took the seven loaves and gave thanks, broke them and gave them to His disciples to set before them; and they set them before the multitude. They also had a few small fish; and having blessed them, He said to set them also before them. So they ate and were filled, and they took up seven large baskets of leftover fragments. Now those who had eaten were about four thousand. And He sent them away, immediately got into the boat with His disciples, and came to the region of Dalmanutha. Then the Pharisees came out and began to dispute with Him, seeking from Him a sign from heaven, testing Him. But He sighed deeply in His spirit, and said, "Why does this generation seek a sign? Assuredly, I say to you, no sign shall be given to this generation." And He left them, and getting into the boat again, departed to the other side. Now the disciples had forgotten to take bread, and they did not have more than one loaf with them in the boat. Then He charged them, saying, "Take heed, beware of the leaven of the Pharisees and the leaven of Herod." And they reasoned among themselves, saying, "It is because we have no bread." But Jesus, being aware of it, said to them, "Why do you reason because you have no bread? Do you not yet perceive nor understand? Is your heart still hardened? Having eyes, do you not see? And having ears, do you not hear? And do you not remember? When I broke the five loaves for the five thousand, how many baskets full of fragments did you take up?" They said to Him, "Twelve." "Also, when I broke the seven for the four thousand, how many large baskets full of fragments did you take up?" And they said, "Seven." So He said to them, "How is it you do not understand?"

I f we were studying the gospel of Mark for the first time, after reading this passage, we might be tempted to ask: "What's happening here? Did a scribe in the early centuries mix up the pages of his manuscript and repeat the same narrative that we find in Mark 6:30–44?"

Actually, many critical scholars have assumed that something like that indeed did happen, simply because there are so many similarities between this narrative and the earlier account of the feeding of the five thousand. On both occasions, a vast multitude gathered to listen to the teaching of Jesus somewhere out in the wilderness. In both narratives, Jesus was moved by compassion for the needs of the people who were gathered. In both instances, the disciples expressed doubts that such a large group could be fed in the wilderness (which, indeed, is very strange in the latter incident, given that they had seen it done in the first incident). In both accounts, He inquired of the disciples as to what provisions were on hand, but they could find only a few loaves and a few fish. In both narratives, Jesus multiplied the loaves and the fishes to such a degree that all of the people were satisfied and a large number of leftover fragments was collected. In both accounts, Jesus left the crowds by boat to go to another part of the Sea of Galilee. Finally, both narratives are followed by an interrogation and confrontation with the Pharisees. So it is not difficult to understand why the critical scholars say there must have been a repetition of the same material.

When I read such criticisms of this text, I recall my first year as a college professor in western Pennsylvania. I had a friend on the faculty who taught the humanities and English. The humanities course was required of all freshmen. In it, they had to study Ovid's *Metamorphoses*, which is filled with ancient mythology. My friend was passionately opposed to the truth claims of Christianity, so every day while his class was working through *Metamorphoses*, he pointed out similarities between the mythological content of Ovid and the New Testament teaching about Jesus. Students from his class would scurry to my class and tell me what he had said, then ask for my response. I began to grow weary of it, so when I saw my friend one day, I asked him why he was pointing out all the similarities between *Metamorphoses* and the New Testament. His reply was simple: "The similarities are there." I acknowledged that the similarities were real, but I pressed him as to whether he was spending an equal amount of time discussing *Metamorphoses* and the New Testament narratives of Jesus. I began to point out difference after difference, not the least of which is a radically different view of history. Finally, he saw my point. In the end, I encouraged him to stick to teaching English and to leave the theology to me, promising that I would not teach literary criticism in my theology class.

In any science, to gain any knowledge, we must use a process called individuation. It involves putting ideas or concepts in groups of similarity, classifying them, if you will, as biologists classify species. Then, after the similarities have been noted, the scientist can begin to differentiate between ideas or concepts by noting the aspects that differ.

This is what happens in medicine. If I have a stomachache, I know that it might be the result of anything from indigestion to stomach cancer. An aching stomach is one similarity among many maladies. Thanks be to God, however, doctors know not just the similarities but the differences between maladies. That is what makes for knowledge. That is what makes for science.

We also need to use this process to properly understand the Word of God. We have seen several of the similarities between the miraculous feedings in Mark 6 and Mark 8, but what of the differences? Some of the most obvious ones are that in the account in Mark 8, the people were with Jesus for three days, not one (v. 2); there were seven loaves, not five (vv. 5–7); and there were fewer baskets of leftovers (v. 8). Also, in Mark 6, a generic Greek word for "fish" was used, whereas in Mark 8 the word translated as "fish" specifically refers to sardines, probably because the feeding of the four thousand took place in a Gentile area that was known for its trade in that species of fish. Finally, the numbers of those who ate were vastly different; in Mark 6, the number was five thousand men, with additional women and children implied, but in Mark 8, the figure of four thousand is inclusive of men, women, and children (v. 9).

Of course, the coup de grace that silences all theories of textual errors is that Jesus later mentioned both feedings in a single discussion with the disciples (vv. 17–21). So I am confident that this account does not indicate a copyist's error. Rather, I believe the Word of God accurately tells of two separate but equally miraculous acts of Christ in multiplying loaves and fishes to feed vast multitudes.

The Pharisees Ask for a Sign

After the people had eaten, **He sent them away, immediately got into the boat with His disciples, and came to the region of Dalmanutha** (vv. 9b–10). This location is not known, but it seems likely that it was somewhere on the western side of the Sea of Galilee, back in Jewish areas. That presumption is bolstered by the fact that, just as they did after the feeding of the five thousand, the Pharisees approached Jesus after He fed the four thousand: **Then the Pharisees came out and began to dispute with Him, seeking from Him a sign from heaven, testing Him** (v. 11). The English word *testing* is weaker than the Greek word it translates, which indicates that the Pharisees were out to harangue Jesus and harass Him, not merely have a polite discussion or debate. They were deeply hostile toward Him. This hostility manifested itself in a demand for a sign, proof of His divinity.

How many signs did the Pharisees need to see? Jesus had been going through the region of Galilee with a blaze of miracles. Everywhere He went He healed the sick and those with various maladies and disabilities. The Pharisees, however, were convinced that Jesus had performed these works by the power of Satan (3:22), so they did not see them as true divine authentications of Jesus as a trustworthy prophet. They wanted what they could judge to be a conclusive sign, one that would settle the matter once and for all. In basic terms, their challenge was this: "Jesus, prove to us that You really are from God." As we will see, the religious leaders kept pressing this demand on Jesus till the final moments of His life (15:32).

In response, **He sighed deeply in His spirit, and said, "Why does this generation seek a sign? Assuredly, I say to you, no sign shall be given to this generation"** (vv. 12). Again, the English language fails to provide a full understanding of how Jesus reacted. The Greek indicates He did more than sigh, even more than give a heavy sigh. It tells us He came to His absolute limit, humanly speaking, of exasperation. He was sick and tired of this kind of response.

We might be tempted to think that because Jesus was sinless He should have been more patient at this point. However, He had been exceedingly patient with these religious leaders. Remember, the Bible often talks about God's patience, His forbearance, His longsuffering, but nowhere does it ever say that His patience is infinite. In the days before the flood, when the wickedness of men was growing exponentially, God said, "My Spirit shall not strive with man forever" (Gen. 6:3). Scripture plainly teaches us there are limits to God's patience. He may forbear with us week after week, month after month, year after year, decade after decade, until we become at ease in Zion and think, "He will always forbear with us." But there have been times in redemptive history when God's patience was exhausted and He gave people over to their sin.

Something like that happened here. Jesus said that for faithlessly asking for yet another sign, the Pharisees would be given no sign at all. Then **He left them, and getting into the boat again, departed to the other side** (v. 13).

Jesus Warns of Pharisaical Leaven

Mark tells us: Now the disciples had forgotten to take bread, and they did not have more than one loaf with them in the boat (v. 14). Perhaps in His grief over the Pharisees' hardness of heart, Jesus left the Dalmanutha area quickly, and the disciples did not discover how short of provisions they were until the boat was well out on the lake. Apparently they became concerned and discussed the problem, and when they did, Jesus seized the opportunity to give a charge to His disciples. Still thinking of His clash with the Pharisees back in Dalmanutha, He said, "Take heed, beware of the leaven of the Pharisees and the leaven of Herod" (v. 15).

All of us have seen signs on gates or doors warning us, "Beware of dog." Perhaps we have read William Shakespeare's tragedy *Julius Caesar*, where the soothsayer cries out in the street: "Caesar! . . . Beware the ides of March." Of course, it is one thing when a sign or a soothsayer bids us to beware, but when God incarnate says, "Beware," we do well to pay attention. What exactly was Jesus warning against when He urged His disciples to beware of the leaven of the Pharisees and Herod?

Leaven, of course, refers to yeast that is added to bread dough to make it rise. The metaphor therefore suggests a small amount of a given substance that can radically alter anything into which it is mixed. In the New Testament, almost every time leaven is mentioned, the context is negative. It is seen as an influence that corrupts and destroys. Leaven is associated with pride (1 Cor. 5:6), malice and wickedness (1 Cor. 5:8), and false teaching on circumcision (Gal. 5:9). Thus, Jesus is saying: "Watch out for false doctrine. Watch out for hypocrisy. Watch out for unbelief." (The "leaven of Herod" may have to do with the tetrarch's desire, like that of the Pharisees, to see a miracle. See Luke 23:8.)

The disciples were taken aback by this strange warning: **And they reasoned among themselves, saying, "It is because we have no bread"** (v. 16). Jesus' mention of leaven seemed, to them, somehow connected to the problem of their lack of bread, which was their immediate pressing concern. Somehow they failed to connect Jesus' mention of the Pharisees with the recent unpleasant incident and those that had gone before.

Jesus perceived their confusion and lack of understanding. He said: **"Why do you reason because you have no bread? Do you not yet perceive nor understand? Is your heart still hardened? Having eyes, do you not see?**

And having ears, do you not hear?" (vv. 17–18a). These rhetorical questions, clearly meant to be answered in the negative, constitute a strong reproach to the disciples. Jesus had been saying to those hearing His teaching, "He who has ears to hear, let him hear!" (4:9; see also 4:23; 7:16). The disciples had heard His teaching with their ears and yet had not understood with their hearts that Jesus is the Son of God, the Messiah. Basically, their view of Him was as faulty as that of the Pharisees.

Jesus Holds Out Hope

He then got even more pointed with them: **"And do you not remember? When I broke the five loaves for the five thousand, how many baskets full of fragments did you take up?" They said to Him, "Twelve." "Also, when I broke the seven for the four thousand, how many large baskets full of fragments did you take up?" And they said, "Seven." So He said to them, "How is it you do not understand?"** (vv. 18b–21). They had seen the mighty miracles by which Jesus fed thousands upon thousands of people on two occasions, yet they were worried because they had forgotten bread. How could they not know, having seen what they had seen, that their Master was fully capable of supplying their need?

This is a humbling rebuke. Yet, it is not without hope. Notice two tiny words in verse 17: *yet* and *still*. Jesus had not given up hope for them. He expected that in time, by the grace of God, they *would* perceive and their hearts *would* grow soft.

By nature, we are deaf and blind to the things of God. Our hearts are recalcitrant, having no pulse for Him, so that the Word of God bounces off our hearts as if they were made of stone. Until the Holy Spirit opens our eyes and ears, we are impervious to the truth of God. The disciples were in this state. They were fallen creatures just like you and me. But Jesus saw the possibility of a change of heart for them.

How is your hearing? How is your perception of the things of God? How is your heart? Does the truth of God bounce off it? Or is your heart softened, so that God's truth penetrates and sinks in? We all need to examine ourselves in the light of God's Word to be sure the deadly leaven of the Pharisees is not working in us, blinding us to the light and making us deaf to the life-giving Word.

26

EYES OPENED

Mark 8:22–30

Then He came to Bethsaida; and they brought a blind man to Him, and begged Him to touch him. So He took the blind man by the hand and led him out of the town. And when He had spit on his eyes and put His hands on him, He asked him if he saw anything. And he looked up and said, "I see men like trees, walking." Then He put His hands on his eyes again and made him look up. And he was restored and saw everyone clearly. Then He sent him away to his house, saying, "Neither go into the town, nor tell anyone in the town." Now Jesus and His disciples went out to the towns of Caesarea Philippi; and on the road He asked His disciples, saying to them, "Who do men say that I am?" So they answered, "John the Baptist; but some say, Elijah; and others, one of the prophets." He said to them, "But who do you say that I am?" Peter answered and said to Him, "You are the Christ." Then He strictly warned them that they should tell no one about Him.

After yet another confrontation with the Pharisees, this time in Dalmanutha (8:10) on the eastern side of the Sea of Galilee, Jesus sailed away, refusing to do any signs there or even to stick around because of the Pharisees' unbelief (vv. 12–13). Mark tells us, **He came to Bethsaida** (v. 22a), another important fishing village located on the northern side of the lake.

However, it must be noted that Jesus did not have a high opinion of Bethsaida. He said: "Woe to you, Chorazin! Woe to you, Bethsaida! For if the mighty works which were done in you had been done in Tyre and Sidon, they would have repented long ago, sitting in sackcloth and ashes. But it will be more tolerable for Tyre and Sidon at the judgment than for you" (Luke 10:13–14). Notice two aspects of this terrible indictment. First, it is yet another indictment for hardness of heart and unbelief. The people of Bethsaida saw mighty miracles, one of which we will study in this chapter, but they did not repent and believe. It seems the leaven of the Pharisees was thoroughly kneaded into their hearts.

Second, Jesus' comments reflect again the idea of degrees of reward and punishment in the judgment. As we saw, Jesus expressed this idea when He said, "It will be more tolerable for Sodom and Gomorrah in the day of judgment than for [a city that rejects apostolic teaching]" (6:11b). When He spoke about Bethsaida, He compared it to the Gentile cities of Tyre and Sidon, which, as we saw in chapter 23, were in what the rabbis considered a region of rank paganism. In that chapter, we saw that Jesus considered His mission to be to the Jews, not to the Gentiles, so even though He visited Tyre and Sidon, and He cast a demon out of a young girl there, He did no major public miracles there. However, speaking hypothetically, He declared that *if* He had performed the same kind of miracles in Tyre and Sidon that He had performed in Bethsaida, those Gentile cities would have expressed abject repentance. But Bethsaida, which actually had seen the miracles, had not believed in Him. Therefore, He said, the final judgment on the Gentiles of Tyre and Sidon would be lighter than the judgment that would fall on the Jews of Bethsaida.

A Dim Perception

Mark tells us that when Jesus arrived in Bethsaida on this occasion, **they brought a blind man to Him, and begged Him to touch him** (v. 22b). So far in Mark's gospel, we have seen Jesus heal a man who was deaf and mute; a woman with a flow of blood; a man with a withered hand; a paralytic; a leper; and many others with unspecified diseases and maladies. We have seen Him cast demons out of people. We have even seen Him bring a dead girl back to life. However, this is the first specific instance of a blind person being brought to Him for help.

Clearly, the request that Jesus touch this man was a request for a healing touch. Yet when Jesus touched him initially, it was not for healing: **So He took the blind man by the hand and led him out of the town** (v. 23a). Jesus took the blind man by the hand so that He could lead him away to a private place. This was unusual. Almost every time Jesus healed someone, He did it openly and publicly, not isolated from the multitude of witnesses. One exception was His most recent healing, the man who was deaf and mute, whom Jesus led apart from the multitude (7:33), though apparently not so far apart as He led the blind man.

Mark writes: **And when He had spit on his eyes and put His hands on him, He asked him if he saw anything. And he looked up and said, "I see men like trees, walking"** (vv. 23b–24). Jesus did two things to this man. First, He used spittle, just as He did in His healing of the man who was deaf and mute, when He apparently spat on His own hands and dabbed the spittle on the man's tongue (7:33). Here, Jesus spat directly on the blind man's eyes. Again, Jesus did not need to do this; there was nothing magical in the spittle that brought healing, but it possibly brought confidence to the blind man because of certain cultural assumptions about the use of spittle as a medium by those endowed with healing powers.

Second, Jesus laid His hands on the man. In Scripture, particularly in the Old Testament, a certain significance is attached to the ritual of the laying on of hands. This practice is used in the Protestant church even today when men are ordained to the ministry or to the church offices of elder or deacon. In the New Testament, we see the laying on of hands accompanying healing (Acts 28:8) and the conveying of spiritual gifts (1 Tim. 4:14). In the Old Testament, the laying on of hands served multiple purposes. The elders of Israel laid hands on sacrifices that were to be offered to God (Lev. 4:15). That ritual signified consecration, the setting aside of a thing to a sacred or holy use. The people laid hands on the Levites (Num. 8:10), again signifying consecration, making something special. One person laid hands on another to communicate a blessing (Gen. 48:14–15). Other uses of this ritual could also be mentioned. However, nowhere in the Old Testament do we see the laying on of hands associated with healing.

Jesus, however, had exercised a very tactile ministry from the moment He did the unthinkable and reached out and touched a leper (1:41). The result was that people had begun trying to touch Him (3:10), including the woman with the flow of blood (5:28). Mark has related that many who touched Him were made well (6:56). Thus, it is not surprising that the word had spread and that those who brought this man to Jesus specifically requested His touch, which Jesus compassionately gave.

When Jesus had anointed the man's eyes and laid His hands on him, He asked whether the man could see anything. In most cases when Jesus healed someone, He gave them a command, saying do this or do that. This is the only instance in the Gospels when Jesus, having touched someone for healing, asked how he or she was doing.

The man gave an exceedingly curious reply: "I see men like trees, walking." This response tells us a couple of things. First, it tells us this man was not born blind; if he had been blind from birth, never having seen anything in the world, he would not have been able to distinguish human beings and trees. Clearly he had once had sight and had lost it. Second, the man's vision was not sharp. Human beings resembled trees in his sight. So the healing Jesus had imparted to him was incomplete.

A Clarified Vision

Mark then tells us: **He put His hands on his eyes again and made him look up. And he was restored and saw everyone clearly** (v. 25). The force of this sentence is that Jesus healed this man to such a degree that when he looked up, he could see clearly from a great distance. His vision was without blur. It was impeccable. His healing was complete. Then, as was usual for Jesus, **He sent him away to his house, saying, "Neither go into the town, nor tell anyone in the town"** (v. 26).

This is the only time in the New Testament when Jesus performed a work of miraculous healing that did not happen instantly. This blind man's healing was gradual rather than instantaneous. Obviously, the fact that the healing was not instantaneous was not due to any lack in the power of Jesus. Why, then, did this miracle happen in a two-step process?

To be honest, I do not have the answer to that question. However, I can make an educated guess based on Mark's apparent goals in his gospel and the themes that are in play in the immediate context of this narrative. I believe Jesus intentionally healed this man in stages as an object lesson for His disciples. In the boat, just before this incident, Jesus had asked the disciples a series of rhetorical questions: "Do you not yet perceive nor understand? Is your heart still hardened? Having eyes, do you not see? And having ears, do you not hear?" (vv. 17b–18a). It is as if, through this two-stage healing, Jesus was saying that the disciples had begun to see dimly. They were not in total darkness as the pagans were. Their eyes had beheld many of the marvelous things of Christ. They had some understanding. But they had not yet seen clearly. If they had been asked to describe Jesus, they might have said, in effect, "I see a mighty oak walking around, but I do not really understand the full measure of who He is."

As we will see in what follows, this miracle seems to have been an eye-opening experience not just for the blind man, but for the disciples as well. After all the mighty works they had seen Him do, after receiving His rebuke for their ongoing hardness of heart and spiritual blindness, and after seeing Him open the eyes of a man who was physically blind, something at last clicked.

A Glorious Confession

From Bethsaida, **Jesus and His disciples went out to the towns of Caesarea Philippi** (v. 27). From Bethsaida, at the northern tip of the Sea of Galilee, they went almost due north for about twenty-five miles to Caesarea Philippi. Herod the Great had built a temple to Caesar Augustus at the foot of Mount Hermon, and his son Philip, tetrarch of Iturea (Luke 3:1), had built the town, which was named in honor of Augustus, with "Philippi" added to distinguish it from the better-known city of Caesarea on the Mediterranean coast.

As they traveled, **He asked His disciples, saying to them, "Who do men say that I am?" So they answered, "John the Baptist; but some say, Elijah; and others, one of the prophets"** (vv. 27b–28). Jesus interrogated His disciples, changing the pattern of most rabbinical schools, in which students questioned their teacher. He asked: "What are people saying? Who do they think I am?" The disciples replied with the current theories: John the Baptist, Elijah, or one of the other prophets of ancient Israel. It is interesting that, as we have seen, Herod Antipas subscribed to the theory that Jesus was John the Baptist returned from the grave (6:14). Apparently others agreed with Herod.

Then Jesus asked the question that clearly was of much greater interest and importance to Him: **"But who do you say that I am?"** (v. 29a). He might have framed His inquiry this way: "Have you seen the truth yet? Do you see who I am? Have you finally perceived My identity? Or am I still just a dim, blurry walking tree to you?" In short, this question brings all the preceding incidents and discussions to a razor-sharp focus. Have the disciples finally perceived what His miracles have demonstrated, what His teaching has proven, and what He has been driving them to see—that He is the Son of God, the long-awaited Messiah?

The next sentence is glorious: **Peter answered and said to Him, "You are the Christ"** (v. 29b). As Matthew reports it in his somewhat more detailed account, Peter said, "You are the Christ, the Son of the living God" (16:16). He was saying: "You are the promised anointed One of God, prophesied from the very beginning, from the third chapter of Genesis, all the way through the Old Testament, the promised Son come to save His people from their sins." It is thrilling to hear Peter make this declaration after the disciples have endured Jesus' rebukes for their hard-heartedness. Finally, their vision is clear.

Mark gives no report of Jesus expressing joy at hearing Peter respond in this way. Matthew, however, tells us that He said, "Blessed are you, Simon Bar-Jonah, for flesh and blood has not revealed this to you, but My Father who is in heaven" (16:17). By the Father's decree, the Spirit had softened Peter's heart, opened his spiritual eyes and ears, and caused him to believe in Jesus.

Note that Matthew also adds these words of Jesus: "I also say to you that you are Peter, and on this rock I will build My church, and the gates of Hades shall not prevail against it" (16:18). The church stands strong and unconquerable as long as it remains committed to its confession that Jesus is the Christ. That confession is the very foundation of the church. A loss of confidence as to the identity of Jesus does not disrupt merely the external trappings of the church; it disrupts the church's foundation. We who confess the name of Christ must remain firm in our conviction that He is God in the flesh.

Mark tells us, **Then He strictly warned them that they should tell no one about Him** (v. 30). It was not yet time for the disciples to spread the Word about His identity. It was not Jesus' wish to see a popular movement develop around Him as a response to the Roman occupation. He had work to do that even the disciples did not fully understand, as we will see in the next chapter.

The question Jesus posed to His disciples is the ultimate question for us: "Who do you say that I am?" Do you believe that Jesus is the Messiah? When we stand up publicly and join a church, we declare to our friends, our neighbors, and all the watching world: "I believe that Jesus is the Messiah. I believe He is the Christ. I believe that He is the Son of the living God." If you believe that, the same benediction that Jesus pronounced on Peter is your benediction. He says, "Blessed are you," because this is not something you learned in kindergarten, from the newspaper, or from the TV news. Flesh and blood do not reveal this kind of information. If you believe in your heart that He is the Christ, you are blessed above all people because God has allowed you to see this truth. If you ever are downcast, if you ever are jealous of someone else's status or possessions, if you ever cry to God, "Why me?" in the midst of affliction, hear these words: "Blessed are you." You have been enabled to recognize the pearl of great price, and if God never gives you another blessing for the rest of your days on this earth, you will have no reason to do anything else but proclaim His glory and His mercy to the whole world, because the greatest blessing a human being can ever receive is the blessing of knowing Him.

27

THE MEANING
OF THE MESSIAH

Mark 8:31–9:1

~

And He began to teach them that the Son of Man must suffer many things, and be rejected by the elders and chief priests and scribes, and be killed, and after three days rise again. He spoke this word openly. Then Peter took Him aside and began to rebuke Him. But when He had turned around and looked at His disciples, He rebuked Peter, saying, "Get behind Me, Satan! For you are not mindful of the things of God, but the things of men." When He had called the people to Himself, with His disciples also, He said to them, "Whoever desires to come after Me, let him deny himself, and take up his cross, and follow Me. For whoever desires to save his life will lose it, but whoever loses his life for My sake and the gospel's will save it. For what will it profit a man if he gains the whole world, and loses his own soul? Or what will a man give in exchange for his soul? For whoever is ashamed of Me and My words in this adulterous and sinful generation, of him the Son of Man also will be ashamed when He comes in the glory of His Father with the holy angels." And He said to them, "Assuredly, I say to you that there are some standing here who will not taste death till they see the kingdom of God present with power."

With Peter's great confession at Caesarea Philippi—"You are the Christ"—the disciples finally grasped that Jesus was the long-awaited and promised Messiah. However, their understanding was still deficient in at least one key way. They understood that He was the Messiah, but they had a very inaccurate understanding of what the word *Messiah* meant and what Jesus' messianic vocation would entail. Thus, it is not surprising that Jesus chose this moment to introduce a new subject into the disciples' course of training.

Mark writes: **And He began to teach them that the Son of Man must suffer many things, and be rejected by the elders and chief priests and scribes, and be killed, and after three days rise again. He spoke this word openly** (vv. 31–32a). Simply put, Jesus began to lay out for the disciples what it meant for Him to be the Messiah. He announced several points. First, He was going to suffer many things. Second, He was going to be rejected by the Jewish religious authorities. Third, He was actually going to be killed. But, fourth, He would rise again from the dead. With these simple statements, Jesus charted the future course of His ministry. Furthermore, He said these things "openly" or plainly, not in parable form, so that the disciples would understand them clearly.

Notice also that Mark says that Jesus told the disciples that these things "must" happen. He told them He *must* suffer, He *must* be rejected, and He *must* die. He saw these events not as mere possibilities in the future but as certainties, things that simply had to occur if He was to fulfill His vocation. Why did Jesus use this language of necessity? He spoke in these terms because, from the foundation of the world, the Father had determined that the Son would suffer, be rejected, and ultimately be killed to redeem His people from God's righteous wrath against their sin. The punishment for sin before almighty God was death, and if Jesus was to save His people, it would be necessary for Him to make full payment for their sin.

I find it interesting that the rabbis of Israel understood that the concept of the Messiah was central to the Old Testament message. They were diligent to examine in close detail every dimension and aspect of the Messiah who was to come. There are many such dimensions; if we look at all of the Old Testament prophecies of the promised Messiah, we see a tapestry woven from a multitude of strands. In other words, the picture of Messiah in the Old Testament is not monochromatic, but a vast complexity of ideas comes together in this promised figure. He would be a King. He would be a Shepherd. He would be a Redeemer. However, there was one element that the rabbis seemed to overlook: the Messiah would suffer.

Writing in the years after Jesus' earthly ministry, when the cross and the resurrection were accomplished facts, the New Testament authors pointed their contemporaries to all the Old Testament prophecies of the Messiah. They directed attention to Isaiah, particularly Isaiah 52–53, which shows that the

Ebed Yahweh, the Servant of the Lord, would bear the sins of the people, would be despised, would be rejected by men, and would be smitten by God Himself, afflicted, and killed. They focused on Psalm 22, which reads like an eyewitness account of the crucifixion. But in the centuries before Jesus came, the rabbis completely missed what these texts were saying. They did not conceive of applying Isaiah 52–53, Psalm 22, or other prophecies to the Messiah. They thought these texts applied to the nation of Israel as it passed through affliction and suffering.

Therefore, when Jesus began to use these Old Testament prophecies to teach His disciples what it meant for Him to be the Messiah, they were shocked. They had never heard such ideas before. Furthermore, they understood that if the Messiah had to suffer, be rejected, and die, that probably meant suffering, rejection, and death for the Messiah's disciples. They received these words of Jesus not only as a death sentence on Him, but a death sentence on themselves, and that was the last thing they wanted to hear.

Minding the Things of God

So, **Peter took Him aside and began to rebuke Him** (v. 32b). It is one thing to disagree with one's teacher. A student might raise his hand and say, "I'm not sure I buy that, professor." It is another thing entirely for the student to rebuke the teacher for his teaching. Yet, that is precisely what Peter did. Keep in mind, too, that this was not just any teacher but the incarnate Word of God, the One who embodies all truth, who speaks nothing except by divine authority. Peter had the gall to confront Him and chastise Him for the things He was teaching.

To make matters even worse, the word that is translated as "rebuke" is used biblically in connection with the denunciation and condemnation of demons from hell. When Jesus silenced demons, He did it by rebuking them, judging them to be worthy of condemnation (see Matt. 17:18; Mark 1:25; 9:25; Luke 4:35; 9:42). It is clear that Peter's protest was not mild by any means; he stood up to Jesus, and he brought the full measure of hostility to his rebuke. The same Peter who so recently had said, "You are the Christ," and who had heard Jesus say, "Blessed are you, Simon Bar-Jonah," presumed to correct and admonish his Master.

What was the nature of Peter's rebuke? Matthew tells us what Peter said: "Far be it from You, Lord; this shall not happen to You!" (16:22b). Peter was saying that all the things Jesus had just said *must* happen to Him most certainly *would not* happen to Him. Why? Because Peter was prepared to prevent them from happening—or so he thought.

How did Jesus respond to this rebuke? Mark tells us: **But when He had**

turned around and looked at His disciples, He rebuked Peter, saying, "Get behind Me, Satan! For you are not mindful of the things of God, but the things of men" (v. 33). Here again is that same Greek word that the gospel writers use to describe how Jesus spoke to demons. Now Mark uses it to describe what Jesus said to Peter, and Jesus' words drive home the severity of this verbal correction, for the Lord called His own disciple "Satan."

Why did Jesus equate Peter with the Devil? I believe it was because Peter presented the same temptation the Devil brought to Jesus in the wilderness at the beginning of His public ministry. In his record of Jesus' final temptation, Matthew writes:

> Again, the devil took Him up on an exceedingly high mountain, and showed Him all the kingdoms of the world and their glory. And he said to Him, "All these things I will give You if You will fall down and worship me." Then Jesus said to him, "Away with you, Satan! For it is written, 'You shall worship the LORD your God, and Him only you shall serve.'" (4:8–10)

Satan asked Jesus to bow down to him, to simply genuflect for a moment. "Nobody will see it," he suggested. "If You'll do it, I will give You all of the kingdoms of this world. You won't have to walk the Via Dolorosa. There will be no cross, there will be no cup of wrath, there will be no suffering, there will be no rejection, there will be no death." The heart of this temptation was the acquisition of a throne without the experience of pain and suffering.

Our Lord withstood that temptation, as He withstood all Satan's offers. But Luke tells us that Satan "departed from Him until an opportune time" (4:13b). There is an element of foreboding there, the hint that Satan was not finished with his temptation, but a day would come when he would return and try to seduce Jesus with the same cheap way to glory.

Who could have foreseen that the "opportune time" would follow right on the heels of the highest confession of faith among the disciples? Who could have foreseen that Satan would come and speak through the spokesman of the disciples, the man who had said, "You are the Christ"? But Jesus recognized the work of Satan right away.

Jesus also told Peter, "You are not mindful of the things of God, but the things of men." Peter was not looking at the Messiah from God's point of view but was still thinking of the Messiah as a political leader who would deliver the Jews from their Roman subjugation. Peter believed that Jesus was the Messiah, but it was still inconceivable for Him that the Messiah should suffer—even though the Old Testament said He would.

Jesus showed Peter that there are basically two ways of looking at things—God's way and man's way. This is the great divide between godliness and godlessness. The godly person is deeply concerned about the things of God, but the godless person has no concern for the things of God. Instead, he is preoccupied with this world. We all need to evaluate ourselves on these criteria from time to time. We need to ask ourselves: "Where is my heart? What is my chief concern? Am I preoccupied with the things of this world, or does my heart beat for the things of God? Am I seeking first the kingdom of God and His righteousness, and letting everything else come as it will? Or is there some other priority that drives me, some ambition that compels me, some goal to which all of my energy is devoted in this world?"

Taking Up the Cross

Seeing that Peter and the other disciples, like the vast multitudes of people who were flocking to Him, were still thinking of Him as a liberator, Jesus decided it was time to lay out for them what following Him would entail. It would not mean taking up the sword and following Him into battle against the Roman legions. Mark writes, **When He had called the people to Himself, with His disciples also, He said to them, "Whoever desires to come after Me, let him deny himself, and take up his cross, and follow Me"** (v. 34).

It may seem odd that Jesus chose to speak of the cross at this point, when it was still well in front of Him. Is this an example of editorial redaction, of the gospel writer adding to the historical record an allusion to the cross that would have had no meaning in the immediate context. Not at all. Every Jew under Roman authority was completely aware of the symbolic significance of the word *cross*, because the chief means of execution by the Roman government at this time was crucifixion. It was normal procedure for the condemned person to carry the crossbeam of the cross from the place of judgment to the place of execution, which Jesus Himself would be required to do at the time of His death. They all knew that when Jesus spoke of the cross, He was talking about execution, about death. He was saying: "If you want to follow Me, do not expect an easy time. Do not expect to have all your hopes, wants, and expectations met. You might as well take up a crossbeam and carry it with you every day, because My disciples must be ready to endure ignominy, shame, and death. If you want to be a Christian, you have to be willing to pick up that crossbeam and follow Me."

He went on, **"For whoever desires to save his life will lose it, but whoever loses his life for My sake and the gospel's will save it"** (v. 35). This is the grand paradox. If we are preoccupied with saving ourselves, the very attempt to save ourselves will result in our destruction. The Christian life is a throwaway life. Every moment that we live without rejection, affliction, and death is grace. But our destiny as the people of God is to be thrown into the garbage by the powers of this world and of this age, and there is no way to glamorize that. So Jesus said: "Count the cost. If you want to follow Me, it will cost you your life."

He added: **"For what will it profit a man if he gains the whole world, and loses his own soul? Or what will a man give in exchange for his soul?"** (vv. 36–37). Here, Jesus gave a lesson in spiritual economics. We may profit to the point of owning the entire world and everything in it. But if gaining that profit happens at the cost of our souls, there is no profit at all. Rather, we have sacrificed that which is supremely valuable for that which is worthless by comparison. If we make this deal, we are bankrupt. To drive the point home, Jesus phrased His question another way: "What will a man give in exchange for his soul?" Literature is filled with fictional tales of men who sell their souls to the Devil, the worst transaction a human being can ever make. We need to consider how valuable our souls are. How can we tell? We can see the true value of souls by noting how much Jesus was willing to pay for the souls of His people.

Finally, Jesus said, **"Whoever is ashamed of Me and My words in this adulterous and sinful generation, of him the Son of Man also will be ashamed when He comes in the glory of His Father with the holy angels"** (v. 38). Here is the ultimate cost of looking at things from the world's perspective. We have a deep desire not to be embarrassed, not to be ashamed, so we hide our devotion to Christ from the world. But despite all the dangers of the Christian life, despite the hate that the world directs at Christ and His followers, we dare not keep our love for Him secret. If we know Him, we must openly profess our allegiance to Him.

Do you know anyone who does not know that you are a Christian? Do your friends and coworkers all know that you are a Christian? If not, take these words of Jesus to heart. If we would be followers of Jesus, we must embrace His suffering, His rejection, His death, and His cross, because that is what it costs to stand with Him.

The Kingdom in Power

The New King James Version places a subhead at the beginning of the ninth chapter of Mark's gospel: "Jesus Transfigured on the Mount." However, Mark's account of Jesus' glorious transfiguration, which happens to be one of my favorite narratives in the New Testament, does not begin until verse 2 of this chapter. Verse 1 properly belongs at the end of chapter 8.

Here, again, we see evidence that the chapter and verse divisions in Scripture were not part of the original inspired documents. Sometimes I think the man who divided the Bible into chapters and verses was an itinerate Methodist minister in the wilderness who did the job while riding along on horseback, and that he came to this portion of Mark as the sun was setting and lost track of where he was. It simply does not make sense to put this verse in chapter 9 rather than chapter 8. It is an enormously important verse.

Mark writes, **And He said to them, "Assuredly, I say to you that there are some standing here who will not taste death till they see the kingdom of God present with power"** (v. 1). With these words, Jesus uttered a prophecy, but not about an event that would take place hundreds or thousands of years later. He attached a time frame to this prophecy when He said, "Some standing here will not taste death till. . . ." In other words, despite the fact that Christ was calling His disciples to take up the cross, to deny themselves and suffer with Him, some of those who heard Him speak these words would not die until the event He prophesied happened. It would happen within the lifetimes of at least some of the disciples.

What event was Jesus talking about when He spoke of the coming of the kingdom of God in power? Before I try to address this question, let me raise the ante by showing that this prophecy is very similar to two other texts in the New Testament that are equally or even more controversial.

In Matthew's gospel, we read: "Now brother will deliver up brother to death, and a father his child; and children will rise up against parents and cause them to be put to death. And you will be hated by all for My name's sake. But he who endures to the end will be saved. When they persecute you in this city, flee to another. For assuredly, I say to you, you will not have gone through the cities of Israel before the Son of Man comes" (10:21–23). Here, as in Mark 8, Jesus foretold suffering and affliction for His followers. He told them that when they came under persecution in one city, they should move on to another. Then He concluded with a promise: "You will not have gone through the cities of Israel before the Son of Man comes."

Here, again, Jesus was prophesying, and once again, He gave a time frame for the fulfillment of the prophecy. In this case, He did not refer to the time when the disciples would see the kingdom of God present in power, but to the coming of the Son of Man. Instead of saying that some of His followers would remain alive until the prophecy came to pass, He said they would not finish going through the cities of Israel before it happened.

Do you see the problem? The Son of Man has not returned from heaven even today, but the disciples finished going through the cities of Israel within the first generation of Christian missionary activity. How, then, are we to understand these words of Jesus?

The most controversial text with a time-frame reference is also found in Matthew's gospel. In chapter 24, we find Matthew's version of the Olivet Discourse, a lengthy teaching that Jesus delivered near the end of His life with His disciples on the Mount of Olives. That discourse is found in all three of the Synoptic Gospels and is easily the most controversial discourse in all of the accounts of Jesus' life.

Jesus began with yet another prophecy. He looked at the temple and said, "Do you not see all these things? Assuredly, I say to you, not one stone shall be left here upon another, that shall not be thrown down" (v. 2). This prophecy of the destruction of the temple was shocking in its magnitude. If anything was unthinkable for the Jews of Jesus' day, it was the destruction of the temple. Thus, it is hardly surprising that His disciples asked Him, "When will these things be?" (v. 3). Jesus gave an elaborate answer, saying in part:

> "Immediately after the tribulation of those days the sun will be darkened, and the moon will not give its light; the stars will fall from heaven, and the powers of the heavens will be shaken. Then the sign of the Son of Man will appear in heaven, and then all the tribes of the earth will mourn, and they will see the Son of Man coming on the clouds of heaven with power and great glory. And He will send His angels with a great sound of a trumpet, and they will gather together His elect from the four winds, from one end of heaven to the other. Now learn this parable from the fig tree: When its branch has already become tender and puts forth leaves, you know that summer is near. So you also, when you see all these things, know that it is near—at the doors! Assuredly, I say to you, this generation will by no means pass away till all these things take place." (vv. 29–34)

Here, again, Jesus set a time frame for a prophecy: "all these things," including the destruction of the temple, would happen within a generation, which, in Jewish terms, was forty years. This prophecy proved astonishingly accurate—at least as far as the temple was concerned. In about forty years, the temple was completely destroyed when Jerusalem was wiped out by the Romans. The problem is that Jesus also listed the coming of the Son of Man among the events that would happen within a generation, but Jesus manifestly has not come to bring the end of the age. Thus, this text is used frequently by skeptics and by higher critical scholars in the academic world to deny the credibility of Jesus and of the New Testament. When Bertrand Russell wrote his essay "Why I Am Not a Christian," he cited this text as his number one argument for not believing in Jesus.

What Did Jesus Mean?

So, we have three critical passages in the New Testament that set forth future events, and they all give time frames, saying the prophesied events would happen within the first generation of believers. However, we cannot be sure that all three of these passages refer to the same historical event. In Mark 9, Jesus said some of His disciples would not taste death until they saw the kingdom of God present with power. In Matthew 10, He said the disciples would not have gone through all the cities of Israel before the Son of Man came. In Mark 14, He declared that not all of the people of the generation then living would die before "these things" happened, including the destruction of the temple.

The gist of scholarly skepticism is this: Jesus foretold several things that would happen during the first generation of believers, including the destruction of the temple and His own return. Yes, the temple was destroyed, but Jesus did not come back to bring history to a close. Therefore, if He was a prophet, He was a false prophet. Not only is His prophecy not fully true, the New Testament documents cannot be trusted.

Evangelicals use all sorts of interpretive gymnastics to get around these problems. Addressing Matthew 24, the most common argument is that Jesus meant the unbelief of that generation would not pass away, that there would be unbelievers in every generation until He came back at the end of the age. In other words, He was not really setting a time frame. But if this is what He meant, He used "this generation" in a way that is utterly foreign to its usage in the rest of the New Testament.

If we take this text and its words seriously, we can only conclude that the disciples understood Jesus to mean one literal generation, about forty years, and that everything He was prophesying would happen within the next forty or so years—with the exception, I believe, of His final coming at the end of the age.

What about Matthew 10? When Jesus said the disciples would not go through all the cities of Israel before the Son of Man came, He clearly was setting a first-century time frame for some kind of coming of the Son of Man. In my judgment, again, He was not referring to His final coming.

In Mark 9, what was Jesus referring to when He said, "There are some standing here who will not taste death till they see the kingdom of God present with power"? It is significant that He did not say, "Some standing here will not taste death until I return." But if "the kingdom of God present with power" does not refer to His second coming, what does it mean?

Through church history, many commentators have argued that since Mark places this prophecy right before his description of the transfiguration, and the transfiguration was the most dazzling manifestation of the presence of the kingdom of God in glory and power that occurred during Jesus' earthly ministry prior to His resurrection, Mark must have seen Jesus' words as a prophecy of the transfiguration. But that interpretation puzzles me. I do not understand why Jesus would have said some of His disciples would not die before the transfiguration, which, Mark tells us, happened a mere six days later (9:2). Was He saying: "Do not worry. Not all of you will die in the next week." It would not have made sense for Him to put such a time frame on an event that was to take place so soon.

Other scholars have said this prophecy refers to the resurrection, which demonstrated the manifestation of Jesus and His kingdom in power even more forcefully than the transfiguration. However, this interpretation suffers from the same problem. None of those who were there at the moment Jesus spoke this prophecy (except Judas Iscariot) died before the resurrection. Even the resurrection was too close to justify a time frame such as Jesus set.

Another view is that this prophecy was fulfilled when the disciples saw the kingdom coming in power on the Day of Pentecost, when they were empowered by the outpouring of the Spirit of God from heaven. That is possible, but again, none of the disciples had died by that time except Judas. Again, the time frame set by Jesus seems to rule out an event that was to happen so soon.

However, it is possible Jesus was talking about the manifestation of the kingdom of God in power in the destruction of Jerusalem and the temple. When these terrible events occurred in AD 70, the Christian church was finally understood as an entity distinct from Judaism. It was no longer considered a subset or a sect within Judaism. The triumph of the Messiah's church was made visible and manifest in power with the judgment of God on the Jews. And some of those who were present when Jesus prophesied the manifestation of the power of the kingdom did, in fact, die between His announcement and the coming of the kingdom in power in 70.

I have to admit that I do not know for certain that this interpretation of Jesus' prophecy is correct. But I know that if you are wrestling with these time-frame passages in the New Testament, you do not need to wrestle any more if you take seriously the fulfillment of Jesus' prophecy concerning the temple. One thing I do know for certain is that the Word of God does not fail. I also know that Jesus was truth incarnate, and when He said that something was going to happen in a certain time frame, I know it happened within that time frame. If that conclusion forces me to challenge some of the constructs of theology in our day, so be it. The mouth of Jesus is the only reliable source of truth.

28

THE TRANSFIGURATION

Mark 9:2–13

〜

Now after six days Jesus took Peter, James, and John, and led them up on a high mountain apart by themselves; and He was transfigured before them. His clothes became shining, exceedingly white, like snow, such as no launderer on earth can whiten them. And Elijah appeared to them with Moses, and they were talking with Jesus. Then Peter answered and said to Jesus, "Rabbi, it is good for us to be here; and let us make three tabernacles: one for You, one for Moses, and one for Elijah"—because he did not know what to say, for they were greatly afraid. And a cloud came and overshadowed them; and a voice came out of the cloud, saying, "This is My beloved Son. Hear Him!" Suddenly, when they had looked around, they saw no one anymore, but only Jesus with themselves. Now as they came down from the mountain, He commanded them that they should tell no one the things they had seen, till the Son of Man had risen from the dead. So they kept this word to themselves, questioning what the rising from the dead meant. And they asked Him, saying, "Why do the scribes say that Elijah must come first?" Then He answered and told them, "Indeed, Elijah is coming first and restores all things. And how is it written concerning the Son of Man, that He must suffer many things and be treated with contempt? But I say to you that Elijah has also come, and they did to him whatever they wished, as it is written of him."

Several years ago, I wrote a book that was somewhat unusual. It was titled *The Glory of Christ*, and I wrote it because, in classical theology, we note that the progress of Jesus' life in general was from humiliation to exaltation. His life began with His birth in the circumstances of poverty and moved toward His rejection by His own people, which rejection reached its peak in His betrayal and crucifixion. The first movement toward exaltation came with the circumstances of His burial in a wealthy man's tomb. It then continued with the resurrection, and finally reached its zenith in the ascension.

Of course, this general progress from humiliation to exaltation was not steady and consistent. Throughout Jesus' life, there were moments when, even in the midst of His humiliation, glory burst forth. For instance, at the time of His birth, the circumstances of poverty were contrasted with the glory God manifested to the shepherds in the surrounding fields. But there was no point in the life of Jesus prior to the resurrection where His glory shined forth so magnificently as it did in His transfiguration.

Mark tells us, **After six days Jesus took Peter, James, and John, and led them up on a high mountain apart by themselves; and He was transfigured before them** (v. 2). It is significant that this event took place "after six days." What had happened six days earlier? At Caesarea Philippi, in response to a question from Jesus, Peter had made his confession of belief in the messiahship of Jesus (8:29). Then, only a little while later, Jesus explained to His disciples that He must suffer and die (v. 31), which left Peter so aghast that he rebuked Jesus (v. 32), prompting Jesus to rebuke him in return (v. 33). Then Jesus began to teach His disciples that they, too, must be prepared to die; if they were to be His followers, they must deny themselves and take up the cross (v. 34).

After these incidents, Jesus and His disciples probably began to move south, back toward the Sea of Galilee, beginning the long journey to Jerusalem, where the cross and death awaited Jesus. We can only imagine that the disciples were filled with a grim foreboding. The terrible words Jesus had spoken to them right after the Caesarea Philippi confession were probably much on their minds. He had said He *must* suffer and die, and now He was heading toward that terrible cup.

In the midst of this despair, Jesus took Peter, James, and John, and went to the top of "a high mountain." We cannot be sure which mountain in Palestine this was. A number of theories have been set forth, but the best seems to be Mount Hermon, which was near Caesarea Philippi and which is indeed a high mountain, being more than nine thousand feet high.

Mark then tells us that Jesus was "transfigured" before His disciples. The Greek word used here is a form of the verb *metamorpheo*, from which we get the English word *metamorphosis*. We learned about metamorphosis in school when we studied the dramatic change that a caterpillar undergoes when it becomes a butterfly. It goes through a change of form. The Greek word for "form" is *morphos*, and so a metamorphosis is a change of form. A transfiguration is also a change of form. The prefix *trans* means "over or across." When we make a transcontinental flight, we go across the continent. If we go transatlantic, we go across the Atlantic Ocean. So Jesus underwent a transformation, a metamorphosis, and suddenly the glory that was hidden and veiled in the cloak of His humanity burst forth, revealing the full deity of Christ to the watching disciples.

Clothes of Brightest White

In his description of the transfigured Jesus, Matthew writes, "His face shone like the sun, and His clothes became as white as the light" (17:2b). Mark says nothing about Jesus' face, but he gives us more detail about His garments: **His clothes became shining, exceedingly white, like snow, such as no launderer on earth can whiten them** (v. 3).

The idea of someone's face shining with unbearable intensity is reminiscent of the Old Testament story of Moses. When Moses was on the mountain with God, he begged to receive the blessed beatific vision. He said, "Please, show me Your glory" (Ex. 33:18). God replied: "You cannot see My face; for no man shall see Me, and live" (v. 20). But God went on to say: "Here is a place by Me, and you shall stand on the rock. So it shall be, while My glory passes by, that I will put you in the cleft of the rock, and will cover you with My hand while I pass by. Then I will take away My hand, and you shall see My back; but My face shall not be seen" (vv. 21–23). When Moses got this momentary glimpse of the backward glance of the glory of God, the experience was so intense, the glory of God from His back was so refulgent, that when Moses gazed on it, his own face began to shine with brilliant radiance so intense the people of Israel were afraid to come near him (Ex. 34:30).

The glow of Moses' face was a mere reflection of the glory he saw in the presence of God. Moses' face was not the source of the light; rather, the light of God was rebounding from the face of the creature. On the mount of transfiguration, however, the disciples witnessed the actual glory of God, not a reflected glory. The source of the light that the disciples saw came from within Christ Himself. His internal, inherent glory was bursting forth before their very eyes. It is this event that John has in mind when he writes, "We beheld His glory, the glory as of the only begotten of the Father, full of grace and truth" (John 1:14b). Likewise, the author of Hebrews calls Jesus "the brightness of His glory and the express image of His person" (1:3). Jesus does not just *reflect* the brightness of the glory of God. He *is* the brightness of the glory of God.

The light that flowed out of Jesus was white and pure. Philosophers argue that color is secondary, not primary. It does not inhere in a substance but is added to the substance by the presence of light. Where does color come from? It comes from the light, from the sun, and all of the hues of the rainbow are found in the pure light of the sun. But when all these colors are mixed together in the purity of light, we have absolute whiteness. Thus, it is not surprising that the light that flowed out of Jesus with an intensity beyond that of the sun was of purest white. Remember, Mark has been at pains to demonstrate to Gentiles that Jesus is the divine Son of God. The whiteness of the light the disciples witnessed there on the mountain said something about who Jesus was.

As far as I am concerned, the most profound chapter in American literature is found in Melville's *Moby Dick*. It is the chapter titled "The Whiteness of the Whale." In this chapter, Melville explores how whiteness is used in history, in religion, and in nature. He describes the whiteness by use of such terms as *elusive, ghastly,* and *transcendent horror,* as well as *sweet, honorable,* and *pure.* He openly states that the whale was the symbol of all these things. Thus, if the whale embodied all that is symbolized by whiteness—that which is terrifying, pure, excellent, horrible, ghastly, mysterious, incomprehensible—he embodied the traits that are found in the fullness of the perfection of God Himself. It is this same deity that Jesus manifests in the purity that contains no spot, no wrinkle, and no blemish.

Elijah, Moses, a Cloud, and a Voice

Mark writes: **And Elijah appeared to them with Moses, and they were talking with Jesus** (v. 4). The disciples were watching the display of light, the breakthrough of glory, when Elijah and Moses appeared and began to talk with Jesus. Luke tells us they discussed "His decease which He was about to accomplish at Jerusalem" (9:31b), that is, the suffering, rejection, and death about which He had told the disciples. Both Elijah, who represents the prophets, and Moses, who represents the law, clearly understood the vocation of the Messiah. They knew Jesus had to die, and they knew why. They came to the second person of the Trinity with their comfort and their encouragement, reminding Him of His destiny that they had foretold centuries before. Elijah, who had been carried up to heaven in a chariot of fire, set foot once more in the Holy Land. Moses, who had been denied entrance into the Promised Land, at last stood there after centuries.

At this point, Mark tells us, **Peter answered and said to Jesus, "Rabbi, it is good for us to be here; and let us make three tabernacles: one for You, one for Moses, and one for Elijah"—because he did not know what to say, for they were greatly afraid** (vv. 5–6). Mark is very honest in telling us that Peter, James, and John were so terrified by what they were seeing that they did not know what to say. Peter spoke, making a suggestion about setting up tents for Jesus, Moses, and Elijah, but the strong implication is that he was babbling, speaking without forethought.

If the disciples were frightened by the transfiguration of Jesus and the appearance of Moses and Elijah, their fear soon turned to abject terror. Mark writes, **And a cloud came and overshadowed them; and a voice came out of the cloud, saying, "This is My beloved Son. Hear Him!"** (v. 7). Luke tells us, "they were fearful as they entered the cloud" (9:34b), and Matthew notes that after they heard the voice of the Father, "they fell on their faces and were greatly afraid" (17:6b). The glory cloud of the presence of God appeared and created a shroud around Jesus, Moses, Elijah, and the disciples. Mark says it "overshadowed" them. We find this word used when the angel Gabriel came to the virgin Mary to announce that she was to be the mother of the Savior. When she asked how such a thing could be possible, he said, "The Holy Spirit will come upon you, and the power of the Highest will overshadow you; therefore, also, that Holy One who is to be born will be called the Son of God" (Luke 1:35). The idea here is the exercise of great power.

From the cloud, the disciples heard a voice saying: "This is My beloved Son. Hear Him!" Just as God the Father audibly commended His Son at His baptism, when He was anointed with power by the Holy Spirit (1:9–11), here on the Mount of Transfiguration the Father audibly commended the Son specifically to the disciples, with the addition of a very pointed exhortation: "Hear Him!"

This is what the Father would say if He were to speak from heaven today. He would tell us, "Listen to My Son, in whom I am well pleased."

Instructions and Questions

The miraculous transfiguration of Jesus ended as abruptly as it began: **Suddenly, when they had looked around, they saw no one anymore, but only Jesus with themselves** (v. 8). Moses and Elijah were gone, the voice was silent, the cloud had lifted, and Jesus was no longer shining. Mark adds: **Now as they came down from the mountain, He commanded them that they should tell no one the things they had seen, till the Son of Man had risen from the dead. So they kept this word to themselves, questioning what the rising from the dead meant** (vv. 9–10). Jesus again commanded the disciples to keep their knowledge about Him to themselves—in this case, Peter, James, and John were not even to tell the other disciples—until after He rose from the dead. They obeyed, but Mark notes that they questioned what He meant by rising from the dead. They still had not understood, partly because the Jews expected a general resurrection at the end of history, not a specific resurrection within history. Indeed, the disciples would not understand that their Lord was to rise again until they saw Him alive after His crucifixion.

As Jesus and the disciples made their way down the mountain, the question of the role of Elijah in the coming kingdom of God was very much in the forefront of the disciples' thoughts: **And they asked Him, saying, "Why do the scribes say that Elijah must come first?" Then He answered and told them, "Indeed, Elijah is coming first and restores all things. And how is it written concerning the Son of Man, that He must suffer many things and be treated with contempt? But I say to you that Elijah has also come, and they did to him whatever they wished, as it is written of him"** (vv. 11–13).

As we have seen, the final book of the Old Testament, the book of Malachi, the last prophet of the Old Testament, said, "Behold, I will send you Elijah the prophet before the coming of the great and dreadful day of the Lord" (4:5). So, for centuries the Jewish community waited for Elijah, knowing that His reappearance would be the harbinger of the breakthrough of the kingdom of God and the appearance of their Messiah. The scribes also believed that Elijah would come first, and that when he came, he would lead the people into a spirit of repentance and would anoint the Messiah for His messianic vocation. The disciples, having seen Elijah on the mountain, were curious why the scribes believed these things.

Jesus affirmed that Elijah had already come. The parallel passage in Matthew adds, "Then the disciples understood that He spoke to them of John the Baptist" (17:13). He was not a reincarnation of Elijah, but he ministered "in the spirit and power of Elijah," as the angel who announced his birth foretold (Luke 1:17). So, John came before Jesus, as Elijah was to come before the Messiah. John's mission was to direct the people to repentance from their sin, again fulfilling the mission of Elijah. Finally, it was John the Baptist who anointed Jesus in the Jordan River to begin Jesus' public ministry as the Messiah. All three expectations attributed to Elijah were in fact fulfilled in the prophetic ministry of John the Baptist. He prepared the way for Jesus, the Savior and Son of God.

What did Jesus mean with His cryptic statement, "And how is it written concerning the Son of Man, that He must suffer many things and be treated with contempt?" Note that He went on to say, "But I say to you that Elijah has also come, and they did to him whatever they wished, as it is written of him." It seems that Jesus was telling His disciples that just as John the Baptist was rejected and ultimately killed, He, too, must be rejected and killed, as the prophets foretold. Here, then, was another reminder that the glorious Lord the disciples had seen on the mountain was about to undergo great agony and distress. Before exaltation, there would be deep humiliation.

29

HELP FOR UNBELIEF

Mark 9:14–29

~~~~~~~~~~

And when He came to the disciples, He saw a great multitude around them, and scribes disputing with them. Immediately, when they saw Him, all the people were greatly amazed, and running to Him, greeted Him. And He asked the scribes, "What are you discussing with them?" Then one of the crowd answered and said, "Teacher, I brought You my son, who has a mute spirit. And wherever it seizes him, it throws him down; he foams at the mouth, gnashes his teeth, and becomes rigid. So I spoke to Your disciples, that they should cast it out, but they could not." He answered him and said, "O faithless generation, how long shall I be with you? How long shall I bear with you? Bring him to Me." Then they brought him to Him. And when he saw Him, immediately the spirit convulsed him, and he fell on the ground and wallowed, foaming at the mouth. So He asked his father, "How long has this been happening to him?" And he said, "From childhood. And often he has thrown him both into the fire and into the water to destroy him. But if You can do anything, have compassion on us and help us." Jesus said to him, "If you can believe, all things are possible to him who believes." Immediately the father of the child cried out and said with tears, "Lord, I believe; help my unbelief!" When Jesus saw that the people came running together, He rebuked the unclean spirit, saying to it, "Deaf and dumb spirit, I command you, come out of him and enter him no more!" Then the spirit cried out, convulsed him greatly, and came out of him. And he became as one dead, so that many said, "He is dead." But Jesus took him by the hand and lifted him up, and he arose. And when He had come into the house, His disciples asked Him privately, "Why could we not cast it out?" So He said to them, "This kind can come out by nothing but prayer and fasting."

We need to be careful in our understanding of the intersection of the demonic world and the natural fallen world. On the one hand, we must be very careful that we do not discount demonic activity in this world. This is the tendency of modern critics, who sometimes reject the testimony of the Bible because, they say, the biblical authors ascribe to Satan things that can be explained by natural science without reference to the supernatural realm. For instance, in Mark 9:14–29, the malady that afflicted the boy, which Mark attributes to demonic possession, strongly resembles the grand mal seizures associated with severe forms of epilepsy. So, the critics say, this boy was not possessed by a demon, he simply was suffering from a disease that we now know as epilepsy.

At the same time, we must not be too hasty in attributing terrible events to the influence of demons. On the day when President Kennedy was assassinated, I noticed that the news commentators constantly reached for language that would adequately express how egregious this act seemed to be. I repeatedly heard the assassination described as satanic, diabolical, devilish, demonic, or hellish.

The assassination may have been inspired by Satan, but we did not have to look to Satan to account for evil of that kind. There is sufficient wickedness in the heart of every human being to produce such a vile act without assistance from the Devil. However, people do not want to recognize that human beings can be that corrupt, that fallen.

Our duty, as always, is to accept what the Bible says, which means that we have no choice but to believe that Jesus dealt with a case of true demonic possession in the incident recorded in this passage, just as He did in earlier events Mark has noted.

However, it is good for us to remember that throughout Scripture, when Satan possesses or troubles a person, he exploits any frailty that is already there. So it may have been that this young man was suffering from epilepsy, but that it was exacerbated by the intervention of the Evil One to torment him all the more. In any case, with this narrative, Mark demonstrates once more the power of the Son of God over the forces of darkness *and* the ravages of disease.

The Disciples' Inability

When Jesus, Peter, James, and John returned from the Mount of Transfiguration and rejoined the other disciples, **He saw a great multitude around them, and scribes disputing with them. Immediately, when they saw Him, all the people were greatly amazed, and running to Him, greeted Him. And He asked the scribes, "What are you discussing with them?"** (vv. 14b–16). He found the disciples involved in some kind of argument or dispute with the scribes, with a large multitude observing. Upon catching sight of Him, the people ran to Him and greeted Him excitedly, but Jesus was concerned about the dispute. He asked, "What are you discussing with them?" but the question was directed not at His disciples but at the scribes. Was Jesus perhaps displeased that the scribes had taken advantage of His absence to dispute with the less-knowledgeable disciples?

The scribes were not given time to answer, for one of the men of the crowd immediately spoke up and said: **"Teacher, I brought You my son, who has a mute spirit. And wherever it seizes him, it throws him down; he foams at the mouth, gnashes his teeth, and becomes rigid. So I spoke to Your disciples, that they should cast it out, but they could not"** (vv. 17b–18). Jesus, as we have seen, had healed a mute man (7:31–37), although that man's muteness was simply a speech impediment; this boy's muteness was caused by a demon. Furthermore, the father reported, the demon occasionally would cause the boy to fall down violently and make him foam at the mouth, gnash his teeth, and become rigid. These symptoms certainly do resemble an epileptic seizure, but there was more than epilepsy going on here, for the testimony of the inspired gospel writer is clear—a demon was involved in these manifestations.

The father had come looking for Jesus to request healing for his son, but since Jesus was on the mountain with Peter, James, and John, the father had appealed to the disciples for aid. However, they had been unable to help the boy. They were impotent to manifest the power of Jesus.

We saw earlier that Jesus had sent the twelve out on a trial mission, and Mark explicitly tells us that on that occasion "they cast out many demons" (6:12). Why, then, could they not help this boy? Jesus provided one specific reason, as we will see later in the narrative, but it appears that the power Jesus gave the disciples for their trial mission was temporary. Their real empowerment for ministry did not happen until Pentecost, when Jesus, having returned to heaven, sent the Holy Spirit on them as He had promised (Acts 1:8; 2:1–4). Thereafter we see many miraculous works of healing at the hands of the disciples, including deliverance from demons.

Today, even though Jesus is no longer present with us touching His human nature, He is never absent from us touching the presence of His Holy Spirit, so that the church has more power at her disposal than even the disciples had before Pentecost.

A Father's Faith
Jesus reacted to this news in a rather curious fashion: **He answered him and said, "O faithless generation, how long shall I be with you? How long shall**

I bear with you? Bring him to Me" (v. 19). This was a lament directed not at the crowds but at Jesus' disciples. He was lamenting not their lack of power but their lack of faith. They had been with Him for some time and had seen scores of miraculous works, but still, in Jesus' judgment, they lacked faith. Humanly speaking, it weighed on Jesus that His own pupils were so slow, not to mention the multitudes who had observed His ministry and still walked around without faith.

Despite His lament, Jesus told the disciples to bring the boy to Him. Mark writes, **when he saw Him, immediately the spirit convulsed him, and he fell on the ground and wallowed, foaming at the mouth** (v. 20b). It seems that the presence of Jesus sent the evil spirit into a paroxysm of rage or terror, which it expressed by sending the boy into another of his horrifying episodes. Then, **He asked his father, "How long has this been happening to him?" And he said, "From childhood. And often he has thrown him both into the fire and into the water to destroy him. But if You can do anything, have compassion on us and help us"** (vv. 21–22). The father had been watching his son suffer like this for some time, sometimes even seeing the boy thrown into a fire or into water, imperiling his life. That motivated the man to appeal to Jesus in moving terms: "If You can do anything, have compassion on us and help us."

Jesus replied, **"If you can believe, all things are possible to him who believes"** (v. 23). This verse has often been ripped from its context and used as a talisman for magic in our age, which is deeply influenced by neo-Gnosticism. The New Age movement seeks to manipulate the external world by mind control. For instance, it puts forth the idea that if we can visualize world peace, we can bring world peace. But even in the Christian world, many hold to simplistic ideas about faith healing. They assert that all we have to do is believe, and if we believe strongly enough, we can move mountains and make anything happen.

I once encountered a young man who was a dynamic, devout Christian, but he suffered from cerebral palsy. He told me that some friends had come to him and said, "We're going to heal you of your cerebral palsy." So, they had laid hands on him and pronounced him whole, but Harvey still had cerebral palsy. Then they had told him: "The problem is that you do not have enough faith, and if you do not have enough faith, you will never be healed. If you really want to be healed, you have to claim your healing in Jesus' name. You have to believe that you are healed before you can be healed." When he remained unhealed, they eventually had concluded that he must be guilty of a heinous sin that was blocking the healing. Finally, they had declared he must be under demonic possession, so they had planned an exorcism and tried to drive the demon out of him, but still he was not healed. Finally he came to me in tears and said, "Dr. Sproul, do you think that I'm possessed by a demon?" I told him I did not think so, then I prayed that he would have peace and that he would trust the Lord with his body and his life, because sometimes God says "no" even to the most ardent prayers.

This kind of thing goes on every day in America and around the world. Blind people are told to believe they can see, and they try their best to do so, but they open their eyes and cannot see a thing. The lame are told to believe they can walk, but they cannot get out of their wheelchairs, though they exert themselves. So, by implication, the problem is within them—they have inadequate faith. Nobody asks the obvious question: If faith is all that is needed, why doesn't the healer himself have enough faith to effect healings? This text is simply not a blanket, universal promise that whatever we believe *can* happen *will* happen.

Years ago, the Orlando Magic team was on the verge of reaching the National Basketball Association finals. The team's publicity department began promoting a motto around Orlando: "You have to believe." The implication seemed to be that all we had to do was close our eyes and work up the faith to believe the Magic were going to win the championship, and it would happen.

However, we cannot make a decision to believe something that we do not, in fact, believe. We can make a decision to repent of our sins. We can make a decision to learn of Jesus, to study the Word of God. We can make decisions to do all kinds of things that will affect our future behavior, but what we cannot do is create faith by a decision. This is why I fault modern evangelistic techniques that suggest that all a person has to do is make a decision and faith will well up in his soul. It does not work like that. Faith comes by hearing. Faith comes by the Word of God. It is God who creates faith in the doubting heart.

This father was in the presence of Jesus, the Author of faith (Heb. 12:2). Jesus called him to trust Him. He had every reason to believe that Jesus had the power to do something for his son, but he was not completely sure that he believed enough. So, he cried out in brutal honesty, with tears, **"Lord, I believe; help my unbelief"** (v. 24b).

Every Christian reading this book has some level of authentic saving faith in his or her heart. However, the intensity of that faith is not constant. It waxes and wanes. It increases and diminishes. No matter how strong your faith is, there are moments in this life when it is assaulted by the enemy. Sometimes it can seem as if your faith is barely hanging on, and you make a prayer much like this man made to Jesus: "I believe, but my belief is not perfect, it is not pure, it is not strong. I need help. Help me with my unbelief."

When you are assaulted with doubts and your faith seems frail, go to the source of faith, the Word of God. There is no time in my life when my faith is stronger than when I am immersed in the Word of God or in prayer. Staying close to the Word, listening to the promises of our Redeemer, and opening my heart to Him are the things that kill unbelief and build a powerful faith that does not let me down in the midst of afflictions.

A Boy's Freedom

Mark writes, **When Jesus saw that the people came running together, He rebuked the unclean spirit, saying to it, "Deaf and dumb spirit, I command you, come out of him and enter him no more!"** (v. 25). Jesus seems to have been motivated to act by the growing size of the crowd; apparently He wished to expel the demon with as little notice as possible. So, He commanded the demon to come out of the boy. At that point, **the spirit cried out, convulsed him greatly, and came out of him. And he became as one dead, so that many said, "He is dead"** (v. 26). The demon made one last attack on the boy and then submitted to Jesus' command. However, the spirit's exit left the boy apparently dead. It seems he was at least unconscious.

Mark tells us, **But Jesus took him by the hand and lifted him up, and he arose** (v. 27). It is not clear whether this was an actual resurrection, but in any case, the revived boy must have been clearly in his right mind, no longer troubled by the evil spirit. I can only imagine that this boy's father looked at his son and then looked at Jesus, and he was filled with faith, because Jesus had done what He said He would do.

In human relationships, it takes a long time to develop trust between people and only five minutes to destroy it. Who do you trust in this world? How much faith do you have in your spouse, in your children, in your friends? When you can come to the place where you can trust people with those things that are most precious to you, you have found something priceless. But people let us down. They break our trust. Unfortunately, we sometimes project the mistrust that we experience in our relationships with other people onto our relationship with God. However, it is reasonable and rational to trust God always. Indeed, nothing is more irrational than *not* to trust God, because God is perfectly trustworthy. He has never broken a promise and He never will. He does not know how to betray His people.

Not surprisingly, the disciples were curious as to why they were unable to cast out the demon. Therefore, **when He had come into the house, His disciples asked Him privately, "Why could we not cast it out?" So He said to them, "This kind can come out by nothing but prayer and fasting"** (vv. 28–29). Again we see that the strength of our faith can never be put on automatic pilot. When we face a formidable foe, it is not enough simply to depend on the reservoir of faith in our souls. We have to get on our knees. We have to plead with God. We have to make use of all of the means of grace that He has given His people, for He strengthens His people through these means.

Years ago, I was speaking at a conference at a large Korean Presbyterian Church in California. We arrived for the conference on Saturday morning about 7:30 to find a traffic jam in the parking lot. However, the traffic was leaving, not arriving. I could not understand why so many people were leaving when the conference had not even started yet. Eventually I discovered that about a thousand people would gather at that church for an hour of prayer each morning at 6:30. The pastor told me, "Nothing builds faith among people like prayer." That is the lesson Jesus taught the disciples on this occasion.

30

THE MEASURE
OF GREATNESS

Mark 9:30–41

⟨⟩

Then they departed from there and passed through Galilee, and He did not want anyone to know it. For He taught His disciples and said to them, "The Son of Man is being betrayed into the hands of men, and they will kill Him. And after He is killed, He will rise the third day." But they did not understand this saying, and were afraid to ask Him. Then He came to Capernaum. And when He was in the house He asked them, "What was it you disputed among yourselves on the road?" But they kept silent, for on the road they had disputed among themselves who would be the greatest. And He sat down, called the twelve, and said to them, "If anyone desires to be first, he shall be last of all and servant of all." Then He took a little child and set him in the midst of them. And when He had taken him in His arms, He said to them, "Whoever receives one of these little children in My name receives Me; and whoever receives Me, receives not Me but Him who sent Me." Now John answered Him, saying, "Teacher, we saw someone who does not follow us casting out demons in Your name, and we forbade him because he does not follow us." But Jesus said, "Do not forbid him, for no one who works a miracle in My name can soon afterward speak evil of Me. For he who is not against us is on our side. For whoever gives you a cup of water to drink in My name, because you belong to Christ, assuredly, I say to you, he will by no means lose his reward."

A s we have seen in the last few chapters, a number of important and noteworthy incidents occurred as Jesus ministered in the area of Caesarea Philippi and Mount Hermon: Peter's confession (8:29), Jesus' first announcement of His coming suffering, death, and resurrection (8:31), Peter's rebuke of Jesus and Jesus' counter-rebuke (8:32–33), the transfiguration (9:1–8), and the healing of a demon-possessed boy (9:14–27). After these things, however, **they departed from there and passed through Galilee** (v. 30a). Having set His face like a flint (Isa. 50:7) to go to Jerusalem, Jesus left the region around Caesarea Philippi and headed south, back into the Galilee area. This is the last time Mark tells us of Jesus spending any time in Galilee until after the resurrection.

As He embarked on this trip, Jesus did His best to keep a low profile: **He did not want anyone to know it. For He taught His disciples and said to them, "The Son of Man is being betrayed into the hands of men, and they will kill Him. And after He is killed, He will rise the third day." But they did not understand this saying, and were afraid to ask Him** (v. 30b–32). It seems Jesus sought to avoid crowds so He could focus on teaching His disciples. What did He teach them? He returned to the message that had so shocked them in Caesarea Philippi—He was going to Jerusalem, there to be betrayed and killed, but to rise on the third day after His death. The disciples, however, did not understand what He was saying to them. They simply could not get their minds around the idea that Israel's Messiah would die. Furthermore, the prospect was so terrifying to them, they could not bring themselves to ask Him for a further explanation.

When Jesus announced again that He would be delivered into the hands of men so that He might be killed, He said, according to the New King James translation, that He was "being betrayed." Jesus used the present tense, showing that His betrayal had already started. He was saying that what would happen to Him at Jerusalem would be the culmination of a process that was already under way.

I do not like the NKJV's use of the term *betrayed* here. Obviously it is not completely inappropriate, because when Jesus arrived in Jerusalem, one from His own group of disciples would betray Him to the authorities who wanted to put Him to death, and it is possible that this course of action was already playing out in Judas' mind. But Jesus did not have the actions of Judas or any other person in this world in mind. He was making the point that He was being handed over or delivered at that very moment, and the One handing Him over was the Father. Jesus was being sent to Jerusalem to fulfill His office as Messiah. Because it was the Father sending Him there, it was not an act of betrayal, because from all eternity it had been agreed among the members of the Trinity that the Father would send the Son into the world to bring about His plan of salvation for His people. At this point, Jesus had to be delivered into the hands of evil men. Jesus was accepting of that deliverance. He had come to do the will of the Father, and to do that, He had to suffer at the hands of sinful people. So the Father's plan to hand Him over to fulfill His destiny was now drawing to its climax.

Greatness through Servanthood

Mark then tells us: **Then He came to Capernaum. And when He was in the house He asked them, "What was it you disputed among yourselves on the road?" But they kept silent, for on the road they had disputed among themselves who would be the greatest** (vv. 33–34). Having arrived at Capernaum on the northwest side of the Sea of Galilee, Jesus entered a house. There, He asked the disciples what they had been disputing about on the road from Caesarea Philippi; Jesus had overheard the dispute and sensed that they were unhappy with one another. What was their answer? There was no answer. There was absolute silence among the disciples because they were overcome with shame and embarrassment—as well they should have been. The Lord had just told them that He was on His way to Jerusalem to suffer and die, but they had fallen into a childish debate over which of them would be the greatest in the coming kingdom. Who would be number one? Who would be at Jesus' right hand?

This question that the disciples debated was concerned with the superlative. This is an issue that we deal with in discussions all the time. We argue about who was the greatest singer of all time. We discuss who was the greatest baseball player ever. It seems that great is not good enough for us; we want to determine who is the best of the best. Sometimes, however, the discussion becomes more personal. This happens when we put ourselves into the debate and begin to evaluate our own merits against those of others.

Notice how Jesus responded to His disciples. Though His question suggests He did not know precisely what they had been talking about, it seems that He knew at least the gist of it, for Mark writes, **And He sat down, called the twelve, and said to them, "If anyone desires to be first, he shall be last of all and servant of all"** (v. 35). When Jesus sat down, He assumed the position and the posture of formal teaching. In those days, rabbis did not stand to teach. They sat down, and their pupils sat around their feet. So, when Jesus sat down and called His disciples to Himself, He was signaling that He was about to teach them something important.

When Jesus said, "If anyone desires to be first, he shall be last of all and servant of all," He turned the values and the aspirations of all human beings upside down. Every one of us is born with an aspiration for significance. We want our lives to count. We do not want to fail to achieve the goals we pursue in our lives. The last thing we want to do is to come in last. We are not satisfied with mediocrity. We dream of glory, of winning, of reaching the pinnacle of success, of getting to the top, of attaining greatness, of being the best. What Friedrich Nietzsche called "the will to power" beats in the heart of every human being. We want to scale the corporate ladder and become king of the hill. But Jesus said, "If you want to be great, if you aspire to significance, if you want your life to count, if you really want to be first in the kingdom, you must choose to be last." This is a paradox, but Jesus used this rhetorical tool again and again: If you want to live, you have to die. If you want to save your life, you have to lose your life. If you want to be great, you have to suffer. He who is first shall be last, and he who is last shall be first. And the way to greatness is the way of service. If we want to be great, we must be the greatest servants we can be.

Of course, we do not associate greatness with servants. Winston Churchill once had a verbal tiff with one of his servants, and Churchill used abusive language as he chastised the man. Finally, the servant had had all he could handle, so he talked back to Churchill in the same tone of voice Churchill had spoken to him. Churchill was stunned and said to his servant, "Who do you think you are, talking to me like that?" The servant cowered, but he said, "Sir Winston, that's the way you talk to me." Churchill looked at the servant and said, "Ah, but I am a great man." That may have been the lowest point of Churchill's life, when he appealed to his own sense of greatness to excuse himself for demeaning one of his servants. Churchill did not understand at that moment that greatness is found in service.

In theology, we make a distinction between a *theologia gloriae* and a *theologia crucis*, between a "theology of glory" and a "theology of the cross." We want glory without a cross. We want greatness without humiliation. But Jesus said we cannot get glory that way. He knew, for what He taught here was not an abstract principle of life. It was the principle He was living out in front of His disciples every day.

To punctuate His point, Jesus used an object lesson: **Then He took a little child and set him in the midst of them. And when He had taken him in His arms, He said to them, "Whoever receives one of these little children in My name receives Me; and whoever receives Me, receives not Me but Him who sent Me"** (vv. 36–37). In most Western cultures today, babies are considered adorable. But in the ancient world, when the mortality rate was so high that a vast number of babies who were born perished before they were five years old, a little child was not considered significant until he reached an age when it was likely he would survive to maturity. So, Jesus took a small child, a person who was not considered to be of great dignity, and said to His disciples, "Whoever receives this child in My name, receives Me." In other words, He did not appoint the twelve to the position of greatness, but a child. He chose a child to be His ambassador, His spokesman to the world. He chose a person of no significance and dignity. The lesson was obvious—the disciples were not to consider themselves great.

Notice also that this teaching of Jesus simply explodes the position of so many scholars and even ordinary believers, who say, "I love Jesus and His teaching, but I cannot stand the Apostles and their teaching." Jesus would have none of that. He said that if we receive those who come in His name, we receive Him. The implication is that if we do not receive those who come in His name, we do not receive Him, and if we do not receive Him, we do not receive the One who sent Him, namely, the Father.

Unity, Not Exclusivity

At that point, John interrupted and said, **"Teacher, we saw someone who does not follow us casting out demons in Your name, and we forbade him because he does not follow us"** (v. 38). Here, again, the same problem manifested itself. John said, in essence, "We forbade someone from healing in Your name because he wasn't part of our group." Whoever was doing this exorcism, though he was not a member of the twelve, was a follower of Jesus. The problem, from John's perspective, was that he was not a follower of Jesus' disciples. He was not part of their little club. This comment reveals a spirit of exclusivism and pridefulness.

Mark tells us: **But Jesus said, "Do not forbid him, for no one who works a miracle in My name can soon afterward speak evil of Me. For he who is not against us is on our side. For whoever gives you a cup of water to drink in My name, because you belong to Christ, assuredly, I say to you, he will by no means lose his reward"** (vv. 39–41). With these profound words, Jesus showed the disciples that they must guard against building walls between believers, but must recognize their essential unity with all who claim the name of Christ.

When I was in graduate school, I was exposed to the great thinkers of traditions different from my own—great Lutheran theologians, great Anglican theologians, and others. As I read their works, I began to see that they concentrated on certain things that were basically ignored in my own tradition. I discovered that there was much to learn from the Lutherans. There were things that I could learn from the Episcopalians. Of course, I could not deny that there were very important differences among us. But we have to distinguish between matters that are important and matters that are of the essence of the Christian faith.

At Saint Andrew's, the church where I minister, we have frequent membership classes. These classes usually include some people coming from Baptist traditions, and their big question is, "Why do you baptize babies here?" Manifestly, the Presbyterian tradition and the Baptist tradition cannot both be right. Either God is pleased with the baptism of infants or He is not pleased. One tradition has it right and one has it wrong. An issue like that is important, because both sides obviously want to please God, but they differ on what does please Him. However, I do not believe that this issue is of the essence of Christianity. We can come down on different sides of this issue and both be redeemed, both be in the kingdom of God, both be justified and adopted into the family of God.

Sadly, I know people who will not tolerate any deviation from their theology. If someone differs at any point, whether it is over baptism, art, justification, predestination, or myriad other issues, that person must not be truly saved. That's not just foolishness, it is sinfulness. To assume that all differences divide us ultimately is nonsense. At the other end of the spectrum are those people who say no difference is essential, that it does not matter what we believe as long as we are sincere. This attitude denies that there is ultimate truth, which is dangerous in the extreme.

The New Testament calls us to recognize the difference between essential issues and nonessential issues. Jesus had to teach His disciples this truth and help them see that this exorcist was not sinning by not following the disciples.

There are many people who do not worship the way we do, who do not share the same confession of faith that we have, who interpret biblical passages very differently, yet they are ministering in the name of Jesus. We have to appreciate and embrace authentic ministry wherever we find it. We also have to distance ourselves from heresy whenever we find it. Simply put, we need discernment.

After years with Jesus, the disciples were still lacking discernment; thus, it is clearly not something that can be developed quickly. However, a good place to start is to appreciate everything that is done in the name of Jesus. Even those who give a cup of cold water to someone who is thirsty are recognized by Jesus if they do it in His name. That does not mean that we get into the kingdom by giving a cup of water to someone, but Christ knows and appreciates any time He is honored. In the case of the disciples, it was imperative for Jesus to get these points across if they were to understand what was waiting for them in Jerusalem.

31

THE PLACE
OF TORMENT

Mark 9:42–50

———⟨⟩———

"But whoever causes one of these little ones who believe in Me to stumble, it would
be better for him if a millstone were hung around his neck, and he were thrown into
the sea. If your hand causes you to sin, cut it off. It is better for you to enter into life
maimed, rather than having two hands, to go to hell, into the fire that shall never be
quenched—where 'Their worm does not die and the fire is not quenched.' And if your
foot causes you to sin, cut it off. It is better for you to enter life lame, rather than having
two feet, to be cast into hell, into the fire that shall never be quenched—where 'Their
worm does not die and the fire is not quenched.' And if your eye causes you to sin, pluck
it out. It is better for you to enter the kingdom of God with one eye, rather than having
two eyes, to be cast into hell fire—where 'Their worm does not die and the fire is not
quenched.' For everyone will be seasoned with fire, and every sacrifice will be seasoned
with salt. Salt is good, but if the salt loses its flavor, how will you season it? Have salt in
yourselves, and have peace with one another."

It seems evident that before the Gospels were written down, there was a
body of what is called *logia*, an oral tradition among the Apostles that
preserved a record of the words and deeds of Jesus Christ. It is fairly well
established that as Jewish rabbis in Jesus' time imparted their teaching, their

students memorized what was said so that they could recall it and apply it later. All the evidence suggests that Jesus and His disciples followed this pattern, with Jesus teaching the twelve as they walked about and the disciples committing His words to memory. These memories were then passed on to others in the early church, forming a robust oral tradition. Later, the Apostles and their associates had the editorial freedom to draw on this oral tradition and record narratives from Jesus' life in the order that best suited the intent of the various gospels. This is the reason the last portion of Mark 9 contains teachings of Jesus that appear in different contexts in the other Synoptic Gospels. Still, it is Jesus' words themselves, not their locations in the Gospels, that need to be our primary concern.

Mark writes: **"Whoever causes one of these little ones who believe in Me to stumble, it would be better for him if a millstone were hung around his neck, and he were thrown into the sea"** (v. 42). At first glance, these words seem to be a warning against mistreatment of children, but that is not the case. When Jesus spoke of "little ones," He was referring to ordinary believers, adult Christians who are not sophisticated in their learning but seek to be faithful and obedient to Jesus with childlike faith. Jesus warned that if people who are puffed up with knowledge or with their status in the church arrogantly cause simple Christians to stumble, they expose themselves to great chastisement from the Lord.

He showed how serious this matter was in His eyes by making a terrifying comparison—it would be *better* for such a puffed-up person to be dragged to the bottom of the sea by a millstone hung about his neck than to make a believer stumble. Ancient Israel was an agrarian society, and some of the most important crops were grains. That grain was ground by a millstone to produce flour. A typical millstone was so big and so heavy that animals were used to turn it; no human being was strong enough to do so, with the notable exception of Samson, who was forced to turn the millstone in the prison of the Philistines (Judg. 16:21). However, Jesus said those who caused believers to stumble would be guilty of such a severe sin that it would be a lesser judgment to have such a heavy stone attached to one's neck and to be thrown into the sea, the place of terror and chaos in Jewish poetry. To say the least, this was a strong metaphor that conveyed Jesus' point with great force.

This warning puts an awesome burden on leaders in the church; pastors, teachers, and others in positions of authority need to be quite careful not to make simple Christians stumble in their faith. Unfortunately, many today do not seem to heed this warning. Every day in our seminaries and our ostensible Christian colleges, students come in excited about Christianity, only to find their faith systematically attacked day in and day out in the classroom. I had this experience as a college freshman and then again when I went to seminary, where the professors told us that if we believed in the substitutionary atonement of Christ, we were fools. We saw the orthodox faith systematically attacked every single day. I dread to think of the future of those teachers and leaders who go about this task of trying to undermine the faith of believers in Christ.

Warnings about Hell

Jesus went on to give an even more striking series of warnings. He said: **"If your hand causes you to sin, cut it off. It is better for you to enter into life maimed, rather than having two hands, to go to hell, into the fire that shall never be quenched"** (v. 43). Here, again, Jesus made a point by use of a comparison—it is better to cut off one's own hand than to sin with that hand and go to hell. In like manner, He said, **"If your foot causes you to sin, cut it off. It is better for you to enter life lame, rather than having two feet, to be cast into hell"** (v. 45a), and **"If your eye causes you to sin, pluck it out. It is better for you to enter the kingdom of God with one eye, rather than having two eyes, to be cast into hell fire"** (v. 47).

We need to understand some background facts in order to appreciate how these words impacted Jesus' original hearers. The Old Testament declared that it was a serious sin for people to disfigure their bodies (Lev. 19:28). Unlike the Greeks, who despised all things physical, the Jews placed a high value on the body. In the Jewish mind, the hands, feet, eyes, and other body parts were gifts of God to be enjoyed in this life; they were regarded as precious possessions. Yet Jesus said it would be better to cut off one's own hand than to go to hell with it intact. Jesus clearly was telling His hearers that bodily disfigurement is better than spending eternity in hell, and that whatever is most precious to us is not worth having compared with the kingdom of God. Simply put, the worst calamity that can befall any human being is to go to hell.

In former generations, preachers often delivered fire-and-brimstone sermons warning their flocks about the danger of going to hell. But in the twenty-first century, the doctrine of hell has all but disappeared from Christian preaching. If it is discussed, it is often watered down to such a degree that people no longer fear going to hell. Jonathan Edwards, who was an expert on this subject, said that impenitent sinners constantly assure themselves that they will escape the judgment of God. This complacency is exacerbated by God's patience. Instead of leading men to repentance, it breeds in some a false sense of security. They think, "God hasn't punished me yet, so obviously all the talk about everlasting punishment is just a scare tactic with no correspondence to reality."

Many Christians would be surprised to learn that no one in the Bible talked more about hell than Jesus. Even though He is popularly regarded as a fount of love and mercy, Jesus is the source of much of the biblical information about the doctrine of hell. Not only that, Jesus talked more about hell than He talked about heaven. I can only guess the reason for that, but it may be that we would scarcely believe His teaching about hell if it came from anyone else. Sadly, we hardly believe it even when it comes from Jesus.

We often glibly describe calamitous earthly situations in terms of hell. People who have been exposed to warfare often say, "War is hell." Likewise, people who have been through afflictions sometimes say, "My life has been hell on earth." I certainly do not want to discount the horrors of war and the suffering of any person, but those who make such comments do not have a clue about the reality of hell. The person who is enduring the worst suffering in the world right now still enjoys a large measure of grace from the hand of God. By contrast, the person in hell is totally removed from the mercy of God, and that is an experience that I would not wish on anyone.

People often ask me whether I believe hell is a literal lake of fire, as it is described in the book of Revelation (19:20; 20:10, 14, 15; 21:8). I usually tell them that I doubt it, and I can always sense their relief. However, I think their relief is premature. The Bible uses a number of ghastly images for eternal punishment, of which the lake of fire is only one. However, in most cases when we use symbolic or figurative language, the reality that we are describing is more intense than the symbol, and that is the case with the symbolic language the Bible employs for hell. Frankly, I would not be surprised to learn that a sinner in hell would do anything possible to trade his circumstances for a lake of fire.

Others ask me, "Is hell simply the absence of God?" Admittedly, it is a dreadful thing to be totally separated from God. On the other hand, there is nothing the sinner in hell would prefer to separation from God. The condemned sinner hates God and wants nothing to do with Him. What makes hell so terrible for the condemned is that God *is* there. He is there in His wrath. It is a dreadful thing to fall into the hands of the living God (Heb. 10:31).

There has been a small movement in the evangelical world over the past twenty years to discount hell in favor of the doctrine of annihilation. This doctrine says that when a sinner who is not redeemed draws his last breath, he is blotted out of existence. His punishment consists of missing the great joy of everlasting life in the presence of God and Christ. However, he endures no ongoing punishment after death. In my opinion, if this doctrine is true, there is a very real sense in which unrepentant sinners get away with their cosmic rebellion against God in their earthly lives.

Over against that view is the biblical idea that hell has no ending point in time, that the punishment goes on forever. I have to admit, I struggle with that. I can hardly contemplate such a dreadful thing. I cringe when I hear people ask, "How can God be good if He allows people to suffer His punishment forever?" The answer, of course, is that one of the reasons God is good is because He is holy, and He does not overlook human sin. Therefore, as much as I struggle with the idea of hell, if God spoke to me and told me that hell is my destiny, I would have no right to complain. Of course, I would be devastated and terrified, but I know that if God sent me there, He would be perfectly just in doing so. That is why I cling to the cross; it is my only hope to escape the wrath that is to come.

The Torments of Hell

As Jesus issued His warnings about hell, He used a refrain three times. Quoting Isaiah 66:24, He said hell is a place where **"Their worm does not die and the fire is not quenched"** (vv. 44, 46, 48). This is symbolic language that paints a picture of ceaseless torment, but it has an interesting and instructive connection to Jewish history.

In ancient Israel, during the reigns of Kings Ahaz and Manasseh in the southern kingdom of Judah, the people became involved in one of the worst of all pagan practices—the sacrifice of children to the pagan deity Molech. These sacrifices occurred in a deep ravine south of Jerusalem. That ravine came to be called Gehenna, an English transliteration of the Greek form of an Aramaic word. This practice of sacrificing children was roundly condemned by the prophet Jeremiah and was finally halted by King Josiah. To make sure it did not begin again, Josiah sought to desecrate the ravine where these sacrifices were made by turning it into the city garbage dump. The refuse from the city, including the carcasses of animals and even the corpses of criminals, was carted out on a regular basis and tossed into this massive garbage dump. To keep the dump from overflowing, the refuse there was burned, with the fires constantly fed by incoming garbage. Meanwhile, worms stayed busy devouring the carcasses of the animals and criminals that were dumped in Gehenna. Thus, the imagery in Isaiah 66 is a picture of this terrible place. Eventually, Gehenna became a Jewish metaphor for the place of final punishment.

We have to understand these metaphors in terms of physical pain. The Bible teaches not only the resurrection of the bodies of the saints but the resurrection of the bodies of the damned, that they may be fit to receive their everlasting punishment in hell in a physical state. In hell, the worm does not die because the host is never consumed. In hell, the fire is never quenched, meaning the torment is constant. Hell, then, is a place of searing, unceasing pain.

By use of these ghastly images, Jesus made it plain that hell is a terrible place. Indeed, it is far better to cut off one's hand, cut off one's foot, or pluck out one's eye than to go to that place. There is nothing worse than the abode of the damned. By the same token, of course, there is no place more wonderful, more blessed, than the abode of the redeemed, the kingdom of God.

Have you ever asked yourself where you will be a hundred years from now? You will be somewhere and you will be conscious. You will either be among the damned or in the state where joy never ends and felicity is never dampened, where your eyes will behold the beautiful vision of the loveliness of Christ forever. If it takes the loss of a hand, a foot, or an eye to make sure you are there, the trade is worth it many times over.

32

MARRIAGE
AND DIVORCE

Mark 10:1–12

⬱

Then He arose from there and came to the region of Judea by the other side of the Jordan. And multitudes gathered to Him again, and as He was accustomed, He taught them again. The Pharisees came and asked Him, "Is it lawful for a man to divorce his wife?" testing Him. And He answered and said to them, "What did Moses command you?" They said, "Moses permitted a man to write a certificate of divorce, and to dismiss her." And Jesus answered and said to them, "Because of the hardness of your heart he wrote you this precept. But from the beginning of the creation, God 'made them male and female.' 'For this reason a man shall leave his father and mother and be joined to his wife, and the two shall become one flesh'; so then they are no longer two, but one flesh. Therefore what God has joined together, let not man separate." In the house His disciples also asked Him again about the same matter. So He said to them, "Whoever divorces his wife and marries another commits adultery against her. And if a woman divorces her husband and marries another, she commits adultery."

In the mid-twentieth century, the Harvard sociologist Pitirim Sorokin wrote a book in which he sounded an alarm about the impending disintegration of American culture and civilization. The central concern of Sorokin's book was the radical proliferation of divorce and the breakup of the American home between 1910 and 1948. He pointed out that in 1910, 10 percent of U.S. marriages ended in divorce, but that number rose to 25 percent in 1948. Sorokin, speaking as a historian of culture, said that no civilization can long survive when one-fourth of its marriage units are disintegrating.

Of course, the situation has only grown worse since Sorokin wrote. Now the divorce rate in America is more than 50 percent. It is so high that for the first time in American history, and arguably even in Western history, masses of young people are repudiating the institution of marriage altogether and are opting to cohabit without a marriage contract to unite them. Cohabitation is now commonplace, and there are no societal sanctions against the practice. It is a matter of course, even among professing believers. This is not how it should be. When Christian men and women choose to cohabit outside the institution of marriage, they commit a gross and heinous sin against God, something that should be absolutely unheard of in the Christian community. As Christians, we are called to take our cues from the Word of God, not from the culture around us. We are called to march to a different drummer.

Even though divorce has become widespread only in the past century or so, it has been a flashpoint for controversy for ages, as we see in the first few verses of Mark 10. The Pharisees, looking for an opportunity to condemn Jesus, seized on the issue of divorce to test Him.

The Pharisees Set a Trap

Jesus continued His march toward Jerusalem, where He knew He would be betrayed and executed. Mark tells us, **He arose from there and came to the region of Judea by the other side of the Jordan** (v. 1a). He left Capernaum (9:33) on the shores of the Sea of Galilee and went south, entering Judea on "the other side of the Jordan," that is, the eastern side, the area where John the Baptist had administered baptism. Even there in Judea, **multitudes gathered to Him again, and as He was accustomed, He taught them again** (v. 1b). Jesus' fame was not confined to Galilee, where, as we have seen, He attracted such enormous crowds He could hardly move. Even in Judea, well to the south, He was well known and sought after.

By moving into Judea, the region around Jerusalem, Jesus moved closer to the epicenter of Pharisaic opposition to His ministry. Scribes and Pharisees had journeyed north to observe Him as rumors of His ministry drifted down to Jerusalem (3:22; 7:1), so they were ready when He came onto their home turf. Mark tells us: **The Pharisees came and asked Him, "Is it lawful for a man to divorce his wife?" testing Him** (v. 2). The Pharisees did not come to Jesus because they wanted to know His views on marriage and divorce. Mark informs us that they brought this question to test Him or, rather, to trap Him. But what was the nature of the trap?

I see two possibilities. On the one hand, if Jesus replied that it was not lawful for a man to divorce his wife and to marry another, He would place Himself in opposition to Herod Antipas, who had done just that and who had been confronted by John the Baptist (see Matt. 14:1–12). For speaking out against the tetrarch's adultery and divorce, John the Baptist was imprisoned and eventually executed. Thus, if Jesus said divorce and remarriage were not permissible, that message would go straight back to Herod, and the Pharisees could then hope that the same fate that befell John the Baptist might befall Jesus. I think that is the more likely possibility.

On the other hand, the Pharisees may have been setting a theological trap. At that time, there was an ongoing theological controversy among the rabbis concerning marriage and divorce, a dispute that had to do with the understanding of Old Testament legislation with respect to divorce. We read in Deuteronomy:

> When a man takes a wife and marries her, and it happens that she finds no favor in his eyes because he has found some uncleanness in her, and he writes her a certificate of divorce, puts it in her hand, and sends her out of his house, when she has departed from his house, and goes and becomes another man's wife, if the latter husband detests her and writes her a certificate of divorce, puts it in her hand, and sends her out of his house, or if the latter husband dies who took her as his wife, then her former husband who divorced her must not take her back to be his wife after she has been defiled; for that is an abomination before the LORD. (24:1–4a)

Here God sets forth certain rules in the matter of divorce, and He says that the violation of these rules is an "abomination" in His sight. But the rabbis disagreed as to the nature of the "uncleanness" or the "unclean thing" in the woman that could serve as the grounds for the husband to divorce her. This text does not specifically say that the uncleanness is adultery. Indeed, the law very clearly stipulated a penalty for adultery—execution (Lev. 20:10). If a man's wife committed adultery, he did not have to bother with a divorce. He could just have her stoned to death. This provision of the law was still practiced at the time of Jesus' birth, and Joseph could have had Mary stoned for becoming pregnant before the consummation of their betrothal. However, he wanted to be merciful to her, so he thought of divorcing her quietly, so that the scandal of alleged adultery would not accompany her name (Matt. 1:18–19). So, divorce was an option in that situation. However, the passage in Deuteronomy seems to have something else in view.

There were two schools of thought among the rabbis—the conservatives and the liberals (just as there are always conservatives and liberals when it comes to interpreting the Word of God). The Shammai school, the conservatives, argued that the only thing that would justify a divorce was a shameful act of sexual infidelity. Anything less than that was not grounds for divorce, and the couple, even though they might be bitter and unhappy, had to stay together. The Hillel school, the liberals, took a much broader view of the uncleanness mentioned in Deuteronomy 24. They said it referred to anything a woman did that embarrassed, disgraced, or merely displeased her husband. Thus, the Hillel school permitted divorce on virtually any ground. By Jesus' time, the prevailing view was that of the Hillel school, which was why Herod Antipas was able to get away with his illegitimate divorce.

So, what was the possible nature of the Pharisees' theological trap? If Jesus sided with the liberal school, suddenly the Pharisees would become conservatives and say Jesus was going against the law of Moses. If He sided with the conservatives, they would say He was going against public opinion. There was no way Jesus could win, no matter how He answered the Pharisees.

Jesus Interprets Deuteronomy

Jesus, of course, was never very concerned about public opinion or about appeasing theologians or politicians. His food was to do the will of the Father (John 4:34), and He was concerned for truth and holiness, Therefore, **He answered and said to them, "What did Moses command you?"** (v. 3). His first order of business was to point the Pharisees back to the Word of God. In reply, **They said, "Moses permitted a man to write a certificate of divorce, and to dismiss her"** (v. 4). This was how the Pharisees interpreted the directives in Deuteronomy 24, a very inadequate understanding. Jesus had to show them how that passage was meant to be understood.

Mark writes: **And Jesus answered and said to them, "Because of the hardness of your heart he wrote you this precept. But from the beginning of the creation, God 'made them male and female.' 'For this reason a man shall leave his father and mother and be joined to his wife, and the two shall become one flesh'; so then they are no longer two, but one flesh. Therefore what God has joined together, let not man separate"** (vv. 5–9). Jesus declared that Moses' words about divorce were not a command or even an enumerated liberty, but a divine concession because of human hardness of heart. He then referenced the institution of marriage in Genesis, reminding the Pharisees that God made both men and women, infusing both genders with dignity, and that God Himself instituted marriage, sanctifying the relationship.

Then, in plain terms, He gave His conclusion: "What God has joined together, let not man separate."

This declaration is so simple and direct, we might expect the Christian church to be completely united in its view of marriage and divorce. Would that it were so. Unfortunately, conservatives and liberals in the church are battling today over the question of divorce and over what exactly Jesus meant when He uttered these words.

Many churches and theologians today do not permit divorce on any grounds. They often cite this passage, declaring that Jesus overruled Moses' concession to human hardness of heart and absolutely banned divorce. Marriage, they say, is to be forever, for Jesus restored the original view of marriage, removing all provisions for divorce.

That would be a sound understanding of Jesus' words except for the parallel text in Matthew's gospel, where we find an expanded version of Jesus' answer. According to Matthew, He told the Pharisees: "Moses, because of the hardness of your hearts, permitted you to divorce your wives, but from the beginning it was not so. And I say to you, whoever divorces his wife, except for sexual immorality, and marries another, commits adultery; and whoever marries her who is divorced commits adultery" (19:8–9). Here Jesus uttered what is known as "the exceptive clause," by which He permitted divorce but defined the grounds on which it was permissible. The only permissible ground for divorce, He said, is "sexual immorality." That was Jesus' interpretation of the "uncleanness" of Deuteronomy 24.

So, most churches historically have allowed divorce on the grounds of sexual immorality. Many of these churches have defined sexual immorality strictly in terms of adultery, marital infidelity. The only other ground for divorce for which biblical teaching is cited is desertion of a Christian by a non-Christian (1 Cor. 7:15).

What exactly did Jesus mean by "sexual immorality"? That question is difficult to answer. The Greek word that is translated as "sexual immorality" is *porneia*, from which we get the English word *pornography*. Scholars are divided over the precise meaning of this term. Many believe that *porneia* is simply a synonym for adultery. Other scholars argue that it encompasses more than adultery and should be understood as referring to a wide variety of sexual sins.

So, if a man commits adultery and his wife finds out about it, and if the husband repents in tears and begs for forgiveness, is the wife obligated to remain in the marriage? I would venture to say that 99 percent of evangelical Christians would answer that question by saying, "Yes, the wife must not divorce her husband." I disagree. I think that if the husband repents, the wife is obligated to receive him as a brother in Christ, but not as a husband, because God gave the provision for ending a marriage if the trust that is at the very heart and foundation of the marital union is violated. Sometimes the church and individual believers put heat on people whose marriages are in crisis, exhorting them that it is not right for them to divorce. I think that is wrong. We cannot take away rights Jesus gives to His people. Likewise, we sometimes say, "Okay, you're allowed to get a divorce, but I think you should take the higher ground and stay." In that case, we are subtly pressuring the spouses by putting a guilt trip on them, even though God has given them clearance to divorce.

Of course, we have the opposite problem today—there is too much freedom, with people in the church divorcing for reasons the Bible does not recognize. That God allows us to end our marriages when they are violated by sexual immorality is an amazing concession to human sin, but that concession does not go so far as no-fault divorce or divorce on the grounds of incompatibility.

The Need for Wisdom and Compassion

The application of this teaching of Jesus in the life of the church is not easy. I wish every church had a group of experts on biblical ethics that could study every individual case and give a judgment, because I have never seen two cases that are the same. Church leaders need the wisdom of Solomon to apply these principles to real-life situations.

Even more than that, we should be doing everything in our power to prepare our children to be good spouses and to strengthen existing marriages. We have lost touch with something that God has called holy, a gift from His hand that is at the very foundation of human society. Though the whole world should set aside the institution of marriage, let every Christian determine to be committed to the sacred bonds of matrimony.

Finally, we must not forget the vital role of the gospel in these matters. Anyone who has been through an illegitimate divorce or sinned sexually against his or her spouse needs to know that these are not unforgivable sins. These sins are what sent Christ to the cross, and all who put their trust in Him are forgiven. The kingdom of God is not closed to those who are divorced, and all of us in the church should be quick to share this good news with those whose marriages have failed or are hurting.

33

THE KEY
TO ETERNAL LIFE

Mark 10:13–22

～

Then they brought little children to Him, that He might touch them; but the disciples rebuked those who brought them. But when Jesus saw it, He was greatly displeased and said to them, "Let the little children come to Me, and do not forbid them; for of such is the kingdom of God. Assuredly, I say to you, whoever does not receive the kingdom of God as a little child will by no means enter it." And He took them up in His arms, laid His hands on them, and blessed them. Now as He was going out on the road, one came running, knelt before Him, and asked Him, "Good Teacher, what shall I do that I may inherit eternal life?" So Jesus said to him, "Why do you call Me good? No one is good but One, that is, God. You know the commandments: 'Do not commit adultery,' 'Do not murder,' 'Do not steal,' 'Do not bear false witness,' 'Do not defraud,' 'Honor your father and your mother.'" And he answered and said to Him, "Teacher, all these things I have kept from my youth." Then Jesus, looking at him, loved him, and said to him, "One thing you lack: Go your way, sell whatever you have and give to the poor, and you will have treasure in heaven; and come, take up the cross, and follow Me." But he was sad at this word, and went away sorrowful, for he had great possessions.

The Reformation Park in the old city of Geneva, Switzerland, is adorned by the Reformation Wall, which includes statues and bas-reliefs of several of the magisterial Reformers. On either side of the central statues is carved the motto of the sixteenth-century Protestant Reformation, *Post Tenebras Lux*, which means "After darkness, light." That motto was adopted because it so well expressed what the Reformation achieved—the recovery of the gospel in its purity after it had been hidden for centuries by accretions of man-made traditions in the church. In the final analysis, the Reformation was not about the church's authority, about worship, or about the virgin Mary. It was about the gospel, specifically the doctrine of justification by faith alone, which Martin Luther described as the article on which the church stands or falls.

This doctrine answers the question, "What must we do to be saved?" This, of course, is an age-old question, and we see it voiced yet again in the passage we are considering in this chapter, wherein we read of Jesus' interaction with the man so often described as the rich young ruler. But even before Jesus dealt with this man, He touched on the manner in which we are saved as He received and blessed a number of children.

Jesus Receives Little Children

Mark tells us, **Then they brought little children to Him, that He might touch them; but the disciples rebuked those who brought them** (v. 13). Repeatedly throughout Mark, we have seen people begging Jesus for His touch or else actively seeking to touch Him. One day, some parents brought their children for Him to touch. We are not told that these children had any specific needs, such as medical problems for which they needed healing. It appears they were healthy and the parents simply wanted Jesus to touch them for the sake of His blessing.

Jesus' disciples were not pleased by what these parents were doing, so they sought to prevent the parents from getting to Jesus. Perhaps they simply wanted to protect Jesus' time, so that He could minister to the people they regarded as most needy. They were so strongly displeased they actually rebuked the parents for seeking to impose on Jesus' time so frivolously.

However, Mark writes: **But when Jesus saw it, He was greatly displeased and said to them, "Let the little children come to Me, and do not forbid them; for of such is the kingdom of God. Assuredly, I say to you, whoever does not receive the kingdom of God as a little child will by no means enter it." And He took them up in His arms, laid His hands on them, and blessed them** (vv. 14–16). Somehow Jesus detected that the disciples were limiting access to Him, and He was "greatly displeased." The Greek word Mark uses here means "indignant," which is a state of anger that is aroused by injustice. He forcefully directed the disciples *not* to prevent the children from coming to Him, for, He said, "of such is the kingdom of God."

What did Jesus mean by this curious statement? Was He saying that all children are saved or that children are more naturally drawn to the things of God? No. Jesus Himself gave the best clue to His meaning in His next sentence: "Assuredly, I say to you, whoever does not receive the kingdom of God as a little child will by no means enter it." Most evangelical commentators believe Jesus was saying that we must trust in Christ with simple, childlike faith if we are to be saved. So, Jesus received the children and blessed them.

Jesus Counsels a Ruler of the Jews

Mark then writes, **Now as He was going out on the road, one came running, knelt before Him, and asked Him, "Good Teacher, what shall I do that I may inherit eternal life?"** (v. 17). Obviously, this man was no disinterested bystander at one of Jesus' public orations. A question was burning in his soul: "What must I do to gain eternal life?" So, He came to Jesus eagerly. He came willingly. He came respectfully, falling on his knees before Jesus. Then, when he spoke to our Lord, he used a form of address that was unusual but clearly was intended to show honor: "Good Teacher" or "Good Rabbi."

Those who held the office of rabbi in the Jewish community were regarded as distinguished and honorable men. It was the custom of the Jews that whenever a father, the patriarch of his family, entered a room, his children would stand out of respect for him. However, so great was the Jewish respect for the office of rabbi, if a man who was a rabbi entered a room, even his father would stand out of respect for him because of his elevated office. This cultural attitude explains the great respect with which the rich young ruler came to Jesus.

This man had a question for Jesus: "Good Teacher, what shall I do that I may inherit eternal life?" He had riches and a position of authority even though he was still a young man, but he knew he lacked salvation. However, he came with the typical assumption that there was something he must do, that eternal life must be earned. It seems he was thoroughly infected by the legalism of the scribes and Pharisees.

Jesus gave an interesting answer. He said: **"Why do you call Me good? No one is good but One, that is, God"** (v. 18). Some of the critics of the Christian faith point to this text as manifest evidence that Jesus did not consider Himself sinless, that He recognized there were weaknesses in His character because He disavowed that He was good. However, I am quite convinced Jesus spoke these words with a very different intent. He knew that this man did not know to whom he was asking his question. He knew this man did not know that he was talking to God incarnate. So, Jesus was calling attention to the rich young ruler's superficial understanding of true goodness, a superficial understanding we all share.

We are quick to call one another good without giving thought to what goodness entails. Usually we employ the term *good* in a comparative way. If I say that my dog is a good dog, I do not mean that my dog has a highly refined ethical sense of propriety. I simply mean that, as dogs go, she is fairly well behaved. She comes when I call her. She does not bite the mailman. She is housebroken. So, compared with many dogs, she is a good dog. The same applies when we say that a person is good. We simply mean that, compared with many other people, he or she is a good person.

However, we dare not judge ourselves or others in relation to other human beings. Ultimately, genuine goodness is defined by the character of God, and His character is made manifest in the law. Therefore, we need to judge ourselves against that standard, the standard of the ultimate righteousness of God. When we do so, we very quickly see what the psalmist and then the Apostle Paul declared: "There is none righteous, no, not one; there is none who understands; there is none who seeks after God. They have all turned aside; they have together become unprofitable; there is none who does good, no, not one" (Rom. 3:10b–12; cf. Ps. 14:1–3).

Of course, we see all kinds of self-sacrificial actions among the pagans, acts of what we call civic virtue. People give to good causes, abide by the laws of the land, help one another, pursue justice, and so on. These are good things—in a sense. Even though people do things that correspond to the law of God, He requires that everything we do be motivated by love for Him and a desire to glorify Him. So, God looks not only at our outward conformity to His law, He looks at our hearts. Unfortunately, when He does, He finds not hearts that are wholly committed to honoring Him. So, He can truly say that there is no one who does good, not even one. As Jesus affirmed to the rich young ruler, only God is truly good. It is ironic, then, that this young man called Jesus "good Teacher"; his words were accurate, but he did not understand why.

Jesus Presents Law, Then Gospel

Before Jesus set forth the gospel to this young man, he took him straight to the law: **"You know the commandments: 'Do not commit adultery,' 'Do not murder,' 'Do not steal,' 'Do not bear false witness,' 'Do not defraud,' 'Honor your father and your mother'"** (v. 19). It is interesting that Jesus cited a number of commandments from the second table of the Ten Commandments, those that govern how we relate to one another. In other words, He started with the easy ones, the ones that even the pagans sometimes keep by means of civic virtue. For the moment, He said nothing about the first table of the Ten Commandments, those that govern how we relate to God, which commandments can be kept only by those whose hearts have been regenerated by God's Holy Spirit.

The rich young ruler replied, **"Teacher, all these things I have kept from my youth"** (v. 20). I can almost hear his sigh of relief. It is as if he said: "Is that all I have to do? I have never committed adultery. I have never stolen anything. I have never murdered anyone. I'm not a covetous person. I have kept all these laws since I was a boy." Hearing Jesus refer him to the commandments must have pleased him.

At this point, I would have expected Jesus to say: "My friend, you are sadly mistaken. You haven't kept these commandments since you got out of bed this morning." It is obvious this man had not heard Jesus' Sermon on the Mount, where Jesus explained that even if we refrain from full-orbed adultery but have lust in our hearts, we have broken the law; that even if we have never taken a human life, if we have been angry without cause, we have broken the law against murder; and so on. Jesus revealed that the demands of God's law are far deeper than simple outward obedience. The rich young ruler did not understand that. He had a superficial understanding of the good and a superficial understanding of the law. He harbored the hope within himself that he could earn his way to heaven. In that, he was no different from the vast majority of people who walk this planet today and even the overwhelming majority of people who are in churches on Sunday morning.

The Evangelism Explosion program uses two diagnostic questions to determine where people stand in their relationship to God and to provide an entry point for a presentation of the gospel. One of those questions is: "If you were to die tonight and stand before God, and He were to say to you, 'Why should I let you into My heaven?' what would you say?" When I was training people in the Evangelism Explosion method years ago, I kept track of the answers to that question I heard from people who already were affiliated with churches. Eighty percent of them gave what we call a works-righteousness answer. They said something along these lines: "I have tried to live a good life. I'm not a criminal. I have never murdered anyone. I go to church almost every Sunday. I go to Sunday school. I'm a deacon. I'm an elder." In short, these people were relying on their performance, their good deeds, their obedience to get them to heaven. As I heard these kinds of answers over and over again, it seemed to me that the gospel had not been adequately communicated to people and that once again the doctrine of justification by faith was going into the darkness, just as it had in the centuries before its recovery in the Protestant Reformation.

I was so alarmed by this discovery, I wanted to make sure my family understood the gospel, so I asked my son, who was about five years old at the time, "Son, if you were to die tonight and stand before God, and He were to say to you, 'Why should I let you into My heaven?' what would you say?" He thought that was the easiest question I had ever asked him. He said, "Well, I would say, 'Because I'm dead.'" In our Reformed household, the prevailing understanding of salvation among my children was "justification by death." They had formed the idea that all we have to do to go to heaven is to die. That's the prevailing view in Western culture.

Jesus Has Compassion on a Sinner

Yet, Jesus did not choose to highlight this man's faulty understandings. Mark tells us, **Then Jesus, looking at him, loved him** (v. 21a). Isn't that interesting? This young man dared to say to the Lord of heaven and earth, "I have kept your law since I was a boy," but despite his misplaced self-confidence, Jesus loved him. Why did Jesus react this way? Was it because He was happy to have finally found an Israelite in whom there was no guile, someone who had kept the law scrupulously and therefore had earned Jesus' love? No, of course not. Rather, I think Jesus felt compassion for the man. I do not believe the rich young ruler was arrogant. He really wanted to know how to inherit eternal life and he really believed that he had kept the law. In short, he was thoroughly lost, and whenever our Lord met people who were as lost as this man, He reacted with compassion. We have already seen several examples of Jesus' compassion in Mark's gospel (1:41; 6:34; 8:2), and I think we are seeing it again here.

Jesus' way of helping the young man was to show him his error by putting his assertion to the test. It was as if Jesus said, "Okay, you say you have kept the law. Let's check it out." He therefore said: **"One thing you lack: Go your way, sell whatever you have and give to the poor, and you will have treasure in heaven; and come, take up the cross, and follow Me"** (v. 21b).

As we think through what Jesus was saying here, we must understand that He was not setting down a universal rule. He was not saying that anyone who wishes to be saved must divest himself of all private property and become an ascetic, living in poverty and self-denial. Rather, He was addressing a specific person with unique heart attitudes.

In a sense, Jesus was taking the rich young ruler to the first table of the Ten Commandments. In essence, He was saying to him: "You say you have kept all of the law. What about the first commandment: 'You shall have no other gods before Me'?" (Ex. 20:3). Jesus knew that money was this man's god. He probably went to synagogue. Maybe he went to temple worship. But all week long, his mind was consumed with questions of wealth. His money ranked ahead of God. As we have seen, Jesus taught that it is to our profit to get rid of anything that keeps us from the kingdom of God, even if it is a hand, foot, or eye (9:43–48). In simple terms, this young man needed to get his priorities right.

When he heard these words, the young man's sigh of relief turned to a groan of despair: **But he was sad at this word, and went away sorrowful, for he had great possessions** (v. 22). The word *sad* is not strong enough. The Greek word Mark uses here communicates several nuances: he was downcast, appalled, shocked, and devastated. So, this one who ran to Jesus walked away from Him in sorrow. Yes, he walked away from *Jesus*. The pearl of great price was standing in front of him, but he turned his back on Him. He was like a man who would not trade a wooden nickel for a billion dollars, and even that is a poor analogy. He thought his own possessions were worth more than Jesus. He preferred his own bank account to the riches of the kingdom of God.

The Bible says the rich young ruler was a wealthy man. In reality, he was bankrupt. That is the condition all men are in naturally; we are all debtors to God who have no hope of paying what we owe. God requires from us that we be holy even as He is holy. The minute we sin, we are infinitely in debt to the righteousness of God. But we keep on sinning, "storing up wrath for [ourselves] on the day of wrath" (Rom. 2:5, ESV).

The tragedy for the rich young ruler was that the answer to his debt problem was standing in front of him. Christ was the only possible debt relief for him. Likewise, He is the only possible debt relief for us, and He is at hand, waiting for us to call on Him for aid. That is what the gospel is about. Christ pays our debt and He gives to us His righteousness, which is the only thing that will satisfy the demands of God's law. By faith, when we put our trust in Christ alone, we receive what we need to get into the kingdom of God. So, we "inherit" eternal life through Christ. Like any inheritance, it is a gift, not a payment that we earn.

34

THE GOD
OF THE POSSIBLE

Mark 10:23–31

Then Jesus looked around and said to His disciples, "How hard it is for those who have riches to enter the kingdom of God!" And the disciples were astonished at His words. But Jesus answered again and said to them, "Children, how hard it is for those who trust in riches to enter the kingdom of God! It is easier for a camel to go through the eye of a needle than for a rich man to enter the kingdom of God." And they were greatly astonished, saying among themselves, "Who then can be saved?" But Jesus looked at them and said, "With men it is impossible, but not with God; for with God all things are possible." Then Peter began to say to Him, "See, we have left all and followed You." So Jesus answered and said, "Assuredly, I say to you, there is no one who has left house or brothers or sisters or father or mother or wife or children or lands, for My sake and the gospel's, who shall not receive a hundredfold now in this time—houses and brothers and sisters and mothers and children and lands, with persecutions—and in the age to come, eternal life. But many who are first will be last, and the last first."

When the rich young ruler turned his back on Jesus and walked away, refusing to cast away the idol of his wealth for the sake of obtaining the pearl of great price, I imagine that Jesus watched him closely, still feeling compassion for him. The young man's unwillingness to part with his riches then prompted Jesus to give His disciples some important instruction about the dangers of material wealth and the things that matter most.

Mark tells us, **Jesus looked around and said to His disciples, "How hard it is for those who have riches to enter the kingdom of God!"** (v. 23). Hearing this, the disciples were astonished (v. 24a), for Old Testament Jews looked on riches as a blessing from God. Therefore, Jesus repeated Himself and expanded on His suggestion that riches can be an obstacle to entering the kingdom of God: **"Children, how hard it is for those who trust in riches to enter the kingdom of God!"** (v. 24b). Note that Jesus changed His words slightly but significantly: in His first comments, He spoke of those who "have riches"; in His second comments, He referred to those who "trust in riches." This small variation is the key to understanding Jesus' warning here.

Four Categories of the Poor

As we begin to unpack these weighty words, let me review the biblical position on wealth and poverty. It is a view we need to understand, particularly in our time, which is saturated by the politics of envy.

We tend to be simplistic about questions involving wealth and poverty. We generally assume that if any person among us is poor, it must be because he is indolent, for only the lazy fall into poverty. From the biblical perspective, that is not always the case. Conversely, we often hold the idea that a person can become wealthy only by means of corruption and exploitation of others, by trampling on the poor and weak to accumulate riches. That, too, is a generalization that does not square with the biblical perspective.

If we look at the words for "poverty" or "the poor" in the Old Testament, we see that there are four distinct types of people who are poor. It is true that the first category is those who are poor because they are lazy. They are poor because they will not work and are irresponsible. The Old Testament looks on these people with disfavor and judgment. Likewise, in the New Testament, it is these of whom Paul speaks when he writes, "If anyone will not work, neither shall he eat" (2 Thess. 3:10).

In the second category are those who are poor because of calamity, illness, natural disasters that ruined their crops, and other events beyond their control. These people receive the compassion of God, and in His law He declares that those who are better off should make provision for these who are poor through no fault of their own.

In the third category are those people who are poor as a direct result of the exploitation of the rich and the powerful. In the Old Testament, the rich and powerful were usually not merchants but rulers and other government officials, such as the pharaoh in Egypt or King Ahab in Israel. These poor people have God as their defender, for He refuses to tolerate the exploitation of the weak by the strong. The exodus of Israel from Egypt was an example of God coming to the aid of those who were exploited as slaves. As believers, we, too, must be defenders of those who face exploitation. James tells us, "Pure and undefiled religion before God and the Father is this: to visit orphans and widows in their trouble, and to keep oneself unspotted from the world" (1:27).

In the fourth category are those who are poor for righteousness' sake; that is, they willingly embrace poverty that they might devote themselves to spiritual things and not be distracted by the pursuit of wealth.

The most fundamental truth about wealth, according to the Bible, is that "every good gift and every perfect gift is from above, and comes down from the Father of lights" (James 1:17). There is no such thing as a bootstrap ethic in the Bible. No one pulls himself up by his own bootstraps apart from the grace of God. Everything that we have comes to us from His bounty and from His goodness. For this reason, God cares deeply about what we trust and what we do with that which He entrusts to us.

If we put our confidence in material wealth, we are trusting in something that cannot possibly redeem us. Jesus warned people against trying to serve God and mammon (Matt. 6:24), and against storing up riches in this world, where thieves break in and steal, and moths and rust destroy. Instead, we should seek to stockpile treasure in heaven (vv. 19–21).

The Camel and the Needle's Eye

Jesus used a strange aphorism in speaking about these things: **"It is easier for a camel to go through the eye of a needle than for a rich man to enter the kingdom of God"** (v. 25). Around the ninth century, a legend developed that Jesus was talking about an obscure point of entry to the walled city of Jerusalem, a small "gate" called the Eye of the Needle. Jerusalem had several gates in its wall, and each of the gates had a name, such as the East Gate, the West Gate, or the Dung Gate. All of these were traditional city gates, but the Eye of the Needle was a small opening in the wall. If a merchant was leading a camel and wished to enter the city through the Eye of the Needle, he had to force the camel to bend its knees. Then, in that awkward position, with much pushing and shoving, the camel could just squeeze through.

It is a nice story, making the point that rich people can get into the kingdom of heaven only on their knees, but there is no mention of such a gate in Jerusalem until long after Jesus' time, so the story is very iffy. I believe Jesus was simply using hyperbole by raising the ridiculous possibility of one of the largest commonly known animals of His time passing through what all of His hearers knew to be a very small opening. His point was that it can be very hard for the rich to enter the kingdom of heaven because they are so strongly tempted to rely on their wealth rather than God to provide for and protect them, even unto eternity.

We who are Americans need to heed our Lord's warning at this point because we are the most prosperous people in the history of the world. Even some who would be classified as poor in America have a better standard of living than some kings had two hundred years ago. The wealth with which we have been blessed by God can become a snare to us, so we need to think about the eye of the needle and take stock every now and then of where our hearts are.

The disciples were flabbergasted by these statements from Jesus. Mark writes: **They were greatly astonished, saying among themselves, "Who then can be saved?" But Jesus looked at them and said, "With men it is impossible, but not with God; for with God all things are possible"** (vv. 26–27). The disciples, again reflecting the Jewish belief that the rich were blessed of God, asked a question out of their astonishment: "Who then can be saved?" Jesus answered them with one of the great statements in all of Scripture: "With men it is impossible, but not with God; for with God all things are possible." Humanly speaking, no one can be saved. But with God, salvation is possible even for the one who has entrusted himself wholeheartedly to material wealth. It may be difficult, but the Holy Spirit intervenes in the lives of people and cuts through the hardness of their hearts. By God's power and grace, a camel *can* go through the eye of a needle, in a manner of speaking.

The Bible gives us examples of men who were both wealthy and faithful, men who trusted God, not their riches. Abraham, for example, was both the father of the faithful and one of the richest men in the world in antiquity (Gen. 13:2). His riches may have been exceeded by those of Job (1:3). Later, in the New Testament, we read of Joseph of Arimathea, who also was a wealthy man (Matt. 27:57). All three men are good examples of the proper way to handle wealth.

Abraham's wealth lay in his vast herds and flocks of livestock. His nephew, Lot, was also quite wealthy in this way, but his attitude toward his wealth was quite different from his uncle's. At one point, it became difficult for the herdsmen for all these flocks to find adequate grazing land, and there were clashes between the servants of the two masters. It was so serious that Abraham said to Lot: "Is not the whole land before you? Please separate from me. If you take the left, then I will go to the right; or, if you go to the right, then I will go to the left" (Gen. 13:9). The land was all Abraham's by divine gift, but he was willing to share it with his nephew to keep the peace. Lot surveyed the land

and saw the rich, well-watered Jordan Valley, so he chose to go there. He moved his family to Sodom, which was a fantastic place to raise cattle, but a terrible place to raise a family, as Lot found out. Abraham, true to his word, kept his flocks in the hills. As wealthy as he was, he counted his family, his faith, and his integrity of much greater value than his cattle.

Job was fabulously wealthy by ancient standards. When God said to Satan, "Have you considered My servant Job, that there is none like him on the earth, a blameless and upright man, one who fears God and shuns evil?" (1:8), Satan scoffed. He said: "Does Job fear God for nothing. Have You not made a hedge around him, around his household, and around all that he has on every side. You have blessed the work of his hands, and his possessions have increased in the land. But now, stretch out Your hand and touch all that he has, and he will surely curse You to Your face!" (vv. 9–11). God allowed Satan to unleash a reign of terror on Job, his family, his livestock, and everything that was precious and dear to him. However, Job cried out, "Though He slay me, yet will I trust Him" (13:15). Job did not trust in his wealth. He trusted in his Redeemer.

Joseph of Arimathea is almost unknown to history. He is mentioned in all four Gospels but nowhere else in the New Testament. The Gospels agree that he was both wealthy and a disciple of Jesus. He is remembered in the Christian world for what he did with his wealth, for donating a highly expensive sepulcher so that the body of the Lord Jesus Christ might be buried in dignity. In other words, he is remembered not for what he had, but for what he gave to the Lord Jesus Christ. His priorities were in their proper order.

Letting Goods and Kindred Go

Peter then said, **"See, we have left all and followed You"** (v. 28). The ever-impetuous Peter spoke up, almost as if he felt Jesus was rebuking him for retaining some wealth from his family business. Jesus replied, **"Assuredly, I say to you, there is no one who has left house or brothers or sisters or father or mother or wife or children or lands, for My sake and the gospel's, who shall not receive a hundredfold now in this time—houses and brothers and sisters and mothers and children and lands, with persecutions—and in the age to come, eternal life. But many who are first will be last, and the last first"** (vv. 29–31).

Years ago, I became involved in a particularly furious theological battle, and it cost me a number of friends, friends who were very important to me. I became quite depressed about it. But one night, in the midst of that controversy, I thought of one of the lines in Martin Luther's great hymn, "A Mighty Fortress Is Our God." That line says, "Let goods and kindred go, this mortal life also."

This is what Jesus calls us to do. He said, "No one, having put his hand to the plow, and looking back, is fit for the kingdom of God" (Luke 9:62). We are to let all our material goods go (in terms of trusting them) and never look back. We are to look to Him, being willing to forsake all other things in this world for Him.

Jesus gave Peter a tremendous promise, one that applies to us, too. If we are willing to give up all for Him, we will receive a hundredfold more in return. Jesus says: "You cannot leave these things for Me without My taking notice. What you leave, I will replace a hundredfold." Yes, Jesus acknowledges that following Him will bring persecution, but we will have the pearl of great price and eternal life.

In the end, there will be surprises in the kingdom. Some who are now first—the rich, the powerful, the beautiful—will be last, while the lowly in this life—the poor, the weak, the undesirable—will be first. In that kingdom, the only thing that will matter is faithfulness to Christ.

35

TRUE GREATNESS

Mark 10:32–45

Now they were on the road, going up to Jerusalem, and Jesus was going before them; and they were amazed. And as they followed they were afraid. Then He took the twelve aside again and began to tell them the things that would happen to Him: "Behold, we are going up to Jerusalem, and the Son of Man will be betrayed to the chief priests and to the scribes; and they will condemn Him to death and deliver Him to the Gentiles; and they will mock Him, and scourge Him, and spit on Him, and kill Him. And the third day He will rise again." Then James and John, the sons of Zebedee, came to Him, saying, "Teacher, we want You to do for us whatever we ask." And He said to them, "What do you want Me to do for you?" They said to Him, "Grant us that we may sit, one on Your right hand and the other on Your left, in Your glory." But Jesus said to them, "You do not know what you ask. Are you able to drink the cup that I drink, and be baptized with the baptism that I am baptized with?" They said to Him, "We are able." So Jesus said to them, "You will indeed drink the cup that I drink, and with the baptism I am baptized with you will be baptized; but to sit on My right hand and on My left is not Mine to give, but it is for those for whom it is prepared." And when the ten heard it, they began to be greatly displeased with James and John. But Jesus called them to Himself and said to them, "You know that those who are considered rulers over the Gentiles lord it over them, and their great ones exercise authority over them. Yet it shall not be so among you; but whoever desires to become great among you shall be your servant. And whoever of you desires to be first shall be slave of all. For even the Son of Man did not come to be served, but to serve, and to give His life a ransom for many."

Throughout the gospel of Mark, we have seen frequent instances of astonishment and amazement over the things Jesus said and did. Various people were astonished at Jesus' teaching (1:22; 6:2) and at His power to heal (2:12; 7:37), to raise the dead (5:42), and to calm the wind (6:51). We can understand how these activities would produce astonishment. In Mark 10:32, however, we encounter another example of amazement, this time among the disciples, but in this instance, the reason for their amazement is not readily apparent.

Mark writes: **Now they were on the road, going up to Jerusalem, and Jesus was going before them; and they were amazed. And as they followed they were afraid** (v. 32a). Jesus was making His way from the area north of the Sea of Galilee southward through Israel toward Jerusalem. By this point, He was nearing the end of this journey. As we have seen, it was Jesus' custom to teach His disciples as He walked about, the disciples following, listening, and committing His teaching to memory. So, at first glance, nothing seems out of the ordinary in this verse. Why, then, were the disciples amazed and even afraid?

I believe Mark gives us this curious detail because of the resolute determination that the disciples saw in Jesus to go to His destiny. He had set His face like flint (Isa. 50:7) to go to Jerusalem, for He knew He was called to give Himself over to His enemies there, and He had taught His disciples what would happen to Him on more than one occasion (8:31–33; 9:30–32). Now, as He approached Jerusalem, Jesus did not linger. He moved quickly, keeping ahead of His disciples, going to His death with a firm step. Most of us, if we knew we were going to our deaths, would drag our feet. Not Jesus. He was prepared to obey the Father to the utmost end. The disciples could not get over it. They were amazed by His resolution and were terrified at what might befall Him at Jerusalem.

At this point, Jesus once again made clear to them what was about to happen: **Then He took the twelve aside again and began to tell them the things that would happen to Him: "Behold, we are going up to Jerusalem, and the Son of Man will be betrayed to the chief priests and to the scribes; and they will condemn Him to death and deliver Him to the Gentiles; and they will mock Him, and scourge Him, and spit on Him, and kill Him. And the third day He will rise again"** (vv. 32b–34). With this warning, Jesus was more specific about what He faced than He had been previously. Before, He spoke generally about being put to death and then rising again. Here He told the disciples that He would be betrayed, delivered to the Gentiles (the Romans), mocked, scourged, and spat upon. If the disciples were afraid before, I can only imagine how terrified they must have been after hearing these details.

Jesus was so specific about what would occur in Jerusalem that liberal critics of the Bible declare that these words must have been attributed to Him after the fact. They deny that Jesus could have foreseen what would happen to Him in such precise detail. They are so allergic to anything supernatural, and so opposed to the idea of predictive prophecy, that they prefer to assume that Mark committed fraud in writing this gospel.

In reality, however, it is entirely possible that Jesus could have known what He faced even without supernatural revelation. In the first instance, if He knew He was going to be betrayed into the hands of His enemies, it was clear what the method of execution would be—a Roman cross. Furthermore, Jesus was not just a student of the Old Testament Scriptures, He was the actual subject of those books, so He was aware of passages such as Isaiah 52–53, which describes the sufferings of the Servant of Yahweh in great detail. The Jews did not associate the Suffering Servant passages of Isaiah with their hope of the coming Messiah, but Jesus knew that those texts applied to Him. So even without any direct revelation from the Father, He knew that He would be treated with scorn, that He would be scourged, and that He would be spat upon.

Perhaps the most important detail in this text is His announcement that He would be delivered into the hands of the Gentiles. First, He would be betrayed into the hands of His enemies among the Jewish hierarchy, the chief priests and the scribes. They, in turn, would deliver Him to the Gentiles. The Jewish leaders did not have the authority to set a death sentence under Roman occupation, so they would hand Him over to Pontius Pilate to be put to death. On the Day of Atonement in ancient Israel, an animal was killed and its blood was spread on the mercy seat in the Holy of Holies, then the sins of the people were symbolically transferred to the back of the scapegoat, which then was driven out into the wilderness, outside the camp, into the outer darkness (Leviticus 16). That was what it meant to a Jew to be delivered to the Gentiles. To be placed into the hands of the Gentiles was to be sent outside the covenant community, outside the camp, outside the place where the presence of God was concentrated and focused. So, the disciples must have been aghast when Jesus told them that He was going to be handed over to the Gentiles.

Craving Power and Position

This, then, was the third instance in which Jesus set before His disciples His *theologia crucis*, His theology of the cross, which affirms that the way of salvation is by suffering and death. However, no sooner had He said these things than two of His most trusted disciples came to Him with a request based on their *theologia gloriae*, the theology of glory. The disciples still were not getting the message; they still were hoping Jesus would assert His messianic reign and bring in the kingdom of God with all of its glory so that they not only might participate in it but have high positions in it.

Mark tells us: **Then James and John, the sons of Zebedee, came to Him, saying, "Teacher, we want You to do for us whatever we ask"** (v. 35). It seems that these disciples saw Jesus as a celestial bellhop, someone who was there to fulfill their orders and give them whatever their hearts desired. They came to Him with a request that sounds more like a demand. We, of course, often fall into the same pattern, bombarding God with request after request, demand after demand, as we focus on our own needs and wants. We know better. We should focus on God and His glory, as well as the good of our neighbors, before our own needs.

Mark goes on: **And He said to them, "What do you want Me to do for you?" They said to Him, "Grant us that we may sit, one on Your right hand and the other on Your left, in Your glory"** (vv. 36–37). James and John had a rather extraordinary request. They were asking that when Jesus was enthroned as the King of kings, He would choose one of them to sit at His right hand, the penultimate place of authority in a kingdom, and the other at His left, the next highest rung on the political ladder. In simple terms, they wanted status. They wanted eternal positions of power.

When I read this text, I cannot help but think of the pagan philosopher Friedrich Nietzsche, who said in the nineteenth century that what distinguishes man from the animals is not our ability to think but the will to power, the drive within every human being to conquer, to climb the ladder, to reach the highest place of exaltation. Some theologians have argued that sin is simply virtue run amok, because God plants in the heart of every creature an aspiration for significance, but we bend that good aspiration into a desire to dominate others. That seems to be what motivated James and John.

When Jesus heard this audacious request, He said: **"You do not know what you ask. Are you able to drink the cup that I drink, and be baptized with the baptism that I am baptized with?"** (v. 38). Jesus knew that James and John did not understand all the implications of what they were requesting. So, He asked them a question to begin to bring out their faulty ideas. In this question, He employed two metaphors to reference His forthcoming experience, which experience they, too, would have to undergo if they wished to sit at His right and left in glory.

First, Jesus asked, "Are you able to drink the cup that I drink?" This was before Gethsemane, when Jesus, in agony, asked the Father, "Take this cup away from me; nevertheless, not what I will, but what You will" (14:36), so the disciples possibly did not know that Jesus thought of His passion as a cup He must drink. Still, His remark was clearly referencing the upcoming events in Jerusalem that He had been telling them about. Second, He asked, "Are you able to be baptized with the baptism that I am baptized with?" He was not talking about the baptism of John that He underwent at the River Jordan. He was talking about being flooded in the fury of God's wrath, inundated by the Father's judgment. Jesus was telling them: "You say you want to be at My right hand and My left hand in My glory, but there is no *theologia gloriae* without first a *theologia crucis*. There is no glory without the cross."

The disciples' reply is stunning in its ignorance: **They said to Him, "We are able"** (v. 39a). They thought they were strong. They thought they were committed to Jesus. They did not know that they would abandon Him at the first sign of serious trouble and leave Him to drink the cup and undergo the baptism utterly alone.

Jesus did not chide them. He said: **"You will indeed drink the cup that I drink, and with the baptism I am baptized with you will be baptized"** (v. 39b). Here Jesus gave a hint that these disciples would go through a great deal of suffering that, on the surface at least, would be like His own. Yet, they would not have to endure the agony of the Father turning His face away. No one of us has ever been asked by God to drink the cup that Jesus drank or to be baptized with the baptism Jesus experienced. Nonetheless, we are called to identify with that cup and that baptism. Our water baptism, which is the sign of the new covenant, signifies that we are united with Christ in His death and in His resurrection. We must be willing to identify with Jesus in His disgrace and humiliation or we will never participate in His exaltation and glory. But He promises that all who identify with Him in His suffering will indeed participate with Him in His glory (Rom. 8:16–18). That is the Christian hope.

Then Jesus added, **"But to sit on My right hand and on My left is not Mine to give, but it is for those for whom it is prepared"** (v. 40). Jesus told James and John He could not grant their request because the decision was not up to Him. It was the Father's choice to make, and indeed, He had already made it, for those positions had been "prepared." The choice had been settled from all eternity.

Greatness by Servanthood

Sometimes the biblical writers make amazing understatements. Mark uses one when he writes, **When the ten heard it, they began to be greatly displeased with James and John** (v. 41). It is tempting to speculate that the other ten disciples were indignant that James and John had made such a request because they would have liked to ask for the same thing. The text does not say that explicitly, but we know that none of the disciples had fully grasped what Jesus was about to undergo and that they had debated among themselves about who would be regarded as the greatest of them (9:33–34). In any case, the unity of Jesus' disciple band was strained because of the selfish request of James and John.

Jesus used this occasion to teach His disciples a lesson we all need to learn. Mark tells us: **Jesus called them to Himself and said to them, "You know that those who are considered rulers over the Gentiles lord it over them, and their great ones exercise authority over them. Yet it shall not be so among you; but whoever desires to become great among you shall be your servant. And whoever of you desires to be first shall be slave of all. For even the Son of Man did not come to be served, but to serve, and to give His life a ransom for many"** (vv. 42–45).

Jesus began by citing the example of the secular authorities among the Gentiles, saying that they tended to "lord it over" those under their rule, that is, misusing their power. They had no sense of responsibility, no willingness to serve. However, Jesus left no doubt that this leadership style is to be unknown in the church: "It shall not be so among you." He said, in essence, "That may be the way of the world, but I will not put up with that in My house." Jesus really hammered the disciples with these words, and that should tell us this topic was extremely important to Him.

What, then, is the manner of leadership that is to be practiced among believers? Jesus said: "Whoever desires to become great among you shall be your servant. And whoever desires to be first shall be slave of all." I do not like this text. I prefer the secular way because, in my heart, I prefer to be served rather than to serve. But Jesus will have none of that. He said that if we want to be great, we must be small. If we want to be exalted, we must be abased. If we want to rule, we must serve. That is the ethic of Jesus. Leaders have to see themselves as slaves.

Finally, Jesus said, "For even the Son of Man did not come to be served, but to serve, and to give His life a ransom for many." As we look at the life of Jesus, at times we scratch our heads and wonder why Jesus said what He said, why He did what He did, what made Him tick, what He was about. Well, here He made it clear. Here He told His disciples why He had come and why He was resolutely going to Jerusalem. In the simplest possible terms, He came to serve—to give His life on a cruel cross as a ransom for many.

In the early church, one of the terrible distortions of the work of Christ was the ransom theory of the atonement, which declared that when Jesus was crucified, He made a payment to the Devil, just as we might make a ransom payment to a kidnapper. The idea was that the Devil is the prince of the world and that he held humanity in captivity, so Jesus paid the ransom to the Devil to set us free. However, the Bible never says anything like this. Jesus did not pay a ransom to Satan. He crushed Satan's head. The ransom was paid to the Father. Christ gave Himself to satisfy the demands of God's justice, so He purchased our freedom from the just wrath of God. This is why Paul declares, "You were bought at a price" (1 Cor. 7:23a). Thus, we who were hopelessly in debt to God are not required to pay. The debt has been paid for us by the Suffering Servant of Israel.

36

A BLIND MAN SEES

Mark 10:46–52

⟨⟩

Now they came to Jericho. As He went out of Jericho with His disciples and a great multitude, blind Bartimaeus, the son of Timaeus, sat by the road begging. And when he heard that it was Jesus of Nazareth, he began to cry out and say, "Jesus, Son of David, have mercy on me!" Then many warned him to be quiet; but he cried out all the more, "Son of David, have mercy on me!" So Jesus stood still and commanded him to be called. Then they called the blind man, saying to him, "Be of good cheer. Rise, He is calling you." And throwing aside his garment, he rose and came to Jesus. So Jesus answered and said to him, "What do you want Me to do for you?" The blind man said to Him, "Rabboni, that I may receive my sight." Then Jesus said to him, "Go your way; your faith has made you well." And immediately he received his sight and followed Jesus on the road.

Throughout the Synoptic Gospels, we read passage after passage that tell of occasions when Jesus employed His miraculous power to heal people of various afflictions. However, in only one instance are we given the name of a person whom Jesus healed, and it is in this passage that describes the healing of a blind man named Bartimaeus. It is impossible not to wonder whether this is simply a coincidence or whether Mark intentionally gave us the name of this man.

It certainly seems that Mark was very intentional in including this narrative in his gospel. At first glance, it is puzzling that Mark chose to recount yet another of Jesus' healings, especially at this point in time, when Jesus was moving so resolutely toward Jerusalem and the conclusion of His ministry. What was so important about this incident?

I think the answer lies in the fact that this account follows Mark's narrative of Jesus' discussion with His disciples after James and John requested that He allow them to sit on His right and left in His glory. As we saw in the previous chapter, Jesus took time to teach His disciples that real discipleship does not mean seeking to sit in the place of power and authority. Instead, the greatest in the kingdom of God are the servants. In this context, Bartimaeus stands in stark contrast with the behavior of the disciples as they squabbled among themselves for status and for rank. This man was a beggar by the road; in Hebrew categories, he was the lowest of the low in terms of his station in life, in terms of public exaltation and status. Presumably he was clothed in nothing more than rags as he sat there hoping against hope that someone would drop a coin into his cup, so that he might have his next meal or a place to rest for the evening. By taking time to serve this lowly man, Jesus set a powerful example for His disciples.

"Son of David, Have Mercy"

Mark writes, **Now they came to Jericho** (v. 46a). Note that this was not Old Testament Jericho, the first city the Israelites attacked when they came into the Promised Land, where God so memorably caused the walls to fall down flat. Rather, this was New Testament Jericho, which was situated about eighteen miles north of Jerusalem. Archaeologists believe that this town is one of two that have been inhabited by people longer than any others on the face of the earth, Damascus being the other. Jericho sits in the desert, but anyone who approaches it can tell right away why there is a village there. Even from a distance, travelers can see the mass of palm trees that grows alongside one of the richest and largest oases to be found in that region. This was a place of refreshment for weary pilgrims heading up to Jerusalem.

Then Mark tells us, **As He went out of Jericho with His disciples and a great multitude, blind Bartimaeus, the son of Timaeus, sat by the road begging** (v. 46b). Jesus was leaving the city, accompanied by a great multitude of people, when He passed a blind beggar. Mark tells us his name was Bartimaeus and he was the son of Timaeus. In telling us this, Mark commits literary redundancy. Every Jew who read this story would know that the name Bartimaeus meant "Son of Timaeus." The prefix *bar* meant "son of." This is why Jesus identified Peter as "Simon Bar-Jonah" (Matt. 16:17); he was the son of Jonah. Likewise, someone who had been through a *bar mitzvah* was a "son of the covenant." It would seem that it was unnecessary for Mark to explain that the name Bartimaeus meant "son of Timaeus," but, as we have seen, Mark was writing for Gentiles who were not always aware of Hebrew ancestry, customs, or names.

Mark also tells us that Bartimaeus was blind and that he begged for his sustenance. When I was a doctoral student in Holland, I traveled into Amsterdam by train. Passengers leaving Central Station in Amsterdam must cross a bridge that leads into the downtown area. Every time I went over that bridge, I passed a blind man who had his hat on the sidewalk to receive alms. When I left Holland, I did not return for four years, but when I finally did go back and walked out of Central Station on my way into the city, that same blind man was still there collecting alms. A few years later, a friend from Holland sent me a book that contained photographs of Amsterdam, and one of the photos featured the bridge to Central Station—and there was the man on the bridge. The constant sight of that man over a long period of time gave me a sense of the helplessness of those who are blind and must beg for their sustenance.

There was at least one positive aspect in Bartimaeus' situation—his location. Jericho was situated on one of the major thoroughfares of that day, so there was steady traffic passing through the city. For this reason, it was an ideal place for a beggar to request alms. Bartimaeus was probably as much a fixture on that road as was the beggar on the Amsterdam bridge. I imagine he sat by the road all day, not seeing anyone but listening for footsteps as people came near so he could ask them for alms.

It seems that the sounds of the multitude moving along with Jesus attracted his attention and curiosity. In the parallel passage in Luke's gospel, we are told, "hearing a multitude passing by, he asked what it meant" (18:36). Apparently someone told him that Jesus was walking by, and it seems he had heard of Jesus, for Mark writes: **When he heard that it was Jesus of Nazareth, he began to cry out and say, "Jesus, Son of David, have mercy on me!" Then many warned him to be quiet; but he cried out all the more, "Son of David, have mercy on me!"** (vv. 47–48).

When Bartimaeus learned that Jesus was passing by, he raised quite a hullabaloo. He began crying out, "Jesus, Son of David, have mercy on me!" Some in the crowd told him to keep quiet, perhaps thinking Jesus would not want to have anything to do with a poor beggar. But Bartimaeus would not be dissuaded. He kept on crying out for mercy.

I am fascinated by the soundness of the theology that was reflected in Bartimaeus' appeal. He knew that the Messiah, the long-promised Deliverer of Israel, would come out of the family and lineage of David (2 Sam. 7:12–13; Isa. 9:7), that He would be David's greater son, that He would be David's son and yet at the same time David's Lord (Ps. 110:1; Matt. 22:42–45). Furthermore, he cried out for mercy. How very different was his request from that of James and John; the two disciples asked for positions of power and authority with a sense of entitlement, whereas Bartimaeus asked for mercy with no suggestion that he deserved Jesus' help. Clearly, Bartimaeus came to Jesus in the better posture.

As we have seen, Jesus was marching toward Jerusalem with resolute determination to face the shame, pain, suffering, and ignominy of the cross. But when He heard Bartimaeus' plaintive cry, Jesus stopped in His tracks. Mark writes that when He heard the beggar cry out to the "Son of David," **Jesus stood still and commanded him to be called** (v. 49a). He told His disciples, "Find out who is calling Me. Bring him to Me. I'm not moving another foot toward Jerusalem until I see this man."

Mark continues: **Then they called the blind man, saying to him, "Be of good cheer. Rise, He is calling you"** (v. 49b). It is one thing for us to call on the Lord. It is something else when He calls on us. That is where our true redemption lies. The crowd had it right—Bartimaeus had cause for good cheer when Jesus called for Him. Mark tells us, **throwing aside his garment, he rose and came to Jesus** (v. 50). That is precisely what everyone should do when Jesus approaches. They should throw aside whatever is hindering them, stand up, and run to Jesus.

"My Lord and My Master"

Then Mark writes, **So Jesus answered and said to him, "What do you want Me to do for you?"** (v. 51a). Does that question ring a bell? When James and John came to Him with a request, Jesus said, "What do you want Me to do for you?" (10:36). They went on to make their audacious request that one of them might sit on Jesus' right hand and the other on His left hand in glory. How different was Bartimaeus' answer when Jesus asked him the same question He had so recently put to His two disciples. Bartimaeus said, **"Rabboni, that I may receive my sight"** (v. 51b). He was not asking for status. He was not asking for glory. He was not asking to be exalted in Jesus' kingdom. He was not even asking to be delivered from his poverty. He was begging the Lord for something that almost every human being already enjoyed. He simply wanted to be able to see. Bartimaeus was a simple man. He had one driving passion—to get out of the impenetrable darkness that defined his life, where he groped in danger, always dependent on someone else to take him by the hand and to lead him. So he cried, "All I want, Lord, is to receive my sight."

However, that is not exactly the way he said it. Again and again in the Gospels we see that when people spoke to Jesus, they addressed Him as "Teacher" or "Rabbi." But Bartimaeus called Him "Rabboni." This is the same title Mary

Magdalene exclaimed when, beyond all hope and expectation, she encountered the Lord Jesus on the morning of His resurrection (John 20:16).

This slight alteration from the title "rabbi" is very significant; *rabboni* means far more than "professor" or "teacher." It has an intense personal significance and is actually a confession of faith. Bartimaeus was saying to Jesus, "My Lord and my Master, let me see." In this passage, Mark gives us a portrait of a true disciple who was ragged, poor, and blind, but who recognized the Messiah and addressed Him as "My Lord and my Master." Jesus had just taught His disciples about the importance of being servants. To be a servant is to serve a master. Whereas the disciples failed to grasp that, this blind man succeeded.

Finally, Mark writes: **Jesus said to him, "Go your way; your faith has made you well." And immediately he received his sight and followed Jesus on the road** (v. 52). With a word of commendation for Bartimaeus' faith, Jesus pronounced him healed, and the beggar was able to see, perhaps for the first time. Most blind people, having their sight restored, would want to run through the city in order to see all the sights that they have known only by the descriptions of others. Not Bartimaeus. As soon as he received his sight, he saw Jesus, and he wanted nothing more than to follow Him to Jerusalem to His death. That is the desire of all who are given eyes to see and ears to hear the truth of the gospel of Jesus Christ.

37

BEHIND JESUS'
TRIUMPHAL ENTRY

Mark 11:1–11

Now when they drew near Jerusalem, to Bethphage and Bethany, at the Mount of Olives, He sent two of His disciples; and He said to them, "Go into the village opposite you; and as soon as you have entered it you will find a colt tied, on which no one has sat. Loose it and bring it. And if anyone says to you, 'Why are you doing this?' say, 'The Lord has need of it,' and immediately he will send it here." So they went their way, and found the colt tied by the door outside on the street, and they loosed it. But some of those who stood there said to them, "What are you doing, loosing the colt?" And they spoke to them just as Jesus had commanded. So they let them go. Then they brought the colt to Jesus and threw their clothes on it, and He sat on it. And many spread their clothes on the road, and others cut down leafy branches from the trees and spread them on the road. Then those who went before and those who followed cried out, saying: "Hosanna! Blessed is He who comes in the name of the LORD! Blessed is the kingdom of our father David that comes in the name of the Lord! Hosanna in the highest!" And Jesus went into Jerusalem and into the temple. So when He had looked around at all things, as the hour was already late, He went out to Bethany with the twelve.

Traditionally, during the Christmas season, many churches celebrate the advent, the coming of Jesus to this world as a baby, born to be a King. That is why angelic greetings came from on high, heralding the birth of a child who was the Savior (Luke 2:11). Some thirty or so years later came the advent of that King into David's royal city, as Mark describes in this passage. We discover here a connection between Jesus' advent into the world to fulfill the kingly prophecies of the Christ child and His advent into Jerusalem.

Chapter 11 begins the last third of the gospel of Mark. This part of Mark's gospel focuses on what appear to be the last seven days of Jesus' life. (Similarly, fully half of John's gospel focuses on the last week or so of Jesus' life.) The gospel writers understood that the events that happened in the short time between Jesus' arrival in Jerusalem and His ascension into heaven fulfilled God's promise of redemption.

Some scholars maintain that Mark compresses the time that Jesus spent in Jerusalem before His death. Churches typically celebrate Holy Week as starting on Palm Sunday, with the crucifixion following on Good Friday, and then Christ's resurrection on Sunday. John's gospel shows Jesus in Jerusalem for four months before He was executed. Adding to the idea that Mark probably is compressing this event is the fact that Jesus' triumphal entry likely took place not in spring but in the fall, during the time of the Feast of Tabernacles, for people characteristically had palm branches as part of the celebration of that festival. Be that as it may, this is a significant event in the history of redemption.

A Colt Only for the King

Mark begins his account, saying, **they drew near Jerusalem, to Bethphage and Bethany, at the Mount of Olives** (v. 1a). Note that Mark mentions first Bethphage, which means "house of unripe figs," then Bethany, which means "house of sorrow." It seems as though, on His journey to Jerusalem, Jesus first traveled through Bethphage and then through Bethany. Critical scholars look at the roads that come from the north into Jerusalem today, and they insist that Mark has the order reversed. One has to go through Bethany and then through Bethphage to get to Jerusalem. But these critics forget that Jesus was not traveling on modern highways. He was traveling on a Roman road, and we know now that the Roman road went just as Mark says it did.

In any case, they came to the Mount of Olives, and **He sent two of His disciples; and He said to them, "Go into the village opposite you; and as soon as you have entered it you will find a colt tied, on which no one has sat. Loose it and bring it"** (vv. 1b–2). These instructions that Jesus gave to His disciples sound strange. It is almost as if Jesus were telling His disciples to go and steal a donkey for Him. But that was not what was going on at all. He was consciously fulfilling prophecy. The Old Testament clearly indicated that the Messiah would enter the city riding on a donkey. For example, Zechariah said, "Behold, your King is coming to you; He is just and having salvation, lowly and riding on a donkey, a colt, the foal of a donkey" (9:9). That prophecy was well known among the people who were waiting for their coming King. Most kings in the ancient world, such as Alexander the Great, rode on magnificent horses, but not the King of the Jews. He came riding on a donkey.

Zechariah's prophecy has roots much earlier in the Old Testament. Genesis 49 provides a record of the patriarchal blessing that Jacob pronounced on his sons. The firstborn son, Reuben, was denied the patriarchal blessing because of his sin, then Simeon and Levi were likewise denied. Then Jacob came to Judah:

> "Judah, you are he whom your brothers shall praise; your hand shall be on the neck of your enemies; your father's children shall bow down before you. Judah is a lion's whelp; from the prey, my son, you have gone up. He bows down, he lies down as a lion; and as a lion, who shall rouse him? The scepter [that is, the sign of royalty] shall not depart from Judah, nor a lawgiver from between his feet, until Shiloh comes; and to Him shall be the obedience of the people. Binding his donkey to the vine, and his donkey's colt to the choice vine, he washed his garments in wine, and his clothes in the blood of grapes." (Gen. 49:8–11)

Deeply rooted in the Jewish consciousness of the Old Testament was the hope of the King who would enter Jerusalem as their coming Messiah while riding on a donkey.

In the ancient world, including Israel, one of the prerogatives of the king was to commandeer a beast of burden whenever he needed it. As the King, Jesus exercised that right and commanded His disciples to get a colt. Something else is significant: the colt had never been ridden. Donkeys, just like horses, usually had to be broken in to become functional beasts of burden. Yet the principle in the Jewish culture was that no one was allowed to ride on the king's horse or the king's donkey. Only the king could ride his beasts. That is why Jesus specifically asked for a colt that had never been ridden; it was the colt prepared for the King.

Jesus added, **"If anyone says to you, 'Why are you doing this?' say, 'The Lord has need of it' and immediately he will send it here"** (v. 3). There is some ambiguity regarding the word that is translated as "Lord" here, *kurios*. It can mean simply "sir" or "master." It also can signify "the supreme ruler and sovereign" over the people. Only rarely does Mark use this term with respect to

Jesus, but here Jesus used it for Himself. It seems as though He was not simply saying, "Tell them the Master needs it," but rather He was saying, "Tell them that the Sovereign One, the King of the Jews, requires that donkey." Mark tells us the disciples **went their way and found the colt tied by the door outside on the street, and they loosed it. But some of those who stood there said to them, "What are you doing, loosing the colt?" And they spoke to them just as Jesus had commanded. So they let them go** (vv. 4–6).

Note what happened when they brought the donkey to Jesus. Mark writes, **then they brought the colt to Jesus and threw their clothes on it, and He sat on it** (v. 7). Jesus' disciples put their own garments on the back of the donkey as a saddle for Jesus. The other gospels also tell us that the people, when Jesus began His procession, took off their outer garments and threw them on the pathway of the donkey. So, on Palm Sunday, when Jesus made His triumphal entry into the city, the donkey walked over the equivalent of a red carpet created by the clothes of the people.

That practice also had roots in the Old Testament. When Jehu was anointed king over Israel in place of Ahab, the people blew trumpets, proclaimed him king, then took off their outer garments and put them in Jehu's path. As he came down the steps after his anointing, he walked over the people's garments (2 Kings 9:13). That same ritual happened again when the people laid their garments in front of Jesus.

According to Mark, **many spread their clothes on the road, and others cut down leafy branches from the trees and spread them on the road. Then those who went before and those who followed cried out, saying: "Hosanna! Blessed is He who comes in the name of the LORD!"** (v. 8). We remember this event every year on Palm Sunday—the waving of the palms and the people crying, "Hosanna," which means, "Lord, save us now."

The Return of God's Glory

Jesus' triumphal entry began at Bethany, a little village at the top of the Mount of Olives. It looks out across the Kidron Valley, down to the city of Jerusalem, three hundred feet below. There is special significance to that.

In 586 BC, at the time of Jerusalem's destruction and the forced exile of its people to Babylon, God gave a vision to the prophet Ezekiel. In that vision, Ezekiel saw the glory of God rise up from the temple in Jerusalem. The glory departed from the east side of the city and ascended three hundred feet to rest on the Mount of Olives (Ezek. 11:23).

When I was in Jerusalem, I stayed on the Mount of Olives, at a hotel overlooking the Holy City. One night, while standing on the patio of the hotel, I looked down across the Kidron Valley and saw the illuminated walls of Jerusalem, and I remembered that vision of Ezekiel. In my mind's eye, I imagined the glory of God departing from the temple, coming from the East Gate, then rising up to where I was on the Mount of Olives and settling there.

Hold that thought for a moment. After Mark describes the triumphal entry, he tells us: **Jesus went into Jerusalem and into the temple. So when He had looked around at all things, as the hour was already late, He went out to Bethany with the twelve** (v. 11). Mark's conclusion of this episode appears anticlimactic at first. It looks as though Jesus got into Jerusalem, went to the temple, looked around, and went back to Bethany, as if nothing significant had taken place. However, we need to remember where Jesus was. Earlier, He had set His face like a flint (Isa. 50:7) to go to Jerusalem, knowing that He would suffer and die there. But Jerusalem was not His ultimate destination. Rather, it was the temple. When He went into Jerusalem and then into the temple, He looked around at the place where historically the sacrifices were offered. He went to the temple that had replaced the tabernacle, which was a living prophecy of the Messiah who was to come.

John's gospel tells us, "the Word became flesh and dwelt among us . . . full of grace and truth" (John 1:1, 14). The phrase that is translated "dwelt among us" literally reads "tabernacled among us." That is because Jesus fulfilled everything the tabernacle pointed to. He is the sanctuary. When He said, "Destroy this temple, and in three days I will raise it up" (John 2:19), He was speaking of Himself.

Here is the supreme irony: In 586 BC, Ezekiel saw the glory of God leave the temple, leave the holy city, and ascend to Bethany on the Mount of Olives. At the triumphal entry, the One whom the Scriptures define as the brightness of God's glory (Heb. 1:3) descended from Bethany and the Mount of Olives, entered the East Gate of the Holy City, and went to the temple. Do you see it? In 586 BC, the glory of God left the temple, but when Jesus came, the glory of God came back. Yet no one understood that the King of glory was in their midst, about to meet the destiny to which He was called and for which He was born.

38

THE LESSON OF
THE FIG TREE

Mark 11:12–21

⌒⌒

Now the next day, when they had come out from Bethany, He was hungry. And seeing from afar a fig tree having leaves, He went to see if perhaps He would find something on it. When He came to it, He found nothing but leaves, for it was not the season for figs. In response Jesus said to it, "Let no one eat fruit from you ever again." And His disciples heard it. So they came to Jerusalem. Then Jesus went into the temple and began to drive out those who bought and sold in the temple, and overturned the tables of the money changers and the seats of those who sold doves. And He would not allow anyone to carry wares through the temple. Then He taught, saying to them, "Is it not written, 'My house shall be called a house of prayer for all nations'? But you have made it a 'den of thieves.'" And the scribes and chief priests heard it and sought how they might destroy Him; for they feared Him, because all the people were astonished at His teaching. When evening had come, He went out of the city. Now in the morning, as they passed by, they saw the fig tree dried up from the roots. And Peter, remembering, said to Him, "Rabbi, look! The fig tree which You cursed has withered away."

The biblical accounts of Jesus' cursing of the fig tree have vexed schol-ars for centuries. For one thing, this perplexing narrative records for us the only miracle in the New Testament that involves destruction.

Furthermore, on the surface, it seems that Jesus overreacted to this innocent fig tree for not bearing fruit when it was not the season for figs. The late Bertrand Russell, who wrote an essay titled "Why I Am Not a Christian," cited this narrative as one of his reasons for repudiating Christianity. He said this incident displays Jesus as a man who expressed vindictive fury to an innocent plant, manifesting behavior that was not that of a righteous man, let alone the Son of God. Even Christian scholars who are sanguine in their evaluation of Jesus are perplexed by this story. Some have said that this incident represents a waste of supernatural power. Certainly it is a challenge for us to understand why Jesus reacted as He did.

A Fruitless Fig Tree

Mark writes: **The next day, when they had come out from Bethany, He was hungry. And seeing from afar a fig tree having leaves, He went to see if perhaps He would find something on it. When He came to it, He found nothing but leaves, for it was not the season for figs** (vv. 12–13). When Jesus found no figs, only leaves, He cursed the fig tree, saying, **"Let no one eat fruit from you ever again." And His disciples heard it** (v. 14).

Some who believe in the sinlessness of Jesus and in the inspiration of the New Testament text have come to the defense of our Lord and tried to explain this somewhat bizarre incident in terms of the growth cycle of figs. Fig season occurs in the fall in Palestine, yet in the spring fig trees send out little knobs or buds called *paggim*, and then a growth of foliage follows. Hungry travelers from time to time pluck these *paggim* from the fig trees and eat them. Even though they are not fully developed figs, they are edible. Some commentators say that these knobs should have been present when Jesus approached the fig tree, but since they were not, Jesus was angry. However, I do not think this is the answer.

One of my professors in seminary, a man who was in his mid-eighties at the time, was one of the most distinguished archaeologists of the twentieth century. He was also perhaps the greatest living expert on the customs of the ancient Near East. When we looked at this text in Mark's gospel, he explained that in Palestine there is a clearly defined season for figs, and the vast majority of fig species bear fruit within that season. However, a few rare species of fig trees bear fruit outside the normal season. The test of whether one could expect figs from a fig tree was not the time of year but whether the foliage of the tree was in full bloom. Jesus, knowing the characteristics of Palestine fig trees even better than my professor, saw this fig tree in full bloom and expected that mature figs would be present on it. When He turned aside to satisfy His hunger from these figs, He found a barren tree.

Why did He curse it? Jesus, among other things, was a prophet. One of the most graphic forms of prophetic communication in the Old Testament was the object lesson. The prophet would take something from nature or everyday life, as Amos did with a plumb line, and use it to communicate God's truth. Here Jesus found an object that illustrated the sin of hypocrisy. It had the appearance of fruitfulness, but it was actually barren. Throughout His earthly ministry, Jesus strongly denounced the sin of hypocrisy. That was His basic critique of the Pharisees of His day (Luke 12:1). On several occasions, Jesus chastened religious leaders for their show of spirituality and righteousness despite their underlying lack of fruit.

That should be a lesson to us. One of the top ten objections to Christianity that one evangelistic ministry learned over many years is the supposition that the church is filled with hypocrites. People who were watching the lives of church members throughout the week said they were turned off to Christianity because they believed Christians did not live out their profession.

Admittedly, the church is full of sinners. In fact, I know of no other organization in the world that requires a person to be a sinner in order to join it. However, while all hypocrites are sinners, not all sinners are hypocrites. Hypocrisy is just one of many sins. It is unfair of our critics to say, "So and so is a professing Christian, and we saw him sin during the week; therefore, he's a hypocrite." That is not necessarily so. If I claim not to do something sinful and then you see me do it, I am guilty of hypocrisy. But if you see me do something sinful that I never claimed I do not do, I am a sinner but I am not a hypocrite. We need to draw that clear distinction.

However, having said that in defense of Christians who by their fallen nature continue to sin even after embracing the Savior, I still urge that we all take care to avoid the sin of hypocrisy. Paul spoke about this when he said, "The name of God is blasphemed among the Gentiles because of you" (Rom. 2:24). Unbelievers see us talking the talk and not walking the walk, and that should not be so among us.

In any case, when Jesus cursed the fig tree, He was addressing hypocrisy—but not hypocrisy within His church. What, then, was the source of the hypocrisy He was addressing? The answer appears, I think, when we see that there is a direct link in this narrative between the cursing of the fig tree and the cleansing of the temple. That is why Mark interjects his account of the cleansing of the temple between the cursing of the fig tree and the discovery of the withered tree the following day.

A Misused Temple

Mark describes what happened in the temple: **So they came to Jerusalem. Then Jesus went into the temple and began to drive out those who bought**

and sold in the temple, and overturned the tables of the money changers and the seats of those who sold doves. And He would not allow anyone to carry wares through the temple (vv. 15–16). When Jesus came into the temple, the house of God, on the morning after His triumphal entry, He was furious with what He found people doing there. The sight provoked Him to righteous indignation.

The Herodian temple was one of the wonders of the ancient world. It was a huge complex that was divided into four parts: the court of the Gentiles; the court of the women; the court of the Jews; and the Holy of Holies. The court of the Gentiles was the largest part of the temple complex. The design of the temple included this place for Gentiles to congregate because God had called Abraham, the patriarch of the Jewish people, to be a blessing to all the nations. The people of Israel had the mission of proclaiming the truth of God not just to themselves but to all people. The court of the Gentiles was on the outer edges of the temple complex, to be sure, but the Gentiles were still able to be present so that they might know and fear the Lord (1 Kings 8:43). However, the Jews, who hated the Gentiles, hoped that when the Messiah came, He would cleanse the temple of all Gentiles and get rid of them once and for all.

Acting on that disregard for the Gentiles, the Sadducees and the Sanhedrin basically had turned the court of the Gentiles into a stockyard for commercial purposes. The sale of animals for sacrifice had become one of the most lucrative sources of revenue for the Sanhedrin. For the celebration of Passover, a feast of obligation for every Jew, the Jews streamed into Jerusalem from all quarters of the ancient world, needing to buy sheep for the sacrifice and to exchange their currency to be able to buy the animals. The animals were sold for a premium because the people needed them, and the exchange rates were extortionate. The Jewish historian Josephus recorded that in AD 66, as the Roman armies were coming against Jerusalem, 255,000 lambs were slaughtered in Jerusalem during the Passover. Can you imagine what a huge business was going on there?

It is little wonder, then, that Jesus took such drastic action, **saying to them, "Is it not written, 'My house shall be called a house of prayer for all nations'? But you have made it a 'den of thieves'"** (v. 17). Jesus quoted from Isaiah 56:7 in saying that His house was meant to be called a house of prayer "for all nations," including Gentiles. But the whole purpose of God's temple had been distorted and corrupted. So, our Lord, as the other gospels tell us, made a whip of cords, kicked over the tables, and drove the money changers and the animals out of the temple, cleansing it. The Jews hoped that the Messiah would cleanse the temple *of* Gentiles, but Jesus cleansed the temple *for* the Gentiles. It was to be a place for people, not for sheep and goats.

Mark then writes: **And the scribes and chief priests heard it and sought how they might destroy Him; for they feared Him, because all the people were astonished at His teaching. When evening had come, He went out of the city** (vv. 18–19). The rulers were angered when Jesus upset the status quo, and they feared His influence with the people. They plotted against Him to take His life. In just a few days, they would accomplish their goal.

Mark tells us that the next morning, as Jesus and His disciples passed by on their way back toward Jerusalem, **they saw the fig tree dried up from the roots. And Peter, remembering, said to Him, "Rabbi, look! The fig tree which You cursed has withered away"** (vv. 20–21). The barren fig tree had been cursed, and it was worthy only to be cast into the fire as firewood. It would never bring forth fruit again.

Do you see the connection here? The lesson of the tree applies to Israel, symbolized in the Old Testament as God's fig tree. Just like the barren fig tree Jesus cursed, Israel had proven unfruitful with respect to God's purpose for her. Her worship had become an exercise in hypocrisy. As the fig tree was cursed, so was the nation of Israel, fit only to be cast into the fire.

39

FAITH AMID FAITHLESSNESS

Mark 11:22–33

⁂

So Jesus answered and said to them, "Have faith in God. For assuredly, I say to you, whoever says to this mountain, 'Be removed and be cast into the sea,' and does not doubt in his heart, but believes that those things he says will be done, he will have whatever he says. Therefore I say to you, whatever things you ask when you pray, believe that you receive them, and you will have them. And whenever you stand praying, if you have anything against anyone, forgive him, that your Father in heaven may also forgive you your trespasses. But if you do not forgive, neither will your Father in heaven forgive your trespasses." Then they came again to Jerusalem. And as He was walking in the temple, the chief priests, the scribes, and the elders came to Him. And they said to Him, "By what authority are You doing these things? And who gave You this authority to do these things?" But Jesus answered and said to them, "I also will ask you one question; then answer Me, and I will tell you by what authority I do these things: The baptism of John—was it from heaven or from men? Answer Me." And they reasoned among themselves, saying, "If we say, 'From heaven,' He will say, 'Why then did you not believe him?' But if we say, 'From men'"—they feared the people, for all counted John to have been a prophet indeed. So they answered and said to Jesus, "We do not know." And Jesus answered and said to them, "Neither will I tell you by what authority I do these things."

Jesus cursed the fig tree, as we saw in the previous chapter, to give a prophetic object lesson about the end to which hypocrisy leads. The fig tree, a symbol for Israel, had the appearance of health, but it was fruitless, so Jesus cursed it, causing it to dry up from its roots. As we saw, Mark wrapped the two episodes of the cursing of the fig tree and the discovery of the withered tree around his account of Jesus' cleansing of the temple. His aim was to show that the hypocrisy of the fig tree was evident even down to the heart of Jewish worship, the temple, which the religious authorities had turned into a house of commerce rather than a house of prayer for all nations. Judaism seemed magnificent, but it was rotten at the core and therefore fruitless.

When Peter discovered the withered fig tree, Mark tells us, **Jesus answered and said to them, "Have faith in God"** (v. 22). This was an imperative, a command from our Lord to His disciples and, by extension, to us. He was saying, "Trust God." Trusting God is the obligation of every creature made in His image. It is a moral, ethical, and spiritual duty, because not to trust God is to impugn the integrity of His Word, His promises, and His character. What possible justification could there be for any creature not to trust the word of an eternal, omnipotent Creator?

Why did Jesus give His disciples this command at this point, immediately following the cursing of the fig tree and the cleansing of the temple? Perhaps His next words provide a clue.

Faith Can Move Mountains

According to Mark, Jesus went on to say: **"For assuredly, I say to you, whoever says to this mountain, 'Be removed and be cast into the sea,' and does not doubt in his heart, but believes that those things he says will be done, he will have whatever he says"** (v. 23). Jesus probably spoke these words while He and His disciples were standing near the withered fig tree, which was on the Mount of Olives overlooking Jerusalem. From that vantage point, they could see the Herodian fortress, built by King Herod the Great. Even to this day, the ruins of that massive fortress are apparent in the landscape. When Herod built it, he used slave labor to transfer the earth from a hill to form the foundation and support structure for the fortress. In literal terms, Herod the Great moved a mountain to build his fortress. The people were aware of that prodigious feat, and Jesus took advantage of that knowledge to provide an object lesson, teaching them that if they had faith in God, they could do similarly amazing deeds.

It is possible that Jesus commanded the disciples to have faith because both the cursing of the fig tree and the cleansing of the temple illustrated infidelity, which is faithlessness. The temple, which was meant to be the place where God's people focused their faith and trust on Him, had become a den of thieves. It had become a monument not to fidelity but to unbelief. The fig tree, which was designed to obey its Creator by bearing figs, also had proved faithless to its Creator. So, perhaps these two examples of faithlessness prompted Jesus to issue this command.

Another possibility is that the disciples may have been astonished—as they were so often astonished by the things Jesus said and did—at the power of Jesus to cause a fig tree to die by His spoken curse. Perhaps they were saying to themselves, "What kind of power is this?" and Jesus was saying to them that the power of faith makes possible deeds far greater than the killing of a fig tree. Faith acting through prayer, He said, is able to move mountains. I believe this is probably the best explanation.

Jesus added, "**Therefore I say to you, whatever things you ask when you pray, believe that you receive them, and you will have them**" (v. 24). We have to be very careful with this verse. A whole theology based almost exclusively on this text has permeated the Christian world in our day. The word of faith movement, which espouses the idea of "name it and claim it," tells us that all we have to do to receive something we want is to claim it as ours in Jesus' name, and it will be ours. This movement is, in some ways, the Christian parallel to the New Age movement in the secular world. The New Age movement teaches that by visualizing what we want to happen, we can actually change the world around us. The force that is at the bottom of New Age thinking is really magic, and the basis of the word of faith movement is not very different. It seizes on this statement by Jesus to assert, "Whatever you believe, if you believe it truly, you will have it."

What's wrong with this picture? The Bible gives us a wealth of instruction about prayer, repeatedly stressing the importance of trusting God for the answers to our prayers. Therefore, an aphoristic statement like this has to be understood in the light of all of that teaching, especially the New Testament qualifications about how God answers our prayers. Something like the word of faith movement results when we lift a verse like this out of its particular context and ignore the rest of the teaching of Scripture.

Consider this statement by Jesus: "Again I say to you that if two of you agree on earth concerning anything that they ask, it will be done for them by My Father in heaven" (Matt. 18:19). That's easy to test. It would not be difficult to find two people who would agree that war should be abolished, that cancer should be cured, or that poverty should be eliminated. Does this agreement mean that these aspirations will be granted by the Father? No, the verse is not saying that. This verse must be understood in light of the consistent teaching of Scripture that we must pray in accordance with the will of God.

The Relationship of Faith and Prayer

What was Jesus saying about the relationship between faith and answers to prayer? When we fall on our knees and cry out to God, and we give Him the concerns of our hearts, we can know for sure that He hears and He answers, and His answers are always perfect. But we tend to think that if God does not do what we ask Him to do, He has not answered. Jesus, in agony, prayed in the garden of Gethsemane, asking, "O My Father, if it is possible, let this cup pass from Me" (Matt. 26:39b). Does the fact that Jesus went to the cross the next day mean the Father did not answer Him? No, the Father did answer Jesus' prayer. His answer was "no." We need to remember that Jesus also prayed, "Nevertheless, not as I will, but as You will" (v. 39c). Jesus' response was this: "If You say 'no' to My request, I say 'yes' to what You want Me to do." That is the prayer of faith. That is trusting God.

Many promises in Scripture assure us as to how God will answer our prayers; we simply need to believe them. Many years ago, when I was on staff at a church, a woman came to me for counsel because of her unrelieved feelings of guilt over a sin she had committed in the past. I advised her that she needed forgiveness from God, and the only possible way for her to receive it was for her to repent. When I told her that, she became irritated. She said, "I thought you were a theologian." She was looking for a technical, sophisticated answer to her moral dilemma, something that she could not expect to find from people in her prayer group. She said, "I have asked God fifty times to forgive me for this sin, and I'm still overwhelmed by my guilt." So I told her she needed to pray one more time and repent of her sin. At that point, she became very irritated and said: "I have told you that I have asked God to forgive me many times. I have repented. Why do I still feel guilty?" So, I said to her: "Yes, you need to pray for forgiveness one more time, but this time you need to pray that God will forgive you for another sin—your arrogance." Of course, she did not understand the point I was making and became even more irate, so I asked her to read 1 John 1:9: "If we confess our sins, He is faithful and just to forgive us our sins and to cleanse us from all unrighteousness." Then I explained to her that she had confessed her sin but she did not feel forgiven because she did not believe God's promise of forgiveness. She could not accept that forgiveness is so easy. She thought she needed to do more, and that was arrogance. She simply needed to pray in faith, believing that God would forgive her just as He had promised He would.

The world today is full of guilt-ridden people. Unfortunately, too many preachers today simply tell those who are plagued by guilt to get over it, to not worry about it. As Jeremiah said, "They have also healed the hurt of My people slightly, saying, 'Peace, peace!' when there is no peace" (6:14). Denying the problem does not help. Denying our guilt will never relieve our souls. The only cure is forgiveness. The prayer of faith trusts the God of grace to forgive us of our sins when we ask Him.

Jesus continued: **"Whenever you stand praying, if you have anything against anyone, forgive him, that your Father in heaven may also forgive you your trespasses. But if you do not forgive, neither will your Father in heaven forgive your trespasses"** (vv. 25–26). This statement may sound completely outrageous, but I do not believe that this text or any text in the New Testament teaches that we are obligated to forgive people who sin against us unilaterally without their repentance. All the New Testament teachings on confronting brothers who sin against us, seeking restitution, carrying out church discipline, and so forth do not mean that if someone harms us, we have to say, "I forgive you." We may do that, but there is an analogy between our forgiveness of others' sins and God's forgiveness of our sins. God does not forgive us unilaterally; He requires repentance. But when we repent, He does forgive. We must do the same. If someone injures us or offends us, but then he apologizes, confesses his sin, and asks for our forgiveness, we cannot hold a grudge. If we do, we can expect the same from God. Jesus' point is that every Christian is to be standing ready at any moment to forgive any offense if the offending person repents.

A Question about Authority

In Jerusalem, the religious leaders of the Jews came to Jesus to make another attempt to trap Him in His words. Mark tells us: **Then they came again to Jerusalem. And as He was walking in the temple, the chief priests, the scribes, and the elders came to Him. And they said to Him, "By what authority are You doing these things? And who gave You this authority to do these things?"** (vv. 27–28). This question of authority was a point of contention throughout Jesus' ministry. He said, "I have not spoken on My own authority; but the Father who sent Me gave Me a command, what I should say and what I should speak" (John 12:49). He also said, "All authority has been given to Me in heaven and on earth" (Matt. 28:18). Of course, this was not just a question for first-century scribes and Pharisees. It is the supreme question that unbelievers face today. Perhaps you are one who has not yet submitted to Christ because you doubt His authority. You are thinking in your heart, "Who is Jesus to tell me what to do?" Simply put, He is the eternal Son of God, and He speaks and acts by the authority that has been given to Him by God the Father.

Mark continues: **But Jesus answered and said to them, "I also will ask you one question; then answer Me, and I will tell you by what authority I** do these things: **The baptism of John—was it from heaven or from men? Answer Me"** (vv. 29–30). Jesus cleverly evaded the trap that had been set for Him by asking the Pharisees and scribes a question of His own. That put them in a dilemma, as Mark explains: **And they reasoned among themselves, saying, "If we say, 'From heaven,' He will say, 'Why then did you not believe him?' But if we say, 'From men'"—they feared the people, for all counted John to have been a prophet indeed** (vv. 31–32). They were trapped between admitting that they should have listened to John or facing the wrath of the people for admitting their doubts about John, for if anything was a given in Israel at this time, it was that John the Baptist was a prophet sent by God. Seeing no way out of Jesus' trap, **they answered and said to Jesus, "We do not know"** (v. 33a).

Jesus knew they were lying. He could have said: "Yes, you do know. You know very well that he was a prophet." Perhaps He judged that the duplicity of the Pharisees and scribes was exposed by their pathetic answer. But since they chose not to answer His question, **Jesus answered and said to them, "Neither will I tell you by what authority I do these things"** (v. 33b). This was a wise move, for the religious leaders were set in their belief that Jesus had no authority to preach and do miracles, and nothing He could say would change their minds. They would continue to try to trap Him in His words.

40

THE FATE OF THE
WICKED VINEDRESSERS

Mark 12:1–12

Then He began to speak to them in parables: "A man planted a vineyard and set a hedge around it, dug a place for the wine vat and built a tower. And he leased it to vinedressers and went into a far country. Now at vintage-time he sent a servant to the vinedressers, that he might receive some of the fruit of the vineyard from the vinedressers. And they took him and beat him and sent him away empty-handed. Again he sent them another servant, and at him they threw stones, wounded him in the head, and sent him away shamefully treated. And again he sent another, and him they killed; and many others, beating some and killing some. Therefore still having one son, his beloved, he also sent him to them last, saying, 'They will respect my son.' But those vinedressers said among themselves, 'This is the heir. Come, let us kill him, and the inheritance will be ours.' So they took him and killed him and cast him out of the vineyard. Therefore what will the owner of the vineyard do? He will come and destroy the vinedressers, and give the vineyard to others. Have you not even read this Scripture: 'The stone which the builders rejected has become the chief cornerstone. This was the LORD's doing, and it is marvelous in our eyes'?" And they sought to lay hands on Him, but feared the multitude, for they knew He had spoken the parable against them. So they left Him and went away.

The vast majority of Jesus' parables are recorded in the Gospels of Matthew and Luke. Mark recounts only a few of them; the last parable we saw in our study of this gospel was in Mark 7. But here in chapter 12 we find another, and a very unusual one at that.

Earlier, when Jesus explained His use of parables to His disciples, He said: "To you it has been given to know the mystery of the kingdom of God; but to those who are outside, all things come in parables, so that 'Seeing they may see and not perceive, and hearing they may hear and not understand; lest they should turn, and their sins be forgiven them'" (4:11–12). In other words, most of Jesus' parables were designed to present a truth about the kingdom of God in a subtle way so that believers would understand but those outside the kingdom would not. However, the meaning of the parable of the wicked vinedressers is plain, and those whom it targeted, namely, the religious leaders of Israel, understood it clearly.

With this parable, Jesus deliberately provoked His enemies to greater opposition against Him. He might have spared Himself from some hatred, but whenever He witnessed blatant sin, He did not hesitate to call attention to it. It is true that He adopted different tones depending on whom He was addressing. With the ordinary people, the lowly of heart, He was gentle, tender, and mild. With those who sat in the seats of religious authority, who corrupted the things of God, He pulled no punches. Thus it was with this parable, which only thinly veiled His wrath and the Father's wrath against the rulers over Israel.

Untrustworthy Hired Hands

Mark writes: **Then He began to speak to them in parables: "A man planted a vineyard and set a hedge around it, dug a place for the wine vat and built a tower. And he leased it to vinedressers and went into a far country"** (v. 1). This brief introduction reveals that Jesus was quite familiar with the wine industry in Israel. He knew something about how grapes were grown and processed into wine. He even knew that vineyards typically included a tower where a watchman could stand to keep an eye out for animals that might destroy the grapes or thieves who might steal them.

It is worth noting that the Jews produced real wine, not mere grape juice. One must completely distort the text of sacred Scripture because of a contemporary cultural bias to conclude that the Jews did not produce real wine, that they did not use real wine in the Passover, and that Jesus did not make real wine at the wedding feast of Cana (John 2). The Jewish moral code was very strict against drunkenness, considering it a profound sin, but the fact that drunkenness was possible in Israel shows us that the beverage that was produced from the vine was wine.

In Jesus' parable, the owner of the vineyard had to go away to another country. In his absence, he leased the vineyard and the whole wine-making operation to vinedressers. The vinedressers were tenant farmers. They were the equivalent of "hirelings," men who were hired to watch sheep. Just as there were shepherds who cared for their own sheep, there were hirelings who were engaged to watch over the sheep owned by others. Hirelings were notorious for not having the same care and love for the sheep as the owners; at the first sign of danger to the sheep, they would abandon them and flee to save their own lives (John 10:12–13). So, the owner of the vineyard put his operation in the hands of men who were not completely trustworthy.

Jesus continued: **"Now at vintage-time he sent a servant to the vinedressers, that he might receive some of the fruit of the vineyard from the vinedressers"** (v. 2). The owner was on pins and needles to learn how the latest vintage of wine had turned out, so at the time when the vintage was produced, he sent a servant from the far country to ask the vinedressers to send him samples of the wine. The result was shocking: **"And they took him and beat him and sent him away empty-handed"** (v. 3). For unspecified reasons, these vinedressers, men who were tenant farmers for another man, refused to honor the request of their landlord and even beat his servant. Not only were they not trustworthy, they were evil.

The vineyard owner showed extraordinary patience, but the results only got worse: **"Again he sent them another servant, and at him they threw stones, wounded him in the head, and sent him away shamefully treated. And again he sent another, and him they killed; and many others, beating some and killing some"** (vv. 4–5). The owner sent "many" servants to the vinedressers, who became more and more cruel. After beating the first servant, the vinedressers stoned the second and actually killed the third. Thereafter, they continued on, injuring some and killing others.

Unsettling Prophetic Imagery

The prophet Isaiah gave a prophecy about a vineyard that is very interesting in light of this parable. Under the subtitle "God's Disappointing Vineyard," it reads:

Now let me sing to my Well-beloved a song of my Beloved regarding His vineyard:

My Well-beloved has a vineyard
on a very fruitful hill.
He dug it up and cleared out its stones,
and planted it with the choicest vine.
He built a tower in its midst,

and also made a winepress in it;

so He expected it to bring forth good grapes,

but it brought forth wild grapes.

"And now, O inhabitants of Jerusalem and men of Judah,

judge, please, between Me and My vineyard.

What more could have been done to My vineyard

that I have not done in it?

Why then, when I expected it to bring forth good grapes,

did it bring forth wild grapes?

And now, please let Me tell you what I will do to My vineyard:

I will take away its hedge, and it shall be burned;

and break down its wall, and it shall be trampled down.

I will lay it waste;

it shall not be pruned or dug,

but there shall come up briers and thorns.

I will also command the clouds

that they rain no rain on it."

For the vineyard of the Lord of hosts is the house of Israel,

and the men of Judah are His pleasant plant. (Isa. 5:1–7a)

Notice that in this prophecy, God's anger was directed against the vineyard, because it was barren. Even though God planted choice vines and tended them with great care, the vineyard brought forth wild grapes (the Hebrew literally means "stinking things," which is best understood as "rotten grapes"). In the end, the fruit was worthless. So, God decided to burn down the hedge, break down the wall, and lay the vineyard waste. He would not let it be tended and would not let rain fall on it. This was a prophecy of God's judgment on Israel.

Jesus clearly borrowed much of this imagery for His parable of the wicked vinedressers, but in His account, judgment is directed not at the vineyard but at the vinedressers. These vinedressers were clearly representative of the clergy of Israel, who, for centuries, had mistreated the servants (the prophets) sent by the owner (God). Jesus was saying that God was not going to destroy His church but the corrupt clergy who had been placed in charge of it to nurture it, feed it, and tend it, tasks they had failed to carry out.

Unyielding Antipathy

Jesus then introduced another variation from the prophecy: **"Therefore still having one son, his beloved, he also sent him to them last, saying, 'They will respect my son'"** (v. 6). In his continuing efforts to deal with the vinedressers, the owner decided to send his only son, "his beloved." I wonder whether any of those standing there remembered how God the Father spoke from heaven at Jesus' baptism, saying, "You are My beloved Son" (Mark 1:11), and at His transfiguration, saying, "This is My beloved Son" (9:7). There is no doubt that the son in the parable was representative of Jesus.

The owner expected that despite all the evil they had committed against his servants, the vinedressers would not go so far as to mistreat or harm his son. Besides, the son had legal claim to the vineyard, for he was the heir. He was not just a servant who could only pass along a message from the owner. The hired hands had to submit to the son's authority because he was the son of the owner.

However, the owner underestimated the depth of evil in the vinedressers' hearts. Jesus said: **"But those vinedressers said among themselves, 'This is the heir. Come, let us kill him, and the inheritance will be ours.' So they took him and killed him and cast him out of the vineyard"** (vv. 7–8). This must have been a shocking twist to the story for many of those who heard Jesus, but for the Pharisees, the scribes, and the other religious leaders, it must have been chillingly revealing, given their plots to do away with Jesus. In fact, by this point, everything must have been clear to them. The owner was God. The vineyard was the people of God. The servants were the prophets. The son was Jesus Himself. And the vinedressers, the ones causing all the trouble, the ones who ignored and mistreated the prophets, and the ones who were planning to do away with the Son, were the religious leaders themselves. We can only imagine how enraged they were that Jesus knew what was in their hearts and so blatantly portrayed their hypocrisy and wickedness.

When the Son of God walked the earth, from the time of His birth until the time of His execution, there was never a moment when His life was safe among human beings. Our fallen nature is such that we are not simply indifferent to God, we hate God. God is our mortal enemy, and fallen human beings will stop at nothing in their attempts to throw off the sovereignty of their Creator. We should not believe that the world is truly indifferent toward God, as it professes to be. If God Himself came to earth today, and people were given power to destroy Him, He would surely be put to death. I am not speaking theoretically when I say that, because it actually happened. It happened just as Jesus said it would happen. Just a few days after He spoke these words, they seized the Son, abused Him, and killed Him outside the city, outside the vineyard of God.

Unfailing Vengeance

So, Jesus asked, **"Therefore what will the owner of the vineyard do?"** (v. 9a). Unlike in the prophecy of Isaiah, Jesus did not say the owner would come and destroy the vineyard. Rather, **"He will come and destroy the vinedressers, and give the vineyard to others"** (v. 9b). Jesus was saying God would destroy the temple, the Jewish sacrificial system, the priesthood, the Sanhedrin, and all the rest—the very heart of Judaism—and give the vineyard to the Gentiles. All of this occurred when the Romans wiped out Jerusalem in AD 70.

Then Jesus said: **"Have you not even read this Scripture: 'The stone which the builders rejected has become the chief cornerstone. This was the Lord's doing, and it is marvelous in our eyes'?"** (vv. 10–11). Jesus quoted Psalm 118:22–23 here, which speaks of the Messiah as a rejected stone that ends up becoming the cornerstone of God's work. In His parable, Jesus acknowledged that the Son—He Himself—would be killed, but even with that sure knowledge He was confident that God's purpose for Him would be established. Though the "builders"—also known as the vinedressers—might reject Him, He would be the cornerstone. It would be the work of God Himself.

Mark then concludes: **And they sought to lay hands on Him, but feared the multitude, for they knew He had spoken the parable against them. So they left Him and went away** (v. 12). Here Mark confirms that the religious leaders fully understood that Jesus spoke this parable against them. He also confirms that they were enraged by it, for they sought to seize Him then and there, and were restrained only by their fear of the adoring crowd. So, they left Him, only to continue their deliberations as to how they might destroy Him in secrecy.

41

A QUESTION ON TAXES

Mark 12:13–17

⌘

Then they sent to Him some of the Pharisees and the Herodians, to catch Him in His words. When they had come, they said to Him, "Teacher, we know that You are true, and care about no one; for You do not regard the person of men, but teach the way of God in truth. Is it lawful to pay taxes to Caesar, or not? Shall we pay, or shall we not pay?" But He, knowing their hypocrisy, said to them, "Why do you test Me? Bring Me a denarius that I may see it." So they brought it. And He said to them, "Whose image and inscription is this?" They said to Him, "Caesar's." And Jesus answered and said to them, "Render to Caesar the things that are Caesar's, and to God the things that are God's." And they marveled at Him.

fter Jesus told His parable of the wicked vinedressers, which we considered in the previous chapter, the religious authorities in Jerusalem stepped up the pressure on Him. In quick succession, three different parties came to Him with questions: first, a delegation of the Pharisees and Herodians, then some of the Sadducees, and finally a representative of the scribes. These efforts, or at least the first two of them, were intended to trap Jesus, to put Him on the horns of a dilemma that would bring Him into conflict with the people, the government, or the theological authorities. We will consider these clashes in this chapter and the following two chapters.

Mark begins by saying, **Then they sent to Him some of the Pharisees and** the Herodians, to catch Him in His words (v. 13). "They" probably refers to the ruling body of the Jews, the Sanhedrin. The Sanhedrin was composed of men from three major groups of the Jews: the Pharisees, the Sadducees, and the scribes, the same groups that presented questions to Jesus in these narratives in Mark 12. Thus, it seems these successive attacks were coordinated to at least some extent by the Sanhedrin.

It is interesting that the Greek word translated as "sent" in this verse is related to the word normally translated as "apostle." As we have seen, an apostle was not simply a messenger, but a messenger empowered with the authority to speak for the one who sent him. The twelve Apostles carried the authority of Jesus. Thus, this group of Pharisees and Herodians came with the authority of the Sanhedrin behind them.

The Herodians, who we saw mentioned in Mark 3:6, were a party of the Jews that supported the ruling authority of the Herodian dynasty. The Herods, who were not pure Jews, were puppet kings under the authority of the Romans, and they were thoroughly despised by many Jews. The Pharisees normally despised the Herodians for supporting the corrupt dynasty, but as has been said, "The enemy of my enemy is my friend." Mutual hatred of Jesus thrust the Pharisees and the Herodians into a strange alliance.

When representatives of these two groups came to Jesus, their aim was to "catch Him in His words." The word *catch* is a rather feeble and insipid translation of the Greek that is used here, *agreuo*. This word is a *hapax legomenon*, a word that appears in the New Testament only once. That rarity means it is difficult to grasp the full measure of the meaning of this word. The verb Mark uses here means "to take by hunting," and it has connotations of violent pursuit. The idea is something like hunting for a man-eating tiger by digging a pit and putting sharp spikes at the bottom so that the tiger will fall in and be impaled. The Pharisees and Herodians were not just trying to play tag with Jesus. They were trying to destroy Him with violence.

The Trap Is Set

Mark writes, **When they had come, they said to Him, "Teacher, we know that You are true, and care about no one; for You do not regard the person of men, but teach the way of God in truth"** (v. 14a). The first words from the Pharisees and Herodians were designed to flatter Jesus. First, they said, "We know that You are true." Later they added, "[You] teach the way of God in truth." Oh, that they actually had believed this. Of course, if they had, they would not have been coming to Him with questions designed to trap Him. They would have been listening to His word and receiving it.

They added, "[You] care about no one; for You do not regard the person of men." When the Pharisees and Herodians said that Jesus "[cared] about no one," they did not mean that He was hard-hearted, with no affection for people. We know from our study in Mark that such was not the case, for we have seen Jesus moved with compassion on several occasions. Rather, they were saying He was a man of integrity. Such a man refuses to compromise principles and ethics; he does not turn from what is right for the sake of popularity. The Pharisees and Herodians were saying that Jesus would not be swayed from the truth because of concerns that people might find His message unpopular. This was a tremendous tribute. Of course, as the following text shows, they uttered their acclaim of Jesus with total and complete hypocrisy, but in spite of themselves, they spoke the truth about His character.

Finally, the Pharisees and Herodians posed their question: **"Is it lawful to pay taxes to Caesar, or not? Shall we pay, or shall we not pay?"** (vv. 14b–15a). In asking this question, they tasked Jesus with settling one of the most controversial issues among the Jews at that time. No nation enjoys being brought under subjection to a conqueror, but having to pay taxes and other forms of tribute to the occupying country is all the more loathsome to the conquered population. Almost every Jew in Israel hated the very thought of paying any tax whatsoever to Caesar, and many of them, in fact, did not pay. Some of the Pharisees believed that the Jews were under a moral obligation not to pay taxes to Caesar, and so, if Jesus were really a godly man, He would not advocate paying taxes to the ungodly conquering government.

So, there was the trap: if Jesus said it was okay to pay taxes to Caesar, the people would turn against Him, but if He said publicly that no one should pay taxes to Caesar, the religious leaders would hasten to the Roman authorities and say, "This man is propagating rebellion by advising people not to pay their taxes."

The Trap Evaded

Of course, Jesus saw right through the attempt to trap Him. Mark tells us: **But He, knowing their hypocrisy, said to them, "Why do you test Me? Bring Me a denarius that I may see it"** (v. 15b). The denarius was probably the most common coin among the Jews. It was a small silver coin that carried the value of an average day's wage for a laborer in Israel. Apparently Jesus did not have a denarius with Him, so He asked His interrogators to produce one.

When they brought the coin, Jesus asked them: **"Whose image and inscription is this?" They said to Him, "Caesar's"** (v. 16). At that time in Jewish history, the caesar whose image appeared on the denarius was Tiberius, who reigned after Augustus, from AD 14 to 37. His image was pressed on the surface of the coin along with an inscription: *Ti Caesar Divi Aug F Augustus*, which meant, "Tiberius Caesar, son of the divine Augustus." On the reverse side of the coin was the inscription *pontif maxim*, that is, "High Priest." The emperor was not only the supreme political ruler of the Roman Empire, he was the supreme religious leader, seen as a deity. It is noteworthy that the name of Tiberius' father, Augustus, was not a name at all but a title, "August One," that was conferred on him by the Senate. This was a religious honor, indicating that he possessed transcendent majesty. However, it was a term the Jews used only for God; they believed that calling any creature "august" was an act of idolatry. So, the denarius displayed the full depth of the arrogance of the Roman caesars.

Jesus then said: **"Render to Caesar the things that are Caesar's, and to God the things that are God's." And they marveled at Him** (v. 17). Since the caesar's image and inscription were on the coin, according to Roman law, it was his possession. Jesus was telling them: "This is Caesar's coin. Use it to pay Caesar's tax. But you have an even higher responsibility. You must render to God the things that are God's."

The New Testament expands on this important topic of paying taxes. In Romans 13, the Apostle Paul explains that God created two institutions in the world, the church and the state. They have separate responsibilities, separate missions to perform. The church is charged with proclaiming the Word of God and administering the sacraments. The power of the sword to wage war and keep the peace is given to the state. Government, therefore, is legitimate, and Christians ought to support it. For this reason, Paul writes, "Render therefore to all their due: taxes to whom taxes are due, customs to whom customs, fear to whom fear, honor to whom honor" (Rom. 13:7).

Paul wrote these words at a time when the government, the Roman Empire, was corrupt and godless. Obviously, therefore, the moral behavior of the state is to have no bearing on whether Christians pay their taxes. Christians are called to a special level of civil obedience, which includes paying taxes no matter how burdensome or oppressive they may be. Of course, our commitment to civil obedience does not mean we cannot speak out against taxes or anything else the government does, but we do not have the right to refuse to pay.

A Modern Trap

However, taxation is no simple matter in our time. We have to be careful that we do not misuse our voting privileges to support unfair taxing practices.

In the early nineteenth century, the French thinker and historian Alexis de Tocqueville visited America and came away highly impressed by this experiment in government. However, in his book *Democracy in America*, he wrote of a danger that could come on the young republic. He foresaw the possibility that the people would begin to understand that their votes were worth money. What did he mean? He was warning that people who wanted to go to seats of political power would be able to use wealth to bribe people in order to be elected. He said that such bribery could destroy the civic righteousness of the nation.

Today, the problem goes deeper than de Tocqueville ever envisioned. We can use our ballots as bullets. The tenth commandment forbids covetousness with respect to private property. But in America, we have seen the proliferation of the politics of envy, prompting people to think nothing of permitting the government to take from one group and give to another. We do this when we vote for programs that benefit some but not all citizens. It is called social justice, even though it is a manifest injustice. In simple terms, it is theft, because all must pay while only some benefit. People go to the polls every day and think nothing of voting themselves benefits from the government, not thinking or caring that they are asking the government to use its power to take from someone else and give to them. Every day people vote for taxes on others without voting for the same taxes on themselves. That is unjust and immoral.

Even if the whole world does this, the Christian must never do it. Even if we find ourselves exploited and oppressed by this practice, we must not do it ourselves. We must never ask the government to force our neighbors to give us something that belongs to them. I urge you to think about the biblical ethic with regard to taxes. We must pay our taxes even if the government is corrupt, but we are not allowed to participate in the corruption of the system.

Jesus told the Pharisees and Herodians to "Render to Caesar the things that are Caesar's, and to God the things that are God's." The denarius belonged to Caesar Tiberius because it had his image stamped on it. Whose image do you bear? Every one of us has been stamped with an image by the supreme authority in heaven and earth. God Himself has placed His image on us. Caesar owned that denarius, but he did not own the people of his time. Likewise, the state does not own us. God owns us; He has the supreme right to claim our lives as His own. So, then, we are to render to God the things that are God's, including our lives, our liberty, our possessions, and our affections. That is the duty of every Christian.

42

A QUESTION ON THE RESURRECTION

Mark 12:18–27

⚯

Then some Sadducees, who say there is no resurrection, came to Him; and they asked Him, saying: "Teacher, Moses wrote to us that if a man's brother dies, and leaves his wife behind, and leaves no children, his brother should take his wife and raise up offspring for his brother. Now there were seven brothers. The first took a wife; and dying, he left no offspring. And the second took her, and he died; nor did he leave any offspring. And the third likewise. So the seven had her and left no offspring. Last of all the woman died also. Therefore, in the resurrection, when they rise, whose wife will she be? For all seven had her as wife." Jesus answered and said to them, "Are you not therefore mistaken, because you do not know the Scriptures nor the power of God? For when they rise from the dead, they neither marry nor are given in marriage, but are like angels in heaven. But concerning the dead, that they rise, have you not read in the book of Moses, in the burning bush passage, how God spoke to him, saying, 'I am the God of Abraham, the God of Isaac, and the God of Jacob'? He is not the God of the dead, but the God of the living. You are therefore greatly mistaken."

After Jesus foiled the attempt of the Pharisees and Herodians to trap Him with a question about taxes, the Sanhedrin fired its second salvo, sending to Him representatives of the Sadducees. They came with a question about the doctrine of the resurrection of the dead, which was the focus of a serious dispute in the first century between the Pharisees and the Sadducees.

These groups, both of which seem to have begun in the second century BC, were as one in their opposition to Jesus, but that is almost the only thing on which they agreed. First, the Pharisees stressed the sovereignty of God. They were the Augustinians and Calvinists of their day. The Sadducees believed that the affairs of men and of history were determined not by a sovereign God but solely by the unfettered free will of human creatures. They were Pelagians before Pelagius. Second, the Pharisees believed in angels and demons, while the Sadducees categorically denied the existence of both. A third point of dispute had to do with the canon of Scripture. The Pharisees believed that the Scriptures contained the Torah, which was the first five books of the Old Testament, plus the Prophets and the Writings, the Wisdom Literature and such. The Sadducees had a much more restricted view of the canon, recognizing only the Torah as the Word of God. So any writings beyond the book of Deuteronomy could not be used for the construction of theology as far as the Sadducees were concerned.

The Pharisees' and Sadducees' differences on the canon contributed to their disagreement about the resurrection. This doctrine states that the souls of men live on after death, and that when God brings history to a close, He will raise the bodies of all human beings from the grave and reunite them to their souls, with the righteous then being welcomed to eternal life with God and the unrighteous being sent away into eternal torment. Because the Sadducees could see no teaching on life after death in the Torah, they were convinced there would be no resurrection at the end of the age. The Pharisees, building their case largely on the teachings of the prophets, argued for the resurrection and life after death.

Acting on their denial of the resurrection of the dead, the Sadducees brought Jesus a question involving a weird case touching on the resurrection and marriage. Mark tells us: **Then some Sadducees, who say there is no resurrection, came to Him; and they asked Him, saying: "Teacher, Moses wrote to us that if a man's brother dies, and leaves his wife behind, and leaves no children, his brother should take his wife and raise up offspring for his brother. Now there were seven brothers. The first took a wife; and dying, he left no offspring. And the second took her, and he died; nor did he leave any offspring. And the third likewise. So the seven had her and left no offspring. Last of all the woman died also. Therefore, in the resurrection, when they rise, whose wife will she be? For all seven had her as wife"** (vv. 18–23).

This question revolved around the so-called levirate law, which God gave to ancient Israel. It was designed to provide descendants for a man who died childless so that his family line could maintain its property. It is explained in the book of Deuteronony:

> "If brothers dwell together, and one of them dies and has no son, the widow of the dead man shall not be married to a stranger outside the family; her husband's brother shall go in to her, take her as his wife, and perform the duty of a husband's brother to her. And it shall be that the firstborn son which she bears will succeed to the name of his dead brother, that his name may not be blotted out of Israel." (25:5–6)

The Sadducees told Jesus of a case of seven brothers, all of whom married the same woman in succession to protect their other brothers' rights. However, none of them fathered children by her, and finally, the woman herself died childless. We might have expected the Sadducees to use this case, which sounds highly hypothetical, to ask an arcane question about the law, but they actually used it to question Him about the truth of the doctrine that the dead will rise again at the end of history. By asking whose wife the woman would be when they were all raised again, the Sadducees seem to have been suggesting that the resurrection would create unsolvable problems. Perhaps they hoped Jesus would make Himself look silly by trying to defend the doctrine of the resurrection in the face of the problem they had presented.

Knowing Scripture and God's Power

Jesus answered the inquiry of the Sadducees with a rebuke. Mark writes, **Jesus answered and said to them, "Are you not therefore mistaken, because you do not know the Scriptures nor the power of God?"** (v. 24). It is easy for us, looking back from our vantage point in the twenty-first century, to conclude that the Jewish religious leaders were ignorant or arrogant, but Jesus said they had a very simple problem: they did not understand the Scriptures. We have this same problem. I think 100 percent of our theological errors happen because we do not know the Scriptures. We all read the same book, but we do not always agree on what the book teaches because we do not take the time to truly understand it. Every believer should strive with all of his might to have a sound knowledge of the Word of God, lest we hear the same rebuke from Jesus: "You are mistaken because you do not know the Word of God."

Neither did they know "the power of God," Jesus said. I believe we have this problem, too. We live sometimes as if our lives are totally in the grip of the powers and forces of this world. We have not begun to understand the transcendent power of God, the God who said, "Let there be light," and the light appeared. This is the God whose power was manifested throughout the earthly pilgrimage of Jesus as He healed the sick, calmed the storm, and raised the dead. The Apostle Paul prayed that God's people would know "what is the exceeding greatness of His power toward us who believe" (Eph. 1:19a). We need to know and trust our powerful God.

Having rebuked the Sadducees, Jesus began to correct their thinking. He said, **"For when they rise from the dead, they neither marry nor are given in marriage, but are like angels in heaven"** (v. 25). Notice the first words He uttered here: "*When* they rise from the dead." Jesus did not say, "*If* they rise. . . ." This was an affirmation of the resurrection. Furthermore, He said those who rise "are like angels in heaven." Here, again, Jesus contradicted Sadducee dogma; they did not believe in angels, but He affirmed that they exist.

The part of this verse that troubles many believers today is Jesus' statement that those who rise again are like the angels in that they "neither marry nor are given in marriage." It seems clear that Jesus taught here that marriage will be unknown after the resurrection of the dead. However, some scholars see a different meaning in these words. First, they note that when Jesus spoke of His return, He said: "But as the days of Noah were, so also will the coming of the Son of Man be. For as in the days before the flood, they were eating and drinking, marrying and giving in marriage, until the day that Noah entered the ark, and did not know until the flood came and took them all away, so also will the coming of the Son of Man be" (Matt. 24:37–39). Second, they interpret "marrying and giving in marriage" to mean that the sanctity of marriage in Noah's day was tarnished because people were marrying and divorcing, remarrying, and divorcing once again. It was like a merry-go-round. The marriage covenant was not honored at all, and that was one of the reasons God sent the flood. The conclusion of these scholars is that Jesus was simply saying, "It is going to be like that when I come again in judgment." In other words, disrespect for marriage would be one of the signs of Jesus' return.

I grant that this is a possible interpretation of Jesus' words to the Sadducees, but personally I am not persuaded by this argument. For one thing, I do not see how this response would have answered the Sadducees' question. I think Jesus was speaking straightforwardly here, saying there will not be any marriage in heaven because we will be like the angels, who do not marry.

As I said above, this verse troubles many believers who take great delight in their spouses and do not relish the idea that their union in this world will not continue in the next when they rise from the dead. I appreciate their struggle, but I am reminded of a statement my mentor, Dr. John Gerstner, once made to me after a seminary chapel in which a speaker had attacked nearly everything precious to classical Reformed theology. As we were leaving the chapel, I caught up with Dr. Gerstner, and because I was quite distressed about what I had heard from the speaker, I blurted out, "If John Calvin could have heard that address, he would have turned over in his grave." Dr. Gerstner stopped, turned to me, and said, "Young man, don't you know that nothing could possibly destroy the felicity that John Calvin enjoys at this moment?" I was taken aback, but I quickly saw his point. We do not understand the depth of joy and delight that God has prepared for His people in heaven. If you use your imagination and try to think of the greatest possible experience that you will have in heaven, then multiply the joy you will feel in that moment by a million times, you still will not have begun to appreciate what God is preparing for His people in heaven. Our existence there will be filled with joy far, far exceeding that which the marriage relationship provides in this fallen world.

The God of the Living

Finally, Jesus took time to teach the Sadducees about the truth of the resurrection. He said: **"But concerning the dead, that they rise, have you not read in the book of Moses, in the burning bush passage, how God spoke to him, saying, 'I am the God of Abraham, the God of Isaac, and the God of Jacob'? He is not the God of the dead, but the God of the living. You are therefore greatly mistaken"** (vv. 26–27). Jesus asked, "Have you not read . . . ?" Earlier, He told them they did not know the Scriptures. Here He opened the Scriptures to them.

It is very significant that He did not take them to any of the Historical Books, to any of the Prophetic Books, or to the Writings. He took them to the Torah, the one section of the Old Testament Scriptures that the Sadducees accepted and which, they believed, said nothing about the resurrection.

Specifically, He took them to Exodus 3:1–6, the account of God's appearance to Moses in the burning bush, on which occasion God introduced Himself to Moses by saying, "I am the God of your father—the God of Abraham, the God of Isaac, and the God of Jacob," the patriarchs of Israel. He did not say, "I *was* the God of Abraham and the others." Jesus therefore told the Sadducees: "He is not the God of the dead, but the God of the living. You are therefore greatly mistaken." To prove that there will be a future resurrection, Jesus simply argued that God would not speak of Himself in this way were Abraham, Isaac, and Jacob not alive beyond the grave. Their lives were and are in the hand of the God of the living, who does not let death end our personal existence.

This text is more than a magnificent philosophical refutation of the views of those who sought to entrap Jesus. It is a bold and strong answer by our Master to mankind's oldest question: "If a man dies, shall he live again?" (Job 14:14). Without hesitation, without ambiguity, our Lord answered that question in the affirmative. We have life, and we have it forever. To miss that is not only to be mistaken, Jesus said, but to be "greatly mistaken." My prayer is that we may never make that mistake.

43

A QUESTION ON THE COMMANDMENTS

Mark 12:28–34

~~~

Then one of the scribes came, and having heard them reasoning together, perceiving that He had answered them well, asked Him, "Which is the first commandment of all?" Jesus answered him, "The first of all the commandments is: 'Hear, O Israel, the LORD our God, the LORD is one. And you shall love the LORD your God with all your heart, with all your soul, with all your mind, and with all your strength.' This is the first commandment. And the second, like it, is this: 'You shall love your neighbor as yourself.' There is no other commandment greater than these." So the scribe said to Him, "Well said, Teacher. You have spoken the truth, for there is one God, and there is no other but He. And to love Him with all the heart, with all the understanding, with all the soul, and with all the strength, and to love one's neighbor as oneself, is more than all the whole burnt offerings and sacrifices." Now when Jesus saw that he answered wisely, He said to him, "You are not far from the kingdom of God." But after that no one dared question Him.

After dealing with questions of a hostile nature from a group of Pharisees and Herodians, then from a delegation of Sadducees, Jesus was posed a question by a representative of the scribes, the third major group that comprised the Sanhedrin. The scribes were the theologians, the experts in biblical interpretation among the Jews. It is not surprising therefore that a scribe chose to ask Jesus a question about the Scriptures. However, his question does not seem to have been dripping with venom. He was not hostile. Instead, he came to Jesus because he had been profoundly impressed as he listened to the way in which Jesus handled the trick questions posed by the Pharisees, Herodians, and Sadducees.

The Scribe's Question

Mark tells us, **Then one of the scribes came, and having heard them reasoning together, perceiving that He had answered them well, asked Him, "Which is the first commandment of all?"** (v. 28). The scribe was not wondering about chronology. He was not asking, "What was the first commandment that God ever gave?" Rather, he was posing a question of priority. He was asking, "What is the single most important commandment that God has given to this world?" He wanted to know the chief duty not just of members of the household of Israel and, later, the Christian community, but of the entire world, of every human being created in the image of God.

It was common in both the Old Testament writings and in Jewish teaching at Jesus' time for teachers to attempt to summarize man's chief obligation to God. For example, the prophet Micah said, "He has shown you, O man, what is good; and what does the LORD require of you but to do justly, to love mercy, and to walk humbly with your God?" (6:8). God told the prophet Habakkuk, "The just shall live by his faith" (2:4b). Rabbi Hillel, who taught twenty years before the ministry of Jesus, summed it up this way: "What you would not want done to you, do not do to your neighbor," which was simply the Golden Rule articulated not in positive terms as Jesus did but as a prohibition. Hillel added: "This is the essence of the law. Everything else is mere commentary on it." These are just a few of the attempts to sum up the whole duty of man.

When the scribe asked Jesus to do this, Mark writes: **Jesus answered him, "The first of all the commandments is: 'Hear, O Israel, the LORD our God, the LORD is one. And you shall love the LORD your God with all your heart, with all your soul, with all your mind, and with all your strength.' This is the first commandment"** (vv. 29–30). Jesus directed the man's attention to the most fundamental summary of man's obligation that God gave to His people in the Old Testament, the *Shema*, which is found in Deuteronomy 6. That chapter begins with these words:

> "Now this is the commandment, and these are the statutes and judgments which the LORD your God has commanded to teach you, that you may observe them in the land which you are crossing over to possess, that you may fear the LORD

your God, to keep all His statutes and His commandments which I command you, you and your son and your grandson, all the days of your life, and that your days may be prolonged. Therefore hear, O Israel, and be careful to observe it, that it may be well with you, and that you may multiply greatly as the LORD God of your fathers has promised you—'a land flowing with milk and honey.'" (vv. 1–3)

After this preface, we come to the divine summons, the call that begins with the Hebrew word *shema*, which means "Hear" or "Give ear." Israel was commanded: "Hear, O Israel: The LORD our God, the LORD is one! You shall love the LORD your God with all your heart, with all your soul, and with all your strength" (vv. 4–5). I believe it is very significant that Jesus chose to cite this passage when asked to identify the highest-priority commandment.

When the *Shema* was uttered and the Jews were directed to focus their affection on God, the object of their affection was not an impersonal cosmic force, an unnamed, unknown higher power. It clearly stated God's identity: "The LORD our God." This was the God of Abraham, Isaac, and Jacob, the God of Moses, the God who had delivered Israel from their slavery in Egypt.

Of course, the Israelites were not commanded to love Him simply because of what He had done for them, just as we ought not to love God simply for the gifts and benefits we receive from His hand. Neither are we to love Him simply for His attributes—His infinite wisdom, His limitless power, His peerless justice, and so on. Rather, we are to love Him for who He is in Himself. We do not really progress in the Christian life until we understand that we are to love God simply because He is lovely and wonderful, worthy of every creature's unqualified affection.

Comprehensive Love for God

This is why the *Shema* commands the people of God to have a comprehensive love for God. First, we are commanded to love God with all our hearts. The idea is that our love for God is to come from the very root of our beings. Our love for God is to be an affection that is surpassed by no other affection. It is to be an undiluted, unmixed love for God.

Second, we are commanded to love God with all our souls. In other words, our love for Him is not to be tepid or lukewarm. It is to be a blazing fire in our souls. It is good to remember the warning Jesus gave to the Laodicean church in the book of Revelation. He said: "I know your works, that you are neither cold nor hot. I could wish you were cold or hot. So then, because you are lukewarm, and neither cold nor hot, I will vomit you out of My mouth" (3:15–16). Our love for God must be white hot, not cold or even lukewarm.

Finally, the *Shema* tells us to love God "with all of [our] strength." The affection that we are to have for God is not to be a weak, impotent thing. We must call on all of the strength we can muster to express our affection for Him.

It is interesting that the *Shema* lists three dimensions of our love for God—heart, soul, and strength. Jesus, however, listed four—heart, soul, mind, and strength. Some Hebrew scholars say the idea of the mind is implied in the word that is translated as "strength" in the *Shema*. Jesus, however, left no ambiguity. When He quoted the *Shema*, He said, "You shall love the LORD your God . . . with all your mind." We are to love God with the fullness of our understanding. Sometimes I get impatient when I hear people say, "I do not want to study, I just want to have a simple faith." God did not give us the Bible so that we might treat it as a children's story. He calls us to apply our minds to the fullest extent to understand the riches and the depths of His revelation of Himself in His Word. This is what it means to love God with our minds.

If we are honest with ourselves, we all have to admit that we have not kept the Great Commandment for even a single day of our lives. However, we are at ease in Zion about it. We are not really under great conviction in this matter, because we see that no one loves the Lord God with all of his or her heart, soul, mind, and strength. Thus, we think it must not be a big deal if we do not keep this commandment either. We are greatly mistaken in thinking this way.

The Most Serious Sin

The scribe asked Jesus which was the Great Commandment, the first in terms of importance. This was a natural question for him. The Jews taught that there are 613 commandments in the Torah, and the scribes distinguished between the "heavy laws" and the "light laws," with the heavy laws being the more important ones. Even Jesus did that to some degree when He talked about the least of the commandments (Matt. 5:19) and weightier matters of the law (Matt. 23:23). We see this distinction also in the way the New Testament discusses sin. The New Testament recognizes a love that covers a multitude of sins (1 Peter 4:8), meaning sins that do not call for public ecclesiastical discipline. Elsewhere, we find lists of heinous crimes that destroy the church and require ecclesiastical discipline (1 Cor. 6:9–10; 1 Tim. 1:9–10). However, no sin is so small as to be insignificant. John Calvin, responding to the Roman Catholic distinction between mortal and venial sin, said that no sin is so slight that it does not deserve death, but no sin is so great that it actually destroys the grace of God in our souls.

If I were to ask you, "What is the most serious sin of all?" what would you say? Murder? Adultery? Idolatry? Unbelief? It seems to me that if the Great

Commandment is to love the Lord our God with all our heart, soul, mind, and strength, the great transgression is the failure to keep this commandment. That scares me, because I have not kept the Great Commandment for five minutes in my life. I have never loved God with my whole heart. My soul has never overflowed with affection for God. My mind has been lazy with respect to understanding God's Word, and I am often more interested in learning the things of this world. Finally, I have used only a portion of my strength in my affection for God. Were it not for Jesus, I would perish because of this sin, and rightly so.

But consider Jesus. Was there any portion of the Lord's heart that was not completely in love with the Father? Did Jesus restrain His soul from affection for His Father? Was there anything that the Father revealed that Jesus ignored as being unworthy of His attention? Was His affection for His Father a spineless, weak affection, or did He manifest the most powerful, strong affection for the Father ever seen on this planet? You know the answers to these questions. The Lord Jesus kept the Great Commandment perfectly. Every second of His life He loved the Father with all of His heart, all of His soul, all of His mind, and all of His strength. Had He not done that, He would not have fulfilled the law of God and would not have been worthy to save Himself, let alone save us.

After identifying the Great Commandment to answer the scribe's question, Jesus added, **"And the second, like it, is this: 'You shall love your neighbor as yourself.' There is no other commandment greater than these"** (v. 31). Jesus here quoted Leviticus 19:18 to identify the second-greatest commandment. Obviously, Jesus was correct in ranking love for God as the greatest commandment, but it is significant that Jesus felt it was necessary to mention love for one's neighbor. Love for other people is also extremely important. Indeed, as Jesus said in the parallel passage in Matthew's gospel, these two commandments summarize "all the Law and the Prophets" (Matt. 22:40), that is, all of Scripture.

It is worth noting the injunctions that follow the *Shema*: "And these words which I command you today shall be in your heart. You shall teach them diligently to your children, and shall talk of them when you sit in your house, when you walk by the way, when you lie down, and when you rise up. You shall bind them as a sign on your hand, and they shall be as frontlets between your eyes. You shall write them on the doorposts of your house and on your gates" (Deut. 6:6–9). We are never to forget the Great Commandment, as well as the other commands in God's Word. To guard against that, the Scriptures must be an integral part of our lives and something we teach to our children with diligence.

Close to the Kingdom

After Jesus gave these answers, the scribe was duly impressed. Mark writes: **So the scribe said to Him, "Well said, Teacher. You have spoken the truth, for there is one God, and there is no other but He. And to love Him with all the heart, with all the understanding, with all the soul, and with all the strength, and to love one's neighbor as oneself, is more than all the whole burnt offerings and sacrifices"** (vv. 32–33). I do not think the scribe was being patronizing to Jesus. I think he meant what he said. To his great credit, he even admitted that loving God and neighbor was more significant than the sacrificial system that was so important to the Jewish authorities.

Then Mark tells us, **Now when Jesus saw that he answered wisely, He said to him, "You are not far from the kingdom of God"** (v. 34a). Jesus regarded the scribe's response as a wise one. Notice, however, that He did not say, "You are in the kingdom of God." He said: "You are not far from the kingdom of God. You are beginning to see. You are starting to understand what it means that the Lord God omnipotent is the sovereign King and what it means to love Him for who He is." The scribe still needed to be born again to faith in Jesus.

Mark then adds a final word: **But after that no one dared question Him** (v. 34b). Jesus' enemies had enough sense to see that they had utterly failed to catch Him in His words. He was able to spot their snares, with the result that they were embarrassed. Thus, they abandoned their attempts to entrap Him. In the end, they would condemn Him on the basis of false testimony and an improper trial (14:53–65).

44

DAVID'S SON
IS DAVID'S LORD

Mark 12:35–37

Then Jesus answered and said, while He taught in the temple, "How is it that the scribes say that the Christ is the Son of David? For David himself said by the Holy Spirit: 'The LORD said to my Lord, "Sit at My right hand, till I make Your enemies Your footstool."' Therefore David himself calls Him 'Lord'; how is He then his Son?" And the common people heard Him gladly.

I had a professor in seminary who liked to reminisce about a well-known Christian apologist. According to my professor, when this apologist engaged in a debate, he not only won, he annihilated his opponent's position. As my professor put it, he would "dust off the spot" where his opponent stood.

That colorful expression went through my mind as I reflected on the interrogations Jesus endured from delegations of the Pharisees and Herodians, and the Sadducees, and finally from a solitary scribe (vv. 13–34). These men sought to entrap Jesus in His words so they might have a reason to accuse Him and silence Him. However, if any adversaries of truth were ever annihilated in debate, it was these representatives; Jesus truly dusted off the spot where each stood. Not only did they not succeed in trapping Him, He displayed such wisdom and insight, and so thoroughly corrected the questioners' beliefs, that "no one dared question Him" anymore (v. 34b).

After He had silenced the questioners, Jesus went on the offensive and became the interrogator. Mark tells us, **Then Jesus answered and said, while He taught in the temple, "How is it that the scribes say that the Christ is the Son of David?"** (v. 35). Apparently Jesus was speaking to the common people, but it is not unlikely that various Pharisees, Sadducees, and scribes were listening, too. Indeed, Jesus asked a question about the scribes' view of the Messiah. He was asking, "Why have the intellectuals, the theologians, the rabbis of Israel concluded that the coming Messiah is to be the Son of David?"

Most of the people were well aware of the manifold texts of the Old Testament that indicated that the Messiah would be from the line of David. David, of course, was Israel's most illustrious king. He was a shepherd, a poet, a warrior, and a brilliant administrator. He extended the boundaries of the nation, was the greatest military genius of Israel's history, and had the finest public-works program of any king who ruled over the Jewish people. Thus, the Jews regarded the reign of David as the golden age of Israel.

When David died, his kingdom passed to his son Solomon. During his reign, despite his great wisdom (and because of his sometimes-great foolishness), the golden age of Israel began to be tarnished. In the next generation, the kingdom was divided between Jeroboam and Rehoboam, and the golden era turned to rust. The decay continued as corruption penetrated every dimension of the monarchies of both the northern and southern kingdoms. So, a longing for the golden years under David arose in the hearts of the people, and God gave them the promise that the house of David would be restored and that the Davidic dynasty would last forever. In generation after generation, the Jewish people pinned their hopes on the coming Messiah who would be one of David's descendants.

Who Is David's Lord?

So, Jesus posed this question regarding the scribes' reasons for teaching that the Messiah would come from David's line. On the surface, the question seems easily answered by citing any number of Old Testament passages. But Jesus then introduced a qualification, an apparently contradictory Scripture passage. He said: **"For David himself said by the Holy Spirit: 'The LORD said to my Lord, "Sit at My right hand, till I make Your enemies Your footstool."' Therefore David himself calls Him 'Lord'; how is He then his Son?"** (vv. 36–37a). The heart of this question is a quotation of Psalm 110:1, in which David referred to the Messiah as his "Lord." Jesus is asking how the great David can describe one of his descendants as greater than himself. His point is that the scribes have missed something important about the Messiah. To discover what it is, I want to work through this remarkable statement piece by piece.

Before I go further, it is worth noting Jesus' view of sacred Scripture. He did not regard the lyrical poetry of David as inspired merely in an artistic sense. Rather, when He quoted from Psalm 110, He said that David wrote "by the Holy Spirit," that is, under divine inspiration. Those who were God's instruments to give us divine revelation wrote not by their own wisdom but under the supervision and influence of the Spirit.

Our Lord had no objection to the doctrine of the divine inspiration of Scripture, and neither should we. However, we live in a day that the great Dutch theologian Abraham Kuyper, founder of the Free University of Amsterdam, described as a time not simply of biblical criticism but of biblical vandalism, when seemingly every conceivable hostile attack against the normative authority of the Bible has been launched. Those who believe in the inspiration of the biblical text are often considered backwoods fundamentalists or theological obscurantists who have no academic or scholarly credibility. So be it. We must stand our ground and say with Martin Luther, "*Spiritus Sanctus non est scepticus*," or, "The Holy Spirit is not a skeptic." That which the Spirit declares is more certain than life itself.

It is somewhat surprising that Psalm 110 is the Old Testament text that is quoted most frequently in the New Testament. Including direct quotations and allusions, the New Testament books refer to Psalm 110 no less than thirty-three times. The New Testament writers clearly understood how important this text is for understanding the person and work of Jesus.

So, when Jesus had finished answering and silencing His adversaries, He took them to this text, which was the supreme text of messianic expectancy among them. And He said, "Notice what David said about His Son, the Son that you are expecting as your Messiah."

David said by the Holy Spirit, "The LORD said to my Lord." This is the first part of the conundrum. Here we find "the LORD," and the capital letters indicate that this is a reference to Yahweh, or God Himself. This is the sacred name of God, the memorial name, the ineffable name, the name by which God revealed Himself to Moses in the Midianite wilderness when He said, "I AM WHO I AM" (Ex. 3:14). In this verse in Psalm 110, Yahweh is having a conversation with someone who is given the title Adonai, or "Lord." In most cases in the Old Testament, Adonai is the supreme title for Yahweh. It means "the One who is absolutely Sovereign." This is why we sometimes find the words LORD and Lord back to back in Scripture. For example, in Psalm 8 we read, "O LORD, our Lord, how excellent is Your name in all the earth" (v. 1a). This text literally reads, "O Yahweh, our Adonai." It is saying, "O Yahweh, our Sovereign One, how excellent is your name."

So Yahweh (LORD) and Adonai (Lord) usually refer to the same person, namely, God. Yet, here in Psalm 110, we find Yahweh calling someone else Adonai. David certainly is not saying, "The LORD said to Himself." Rather, he says, "The LORD said to my Lord," or "my Adonai." Clearly he is thinking of two different people. Who, then, is David's Adonai? Who is sovereign over the king of Israel? In Hebrew categories, that would be God. So, it seems that God is speaking to someone else who carries the title for God. Thus, Jesus said to the scholars: "What do you think about this? What is the Holy Spirit saying?"

The Session of the Lord

God said to David's Lord, "Sit at My right hand till I make Your enemies Your footstool." When we study the biblical narratives of the life and work of Jesus, as well as the apostolic commentaries on those narratives, we discover moments of supreme importance in terms of redemptive history. These include His birth, His death on the cross, His resurrection, the Day of Pentecost, and His return. However, there is an element in the work of Christ that we almost completely overlook. It is the session of Jesus.

Churches that use the Presbyterian form of church government are led by elders, who collectively constitute what is called the session. The body of elders is known as the session because when they meet to deliberate, to establish policy, and to give supervision to the spiritual lives of the church members under their care, they sit down and discuss these things. Likewise, when we say that Congress is in session, we mean that our representatives are assembled and in their seats, ready to transact the business of the United States. The word *session* is appropriate to describe these situations because it is derived from the Latin *sessio*, which simply means "the act of sitting."

The most important session of all is the session of Jesus Christ in heaven. When Yahweh said to David's Lord, "Sit at My right hand," He was saying, "Be seated in the highest place of authority in the universe." Psalm 110 is a prophetic psalm, and David was saying by the Holy Spirit that when the Messiah had finished His labor in this world, He would be exalted to heaven and enthroned at the right hand of God. We declare that these things took place when we recite the Apostles' Creed, which affirms that Jesus "ascended into heaven and sitteth on the right hand of God." This was the early church's confession of belief in the importance of the session of Christ.

What does this mean for us? In simple terms, it means everything. We Americans pride ourselves on living in a democracy, but as Christians we live in a kingdom, one that is actively ruled by the King of kings. His reign is ongoing. Jesus is King at this moment. He is on His throne even now.

I love the legend of Robin Hood. In one version of the story, King Richard the Lionheart leaves England to fight in the Crusades, leaving his brother, Prince John, in charge of the realm. John mismanages the kingdom for his own benefit, forcing Robin and others to become outlaws. Robin and his compatriots, known as his merry men, live in Sherwood Forest, evading John and his henchman, the sheriff of Nottingham. The merry men are known for their joy, but they are known especially for their loyalty. They want to protect the realm until their king comes home. My favorite part of the story happens near the end, when Richard returns to England in the guise of a monk. At an inn, he hears talk about Robin Hood and his opposition to Prince John, so he purposely travels through Sherwood Forest. Suddenly, Robin and his men waylay Richard and his fellow travelers, and try to relieve the king of his purse. The king asks Robin, "Why are you doing this?" Robin replies, "Because of my allegiance to my king." Then Richard pulls off the monk's garments and displays the lion and the cross on his chest. Robin recognizes him and falls on his knees, saying, "My liege." In the end, Richard knights Robin because of his faithfulness during the absence of the king.

I love that story as a metaphor for the church. Our King is seated on the right hand of God. He expects us, His people, to remain loyal to Him while the whole world goes for Prince John. In time, He will return and put all things right.

Every Tongue Shall Confess

So, in Psalm 110, David writes of a conversation in which God invites David's Lord to sit in the seat of highest authority. That much is clear. Still, we have not answered Jesus' question: "Therefore David himself calls Him 'Lord'; how is He then his Son?" (v. 37a). In other words, how can David describe one of his descendants as greater than himself? In Jewish categories, the son was always subordinate to his father. The son was never greater than the father. By that reasoning, as marvelous as the Messiah would be, if He was to be David's Son, He could not be greater than David. Yet David himself calls his Son "my Lord," indicating that Jesus is not simply the Son of David, He is David's Sovereign. He is David's Adonai. He is David's King, the One before whom even David must bow.

In Philippians 2:5–11, Paul writes what is known as the Kenotic Hymn, because it speaks of Christ's Kenosis, or emptying of Himself. Paul says:

Let this mind be in you which was also in Christ Jesus, who, being in the form of God, did not consider it robbery to be equal with God, but made Himself of no reputation, taking the form of a bondservant, and coming in the likeness of men. And being found in appearance as a man, He humbled Himself and became obedient to the point of death, even the death of the cross. Therefore God also has highly exalted Him and given Him the name which is above every name, that at the name of Jesus every knee should bow, of those in heaven, and of those on earth, and of those under the earth, and that every tongue should confess that Jesus Christ is Lord, to the glory of God the Father.

Paul concludes that Jesus has been given the name that is above every name, and at that name every knee shall bow and every tongue confess that He is Lord. The supreme title, the title that was reserved for God in the Old Testament, is now given to His Son, and every person will recognize Him as Lord someday.

45

THE SCRIBES AND
THE WIDOW

Mark 12:38–44

Then He said to them in His teaching, "Beware of the scribes, who desire to go around in long robes, love greetings in the marketplaces, the best seats in the synagogues, and the best places at feasts, who devour widows' houses, and for a pretense make long prayers. These will receive greater condemnation." Now Jesus sat opposite the treasury and saw how the people put money into the treasury. And many who were rich put in much. Then one poor widow came and threw in two mites, which make a quadrans. So He called His disciples to Himself and said to them, "Assuredly, I say to you that this poor widow has put in more than all those who have given to the treasury; for they all put in out of their abundance, but she out of her poverty put in all that she had, her whole livelihood."

The scribes, the biblical interpreters of Jesus' time, seem to have become more and more the focus for Him as He taught in Jerusalem. After answering one scribe's question about the greatest commandment (vv. 28–34), He then posed a question about the scribes' teaching on the Messiah (vv. 35–37). Then, growing even more pointed, He gave the people a straightforward warning about the scribes.

Mark writes: **Then He said to them in His teaching, "Beware of the scribes, who desire to go around in long robes, love greetings in the marketplaces,**

the best seats in the synagogues, and the best places at feasts, who devour widows' houses, and for a pretense make long prayers. These will receive greater condemnation" (vv. 38–40). Later, the Apostle James gave a similar warning to teachers in the Christian church: "Let not many of you become teachers, knowing that we shall receive a stricter judgment" (3:1). Anyone who is put in a position of ecclesiastical leadership with the responsibility to feed the sheep of Christ has an enormous power to mislead the flock of God, so teachers have a responsibility to watch their doctrine closely and teach only that which is true. However, not all teachers take that responsibility seriously. That is where Jesus' warning comes in. Sheep need to know when their shepherds are misleading them. They, too, need to watch their teachers' doctrine—and their conduct.

Let us consider the specifics of Jesus' warning. The scribes, He said, "desire to go around in long robes." It was customary for a Jew to put on a prayer shawl when he recited prayers, but the scribes had special prayer shawls that were so long they touched the ground. These shawls, which had ornate tassels on the ends, depicted the lofty status these professors enjoyed in the community.

Some things never change. In the academic world, there sometimes is great jealousy among professors with respect to status, position, titles, and even the garments that are worn in academic processions. Academics often expend much energy to gain higher titles. You start out as an assistant or an instructor, then become an assistant professor, and finally a full professor with tenure. In the ecclesiastical world, you start off with nothing except your name. Once you go through seminary and receive a call, you become Reverend so and so. Then perhaps you go to graduate school and get an advanced degree, so that people begin to call you Doctor such and such. Still, you have not really made it in the theological world until you are known simply by your last name, like Luther, or Calvin. Perhaps the greatest tribute to any theologian is to have a theological system named after him; Augustinianism and Calvinism are just two examples.

Furthermore, Jesus said, the scribes "love greetings in the marketplaces." It was customary among the Jews for people to rise in the presence of a dignified scholar such as a scribe. Also, they love "the best seats in the synagogues, and the best places at feasts." In the synagogues, the best seats were the benches along the sides; the common people sat on the floor, but the scribes had what was then a comfortable place to sit. At feasts, they sat at the head tables. They greatly loved these symbols of honor and respect.

A Dreadful Evaluation

In a darker vein, Jesus said that the scribes "devour widows' houses." What did He mean? The Bible reveals that God has a special care for widows and orphans. Among the Jews, they were the most vulnerable, the most dependent, and the most easily exploited. To their shame, some scribes would go to vulnerable widows and basically bilk them out of whatever savings they had.

Years ago, when I was teaching in Jackson, Mississippi, the local newspaper published an exposé about unethical practices at a chain of dance studios. The dance instructors would invite elderly widows to come in for dance lessons and then charge them exorbitant amounts of money. The studio operators promised companionship, and they took the widows to dance contests in New Orleans a couple of times a year, and this became the lives of these widows. The paper reported that one dance instructor went to a woman's house and explained that she needed to take thousands of dollars worth of dance lessons. She did not have the money, but he offered to drive her to the bank so that she could take a second mortgage on her home in order to afford the dance lessons, and she agreed. Widows can fall for scams like that because they are frightened and insecure. If someone promises them an attractive return of some type for an investment, even if the investment is expensive, they often fall for it. That is what the scribes of Jesus' day were doing.

The scribes, Jesus said, disguised their hypocrisy with long, drawn-out prayers in public. They prayed these prayers not to honor God but that their piety might be seen by men. It was as if they peeked while praying to see who was watching, so that they could enjoy their reputations.

This is a dreadful evaluation of a group of people. Jesus' conclusion is devastating: "These will receive greater condemnation." As teachers of the Scriptures, these men were charged with a heavy responsibility, but they had not fulfilled it. They had failed to lead the people into truth and had failed to serve them humbly. As those entrusted with the truths of God, they would incur a harsher condemnation.

A Stark Contrast

Following his account of Jesus' warning about the scribes, Mark records an incident that illustrates the contrast between those who serve God with hypocrisy and those who serve Him with true spiritual devotion.

It happened, Mark tells us, that **Jesus sat opposite the treasury and saw how the people put money into the treasury. And many who were rich put in much** (v. 41). The treasury consisted of thirteen receptacles for donations or alms. It was situated in the temple's court of the women, so named because both men and women could enter that court; thus, everyone was able to make donations.

The practice of giving gifts to God's sanctuary was established in the days and weeks after God brought the people out of Egypt. In fact, He commanded the people to brings gifts to be used in the construction of the tabernacle, the very first sanctuary:

> Then the LORD spoke to Moses, saying: "Speak to the children of Israel, that they bring Me an offering. From everyone who gives it willingly with his heart you shall take My offering. And this is the offering which you shall take from them: gold, silver, and bronze; blue, purple, and scarlet thread, fine linen, and goats' hair; ram skins dyed red, badger skins, and acacia wood; oil for the light, and spices for the anointing oil and for the sweet incense; onyx stones, and stones to be set in the ephod and in the breastplate. And let them make Me a sanctuary, that I may dwell among them." (Ex. 25:1–8)

Later, God gave the people instructions for tithing. Because Israel was an agrarian society, they were told to bring tithes of their grain, new wine, and oil, and the firstborn of their herds and flocks (Deut. 14:22–29). If the journey to the sanctuary was long, they could exchange their gifts for money and bring that. These gifts supported the priests and Levites. Tithes also regularly helped foreigners, orphans, and widows (Deut. 26:12).

In Jesus' time, donations were brought to the temple. So much was given and distributed, the temple was something like the central bank of the nation. In fact, the person who administered the temple treasury was one of the most important officials in Israel.

As Jesus sat in the court of the women, He witnessed wealthy people making very large donations to the temple treasury. However, He also saw a donation of a different kind: **Then one poor widow came and threw in two mites, which make a quadrans** (v. 42). This is the most famous donation in history. It is better known than all the charitable contributions by Bill Gates, all the gifts of hundreds of millions of dollars by the Carnegie and Rockefeller families, or anyone else who has shown great generosity. The most famous gift was made by this poor widow in the temple as Jesus looked on.

The widow's gift was especially amazing because it was made in such stark contrast to the manner of the scribes, who wanted people to see their piety. In all probability, the last thing this poor woman wanted was to be noticed. She may have been ashamed of the meager donation that she gave. Mark tells us she brought two mites, which together made up one thirty-second of a denarius, and a denarius was the average pay for one day's work of a laborer.

An Unusual Value System

Jesus took note: **So He called His disciples to Himself and said to them, "Assuredly, I say to you that this poor widow has put in more than all those who have given to the treasury; for they all put in out of their abundance, but she out of her poverty put in all that she had, her whole livelihood"** (vv. 43–44). Jesus could not resist pointing out the contrast to His disciples. The wealthy people who were putting in much were giving out of their abundance. They gave to God what they could spare. The widow had nothing to spare, but what she had, she gave. For the vast majority of people who came to the treasury, there was no sacrifice involved at all. Their gifts cost them hardly anything in terms of their substance. The poor widow, by contrast, made a very costly sacrifice, even though it was a mere two mites. Seeing this, Jesus said to His disciples that the widow had put in more than anyone.

Jesus was telling His disciples—and us—something about God's balance sheet. Yes, Jesus could add. He knew the wealthy people were giving much greater amounts than the poor widow. However, it was not the money that Jesus valued most. He saw her act of piety and recognized true devotion. She loved her God and wished to obey Him and honor Him. That was why, out of her poverty, she put in all that she had, her whole livelihood.

This is the kind of sacrificial devotion to which we are called. Our Lord, who sacrificed His all for His people, calls us to give of ourselves. Furthermore, He tells us to do it quietly:

> "Take heed that you do not do your charitable deeds before men, to be seen by them. Otherwise you have no reward from your Father in heaven. Therefore, when you do a charitable deed, do not sound a trumpet before you as the hypocrites do in the synagogues and in the streets, that they may have glory from men. Assuredly, I say to you, they have their reward. But when you do a charitable deed, do not let your left hand know what your right hand is doing, that your charitable deed may be in secret; and your Father who sees in secret will Himself reward you openly." (Matt. 6:1–4)

God is not so much concerned with what we give as how we give. We must guard against giving so as to be seen by men. We can rest content, knowing that God sees all that we give, and He rewards those who give from hearts of devotion to Him.

46

THE OLIVET DISCOURSE, PART 1

Mark 13:1–8

～

Then as He went out of the temple, one of His disciples said to Him, "Teacher, see what manner of stones and what buildings are here!" And Jesus answered and said to him, "Do you see these great buildings? Not one stone shall be left upon another, that shall not be thrown down." Now as He sat on the Mount of Olives opposite the temple, Peter, James, John, and Andrew asked Him privately, "Tell us, when will these things be? And what will be the sign when all these things will be fulfilled?" And Jesus, answering them, began to say: "Take heed that no one deceives you. For many will come in My name, saying, 'I am He,' and will deceive many. But when you hear of wars and rumors of wars, do not be troubled; for such things must happen, but the end is not yet. For nation will rise against nation, and kingdom against kingdom. And there will be earthquakes in various places, and there will be famines and troubles. These are the beginnings of sorrows."

I n Mark 13, we find the longest sustained teaching of Jesus in this gospel. This teaching, known as the Olivet Discourse because it was delivered on the Mount of Olives, also appears in Matthew 24 and Luke 21. In it, Jesus discussed the future destruction of the temple and of Jerusalem, and of His coming.

If any text should prove Jesus' claims of divinity, it is this one. He clearly prophesied the destruction of the temple and of Jerusalem, along with numerous accompanying events, years before they happened. This is predictive prophecy of the highest magnitude. Such accuracy also argues strongly for the divine inspiration of sacred Scripture. However, no other New Testament text has been used more often by higher critical scholars and skeptics to raise questions about the identity of Christ and the trustworthiness of the New Testament. So, on one hand, this text is the most powerful apologetic we have for our Christology and for the Scriptures. On the other, it is a controversial text that is used in arguments against the truth claims of Christianity.

The problem is this: In addition to prophesying the destruction of the temple and of Jerusalem, along with many related events (vv. 2–23), Jesus spoke of His coming in clouds of glory (vv. 24–27). Then, near the end of the discourse, He said, "Assuredly, I say to you, this generation will by no means pass away till *all these things* take place" (v. 30). Thus, Jesus seemed to say that the generation of those then living would not die out before He returned. But His glorious return to bring history to a close did not happen before the first generation died; indeed, it has not happened even yet, nearly two thousand years later.

Jesus made other prophecies with a similar time frame. In chapter 27, we discussed this statement from Jesus: "Assuredly, I say to you that there are some standing here who will not taste death till they see the kingdom of God present with power" (Mark 9:1). We also considered this assertion: "Assuredly, I say to you, you will not have gone through the cities of Israel before the Son of Man comes" (Matt. 10:23).

Critical scholars seize on these prophecies, as well as the prophecy of Mark 13, to say that Jesus expected the consummation of His kingdom within a forty-year time frame, but since the consummation has not yet occurred, Jesus was mistaken. I do not think a week went by when I was in seminary that some biblical scholar did not seek to rub our noses in the difficulties of the Olivet Discourse, trying to use the text to disprove the inspiration of the Bible. When Bertrand Russell wrote his essay "Why I Am Not a Christian," he cited the Olivet Discourse as one of the chief reasons for his rejection of Christianity. He declared that even though Jesus' prophecies about the destruction of the temple and of Jerusalem were amazingly accurate, His credibility, and that of the entire New Testament, collapsed when He failed to return within a generation of the delivery of the Olivet Discourse.

I believe that conservative evangelical scholars who have struggled with this text have mostly failed to feel the real weight of this problem. I think it is the most significant problem we face with respect to the questions of the nature of Christ and of Scripture.

There have been many attempts to deal with this difficulty. There have been those who have suggested that Jesus did not include His coming among the events that He said would happen within a generation. Some have proposed that the word *generation* should not be understood in its literal sense but in some sort of figurative way. Others suggest that this prophecy follows the pattern of many Old Testament prophecies that had both a short-term fulfillment and a long-term fulfillment. Still others assert that Jesus was not talking about His final coming at the end of time but His coming in judgment on Israel in AD 70. That view has become more popular as criticism has intensified in our day.

This is a very complicated matter, but it is also a very important one. Therefore, it is important to wrestle with this passage in an effort to come to an understanding of it. As we work through Mark's account of the Olivet Discourse in this and the next two chapters, I will endeavor to point out problems this text presents and, by God's grace, suggest some ways to resolve these difficulties. My main thrust is to show that many, if not all, of the details in this discourse can be understood in terms of first-century events.

A Wonder of the Ancient World

Mark writes, **Then as He went out of the temple, one of His disciples said to Him, "Teacher, see what manner of stones and what buildings are here!"** (v. 1). Jesus had been in the temple complex, where He had answered questions, taught the people, and witnessed the poor widow put her two mites in the temple treasury (Mark 12). As He and His disciples were leaving, heading for the Mount of Olives, one of the disciples turned and looked at the magnificent temple, which truly was one of the wonders of the ancient world. It is difficult to imagine that he had not seen the temple before, but even so, he was amazed by it and expressed his amazement to Jesus.

The temple this disciple saw was not the one Solomon built in the tenth century BC. That temple was destroyed in 587 BC when the Babylonians, led by King Nebuchadnezzar, conquered Jerusalem. After the Israelites returned from the Babylonian exile, the temple was rebuilt, the work being completed around 516 BC. Around 19 BC, Herod the Great began to remodel the temple, and thereafter it became known as Herod's temple. The remodeling work was still going on in Jesus' time.

Herod is remembered for his massive building projects, and the temple was a prime example. The temple complex covered about thirty-five acres. The sanctuary stood one hundred and fifty feet high, as did the temple wall. The columns that held up the portico were so massive that three large men could barely encompass them by touching fingertip to fingertip. Josephus tells us that some of the stones that made up the temple were sixty feet long, eleven feet high, and eight feet deep, with each stone weighing more than a million pounds. Other historians of antiquity said Herod's temple looked like a mountain of marble decorated with gold. The temple complex was architecturally stunning and must have looked strong enough to stand for a thousand years or more.

A Prophecy of Destruction

When the disciple voiced His awe over the temple, perhaps Jesus and the other disciples turned and gazed at the temple, too, sharing their comrade's wonder. Jesus then said a thing that must have amazed them in a different way. Mark writes: **And Jesus answered and said to him, "Do you see these great buildings? Not one stone shall be left upon another, that shall not be thrown down"** (v. 2).

Mark does not give us the disciples' immediate reaction when Jesus made this incredible declaration. However, he notes: **Now as He sat on the Mount of Olives opposite the temple, Peter, James, John, and Andrew asked Him privately, "Tell us, when will these things be? And what will be the sign when all these things will be fulfilled?"** (vv. 3–4). A small group of the disciples came to Him with questions about His prophecy of the destruction of the temple. They did not ask whether they had heard Him correctly; they accepted what He had said. Their first question was about the timing: *Would* the temple stand for a thousand years before destruction came upon it? Or might that terrible event be much sooner? They also asked Him to identify a sign that would tip them off that the fulfillment of the prophecy was at hand.

Note that both of their questions included the words "these things." Jesus used the same term when He uttered the crucial statement recorded in verse 30: "Assuredly, I say to you, this generation will by no means pass away till all these things take place." The question at the heart of the difficulties in this passage is whether Jesus meant the same thing as the disciples when He said "these things." On the surface, it hardly seems possible that He did. The disciples had heard Jesus address only the destruction of the temple when they asked about "these things," but by the time Jesus spoke of "these things," He had addressed the destruction of the temple and of Jerusalem itself, as well as His coming.

Jesus began His response to the disciples with an interesting exhortation. Mark writes, **And Jesus, answering them, began to say: "Take heed that no one deceives you"** (v. 5). His first priority was to alert His disciples that the topic of future things was rife with potential for deception. In what way? Jesus went on, **"For many will come in My name, saying, 'I am He,' and**

will deceive many" (v. 6). So the first sign of the impending fulfillment of His prophecy that Jesus identified for His disciples was the appearance of false messiahs. This aspect of the prophecy definitely had a first-century fulfillment. Historians tell us that many false messiahs appeared before the destruction of the temple. Josephus especially documents these figures who claimed to be the returned Christ.

Wars, Earthquakes, Famines

Jesus went on to list additional signs: **"But when you hear of wars and rumors of wars, do not be troubled; for such things must happen, but the end is not yet. For nation will rise against nation, and kingdom against kingdom. And there will be earthquakes in various places, and there will be famines and troubles. These are the beginnings of sorrows"** (vv. 7–8). The disciples listening to Jesus must have understood "wars and rumors of wars" as harbingers of the destruction of the temple. So, in later years, they must have paid close attention as various conflicts flared up. For instance, in AD 40, the mad Emperor Caligula tried to set up a statue of himself in the sacred precincts of the temple, sparking violent protests in Jerusalem. There were rumors that the Romans were going to use force to stop the protests and carry out Caligula's profound sacrilege. In that instance, the rumors were just that—rumors—and no actual conflict occurred until the Jewish revolt against the Romans in AD 66, which led to the destruction of the temple and of Jerusalem in AD 70. No doubt the disciples paid close attention to these happenings, but Jesus counseled them not to be alarmed by wars and rumors of wars, for "such things must happen, but the end is not yet."

Jesus also listed earthquakes, famines, and "troubles" as signs. A tremendous earthquake hit the region of Phrygia in AD 61, and another leveled the city of Pompeii in the year 63. Also, between AD 41 and 54, during the reign of Claudius, several serious famines affected the Near East. These things, too, were signs of the impending destruction of the temple.

So, in that first generation, in the lifetimes of most of the disciples, wars, rumors of wars, earthquakes, and famines all took place. I believe our Lord was calling attention to things that were going to happen in the first century, things that, in fact, did happen in the first century. These signs were, as Jesus said, "the beginnings of sorrows."

Many evangelicals today have a tendency, every time a war breaks out, to say, "There's another sign of the times; Jesus must be coming back soon." Earthquakes, famines, and such also draw evangelical attention. Obviously, the reason why evangelicals watch for these signs is because of what apparently did *not* happen in the first century, namely, Jesus' coming in the clouds with glory. However, as we are beginning to see, the things of which Jesus spoke in the Olivet Discourse were fulfilled within the lifetimes of the disciples who heard Him speak. We will consider the numerous other events He mentioned and the implications of the first-century fulfillments of those events as we move forward.

47

THE OLIVET DISCOURSE, PART 2

Mark 13:9–23

"But watch out for yourselves, for they will deliver you up to councils, and you will be beaten in the synagogues. You will be brought before rulers and kings for My sake, for a testimony to them. And the gospel must first be preached to all the nations. But when they arrest you and deliver you up, do not worry beforehand, or premeditate what you will speak. But whatever is given you in that hour, speak that; for it is not you who speak, but the Holy Spirit. Now brother will betray brother to death, and a father his child; and children will rise up against parents and cause them to be put to death. And you will be hated by all for My name's sake. But he who endures to the end shall be saved. So when you see the 'abomination of desolation,' spoken of by Daniel the prophet, standing where it ought not" (let the reader understand), "then let those who are in Judea flee to the mountains. Let him who is on the housetop not go down into the house, nor enter to take anything out of his house. And let him who is in the field not go back to get his clothes. But woe to those who are pregnant and to those who are nursing babies in those days! And pray that your flight may not be in winter. For in those days there will be tribulation, such as has not been since the beginning of the creation which God created until this time, nor ever shall be. And unless the Lord had shortened those days, no flesh would be saved; but for the elect's sake, whom He chose, He shortened the days. Then if anyone says to you, 'Look, here is the Christ!' or, 'Look, He is there!' do not believe it. For false christs and false prophets will rise and show signs and wonders to deceive, if possible, even the elect. But take heed; see, I have told you all things beforehand."

A s Jesus continued in the Olivet Discourse, listing signs that would mark the impending fulfillment of His prophecy regarding the destruction of the temple at Jerusalem, He moved on from general signs such as wars, earthquakes, and famines to more personal signs. He began to tell His disciples about things that would happen to them and how they should respond. As we consider these signs, I want to continue to explore ways they may have been fulfilled in the first century.

Mark tells us that Jesus said: **"But watch out for yourselves, for they will deliver you up to councils, and you will be beaten in the synagogues. You will be brought before rulers and kings for My sake, for a testimony to them. And the gospel must first be preached to all the nations. But when they arrest you and deliver you up, do not worry beforehand, or premeditate what you will speak. But whatever is given you in that hour, speak that; for it is not you who speak, but the Holy Spirit"** (vv. 9–11). This portion of the prophecy reads like an overview of the book of Acts. In that book, as he recounts the spread of the gospel in the first century, Luke tells how the Apostles repeatedly were subjected to persecution, first by the Jewish authorities and later by the powers of Rome. Indeed, they were taken before councils, such as when Peter and John were questioned by the Sanhedrin (Acts 4). They were beaten in the synagogues; Paul confessed that he himself beat believers before his conversion (Acts 22:19). They were brought before rulers and kings, such as when Paul stood before King Agrippa (Acts 26). Agrippa said, "You almost persuade me to become a Christian," and Paul replied, "I would to God that not only you, but also all who hear me today, might become both almost and altogether such as I am, except for these chains" (vv. 28–29).

It appears that the Apostles had a strong awareness of the words of Jesus, so they trusted the presence and power of God the Holy Spirit to give them the proper words to say on various occasions. At key moments of heavy persecution, Luke often mentions that the Apostles were "filled with the Holy Spirit" and gave stirring testimonies to the saving work of Christ (4:8; 7:55; 13:9).

How are we to understand verse 10: "The gospel must first be preached to all the nations"? We have to remember that Jesus was answering the question, "What will be the sign when all these things will be fulfilled?" (v. 4), that is, the destruction of the temple, which Jesus had prophesied (v. 2). Thus, Jesus was listing signs the disciples should watch for, events that would signal that the destruction of the temple would happen soon. One such sign, He said, was that the gospel would be preached to all the nations, all the *ethnoi*. This happened in the first century; Paul said in one of his later letters that "the word of the truth of the gospel . . . has come to you, as it has also in all the world" (Col. 1:5b–6).

Certainly the gospel was not preached to every corner of the globe in the first century. The gospel did not go to southern Africa, East Asia, Australia, or the Americas. How then, could Paul write that the gospel had gone to the whole world? He was speaking about the Mediterranean world, the known world of that time, and the gospel was preached across that world in the first century.

Family Betrayals

Jesus went on to say: **"Now brother will betray brother to death, and a father his child; and children will rise up against parents and cause them to be put to death. And you will be hated by all for My name's sake. But he who endures to the end shall be saved"** (vv. 12–13). One of the most difficult problems with which the early church had to wrestle was the issue of those who betrayed the faith under persecution. In fact, some interpreters of the book of Hebrews believe that one of the main reasons the book was written was to address this problem. Of course, we usually hear about those who refused to recant under the Jewish and Roman persecution. We hear about the martyrs who were faithful to death, being made into human torches to illumine Nero's gardens, being fed to the lions in the arena, and meeting other horrible ends. It has been said that the blood of the martyrs is the seed of the church, and there is a great deal of truth in that, for where men have stood firm against opposition to the gospel, the church has flourished. However, it is also a fact of history that not all of the professing Christians who came under persecution in the first century went to their deaths singing hymns. There were those who caved in and betrayed their professions of faith. Some betrayed their friends, their parents, their brothers, and their sisters to save their own necks. Simply put, there were traitors to the faith in the first century, just as Jesus warned that there would be.

Sometimes, once the persecution died down, these unfaithful ones sought to be readmitted to the church. Naturally, those in the church found it difficult to forgive these traitors who had caused others to lose their lives.

I had a taste of how bitterness against such traitors can linger when I was doing graduate studies in Holland in 1965. We were staying in a small village outside Amsterdam. One day, as I was returning from the market with a bag of groceries, I saw a woman approaching me on the sidewalk. Out of common courtesy, I greeted her, saying "Good afternoon." Her face lit up and she stopped in her tracks. It wasn't enough for her to say, "Good afternoon." She began to ask me questions and engage me in conversation. Even though I did not know this woman, I stood there on the sidewalk and talked with her for about fifteen minutes.

Finally, when the conversation ended, I made my way to the house where we had rented a room. When I arrived, our landlady was waiting for me at the door, and she was livid. She began to berate me for talking to the woman I had met in the street. At first I could not understand what I had done wrong, but our landlady soon revealed that the woman had been a Nazi collaborator during World War II. The war had been over for twenty years, but even after all that time, no one in the village would talk to that woman because of her treason. Because of what she did, some of the young men in the village had been carried away to prison camps in Germany. So, I witnessed firsthand the pain that can drive people to withhold forgiveness from those who betray them, and this kind of betrayal occurred in the first century as well.

Jesus also prophesied that widespread hatred against the disciples would be another sign of the impending destruction of the temple. It was this hatred that drove the first-century persecution against the church. The disciples accepted this attitude of the world and took it in stride. John advised, "Do not marvel, my brethren, if the world hates you" (1 John 3:13).

Finally, Jesus said, "He who endures to the end shall be saved." Those who stand firm through persecution and even martyrdom are saved, but not because of their own faithfulness. They are given the grace to stand, and steadfastness is simply the proof that they have been given true faith in Christ.

The Abomination of Desolation

As Jesus continued to set out signs the disciples should watch for in order to know whether the destruction of the temple was imminent, He listed the fulfillment of a particular Old Testament prophecy. Mark tells us that He said: **"So when you see the 'abomination of desolation,' spoken of by Daniel the prophet, standing where it ought not"** (let the reader understand), **"then let those who are in Judea flee to the mountains"** (v. 14).

Jesus referred here to a prophecy that was given to the prophet Daniel by the archangel Gabriel (Dan. 9:20–27). It is clearly a messianic prophecy, but it also speaks of the destruction of the temple and of Jerusalem itself. The concluding verses say:

> "And after the sixty-two weeks Messiah shall be cut off, but not for Himself; and
> the people of the prince who is to come shall destroy the city and the sanctuary.

The end of it shall be with a flood, and till the end of the war desolations are determined. Then he shall confirm a covenant with many for one week; but in the middle of the week He shall bring an end to sacrifice and offering. And on the wing of abominations shall be one who makes desolate, even until the consummation, which is determined, is poured out on the desolate." (vv. 26–27)

There are many different scholarly opinions as to the precise meaning of the term "abomination of desolation," although there is general agreement that it refers to some sort of pagan desecration of the temple. Some believe this prophecy was fulfilled in the second century BC with the sacrilege committed by Antiochus Epiphanes, ruler of the Seleucid Empire, who conquered Jerusalem and sacrificed a pig on a pagan altar in the Holy of Holies. Others believe Daniel's vision had to do with Caligula's attempt to erect a statue of himself in the temple precincts in AD 40. But according to Josephus, the Jewish historian, the greatest desecration of the temple of God took place under the direction of the Roman general Titus, who later became emperor, at the time of the destruction of Jerusalem.

Josephus' account is based on firsthand knowledge. He was a leader in the Jewish resistance until he was captured by the Romans. Because of his great valor and knowledge, he became a friend of Titus, who took over the leadership of the Roman invasion of Palestine when his father was recalled to Rome to become emperor. Josephus pleaded with Titus to save the city. In fact, Titus used him to negotiate with the Jews, asking them to surrender while the Romans besieged the city. Josephus did not intend to betray his people by cooperating with the Romans in this way; he simply knew that all the people in the city would die if they did not surrender, and furthermore, the holy temple would be destroyed. The Jews refused to surrender and, in time, Josephus' worst fears were realized. He believed that Titus' conquest and destruction of the temple and the city in AD 70 fulfilled Daniel's prophecy.

Jesus advised His disciples, upon seeing the "abomination of desolation," to "flee to the mountains." This advice was contrary to the conventional wisdom in the ancient world. In times of invasion, people fled not to the mountains but to the walled cities, which were regarded as the safest places. That is what happened when the Romans invaded and placed Jerusalem under siege. Jerusalem was packed with people fleeing from the countryside and the villages. When Jerusalem fell to the Romans, 1.1 million Jews were slaughtered. However, the Christians were not among them. They had taken note of the sign and heeded Jesus' warning.

A Need for Haste

Jesus made it clear that when the sign appeared, haste was essential. He said: **"Let him who is on the housetop not go down into the house, nor enter to take anything out of his house. And let him who is in the field not go back to get his clothes. But woe to those who are pregnant and to those who are nursing babies in those days! And pray that your flight may not be in winter"** (vv. 15–18). Upon seeing the desecration of the temple, the disciples were not to go back for clothes or other goods, but to leave right away. Whether Jesus literally meant that they should drop everything and run is unclear, but He clearly was counseling haste. Jesus also made it clear that it would be a difficult time, especially for pregnant women and mothers with young children. He counseled the disciples to pray that they would not have to flee in the even more difficult conditions of winter.

He added: **"For in those days there will be tribulation, such as has not been since the beginning of the creation which God created until this time, nor ever shall be. And unless the Lord had shortened those days, no flesh would be saved; but for the elect's sake, whom He chose, He shortened the days"** (vv. 19–20). Here is the origin of the term "Great Tribulation," which many evangelicals foresee happening at the end of time. However, when we consider this teaching in the context of the Olivet Discourse, it seems clear that Jesus was speaking of events surrounding the destruction of Jerusalem. He said it would be a terrible time, the worst time in history. In fact, He said, it was going to be so bad in that time that no one would survive it if God had not determined that the time of most difficulty would be short. For the sake of His elect, His chosen people, God had shortened that time of trouble so that some of them might survive.

Finally Jesus said: **"Then if anyone says to you, 'Look, here is the Christ!' or, 'Look, He is there!' do not believe it. For false christs and false prophets will rise and show signs and wonders to deceive, if possible, even the elect. But take heed; see, I have told you all things beforehand"** (vv. 21–23). Here He mentioned once again (see v. 6) that multiplying false messiahs, as well as false prophets, would be signs that the destruction of the temple was close at hand. These false messiahs and prophets would have the ability to do great miracles that would be so astonishing that even the elect might be fooled.

Having said all these things and having listed numerous signs the disciples should watch for, Jesus declared, "Take heed; see, I have told you all things beforehand." In other words, Jesus was saying: "You are now informed. You know what to watch for. Do not forget My words. Take them to heart. Keep watch." He had answered their question thoroughly.

It is clear that we do not have to look beyond AD 70 to find a fulfillment of all Jesus spoke about in the Olivet Discourse to this point. All of these signs were displayed in the years and days leading up to the fall of Jerusalem. But what of His words about His coming in glory? We will consider that section of the Olivet Discourse in the next chapter.

48

THE OLIVET DISCOURSE, PART 3

Mark 13:24–37

⸻

"But in those days, after that tribulation, the sun will be darkened, and the moon will not give its light; the stars of heaven will fall, and the powers in the heavens will be shaken. Then they will see the Son of Man coming in the clouds with great power and glory. And then He will send His angels, and gather together His elect from the four winds, from the farthest part of earth to the farthest part of heaven. Now learn this parable from the fig tree: When its branch has already become tender, and puts forth leaves, you know that summer is near. So you also, when you see these things happening, know that it is near—at the doors! Assuredly, I say to you, this generation will by no means pass away till all these things take place. Heaven and earth will pass away, but My words will by no means pass away. But of that day and hour no one knows, not even the angels in heaven, nor the Son, but only the Father. Take heed, watch and pray; for you do not know when the time is. It is like a man going to a far country, who left his house and gave authority to his servants, and to each his work, and commanded the doorkeeper to watch. Watch therefore, for you do not know when the master of the house is coming—in the evening, at midnight, at the crowing of the rooster, or in the morning—lest, coming suddenly, he find you sleeping. And what I say to you, I say to all: Watch!"

In the first portions of the Olivet Discourse, Jesus, at the request of four of His disciples, prophesied a number of signs they should watch for in order to know when the destruction of the temple was imminent. We have seen that all of these signs were fulfilled in the years leading up to the Roman siege of Jerusalem that culminated in the destruction of the city and the temple in AD 70.

However, the verses that make the Olivet Discourse so difficult to interpret occur near the end, where Jesus spoke about His "coming in the clouds" and said that "this generation will by no means pass away till all these things take place" (v. 30). As we have seen, Jesus' reference to His coming is usually understood as His final coming at the end of history, but when it is understood that way, His assertion that "all these things"—the destruction of the temple and Jerusalem, as well as His return—would happen within a generation is inaccurate. This problem carries enormous implications with regard to the trustworthiness of both Jesus and sacred Scripture.

The Coming of the Son

Mark tells us that Jesus said: **"But in those days, after that tribulation, the sun will be darkened, and the moon will not give its light; the stars of heaven will fall, and the powers in the heavens will be shaken. Then they will see the Son of Man coming in the clouds with great power and glory. And then He will send His angels, and gather together His elect from the four winds, from the farthest part of earth to the farthest part of heaven"** (vv. 24–27).

What is Jesus speaking about here? On the surface, it seems that He is talking about His second coming. This view is bolstered by the fact that this passage is similar to another New Testament passage that is universally taken to be a reference to the second coming:

> For the Lord Himself will descend from heaven with a shout, with the voice of an archangel, and with the trumpet of God. And the dead in Christ will rise first. Then we who are alive and remain shall be caught up together with them in the clouds to meet the Lord in the air. And thus we shall always be with the Lord. (1 Thess. 4:16–17)

However, before we proceed on the assumption that Jesus was speaking in the Olivet Discourse about the second coming, which would mean He was wrong when He said that "all these things" would take place within a generation, let us explore whether this portion of the Olivet Discourse also had a first-century fulfillment.

First of all, note the unique language Jesus employed in this passage: "the sun will be darkened, and the moon will not give its light; the stars of heaven will fall, and the powers in the heavens will be shaken." This language can be interpreted in a figurative way or a literal way.

The figurative interpretation is possible because this kind of language was characteristically used by the Old Testament prophets to warn of the coming judgment of God. For example:

> "Wail, for the day of the LORD is at hand! It will come as destruction from the Almighty. Therefore all hands will be limp, every man's heart will melt, and they will be afraid. Pangs and sorrows will take hold of them; they will be in pain as a woman in childbirth; they will be amazed at one another; their faces will be like flames. Behold, the day of the LORD comes, cruel, with both wrath and fierce anger, to lay the land desolate; and He will destroy its sinners from it. For the stars of heaven and their constellations will not give their light; the sun will be darkened in its going forth, and the moon will not cause its light to shine." (Isa. 13:6–10)

This passage, part of a proclamation of judgment on Babylon, is typical of Old Testament prophecies of doom. Such passages often include references to astronomical upheavals. It is a principle of biblical interpretation that when the Bible consistently uses a given type of language in a given context, whenever we see that language, we should look for that context. In the case of Mark 13, then, the language seems to be speaking of divine judgment. Certainly the destruction of the temple and the city of Jerusalem were acts of divine judgment. Therefore, the coming of Christ that Jesus spoke about here may be understood as His coming in judgment on Jerusalem in AD 70.

The literal interpretation has some justification because of certain unusual reports from the time of the fall of Jerusalem. In AD 70, there were reports of astronomical perturbations, including a comet that streamed across the sky, which the people of the time regarded as a sign of coming judgment. Even more unusual is the report from Josephus, the Jewish historian:

> A few days after that feast, on the one and twentieth day of the month Arte-misius, a certain prodigious and incredible phenomenon appeared; I suppose the account of it would seem to be a fable, were it not related by those that saw it, and were not the events that followed it of so considerable of a nature as to deserve such signals; for, before sun-setting, chariots and troops of soldiers in their armor were seen running about among the clouds, and surrounding the

cities. Moreover, at the feast which we call Pentecost, as the priests were going by night into the inner [court of the temple] as their custom was, to perform their sacred ministrations, they said that, in the first place, they felt a quaking, and heard a great noise, and after that they heard a sound as of a great multitude, saying, "Let us remove hence."[1]

So, Josephus' testimony is that at the time of the destruction of Jerusalem, multitudes of people saw chariots and armored soldiers moving around the clouds. This account is reminiscent of a biblical narrative from the life of the prophet Elisha. When the king of Syria sent an army to capture Elisha, the prophet's servant saw the horses, chariots, and troops, and he panicked. Elisha calmly prayed, "LORD, I pray, open his eyes that he may see." When God answered that prayer, Elisha's servant saw that "the mountain was full of horses and chariots of fire all around Elisha" (2 Kings 6:17). It is possible that some people in Jerusalem in AD 70 were given a similar vision—a vision of the armies of the Lord, come not to protect God's prophet but to carry out His judgment.

Second, one of the chief reasons this passage is interpreted as speaking of the end of time is because of the way the disciples' questions are worded in Matthew's gospel. In Matthew 24, after Jesus told the disciples that every stone of the temple would be thrown down, they asked Him: "Tell us, when will these things be? And what will be the sign of Your coming, and of the end of the age?" (v. 3). The fact that, according to Matthew's account, the disciples asked about the sign of "the end of the age" leads some to assume they were asking about—and that Jesus was prophesying about—the end of human history.

However, the Bible sometimes refers to the end of the age of the Jews and the beginning of the age of the Gentiles. For instance, in Luke's version of the Olivet Discourse, he records Jesus as saying, "Jerusalem will be trampled by Gentiles until the times of the Gentiles are fulfilled" (21:24). In Romans, Paul speaks of "the fullness of the Gentiles" (11:25) coming into the kingdom of God before the final consummation. The age of the Gentiles stands in bold contrast with the age of the Jews. This is why Paul speaks of "the ends of the ages" (1 Cor. 10:11). So, it is possible that Jesus was discussing signs not of the end of human history but of the end of the Jewish era, which corresponded to the destruction of Jerusalem in AD 70.

What are we to make of verse 27, where Jesus speaks of sending "His angels" to gather "His elect" from all over the world? Yes, this sounds as if it may be referencing the second coming of Christ and the ingathering of believers, as

---

[1] Flavius Josephus, *The Jewish Wars*, 6.5.3.

pictured in 1 Thessalonians 4. However, the Greek word translated as "angel" here, *angelos*, literally means "messenger," so it is also possible that Jesus was speaking of the gospel going forth by human messengers who would be God's instruments to gather in His elect following the fall of Jerusalem.

There is no question that this passage is difficult to interpret in its context. It has been a source of disagreement among Christians for centuries and will continue to be so. Yet, I contend that it need not be interpreted as referring to the end of history. It can be understood as referring to the cataclysmic events that occurred in AD 70.

Watching for the Signs

Jesus went on to say: **"Now learn this parable from the fig tree: When its branch has already become tender, and puts forth leaves, you know that summer is near. So you also, when you see these things happening, know that it is near—at the doors! Assuredly, I say to you, this generation will by no means pass away till all these things take place. Heaven and earth will pass away, but My words will by no means pass away"** (vv. 28–31). The central point of this portion of the discourse was to assure the disciples that the signs Jesus had given them were reliable. It is as if Jesus was saying, "Assuredly, I say to you" after the fact. Just as certain happenings in nature point to something else to come, the signs He had listed would reliably point to the destruction of the temple. Moreover, He said, when the signs began to occur, the destruction of the temple would happen very soon.

Here we find the statement that makes the Olivet Discourse so difficult: "This generation will by no means pass away till all these things take place." Was Jesus speaking literally of those then living? Or was He using the word *generation* in some sort of figurative sense that would encompass the still-future second coming? That question may never be settled in this life, but we have seen no reason in our study of this discourse to rule out a literal sense. Basically, it seems, Jesus was stressing once again that the destruction of the temple would happen relatively soon.

Likewise, when Jesus declared, "My words will by no means pass away," He was saying that His words are more enduring than creation, more solid, more dependable, more reliable. Truly, if Jesus says something, that settles it, and that was the case with His prophecies regarding the destruction of the temple and Jerusalem.

Finally, Jesus said: **"But of that day and hour no one knows, not even the angels in heaven, nor the Son, but only the Father. Take heed, watch and pray; for you do not know when the time is. It is like a man going to a far** country, who left his house and gave authority to his servants, and to each his work, and commanded the doorkeeper to watch. Watch therefore, for you do not know when the master of the house is coming—in the evening, at midnight, at the crowing of the rooster, or in the morning—lest, coming suddenly, he find you sleeping. And what I say to you, I say to all: Watch!" (vv. 32–37). This passage troubles many Christians. If Jesus was God, they ask, why did He say He did not know precisely the day and hour when the things He had been talking about were to take place? Simply put, there was a limitation of His knowledge during His incarnation. As we saw in chapter 15, His human nature was not omniscient, but His divine nature was not diminished. In this case, however, it appears that the Father had simply not revealed the time to the Son.

Others point to this passage and ask how, if Jesus did not know the day and hour, He could have said it would happen within a generation. I am not a prophet, but I believe I can safely predict that the Pittsburgh Steelers will win another Super Bowl in the next forty years. I do not know in which year they will win it, but that has no effect on my prediction. Jesus knew the signs that would mark the destruction of the temple and He knew the season when it would happen, but not the precise date. That did not negate His prophecy in the least.

The central thrust of this final passage of the Olivet Discourse is an exhortation to watchfulness. Jesus was saying that His prophecy could be fulfilled suddenly, with little warning. Therefore, the disciples needed to take heed to the signs He had given them.

The Figurative and the Literal

In the end, there are basically two ways to handle the Olivet Discourse. One is to interpret Jesus' language about His coming in a figurative sense and interpret the time-frame references in a direct, literal sense. Or we can understand the time-frame references figuratively and treat the teaching about Jesus' coming in a literal sense. In other words, either the language of the return is figurative or the time-frame references are figurative.

Through history, many Christians have chosen to view the time-frame references as figurative. They have held that Jesus used the word *generation* in a figurative manner. He was not giving a time frame at all; rather, He probably was saying that a certain type of person, the unbelieving people that we deal with every day in the preaching of the gospel, would still be around until the time this prophecy was fulfilled. This has been a common approach to this text, an effort to save it from criticism. However, I believe that kind of treatment of the text simply makes Christians seem naïve or obscurantist, because it tortures the text too much.

I personally believe that we must understand the time-frame references in the Olivet Discourse in a literal sense and Jesus' coming in a figurative sense. In short, I believe that Jesus was not talking about His final coming at the end of the age, but about His coming in power and in judgment on His own people, which occurred in AD 70. In my judgment, this is the most natural and consistent way to interpret this text, and it vindicates Jesus as a true prophet and Scripture as absolutely reliable.

49

JESUS,
THE PASSOVER LAMB

Mark 14:1–9

After two days it was the Passover and the Feast of Unleavened Bread. And the chief priests and the scribes sought how they might take Him by trickery and put Him to death. But they said, "Not during the feast, lest there be an uproar of the people." And being in Bethany at the house of Simon the leper, as He sat at the table, a woman came having an alabaster flask of very costly oil of spikenard. Then she broke the flask and poured it on His head. But there were some who were indignant among themselves, and said, "Why was this fragrant oil wasted? For it might have been sold for more than three hundred denarii and given to the poor." And they criticized her sharply. But Jesus said, "Let her alone. Why do you trouble her? She has done a good work for Me. For you have the poor with you always, and whenever you wish you may do them good; but Me you do not have always. She has done what she could. She has come beforehand to anoint My body for burial. Assuredly, I say to you, wherever this gospel is preached in the whole world, what this woman has done will also be told as a memorial to her."

The most important feast of Old Testament Judaism was the celebration of the Passover. This feast commemorated God's deliverance of the people of Israel from slavery in Egypt and His protection of them from the destroyer who killed all the Egyptians' firstborn (Ex. 12:23). God instructed

His people to smear the blood of lambs on their doorposts. The destroyer passed over any house marked by the blood, and that household escaped the judgment that was visited on the Egyptians.

It is no coincidence that, in the history of redemption, the Passover was at hand when Jesus Christ, the Lamb of God, came to Jerusalem to suffer and die. By His blood, God's judgment passes over His people.

This is why the mood of Mark's gospel changes dramatically in chapter 14. Chapter 13 contains the Olivet Discourse, in which Jesus taught from the Mount of Olives about the signs that would precede the destruction of the temple, including His coming in clouds of glory. From that scene of triumph and exultation, Mark shifts in chapter 14 to an ominous foreshadowing of our Lord's suffering for the sins of His people.

Chapter 14 is the longest chapter in the gospel of Mark, and it focuses on what theologians have called the passion of Christ. The word *passion* is rooted in the concept of suffering. When we say we have a passion for something, usually we do not mean something that brings us suffering, but rather something about which we have strong feelings. Jesus' suffering, His passion, elicited in His soul and body intense feelings of agony.

With this background, let us look at the text. Mark tells us, **After two days it was the Passover and the Feast of Unleavened Bread** (v. 1a). That is, these important events in the Jewish calendar took place two days after the Olivet Discourse. Jesus' great suffering coincided with the Passover and the Feast of Unleavened Bread.

Many years earlier, God had instructed the Israelites to celebrate this annual feast with bitter herbs to remind them of the bitterness of their experience in bondage, and also to sacrifice a lamb in the afternoon and then consume it in the evening (Exodus 12; Numbers 9). He also commanded them to celebrate this feast by eating unleavened bread. The bread was unleavened to commemorate the historic circumstances of the original Passover. God had commanded the people to be ready to move at a moment's notice for their exodus from Egypt. They had no time to allow the yeast to rise in their bread dough, so they made unleavened bread (Ex. 12:18–20, 33–34).

New Testament accounts of the celebration of the Passover can get a bit confusing. The Passover celebration was observed for an entire week. The Feast of Unleavened Bread took place over a long weekend, not for the entire seven days. The Passover meal itself took place in one afternoon and evening. So, sometimes a mention of the Passover refers to that one day, other times to the entire week.

Immediately after Mark tells us of the time of these events, his account turns ominous: **And the chief priests and the scribes sought how they might take**

Him by trickery and put Him to death (v. 1b). When Mark speaks of the "chief priests and the scribes," he is referring to the Sanhedrin, the ruling body of the Jews. These groups joined together to hatch a plot to capture Him so they could kill Him. **But they said, "Not during the feast, lest there be an uproar of the people"** (v. 2). As much as they wanted to get rid of Jesus, they feared a popular uprising, so they limited their plans with an eye to public opinion.

An Extravagant Anointing of Oil

Suddenly, the narrative changes. Mark interrupts his account of the plot to capture and execute Jesus. Throughout his gospel, Mark uses what some call "a sandwich technique." In the middle of a narrative, he will "sandwich" in something else that directly relates to the broader narrative. Here he recounts for his readers an event that happened in Bethany.

He tells us that Jesus was **in Bethany at the house of Simon the leper** (v. 3a). Simon must have been a healed leper because lepers were not allowed to host dinner meals for uninfected people. Perhaps Simon was hosting this meal because Jesus had healed him.

In any case, Jesus was in that home having a meal, and **as He sat at the table, a woman came having an alabaster flask of very costly oil of spikenard** (v. 3b). Although Mark does not name the woman, John's gospel identifies her as Mary, the sister of Martha and Lazarus, who lived in Bethany. Her alabaster flask, a translucent white bottle, was itself of some value. The very precious perfume it contained, oil of spikenard, was worth more than three hundred denarii. As we have seen, a denarius was typically one day's wage for a laborer in Israel. The people worked six days a week. So, the contents of this flask cost a whole year's wages.

The volume of this perfume was at least twelve ounces, maybe even sixteen, compared with perhaps one ounce in the typical bottles of perfume sold today. In all probability, the overwhelming majority of women who lived in that day did not make enough money to buy such a quantity of precious perfume. Likely this flask of perfume was owned by the woman's family, and perhaps it was even a family heirloom.

As Jesus was dining with Simon, Mary came in and interrupted the meal, which was a breach of Jewish protocol. A woman was allowed to interrupt men at a meal only if she were serving the meal, not for visiting or joining the conversation. However, Mary did not hesitate. Mark tells us, **Then she broke the flask and poured it on His head** (v. 3c).

One of the so-called discrepancies among the Gospels that some like to note is that John's gospel says Mary anointed Jesus' feet and then wiped them with her hair (John 12:3). So, was Jesus anointed on His feet or on His head? Considering the volume of perfume Mary poured on Jesus, it may have covered His body head to toe. He was given a minor bath of precious perfume.

Mark tells us that when she did this, **there were some who were indignant among themselves, and said, "Why was this fragrant oil wasted?"** (v. 4). According to the Greek text, they were not just annoyed or irked, but their irritation rose to the level of fury when they witnessed this episode. They had no idea that they were witnessing the anointing of the Lord of glory as He was entering into His passion. In the eyes of Jesus' contemporaries, this act of devotion by Mary was an inexcusable extravagance.

They continued: **"It might have been sold for more than three hundred denarii and given to the poor." And they criticized her sharply** (v. 5). The term *sharply* is a vast understatement in the English. In a bullfight, when the matador taunts the bull, the bull paws the ground and his nostrils flare in anger. That is the image used here. These people were so angry with Mary for wasting the ointment that their nostrils were flaring in their criticism.

Preparation for Burial

Our Lord had a very different response: **But Jesus said, "Let her alone. Why do you trouble her? She has done a good work for Me. For you have the poor with you always, and whenever you wish you may do them good; but Me you do not have always"** (vv. 6–7).

Several years ago, I was invited to preach in the inner city of Cleveland at a church where the minister had been serving for twenty-five years. The church building was surrounded with signs of poverty, drug dealing, crime, and broken humanity. The minister and I talked about frustrations with his ministry. He mentioned that several young assistant ministers had come to work in that church straight out of seminary. Each stayed about two years and then gave up in frustration. I asked him why he had stayed for twenty-five years. He said, "Because of what Jesus said: 'You have the poor with you always.'" Some people use this verse to justify ignoring the poor, but it had stimulated him to persevere in his ministry in the ghetto. He said: "My young assistants came out of seminary with stars in their eyes, filled with idealism. They were going to come in here like knights in armor and eradicate poverty. When they saw that it did not happen in two years, they burned out, and they left. But I knew when I came here that the poor were always going to be here, and that my mission was not to eradicate poverty but to minister to people in the midst of their poverty."

I believe that minister understood these words of Jesus rightly. In a fallen world, poverty will never be eliminated, though we are called to do what we can to alleviate it. Nevertheless, the ongoing problem of poverty does not mean that extravagant gestures of piety are not permitted.

Jesus then said: **"She has done what she could. She has come beforehand to anoint My body for burial"** (v. 8). Later, we will study the details of Jesus' burial and how it fulfilled specific Old Testament prophecies. We will see that Jesus' body was not thrown into the garbage dump of Gehenna as the corpses of executed criminals usually were; instead, Jesus was laid to rest in a rich man's tomb. However, we also will see that because of the haste with which He was buried after His death, His body was not anointed with spices in typical Jewish fashion. This anointing, then, was the only anointing He received for burial.

Mary came with her priceless possession and gave all of it to anoint Him before He died. This is one of the most sacrificial, extravagant, heart-rending gifts of all time.

Jesus ended the dinner discussion with these words: **"Assuredly, I say to you, wherever this gospel is preached in the whole world, what this woman has done will also be told as a memorial to her"** (v. 9). He was not going to let the world forget what the dinner guests had just witnessed—Mary's act of love, devotion, and sacrifice. She did a great thing that we should applaud and emulate.

50

JESUS' LAST
PASSOVER SUPPER

Mark 14:10–26

━━━⧓━━━

Then Judas Iscariot, one of the twelve, went to the chief priests to betray Him to them. And when they heard it, they were glad, and promised to give him money. So he sought how he might conveniently betray Him. Now on the first day of Unleavened Bread, when they killed the Passover lamb, His disciples said to Him, "Where do You want us to go and prepare, that You may eat the Passover?" And He sent out two of His disciples and said to them, "Go into the city, and a man will meet you carrying a pitcher of water; follow him. Wherever he goes in, say to the master of the house, 'The Teacher says, "Where is the guest room in which I may eat the Passover with My disciples?"' Then he will show you a large upper room, furnished and prepared; there make ready for us." So His disciples went out, and came into the city, and found it just as He had said to them; and they prepared the Passover. In the evening He came with the twelve. Now as they sat and ate, Jesus said, "Assuredly, I say to you, one of you who eats with Me will betray Me." And they began to be sorrowful, and to say to Him one by one, "Is it I?" And another said, "Is it I?" He answered and said to them, "It is one of the twelve, who dips with Me in the dish. The Son of Man indeed goes just as it is written of Him, but woe to that man by whom the Son of Man is betrayed! It would have been good for that man if he had never been born." And as they were eating, Jesus took bread, blessed and broke it, and gave it to them and said, "Take, eat; this is My body." Then He took the cup, and when He had given thanks He gave it to them, and they all drank from it.

And He said to them, "This is My blood of the new covenant, which is shed for many. Assuredly, I say to you, I will no longer drink of the fruit of the vine until that day when I drink it new in the kingdom of God." And when they had sung a hymn, they went out to the Mount of Olives.

When a homicide is committed in America today, one of the first details investigators seek to discern is whether it was an act of sudden anger or whether it was planned and premeditated. Premeditation has significant implications for the investigation and for the potential penalty the court might impose in the event the suspect eventually is convicted.

When we look at this account of the Last Supper, we know that every one of the twelve disciples who sat with Jesus would shortly betray Him. Most of them would do so out of fear, weakness, and the pressure of the moment. One of them, however, would betray Him by premeditation. He would commit premeditated treason against the King of kings. This treason was in his heart as he broke bread with the Lord.

Mark makes that very clear as he writes, **Then Judas Iscariot, one of the twelve, went to the chief priests to betray Him to them** (v. 10). Note that this transaction took place on Judas' initiative. He went out of his way to visit those who he knew were taking counsel together to find a way to get rid of Jesus. He went to the chief priests in order to betray Jesus to them. Not surprisingly, **when they heard it, they were glad, and promised to give him money** (v. 11a). The other gospels make it clear that the amount of money was thirty pieces of silver. Jesus' life was sold at a cheap price, relatively speaking.

Mark goes on to tell us that Judas **sought how he might conveniently betray Him** (v. 11b). He does not simply say, "Judas sought how he might betray Him," but rather how he might *conveniently* betray Him. It was not enough that he intended to deliver Jesus into the hands of those who would kill Him. Not only did he undertake this deed for monetary gain, he also sought to carry it out in a manner that would not inconvenience him.

Preparations for the Passover Supper

Then Mark gives us his record of the actual Passover, as Jesus planned it. He writes, **on the first day of Unleavened Bread, when they killed the Passover lamb, His disciples said to Him, "Where do you want us to go and prepare, that You may eat the Passover?"** (v. 12). As we have seen, the disciples of a rabbi also served his needs, and in this case the disciples of Jesus carried out that function well.

There is similarity between the very specific instructions that Jesus gave His disciples on this occasion and the instructions He gave them for His triumphal entry into the city (11:1–6). Mark writes: **He sent out two of His disciples and said to them, "Go into the city, and a man will meet you carrying a pitcher of water; follow him. Wherever he goes in, say to the master of the house, 'The Teacher says, "Where is the guest room in which I may eat the Passover with My disciples?"' Then he will show you a large upper room, furnished and prepared; there make ready for us"** (vv. 13–15).

So we do not miss the significance of Jesus' directive, let us consider the historical perspective and context. First, let me direct your attention to Jesus' instruction for the disciples to look for a man carrying water. It was highly unusual for a man to carry water in Jerusalem at the time of the Passover. First, the Israelites regarded the carrying of water jugs to be women's work. The only men who carried jars of water were slaves—with one exception. The Essenes, a group of ascetics who lived in the desert, became famous centuries later following the discovery of the Dead Sea Scrolls. This sect of Jews had divorced themselves from the mainstream of Israel. Some have speculated that the Essenes influenced Jesus, and this text has fostered even more speculation because the Essenes had no women among their company. So, the Essenes had to carry their own water. Thus, the man carrying water in Jerusalem was probably a slave or an Essene.

Second, Jesus had a good reason for telling the disciples to look for such a unique sight. Jerusalem was extremely crowded during the festival. Jews from all over the region came to Jerusalem to celebrate the Passover, for it was the only place where it was lawful to do so. Josephus tells us that in AD 66, more than two million people crowded into Jerusalem for the Passover.

In God's providence, Mark tells us, **His disciples went out, and came into the city, and found it just as He had said to them; and they prepared the Passover.** (v. 16).

Mark then focuses in on certain conversations and interactions during the meal: **In the evening He came with the twelve. Now as they sat and ate, Jesus said, "Assuredly, I say to you, one of you who eats with Me will betray Me"** (vv. 17–18). The disciples were gathered around Jesus, celebrating the most sacred feast of the Jewish nation, when Jesus interrupted the mood of worship and thanksgiving with a shocking prophecy. We can only imagine the horror that descended on the disciples. Mark tells us **they began to be sorrowful, and to say to Him one by one, "Is it I?" And another said, "Is it I?"** (v. 19). They looked at Jesus and, one after another, asked about their possible involvement.

Prophecies Coming to Fruition

Mark writes: **He answered and said to them, "It is one of the twelve, who dips with Me in the dish. The Son of Man indeed goes just as it is written of Him"** (vv. 20–21a). Jesus was aware of the Messianic prophecies regarding the Servant of Yahweh in Isaiah 52–53. He knew that He was destined to be betrayed and that the betrayal was not a sudden invention of Judas. By saying "just as it is written of Him," Jesus was letting His shocked and sorrowful disciples know that events were playing out exactly as the Father had ordained them from the beginning of the world.

Many read this text and question how, if God predestined the betrayal by Judas, He could hold Judas responsible for this evil deed. We can imagine Judas saying on the day of judgment: "Lord, I was just carrying out Your will. In fact, if it weren't for my betrayal, the atonement would never have taken place. Your people would still be in their sins. But You used me to bring Jesus to the cross, and through that cross Your people were redeemed. Therefore, I think I deserve the heavenly medal of honor."

Judas would be wrong to say such things. The fact that God ordained Judas' betrayal of Jesus did not relieve Judas of the responsibility for that evil deed. Joseph was betrayed by his brothers, and when they met him later, they feared his wrath. Joseph did not deny that they meant evil against him, but he also understood that God meant it for good (Gen. 50:20). That is why Jesus went on to say: **"woe to that man by whom the Son of Man is betrayed! It would have been good for that man if he had never been born"** (v. 21b). Jesus was proceeding in obedience to God's foreordination, but curses would be on the man whose hand betrayed Him. If any human being ever had reason to curse the day of his birth, it was Judas Iscariot.

In these events, we see the intersection between the secret counsel of God and the machinations of the human will. In God's providence, what we call the mystery of concurrence occurred. Two streams came together—the sovereign will of God and the earthly will of human flesh. It is not as though God in His sovereignty coerced Judas to carry out the evil act of betraying Jesus. Rather, the sovereign God worked His will in and through the choices of His creatures. Judas did exactly what Judas wanted to do, but God brought good out of evil, redemption out of treachery.

Institution of the Lord's Supper

After recounting the betrayal plans, Mark turns his attention to Jesus' institution of the Lord's Supper: **As they were eating, Jesus took bread, blessed it and**

broke it, and gave it to them and said, "Take, eat; this is My body." Then
He took the cup, and when He had given thanks He gave it to them, and
they all drank from it. And He said to them, "This is My blood of the new
covenant, which is shed for many" (vv. 22–24). If He spoke these words in
Aramaic, which He probably did, basically He said, "Eat this My body."

We cannot imagine the number of theological disputes that have occurred
in church history about how to interpret these three verses. One of the great
tragedies of the Protestant Reformation is that the Reformers under the leadership of John Calvin and Ulrich Zwingli could not come to an agreement with
Martin Luther and the German Protestants on the issue of whether the human
nature of Jesus was physically present in the Lord's Supper. Calvin insisted that
His human nature is confined by space and time, so it cannot be in many places
at the same time. His divine nature, yes, but not His human nature, which
is always limited by the attributes of humanity. Thus, Christ is not physically
present in the Lord's Supper. Luther, however, insisted that the divine attribute
of omnipresence is communicated to Jesus' human nature, making it possible for
Him in His humanity to be in many places at the same time, so he insisted that
the presence of Jesus in the Lord's Supper is in some way physical or corporeal
based on the words by which He instituted it.

At one point in these discussions, Luther lost his temper and pounded his
fists on the table, saying, "*Hoc est corpus meum, hoc est corpus meum,*" which is
Latin for "This is My body." The Reformers replied that Jesus also said, "I am
the door," but we do not take that in a literal sense. They held that Jesus meant
that the bread and wine represent His body and blood. Luther believed Jesus'
words meant more than that.

I think the truth is somewhere in between. If we equate the bread and the
wine with the physical body of Jesus, we have christological problems that will
not go away. Calvin understood that Jesus was not saying that the elements are
just His physical person, but that they *are* His person. There is a reality in the
celebration of the Lord's Supper beyond a memorial. Yes, Jesus in His humanity
is in heaven, but in His deity, He is not restricted by time and space. So, we
can have full assurance when we come to the Lord's Table that we come into
His real presence. He is there.

It is true that He is with us every time we worship, every time we gather
together. So what's the difference? It is that when He invites us to His Table,
He invites us to intimacy. He invites us to feed on Him, to be nurtured by
Him, and to be strengthened by Him.

He told His disciples: **"Assuredly, I say to you, I will no longer drink of**

the fruit of the vine until that day when I drink it new in the kingdom of God." And when they had sung a hymn, they went out to the Mount of Olives (vv. 25–26). With these sorrowful words, Jesus indicated that His death was at hand. However, He meets today with all who place their faith in Him as Lord and Savior and come to His Table to be nurtured by Him.

51

THE TWO
NATURES OF JESUS

Mark 14:27–42

Then Jesus said to them, "All of you will be made to stumble because of Me this night, for it is written: 'I will strike the Shepherd, and the sheep will be scattered.' But after I have been raised, I will go before you to Galilee." Peter said to Him, "Even if all are made to stumble, yet I will not be." Jesus said to him, "Assuredly, I say to you that today, even this night, before the rooster crows twice, you will deny Me three times." But he spoke more vehemently, "If I have to die with You, I will not deny You!" And they all said likewise. Then they came to a place which was named Gethsemane; and He said to His disciples, "Sit here while I pray." And He took Peter, James, and John with Him, and He began to be troubled and deeply distressed. Then He said to them, "My soul is exceedingly sorrowful, even to death. Stay here and watch." He went a little farther, and fell on the ground, and prayed that if it were possible, the hour might pass from Him. And He said, "Abba, Father, all things are possible for You. Take this cup away from Me; nevertheless, not what I will, but what You will." Then He came and found them sleeping, and said to Peter, "Simon, are you sleeping? Could you not watch one hour? Watch and pray, lest you enter into temptation. The spirit indeed is willing, but the flesh is weak." Again He went away and prayed, and spoke the same words. And when He returned, He found them asleep again, for their eyes were heavy; and they did not know what to answer Him. Then He came the third time and said to them, "Are you still sleeping and resting? It is enough! The hour has come; behold, the Son of Man is being betrayed into the hands of sinners. Rise, let us be going. See, My betrayer is at hand."

Difficult questions about the nature of Jesus Christ, the God-man, have troubled theologians throughout the history of the church. In some cases, these questions led to outright heresies, which, in turn, produced corrective pronouncements from church councils. Because this chapter raises some of those questions, I am going to depart from my normal practice of verse-by-verse exposition in favor of a theological exposition of matters that arise in this text. There are times and situations when theological exposition is vitally necessary to protect the saints from distortions, errors, and even heresies, and I believe this is one of those times.

Specifically, I want to address the relationship of Jesus' divine and human natures. Questions about this relationship arise from at least two incidents in this passage.

First, Jesus foretold His resurrection when He told His disciples, **"after I have been raised, I will go before you to Galilee"** (v. 28). Also, He told Peter, **"Assuredly, I say to you that today, even this night, before the rooster crows twice, you will deny Me three times"** (v. 30). Jesus showed supernatural knowledge of the future, just as we would expect in the God-man. However, we must remember that just a little earlier, Jesus said, "But of that day and hour no one knows, not even the angels in heaven, nor the Son, but only the Father" (Mark 13:32). Jesus could foretell the destruction of the temple and of Jerusalem (13:2), and even announce in advance His own resurrection and Peter's denial with uncanny accuracy. Nevertheless, there were some things He did not know. By His own testimony, His knowledge was limited. You may have been taught that God is omniscient, that He knows everything, past, present, and future, even all *potential* future events, and that is true. However, that does not seem to have been the case with God the Son, at least during the incarnation. How are we to understand this?

Second, when Jesus went to the garden of Gethsemane, He prayed a curious prayer: **"Abba, Father, all things are possible for You. Take this cup away from Me; nevertheless, not what I will, but what You will"** (v. 36). What was going on when Jesus prayed in this way? If Jesus is God incarnate, how could He have pleaded with God to change the decree of God?

The Council of Chalcedon

In the year 451, the church convened the great Council of Chalcedon, one of the most important ecumenical councils of all time. It was called to combat several heresies, the most significant of which was the Monophysite heresy. The term *monophysite* has a prefix and a root. The prefix, *mono*, means "one," and the root, *phusis*, is translated as "nature." So *monophusis* or *monophysite* simply means "one nature."

The Monophysites claimed that Jesus did not have two natures, a divine nature and a human nature, but only one nature. That one nature was neither completely divine nor completely human. It was, depending on how one looked at it, a deified human nature or a humanized divine nature. This heresy was very serious for two reasons. It denied, on the one hand, the full deity of Christ. On the other hand, it denied the real humanity of Jesus. Against that, the Council of Chalcedon declared that Christ was *vere homo, vere Deus,* that is, "truly man and truly God," having two natures in one person.

How are we to understand the union of a human nature and a divine nature? The Bible says that in the incarnation, the second person of the Trinity took on Himself a human nature. However, when He took flesh, a human nature, He did not deify that human nature. That human nature remained human.

The Council of Chalcedon, in dealing with the mystery of the incarnation and affirming Jesus' two natures, said that His two natures are perfectly united in such a way that they are not confused or mixed, divided or separated. We cannot mix them together as the Monophysites did, deifying the flesh or humanizing the spirit. At the same time, we must never separate them. They are always and everywhere united. Those four negatives of Chalcedon are further qualified by this phrase, "each nature retaining its own attributes." That is, in the incarnation, the Son did not surrender any of His attributes. The divine nature is still eternal, infinite, omniscient, omnipresent, and omnipotent. It manifests all the attributes that belong to deity. God did not stop being God when He took on a human nature in Jesus. At the same time, the human nature retained its own attributes, being finite, contained, unable to be at more than one place at the same time, limited in knowledge, and limited in power. All of those attributes of humanity remained attributes of Jesus' humanity.

Communication of Attributes?

In the last chapter, we looked at Jesus' institution of the Lord's Supper, when He said, "This is My body." We saw that those words sparked a great controversy in the sixteenth century as to whether or not the human, physical nature of Jesus could be present at more than one place. The Council of Chalcedon established that the human nature of Jesus could not be present at more than one place at the same time. That could be possible only if a divine attribute were communicated to the human nature of Jesus. Amazingly, that was precisely what the Roman Catholic Church eventually began to teach.

That idea grew out of the teaching of Thomas Aquinas, the "Angelic Doctor" of the Roman Catholic Church and one of the most brilliant theologians the world has ever known. Aquinas essentially rejected the idea of a limitation of

Jesus' knowledge. Because Jesus was the God-man, with a divine nature and a human nature in perfect unity, He must have known the day and the hour of His coming, Aquinas said. However, he insisted that the knowledge was simply too high, too holy, and too wonderful for Jesus to communicate to mortal souls such as His disciples. So, to accommodate Himself to their weakness, He simply told them He did not know. That saves the idea of Jesus' omniscience, but it raises an even more serious problem. If Jesus told His disciples He did not know something when in fact He did know something, He told a falsehood, and that would disqualify Jesus from being our Savior.

In the wake of Aquinas' accommodation theory, Rome developed a concept called the communication of attributes, the *communicatio idiomata*. This teaching declares that in the incarnation, divine attributes were communicated to Jesus' human nature. That makes it possible, Rome says, for the body of Jesus to be in many places at the same time, as we discussed in the last chapter. However, we cannot accomplish this feat because our humanity is always limited by space and time. The divine attribute of omniscience has not been communicated to our human natures.

It is true that in the incarnation, there was a communication of knowledge from the divine nature to the human nature. Things only God could know were communicated to Jesus' human nature, so that He could foretell the future with perfect accuracy. Of course, this was nothing new. Such communication of knowledge from God to man in a supernatural way happened multitudes of times to the Old Testament prophets. They were given information they could not possibly have learned through their own efforts. In like manner, the Apostles in the New Testament, chiefly the Apostle Paul, served as agents of revelation and communicated to us things that they could not possibly have learned on their own, but which God communicated to them.

However, the communication of *knowledge* from the divine nature to the human nature is one thing. It is something else to say God communicates *a divine attribute*. If Jesus knew tomorrow because the attribute of omniscience was communicated to His human nature, we would expect His human nature to know everything. But He Himself indicated there were limits to what He knew. So if we understand that the divine nature communicates information without communicating omniscience, we will not stumble over these passages.

Distinguishing, Not Separating

Chalcedon also declared that Jesus' divine and human natures must not be divided or separated. We do this when we deny the perfect unity of the two natures. However, while we must not question the unity of the two natures, it is perfectly acceptable to distinguish them.

When we distinguish between the human and the divine natures, it is obvious that Jesus' human nature experienced the agony at Gethsemane. It was the human Jesus praying to the divine Father for relief from His agony, yet at the same time indicating His perfect commitment to obey the Father's will. The two natures, without confusion, mixture, division, or separation, remained intact, but there were certain things that manifested the divine nature and other things that manifested the human nature. His divine nature did not plead with the Father to change His mind. We know that the Father, the Son, and the Holy Spirit, the three persons of the Trinity, were in total agreement from all eternity as to how our redemption was going to be accomplished. Rather, His human nature pleaded that the cup might pass from Him. When Jesus, in His agony, began to sweat, were those beads of perspiration divine sweat? Or did that perspiration manifest the human nature of Jesus? Obviously, His sweat was a manifestation not of the divine nature but of the human nature, and so was His prayer.

This very moment, Jesus is in heaven touching His human nature. But the person of Jesus is perfectly united to His divine nature even here. The divine nature can be everywhere at all times. Wherever the divine nature is, the person is, even though the physical body is in heaven.

I take the time to review this because it has been said that every heresy the church combated in the first eight hundred years is repeated in every generation. If you watch Christian television for one day, you will hear these heresies taught as biblical truth. So we have to be careful in every generation, lest we fall into ideas that distort the truth.

Of course, we do not know all there is to know about the mystery of the incarnation. The Council of Chalcedon drew boundaries. The men who met there set the limits of our speculation. They said, in effect: "If you go over this boundary, you will end up in the Monophysite heresy. If you go over this boundary, you will end up separating the two natures." They wanted to be careful to stay within the boundaries of legitimate reflection. They basically admitted that they did not understand how the divine nature and the human nature are co-joined, but they knew how they are not. There is no confusion, mixture, division, or separation. They knew that no matter how the divine nature and the human nature are united, each nature retains its own attributes in that perfect union. The divine nature does not stop being divine. The human nature does not stop being human.

I sometimes get upset with some of our hymns that speak of God dying on the cross. The God-man died on the cross, but the divine nature did not die. If God actually had died on the cross, not only would Jesus have died, the Father would have died and the Holy Spirit would have died, and the whole universe would have ceased to exist because the universe depends for its moment-to-moment continuation on the upholding hand of God. If God perishes, everything perishes. No, the God-man died in His human nature. Even when He was a corpse in the tomb, He remained united to the divine nature. His human spirit was given to the Father in His last breath. The union of the divine and human was not broken. So, we do not separate the two natures, but we must distinguish them to avoid falling into heresy.

52

A KISS OF BETRAYAL

Mark 14:43–52

∾

And immediately, while He was still speaking, Judas, one of the twelve, with a great multitude with swords and clubs, came from the chief priests and the scribes and the elders. Now His betrayer had given them a signal, saying, "Whomever I kiss, He is the One; seize Him and lead Him away safely." As soon as he had come, immediately he went up to Him and said to Him, "Rabbi, Rabbi!" and kissed Him. Then they laid their hands on Him and took Him. And one of those who stood by drew his sword and struck the servant of the high priest, and cut off his ear. Then Jesus answered and said to them, "Have you come out, as against a robber, with swords and clubs to take Me? I was daily with you in the temple teaching, and you did not seize Me. But the Scriptures must be fulfilled." Then they all forsook Him and fled. Now a certain young man followed Him, having a linen cloth thrown around his naked body. And the young men laid hold of him, and he left the linen cloth and fled from them naked.

One of the most wicked acts in all of history took place, appropriately, not in the light of day but in the darkness of night. It was the betrayal of Jesus by the kiss of Judas, known in history as the kiss of death. Mark tells us, **immediately, while He was still speaking, Judas, one of the twelve, with a great multitude with swords and clubs, came from the chief priests and the scribes and the elders** (v. 43). It was no surprise to Jesus, who had just said that His betrayer was at hand (v. 42).

Presumably, the group with swords and clubs was a mixture of members of the temple guard belonging to the Sanhedrin and soldiers of the Roman garrisons stationed in Jerusalem. They came to this designated place where they could arrest Jesus away from the public, under cover of darkness. Every aspect of this incident indicates an action committed by children of darkness.

Mark writes that Judas **had given them a signal, saying, "Whomever I kiss, He is the One; seize Him and lead Him away safely"** (v. 44). When Judas said the soldiers could lead Jesus away "safely," he was not expressing the desire that Jesus not be harmed. Judas simply meant that the soldiers could make this arrest with little risk to themselves.

Mark goes on to say, **As soon as he had come, immediately he went up to Him and said to Him, "Rabbi, Rabbi!" and kissed Him** (v. 45). What an incredible paradox. It was a gesture of profound honor and affection, customarily given by disciples to their rabbi, that Judas used for his evil mission. The language here describes Judas's kiss as not a brief peck on the cheek, but a kiss lavishly bestowed, signifying an especially deep sense of affection and honor. This kiss was an act of hypocrisy with a vengeance.

Repeating a Name

Consider also the way Judas spoke to Jesus. It reminds me of when Jesus, at the end of the Sermon on the Mount, described a situation that would come to pass on the last day. He said: "Many will say to Me in that day, 'Lord, Lord, have we not . . . done many wonders in Your name?' And then I will declare to them, 'I never knew you; depart from Me, you who practice lawlessness!'" (Matt. 7:22–23). Jesus' warning contained an unusual form of cultural expression. He portrayed those who would come professing to be affectionate toward Him as saying, "Lord, Lord," repeating the word. The Hebraic custom of addressing people by repeating their names occurs only about fifteen times in all of sacred Scripture, but it is very significant.

We see it in the Old Testament, in that poignant moment on Mount Moriah when Abraham laid his son Isaac on the altar, and at the last second God called to him, saying, "Abraham, Abraham! . . . Do not lay your hand on the lad . . . for now I know that you fear God" (Gen. 22:11–12). Later, when Jacob feared to go with his family into the land of Goshen, God came and spoke to him, saying, "Jacob, Jacob! . . . do not fear to go down to Egypt. . . . I will go down with you" (Gen. 46:2–4). Still later, in the Midianite wilderness, when God called Moses to lead the people of Israel in the exodus, He spoke to him out of the burning bush, saying, "Moses, Moses!" (Ex. 3:4). In His midnight summons to Samuel, God called out "Samuel! Samuel!" to which the lad replied, "Speak, for your servant hears" (1 Sam. 3:10). When Elijah was taken up to heaven in the chariot of fire, Elisha stood there looking on and cried out, "My father, my father" (2 Kings 2:12). Then there was David's cry of lament at the news of the death of his son, when he wailed, "O my son Absalom! O Absalom, my son, my son!" (2 Sam. 19:4).

In the New Testament, Jesus spoke tenderly to Martha when she registered her complaint, saying, "Martha, Martha" (Luke 10:41). When Simon Peter told Jesus he would never deny Him, Jesus said: "Simon, Simon! Indeed, Satan has asked for you, that he may sift you as wheat. But I have prayed for you" (Luke 22:31–32). Jesus lamented over the city, saying: "O Jerusalem, Jerusalem. . . . How often I wanted to gather your children together, as a hen gathers her brood under her wings, but you were not willing!" (Luke 13:34). To Saul on the road to Damascus, Jesus said, "Saul, Saul, why are you persecuting Me?" (Acts 9:4). Of course, the most dramatic use of such repetition came from the cross itself, when Jesus cried out, "My God, My God, why have you forsaken Me" (Mark 15:34).

Do you see what is going on in these situations? Every time a name is repeated it communicates an intense and profound sense of personal affection. Jesus was saying that at the last day people will come to Him, people whom He will not know and who will not belong to Him, but they will pretend they belong to Him. They not only will speak His name, they will repeat it as though they are on intimate terms with Him. Jesus said He essentially will say to them: "Please leave. I do not know who you are. I do not know your name. Depart from Me, you workers of iniquity."

In the Christian community, people say, "Do you know Jesus?" Yet the issue is not whether we know Jesus. The issue is whether Jesus knows us. Well, Judas did not know Jesus and Jesus did not know him, even though he came to Jesus saying, "Rabbi, Rabbi!" Jesus did not have to wait until the last day to see His prophecy fulfilled in Judas.

Arresting Jesus

Mark continues his account: **Then they laid their hands on Him and took Him. And one of those who stood by drew his sword and struck the servant of the high priest, and cut off his ear** (vv. 46–47). The one who drew his sword is nameless in Mark's account. Tradition tells us that Mark was the Apostle Peter's secretary, and it was Peter's apostleship that stood behind Mark's gospel. John identifies the nameless one in his gospel as Peter, the impetuous and impulsive disciple (John 18:10). Mark also does not tell us that Jesus rebuked Peter for attacking the servant or that He picked up the ear and restored it (Luke 22:51).

This man whose ear had just been cut off was healed by the very One he was arresting for execution.

Mark tells us: **Jesus answered and said to them, "Have you come out, as against a robber, with swords and clubs to take Me? I was daily with you in the temple teaching, and you did not seize Me. But the Scriptures must be fulfilled"** (vv. 48–49). Jesus told them there was no need for force. He was prepared to go with them quietly, for He knew that what was happening was the Father's will, long prophesied.

What happened next fulfilled what Jesus had foretold earlier, as recorded in verse 27: **Then they all forsook Him and fled** (v. 50). It was not only Judas; it was not only Peter; it was every last one of them. At the moment of His arrest, the disciples turned and fled into the darkness.

Then Mark appends an unusual detail: **Now a certain young man followed him, having a linen cloth thrown around his naked body. And the young men laid hold of him, and he left the linen cloth and fled from them naked** (v. 51). There are some things we can discern from the text about this strange incident. Presumably, this young man was not one of the twelve. He obviously was a man of means because only the wealthy wore linen coverings under their tunics. The fact that he had on only the linen cloth without the undergarments indicated that he had dressed in haste to come and follow this situation. He probably lived nearby, perhaps in Jerusalem.

This is a tantalizing morsel for speculative theologians to chew on, and many of them do so, asking, "Why is this account of this unnamed person in this embarrassing situation included in this gospel?" This young man may have been Mark himself, who was from a family of wealth. Maybe this was Mark's way of inserting himself into the account, to indicate he was an eyewitness of the things that took place that night. If so, it was a harrowing moment for him, as he was nearly caught. His linen garment was grabbed by one of the soldiers, but he spun away and left his garment, just as Joseph fled from Potiphar's wife when she clutched his garment, and he escaped by leaving the garment behind (Gen. 39:11–16).

Nakedness Equals Shame

Many years ago, I wrote a book that was first titled *The Psychology of Atheism*, then later retitled *If There Is a God, Why Are There Atheists?* In it, I included a chapter on the nakedness motif that we find in sacred Scripture and in Western philosophy. I did a word study of *gumnos*, which is the Greek for "naked." In the garden of Eden, the man and the woman were naked but without shame until sin came into their lives. The very first psychological self-awareness of guilt and shame was an uncomfortable awareness of nudity. Since then, human beings have been the only creatures who have adorned and covered themselves with artificial garments, because it is built into our fallen humanity to equate shame and humiliation with nakedness.

Throughout the pages of Scripture, when God speaks of bringing judgment against the guilty, He does it by exposing their sin and stripping them of their clothes. A prime example of this comes from the book of the prophet Amos. Amos gives the Lord's list of transgressions by Moab, Judah, Israel, and so on, then gives God's response: "Behold, I am weighed down by you, as a cart full of sheaves is weighed down." This is God's rebuke of His people. He then says: "Therefore flight shall perish from the swift, the strong shall not strengthen his power, nor shall the mighty deliver himself; he shall not stand who handles the bow, the swift of foot shall not escape." God was foretelling the conditions when He visited His judgment on His people. Then He says, "The most courageous men of might shall flee naked in that day" (2:13–16). As another example, the book of Revelation connects the judgments of God on the wicked to nakedness (Rev. 3:17; 16:15; 17:16).

The motif of clothing and nakedness is at the heart of our understanding of redemption. Our own righteousness, we are told, is like rotten, filthy rags (Isa. 64:6). The only way any of us can stand in God's presence is to be stripped of those rags and then clothed afresh in the garments of Christ's righteousness. That is the gospel. You and I can never stand in the presence of a holy God unless we are clothed from on high with a righteousness that is not our own.

God has provided for us a covering for our shame and our nakedness. He has invited us into His redeeming presence to experience anew that sense of safety that we have in knowing His Son has covered our sin with His blood on the cross and covered our nakedness with His perfect righteousness in His life.

53

JESUS STANDS TRIAL

Mark 14:53–72

———⁓———

And they led Jesus away to the high priest; and with him were assembled all the chief priests, the elders, and the scribes. But Peter followed Him at a distance, right into the courtyard of the high priest. And he sat with the servants and warmed himself at the fire. Now the chief priests and all the council sought testimony against Jesus to put Him to death, but found none. For many bore false witness against Him, but their testimonies did not agree. Then some rose up and bore false witness against Him, saying, "We heard Him say, 'I will destroy this temple made with hands, and within three days I will build another made without hands.'" But not even then did their testimony agree. And the high priest stood up in the midst and asked Jesus, saying, "Do You answer nothing? What is it these men testify against You?" But He kept silent and answered nothing. Again the high priest asked Him, saying to Him, "Are You the Christ, the Son of the Blessed?" Jesus said, "I am. And you will see the Son of Man sitting at the right hand of the Power, and coming with the clouds of heaven." Then the high priest tore his clothes and said, "What further need do we have of witnesses? You have heard the blasphemy! What do you think?" And they all condemned Him to be deserving of death. Then some began to spit on Him, and to blindfold Him, and to beat Him, and to say to Him, "Prophesy!" And the officers struck Him with the palms of their hands. Now as Peter was below in the courtyard, one of the servant girls of the high priest came. And when she saw Peter warming himself, she looked at him and said, "You also were with Jesus of Nazareth." But he denied it, saying, "I neither know nor understand what you are saying." And he went out on the porch, and a rooster crowed. And the servant girl saw him again, and began to say to those who stood by, "This is one of them." But he denied it again. And a little later those who stood by said to Peter again, "Surely you are one of them; for you are a Galilean, and your speech shows it." Then he began to curse and swear, "I do not know this Man of whom you speak!" A second time the rooster crowed. Then Peter called to mind the word that Jesus had said to him, "Before the rooster crows twice, you will deny Me three times." And when he thought about it, he wept.

Following His arrest, Jesus was taken before the most powerful Jewish leaders of that day. Mark writes: **And they led Jesus away to the high priest; and with him were assembled all the chief priests, the elders, and the scribes** (v. 53). It is unthinkable that the Messiah, the Ruler and Sustainer of the universe, should be subjected to a trial by mere men, but in the good providence of God, that is what occurred. Of course, there was nothing with which they could charge Him. As a result, His trial was a travesty.

Mark also tells us: **But Peter followed him at a distance, right into the courtyard of the high priest. And he sat with the servants and warmed himself at the fire** (v. 54). Peter came back from fleeing into the darkness and began to follow the proceedings as an observer, seeking to remain anonymous. He was trying to keep a safe distance between himself and Jesus. He was hoping to preserve his life; he did not want to be executed along with Christ. This is the same Peter who had told Jesus he would follow Him to the death.

Are you following Jesus from a distance? Do the people with whom you interact each day know that you are a Christian? I am not asking whether you wear your Christianity on your sleeve and make a pest of yourself to your friends and coworkers. I am simply asking whether they know where your allegiance lies. If they do not, perhaps you are keeping a safe distance from your Savior.

Peter followed Jesus in this way, trying to keep a safe distance. He was just bold enough to come into the courtyard that surrounded Caiaphas' home and to join a group of servants warming themselves at a fire. You see, he not only wanted to be safe, he also wanted to be comfortable as he was following Jesus.

A Rigged Trial

Mark writes, **Now the chief priests and all the council sought testimony against Jesus to put Him to death, but found none** (v. 55). This language indicates that the Jewish religious leaders were not on a truth-seeking mission. They were not gathering facts. The Greek implies that they were intentionally trying to find something by which they could convict Jesus of a capital offense. In truth, this was a witch hunt.

Mark's vignette about Peter tells us that Jesus was not taken to the Chamber of Hewn Stone, which was the normal meeting place of the Sanhedrin, the ruling body of the Jews. Instead, He was taken to the home of the high priest Caiaphas, the son-in-law of Annas, who was perhaps the most powerful Jew in the land. Caiaphas reigned from AD 18 to 36. Also, this is the only recorded instance of a Jewish trial being conducted at night, which was illegal. Clearly the Sanhedrin did not want the people of Jerusalem to know what was happening lest they march in protest. Jewish law also prescribed that no trial could be held on the Sabbath, a feast day, or the eve of a Sabbath or a feast day, so that regulation was violated as well.

The unfolding of the trial brought further irregularities. Old Testament law required that in a capital case there had to be two eyewitnesses to the crime, and those eyewitnesses had to agree in their testimony, but the testimony in Jesus' trial did not match up. Furthermore, Jewish law required that if a criminal was convicted of a capital crime, the Sanhedrin had to meet again the next day to confirm that judgment. This law was designed to prevent rash and sudden judgments in capital cases, but it was not observed in Jesus' trial. Nearly everything about this hearing went in the face of Jewish law.

Mark writes, **For many bore false witness against Him, but their testimonies did not agree** (v. 56). The supposed witnesses could not get their stories to line up. Next, members of the Sanhedrin took their turn: **Then some rose up and bore false witness against Him, saying, "We heard Him say, 'I will destroy this temple made with hands, and within three days I will build another made without hands.'" But not even then did their testimony agree** (vv. 57–59). The members of the Sanhedrin, the leaders of the Jews, here bore false against Jesus, violating the ninth commandment (Ex. 20:16). But even they could not maintain a consistent story.

The Greek word translated as "witness" in verse 56 is *marturia*, which means "testimony, a bearing witness." It is related to the word *martur*, from which we get the English word *martyr*. Martyrs were so called in the early church because they gave the most eloquent testimony, or witness, to Jesus that they possibly could give by dying for Him. They testified to the truth of Christ with their lives and hence were called martyrs, those who gave testimony. By contrast, the Greek term that is translated as "false witness" in verse 57 is a form of the verb *pseudomartureo*, which means "to bear false witness."

The High Priest's Questions

Finally, the high priest stood up and asked Jesus a question: **"Do you answer nothing? What is it these men testify against you?" But He kept silent and**

answered nothing (vv. 60–61a). We can imagine Caiaphas's agitation when Jesus refused to speak. Jesus was fulfilling the prophecy of Isaiah 53:7: "Yet He opened not His mouth; He was led as a lamb to the slaughter." Furthermore, He knew what these people were doing, and He knew that whatever He said, no matter how accurate or sincere it was, would be twisted and used against Him. It was better to let these false witnesses give their testimony and for Jesus to say nothing rather than to say anything they could use against Him.

At this point, Caiaphas was beside himself, so he pressed the issue: **Again the high priest asked him, saying to him, "Are you the Christ, the Son of the Blessed?"** (v. 61b). The word *Blessed* is circumlocution. It was a word the Jews used to avoid saying, and perhaps misusing, the sacred name of God. Caiaphas was really asking, "Are You the Christ, the Son of God?"

Throughout the gospel of Mark, we have seen that whenever someone came to see that Jesus was the Messiah, He would say, essentially, "Do not tell anyone." At His hearing, there was no more need for secrecy, so when Caiaphas asked Him whether He was the Christ—the Messiah—and the Son of God, Jesus answered: **"I am. And you will see the Son of Man sitting at the right hand of the Power, and coming with the clouds of heaven"** (v. 62). He, too, used a circumlocution, saying "the Power" instead of "God."

However, when Jesus said, "you will see the Son of Man sitting at the right hand of the Power, and coming with the clouds of heaven," He took another step. This was a clear reference to Daniel 7, with which everyone in that court was familiar. It describes a heavenly being who comes to the throne of the Ancient of Days. Jesus was saying, essentially: "Yes, I am the Son of God. I came from heaven and I am going back to heaven. I am appointed to judge the earth." He was letting them know this would not be the last time they would meet in the context of a trial. He would be back with all of the authority of heaven, and He would judge them. That was His clear implication.

Caiaphas lost whatever composure or restraint he may have had at that point. Mark writes: **Then the high priest tore his clothes and said, "What further need do we have of witnesses? You have heard the blasphemy! What do you think?"** (vv. 63–64a). In the Old Testament, whenever someone ripped his garments, it was because he was overcome with profound grief or rage. Caiaphas was furious.

Why did Caiaphas equate Jesus' statement with blasphemy? The Jewish law carefully defined this sin. To be guilty of blasphemy, a person had to curse the name of God directly. Jesus did not do that. Rather, He blessed the name of God. But the Jewish religious leaders believed His identification of Himself as the Son of God to be blasphemous. This charge was without Jewish legal foundation. Nevertheless, **they all condemned Him to be deserving of death** (v. 64b).

Mark then writes: **Then some began to spit on Him, and to blindfold Him, and to beat Him, and to say to Him, "Prophesy!" And the officers struck Him with the palms of their hands** (v. 65). These actions recall Isaiah's description of God's Suffering Servant: "The Lord GOD has opened My ear; and I was not rebellious, nor did I turn away. I gave My back to those who struck Me, and My cheeks to those who plucked out the beard; I did not hide My face from shame and spitting" (Isa. 50:5–6). If someone tries to spit in your face, you shield yourself. However, Jesus took it, following the prophetic utterance of Isaiah of what would happen centuries in the future to the Servant of the Lord. He was beaten and spat on, and He endured it.

Peter's Denial of Jesus

Meanwhile, Mark tells us, **as Peter was below in the courtyard, one of the servant girls of the high priest came** (v. 66). While Jesus' trial was going on upstairs, another one was taking place downstairs in the courtyard. The presiding officer in this trial was not one of the rulers of the Jews, the nobles of the community, or the Sanhedrin members, but a servant girl who had no status, power, or authority.

The trial proceeded quickly: **When she saw Peter warming himself, she looked at him and said, "You also were with Jesus of Nazareth." But he denied it, saying, "I neither know nor understand what you are saying." And he went out on the porch, and a rooster crowed** (vv. 67–68). As soon as Peter denied Jesus for the first time, he moved to what he thought was a safer position, away from this servant girl. At that moment, a rooster crowed. Mark does not state whether Peter took notice of that first crow. Then, Mark tells us, **the servant girl saw him again, and began to say to those who stood by, "This is one of them." But he denied it again** (vv. 69–70a). At this point, Peter had denied Jesus twice, but it does not seem to have registered with him. Mark continues: **And a little later those who stood by said to Peter again, "Surely you are one of them; for you are a Galilean, and your speech shows it." Then he began to curse and swear, "I do not know this Man of whom you speak!"** (vv. 70b–71). The third time he punctuated his denial with cursing. He may have just used crude language. Or, as some commentators suggest, perhaps he uttered a solemn oath, saying, "I swear in the name of God, I do not know the man." It is ironic that Jesus was convicted of blasphemy, but in all probability the one who was committing the blasphemy was down in the courtyard—Simon Peter.

Then we read: **A second time the rooster crowed. Then Peter called to mind the word that Jesus had said to him, "Before the rooster crows twice, you will deny Me three times." And when he thought about it, he wept** (v. 72). Peter did not weep until he remembered what Jesus had said. When he began to contemplate what he had done, he was sick to tears.

Often people do not really feel the force of guilt when there are people around them. Usually they experience the weight of their guilt when they put their heads on their pillows at night, when all of their defensive postures are removed and they are left alone before God. Then the truth pierces their consciences and breaks their hearts.

This was the same Peter who had said he would die with Jesus. Jesus essentially said: "No, you will not die with Me. You will deny that you even know Me. Three times you will deny Me." That is exactly what Peter did. And that is what most people do when they try to follow Jesus at a distance and be safe Christians.

If such a moment of truth ever comes for you, that moment when you have to stand up and identify yourself as one who belongs to Jesus, remember that Jesus said, "For whoever is ashamed of Me and My words in this adulterous and sinful generation, of him the Son of Man also will be ashamed when He comes in the glory of His Father with the holy angels" (Mark 8:38). I cannot imagine anything more embarrassing than to stand in heaven and hear Jesus say, "I am ashamed of this man," to have Jesus look at me and say, "Shame on you." I pray that the grace of God and the power of the Holy Spirit will keep you and me from ever doing that to Jesus.

54

JESUS AND PILATE

Mark 15:1–15

⁂

Immediately, in the morning, the chief priests held a consultation with the elders and scribes and the whole council; and they bound Jesus, led Him away, and delivered Him to Pilate. Then Pilate asked Him, "Are You the King of the Jews?" He answered and said to him, "It is as you say." And the chief priests accused Him of many things, but He answered nothing. Then Pilate asked Him again, saying, "Do You answer nothing? See how many things they testify against You!" But Jesus still answered nothing, so that Pilate marveled. Now at the feast he was accustomed to releasing one prisoner to them, whomever they requested. And there was one named Barabbas, who was chained with his fellow rebels; they had committed murder in the rebellion. Then the multitude, crying aloud, began to ask him to do just as he had always done for them. But Pilate answered them, saying, "Do you want me to release to you the King of the Jews?" For he knew that the chief priests had handed Him over because of envy. But the chief priests stirred up the crowd, so that he should rather release Barabbas to them. Pilate answered and said to them again, "What then do you want me to do with Him whom you call the King of the Jews?" So they cried out again, "Crucify Him!" Then Pilate said to them, "Why, what evil has He done?" But they cried out all the more, "Crucify Him!" So Pilate, wanting to gratify the crowd, released Barabbas to them; and he delivered Jesus, after he had scourged Him, to be crucified.

For thousands of years, Christians have confessed their faith by use of the Apostles' Creed. This creed, as we might expect in an orthodox statement of faith, mentions all three persons of the Trinity. In addition, it mentions two people. First, the creed tells us that our Lord Jesus was "born of the virgin Mary." It is not surprising that the virgin is mentioned, for the fact that she was Jesus' mother speaks to His supernatural conception and to His humanity. Second, and more surprising by far, the creed says that Jesus "suffered under Pontius Pilate." I sometimes wonder why it was, when ancient believers put this creed together, they chose to include the name of Pontius Pilate. They could have noted that Jesus was "betrayed by Judas Iscariot," "denied by Simon Peter," or "delivered by the High Priest Caiaphas." Why was a third-rate Roman politician enshrined in one of the important creeds of the church?

The simple reason, of course, is that Pilate was the presiding officer in Jesus' final condemnation and His execution. In that role, as church historians and theologians agree, he functioned not merely as a Roman provincial governor but as a *persona publica*, a "public person" who issued a judgment that was far more significant in terms of history than his own personal opinion.

Mark, as is his custom, gives us an extremely brief summary of the discussion between Jesus and Pilate—if it can even be properly described as a discussion. Even so, the account is filled with irony.

Jesus Delivered to Pilate

Mark writes, **Immediately, in the morning, the chief priests held a consultation with the elders and scribes and the whole council; and they bound Jesus, led Him away, and delivered Him to Pilate** (v. 1). As we have seen, when the Jewish authorities arrested Jesus, they subjected Him to a late-night trial, but the witnesses could not keep their stories straight. Finally, the high priest asked Jesus, "Are you the Christ?" and Jesus replied, "I am" (14:61–62). Then the council condemned Him, judging that His claim to be the Messiah was blasphemy (14:64).

In the morning, the Sanhedrin discussed the next step. There was really only one thing to be done. Because Israel was under Roman control, the Jewish authorities could not execute anyone. They had to take Jesus to Pilate and try to convince him that Jesus deserved to be put to death. They probably met to devise civil charges that would be more heinous in Pilate's eyes than a charge of blasphemy according to Jewish categories.

Then they bound Jesus and led Him away. There really was no need to bind Him; when they arrested Him, He said, "Have you come out, as against a robber, with swords and clubs to take Me?" (14:48). He went with them willingly.

However, the Jewish religious leaders wanted to humiliate Jesus and portray Him as dangerous in the governor's eyes. So, they took Him to Pilate early in the morning, when Pilate normally heard such cases.

It was the Roman custom to appoint governors over the lands conquered by the legions. Pilate was the fifth governor of Judea. He held the office for eleven years, from AD 26 to 37, the longest tenure of those who served in the post. The governorship of Judea was not a political plum; it was one of the lowest rungs on the ladder for a Roman administrator, so staying in that outpost for eleven years was not so much a sign of success as it was a sign of failure. Pilate's tenure finally ended when he was fired and banished from government by the Emperor Caligula.

The ancient historians Philo and Josephus tell us that Pilate was inflexible, stubborn, and cruel. During his tenure in Judea, he put down several insurrections or protests by the Jews in brutal fashion. There were times when he deliberately provoked them. For example, he invited the legions of Rome to enter Jerusalem and the temple area with banners that proclaimed the Roman caesar, which was seen as blasphemous to the Jewish people. On another occasion, he built an aqueduct that ran for twenty-three miles, bringing water into Jerusalem. That was the good news. The bad news was that he confiscated money from the temple in order to build his aqueduct.

Note that Mark says the Jews "delivered Him" to Pilate. Jesus had told His disciples that He would be delivered to the Gentiles (10:33), but the Old Testament had prophesied this deliverance centuries before. It foretold that the Savior would be judged and killed outside the camp. Just as the sins of ancient Israel were symbolically transferred to the scapegoat, which then was driven out of the camp into the wilderness, into the outer darkness (Leviticus 16), the Messiah was to die at the hands of the Gentiles outside the city of God, symbolically cut off from the presence of God and the people of God. Thus, in one of the most messianic of the psalms, the psalmist cries out, "Dogs have surrounded Me; the congregation of the wicked has enclosed Me" (Ps. 22:16). This prophecy was fulfilled when Jesus was delivered to Pilate.

The King of the Kings

When Jesus was taken to Pilate, a discussion ensued between them that touched on a series of topics. Some of these topics are addressed in some of the Gospels, some in others, and the accounts vary in terms of the amount of detail the authors include. Therefore, I will look to all four Gospels, not just Mark, to address these portions of the discussion. First, they talked about whether Jesus was a king. Second, they discussed the nature of truth. Third, they talked about Jesus' guilt or innocence. Fourth, there was a discussion about amnesty.

First, regarding Jesus' kingship, Mark writes: **Then Pilate asked Him, "Are You the King of the Jews?" He answered and said to him, "It is as you say." And the chief priests accused Him of many things, but He answered nothing. Then Pilate asked Him again, saying, "Do You answer nothing? See how many things they testify against You!" But Jesus still answered nothing, so that Pilate marveled** (vv. 2–5). Luke tells us that the Jewish authorities presented this accusation when they brought Jesus to Pilate: "We found this fellow perverting the nation, and forbidding to pay taxes to Caesar, saying that He Himself is Christ, a King" (23:2). These obviously false charges were designed to cast Jesus as a revolutionary, angering Pilate. So, Pilate asked: "Is it true? Are you the King of the Jews?"

In Mark's terse record, Jesus' reply is very simple: "It is as you say." I think that every translation of this sentence misses the force of Jesus' reply. When Pilate asked whether He was a King, He basically replied, "You said it!" He was not saying, "Well, *you* say I am a King, but *I* do not say that." No, He was strongly affirming that He is a King.

As we read in John's account, Jesus qualified that statement by saying: "My kingdom is not of this world. If My kingdom were of this world, My servants would fight, so that I should not be delivered to the Jews; but now My kingdom is not from here" (18:36). Jesus was saying to Pilate, "You have nothing to fear from Me in terms of your political power. My kingdom is not of this world. It is a transcendent kingdom." He could have gone on to say: "My kingdom is higher than the Roman Empire. My kingdom is the ultimate kingdom, because I am the King of the kings. I am the Lord of the lords. Every emperor, king, prince, and governor will someday stand before My judgment."

Of course, He did not say all that. In fact, Mark tells us, He said almost nothing at all, refusing to respond to the accusations of the Jews. He was so peaceful in the face of these accusations that Pilate marveled. He had never seen this demeanor in a prisoner.

The Truth Incarnate

According to John, after Jesus said, "My kingdom is not from here," Pilate replied, "Are You a king then?" Jesus said, "You say rightly that I am a king," but then He introduced another topic: "For this cause I was born, and for this cause I have come into the world, that I should bear witness to the truth. Everyone who is of the truth hears My voice" (18:37). It is interesting that Jesus changed the focus on the discussion in this way. He basically said to Pilate: "Do you want to know what I am about? Do you want to know what My mission is? Do you want to know why I came into the world? I will tell you—I came to bear witness to the truth."

During His ministry, Jesus explained His mission in different ways. For instance, He said, "I have come that they may have life, and that they may have it more abundantly" (John 10:10b). Earlier in Mark, we saw that Jesus said, "The Son of Man did not come to be served, but to serve, and to give His life a ransom for many" (10:45). However, when He was on trial for His life, He said, "I came to this world to bear witness to the truth."

We desperately need to hear Jesus' witness to the truth. I know of no time in Christian history when the church has been less interested in truth than it is today. There is a negative attitude toward doctrine, toward theology. People say: "Doctrine divides. Christianity is about personal relationships." However, we cannot define a good personal relationship without some understanding of truth. The Old Testament is the history of warfare between the speakers of truth and the false prophets who lied. When the false prophets got the upper hand in Israel, it was said that "truth is fallen in the street" (Isa. 59:14). That is where we are today. It seems that almost no one wants to know the truth.

When Jesus said, "I came to bear witness to the truth," Pilate asked, "What is truth?" (John 18:38). John does not describe Pilate's facial expression or the tone of voice he used when he asked this question. Given how cynical Pilate was and what a corrupt politician he was, he was probably the last person on the planet who normally was concerned about truth. So, was his question sarcastic, jaded, or discouraged? Actually, I think that for one moment in his life, having interacted with this unusual man, Pilate really was curious to know the truth. Ironically, the truth incarnate was standing right in front of him.

The Man with No Fault

Luke tells us that after hearing all the accusations of the Jews and examining Jesus himself, Pilate came to a verdict: "I find no fault in this Man" (23:4). Likewise, Matthew records an interesting vignette: "While [Pilate] was sitting on the judgment seat, his wife sent to him, saying, 'Have nothing to do with that *just* Man, for I have suffered many things today in a dream because of Him'" (27:19). Even after he yielded to the crowd's desire that Jesus be crucified, Pilate still felt Jesus was innocent. Matthew tells us, "He took water and washed his hands before the multitude, saying, 'I am innocent of the blood of this *just* Person'" (Matt. 27:24b). Never in his life did Pilate speak more truthfully than when he said of Jesus, "I find no fault in this Man."

Why could Pilate not find any fault in Jesus? Was it because he did not look hard enough? No. There was no fault in Him to be found. No one can find what does not exist, and there was no fault, no blemish in Jesus.

The Son of the Father

Mark then writes, **Now at the feast he was accustomed to releasing one prisoner to them, whomever they requested. And there was one named Barabbas, who was chained with his fellow rebels; they had committed murder in the rebellion. Then the multitude, crying aloud, began to ask him to do just as he had always done for them. But Pilate answered them, saying, "Do you want me to release to you the King of the Jews?" For he knew that the chief priests had handed Him over because of envy** (vv. 6–10). Pilate had a strange tradition that, during the Passover festival, he would grant full amnesty to one prisoner whose release the Jews requested. Because he judged Jesus was innocent, and because he knew the Jewish leaders had brought Jesus to him because they were envious of Jesus' popularity, he assumed that the crowds were on Jesus' side and would be open to his suggestion that he grant amnesty to Jesus.

However, Pilate overlooked the Jewish leaders' ability to manipulate the people. Mark tells us, **But the chief priests stirred up the crowd, so that he should rather release Barabbas to them** (v. 11). It is unclear how the priests did this. Did they threaten the people? Did they promise them something? In any case, they successfully motivated the people to reject Pilate's offer of amnesty for Jesus and to demand the release of Barabbas instead.

This part of the narrative is filled with irony. First, the Greek New Testament indicates that Barabbas was this man's last name; his first name was actually Jesus. So, the choice Pilate offered to the crowd was Jesus Barabbas or Jesus of Nazareth. Second, the name Barabbas itself is ironic. When the Spirit enables us to address God as Father, we cry, "Abba, Father" (Rom. 8:15), which is basically a repetition, although *Abba* is a term that carries more endearment. In Jewish names, *Bar* means "son of." Therefore, Jesus is called Jesus Bar-Joseph. Similarly, the name Barabbas means "son of the father." So, Pilate offered the people Jesus, son of the father, or Jesus of Nazareth, who was the true Son of the Father.

Barabbas, we are told, was a rebel who "had committed murder in the rebellion." It seems he was an insurrectionist who had taken up arms against Rome in an unnamed uprising. Here, then, is yet another irony: Pilate offered the people a man who wanted to give them political freedom and a man who could give them spiritual freedom.

Perhaps Barabbas was a hero of the people for his opposition to Rome (the very thing they had looked for in Jesus). Perhaps the priests were able to exert just enough leverage on the crowd by some means. In any case, the crowd foiled Pilate's plan for Jesus' release by demanding that he grant amnesty to Barabbas. They did not want the true Son of the Father. They wanted a different Jesus, a Jesus they could live with, a Jesus who would not make them feel guilty, a Jesus of this world. For two thousand years, the world has cried for a different Jesus, one more like us.

Mark writes: **Pilate answered and said to them again, "What then do you want me to do with Him whom you call the King of the Jews?" So they cried out again, "Crucify Him!" Then Pilate said to them, "Why, what evil has He done?" But they cried out all the more, "Crucify Him!" So Pilate, wanting to gratify the crowd, released Barabbas to them; and he delivered Jesus, after he had scourged Him, to be crucified** (vv. 12–15). Having recognized the crowd's desire for Barabbas' release, Pilate foolishly and inexplicably asked the crowd to pronounce judgment on Jesus. Perhaps the priests were able to exert influence again, for the crowd cried for Jesus' crucifixion. Pilate tried briefly to reason with them, but he was shouted down. In the end, "wanting to gratify the crowd," Pilate pronounced the death sentence. He released Barabbas, then had Jesus scourged and delivered Him to be crucified.

Pilate failed in his leadership by doing the politically correct thing. This was a travesty of justice and one of the most wicked acts in human history. However, even in that very moment, Pilate was putty in the hands of God, a tool to bring about the redemption that God had ordained from all eternity.

55

ABUSE, MOCKERY, AND TORMENT

Mark 15:16–33

⧓

Then the soldiers led Him away into the hall called Praetorium, and they called together the whole garrison. And they clothed Him with purple; and they twisted a crown of thorns, put it on His head, and began to salute Him, "Hail, King of the Jews!" Then they struck Him on the head with a reed and spat on Him; and bowing the knee, they worshiped Him. And when they had mocked Him, they took the purple off Him, put His own clothes on Him, and led Him out to crucify Him. Then they compelled a certain man, Simon a Cyrenian, the father of Alexander and Rufus, as he was coming out of the country and passing by, to bear His cross. And they brought Him to the place Golgotha, which is translated, Place of a Skull. Then they gave Him wine mingled with myrrh to drink, but He did not take it. And when they crucified Him, they divided His garments, casting lots for them to determine what every man should take. Now it was the third hour, and they crucified Him. And the inscription of His accusation was written above: THE KING OF THE JEWS. With Him they also crucified two robbers, one on His right and the other on His left. So the Scripture was fulfilled which says, "And He was numbered with the transgressors." And those who passed by blasphemed Him, wagging their heads and saying, "Aha! You who destroy the temple and build it in three days, save Yourself, and come down from the cross!" Likewise the chief priests also, mocking among themselves with the scribes, said, "He saved others; Himself He cannot save. Let the Christ, the King of Israel, descend now from the cross, that we may see and believe." Even those who were crucified with Him reviled Him. Now when the sixth hour had come, there was darkness over the whole land until the ninth hour.

Once Pilate accepted the demand of the mob and delivered Jesus to be crucified, things turned ugly very quickly. Jesus was subjected to terrible abuse and mockery as His enemies gloated over Him.

Isaiah gave a prophetic preview of these things when he wrote of the Suffering Servant:

He is despised and rejected by men, a Man of sorrows and acquainted with grief. And we hid, as it were, our faces from Him; He was despised, and we did not esteem Him. Surely He has borne our griefs and carried our sorrows; yet we esteemed Him stricken, smitten by God, and afflicted. But He was wounded for our transgressions, He was bruised for our iniquities; the chastisement for our peace was upon Him, and by His stripes we are healed. All we like sheep have gone astray; we have turned, every one, to his own way; and the LORD has laid on Him the iniquity of us all. He was oppressed and He was afflicted, yet He opened not His mouth; He was led as a lamb to the slaughter, and as a sheep before its shearers is silent, so He opened not His mouth. (53:3–7)

Despite this prophecy, it is still difficult to read of the mistreatment the Lord of glory endured. He should have been honored and worshiped, but He was abused and mocked. However, Isaiah makes it clear that this suffering was not without purpose. Christ went through His passion to bear our griefs and sorrows. He was wounded for our transgressions, bruised for our iniquities. By His suffering and death, He atoned for the sins of His people.

In this chapter, I will consider the portion of Mark's crucifixion narrative to the point of Jesus' death. In the next chapter, I will examine His death and burial, and touch on the significance of the crucifixion.

Scourging and Mockery

We saw in the previous chapter that Pontius Pilate had Jesus scourged before he delivered Him to the soldiers to be crucified. Scourging was a terrible thing. The prisoner was tied to a post and his back was bared, then a guard began to lash the prisoner with a braided leather thong that had pieces of bone and metal inserted in the braids. The lashing literally ripped chunks of skin off the prisoner's body. The scourging was intended to humiliate the prisoner, but also to weaken him so that the crucifixion itself would not last too long. In many cases, a prisoner sentenced to crucifixion never made it past the scourging. This is what Jesus endured before He was handed over to the soldiers.

The soldiers were not content to simply carry out the crucifixion. Mark tells us: **Then the soldiers led Him away into the hall called Praetorium, and they called together the whole garrison. And they clothed Him with purple; and they twisted a crown of thorns, put it on His head, and began to salute Him, "Hail, King of the Jews!" Then they struck Him on the head with a reed and spat on Him; and bowing the knee, they worshiped Him. And when they had mocked Him, they took the purple off Him, put His own clothes on Him, and led Him out to crucify Him** (vv. 16–20).

The soldiers took Jesus to the Praetorium, which was probably a portion of Herod's palace, and they called together the whole garrison, which was one-tenth of a Roman legion, or six hundred soldiers. So, the mockery and mistreatment that was heaped on Jesus came not from a small group but from a large crowd.

The soldiers clothed Jesus with a purple garment, which was the clothing color reserved for royalty; they were mocking Him for claiming to be a King. They also made a makeshift crown of thorns from a plant that had exceedingly sharp thorns and pressed it on His head. They began to salute Him in a mocking way; just as the emperor was greeted by the words, "Hail, Caesar!" the soldiers saluted Jesus by saying, "Hail, King of the Jews." They struck Him on the head with a reed, they spat on Him, and they got down on their knees and feigned worship of Him. Finally, they had enough of their fun and led Him out to be crucified.

Mark gives us an interesting detail: **Then they compelled a certain man, Simon a Cyrenian, the father of Alexander and Rufus, as he was coming out of the country and passing by, to bear His cross** (v. 21). Simon of Cyrene happened to be passing by, and he was enlisted by the soldiers to carry Jesus' cross. Normally, the prisoner who was to be crucified was compelled to carry his own cross to the place of execution. In fact, it was not the full cross that was carried, but only the horizontal crossbeam, which was affixed to the vertical beam at the site of the crucifixion. In any case, it is clear that Jesus was so weakened from the scourging He had endured that He was not able to carry the crossbeam Himself, and so the soldiers enlisted Simon to help. However, they did not merely ask him to help. Mark tells us they "compelled" him to do it, and the language Mark uses speaks of the way in which animals were forced to go to their slaughter. Ironically, Jesus had told His disciples that they must take up their crosses and follow Him (8:34). Simon had to do that literally.

Mark also identified Simon as the father of Rufus. Paul sent greetings to a Rufus in the church at Rome (Rom. 16:13), which would have been in the middle of the decade of the 50s. Scholars largely agree that Mark mentioned Rufus because he was writing to the Christians at Rome, who would have known Rufus and his father, Simon of Cyrene.

The Crucifixion of the King

Mark continues, **And they brought Him to the place Golgotha, which is translated, Place of a Skull** (v. 22). The precise location of Golgotha is not known, but it was not far outside the walls of Jerusalem. The reason why it was known as "Place of a Skull" is also unclear; some have suggested it was on a rocky hill that had the appearance of a skull. At Golgotha, in preparation for the crucifixion, **they gave Him wine mingled with myrrh to drink, but He did not take it** (v. 23). The wine-myrrh mix was a narcotic that was given to condemned prisoners to dull their senses to the pain they were about to endure. It was one of the very few humane elements the Romans allowed. Jesus, however, did not take it. He willingly suffered the full measure of the torment of crucifixion. Mark also tells us, **they divided His garments, casting lots for them to determine what every man should take** (v. 24). This was prophesied in Psalm 22:18.

Finally, all the preparations were finished. Mark says, very simply, **Now it was the third hour, and they crucified Him** (v. 25). He provides no details about this grisly act itself, simply noting that it happened at the third hour, which was 9 a.m. Then it was that our Lord, already weakened from His terrible scourging, was nailed to a cruel cross and entered a whole new level of suffering for the sake of His people.

Mark writes, **And the inscription of His accusation was written above: THE KING OF THE JEWS** (v. 26). It was the custom of the Romans, when someone was crucified, to affix a statement of the charges against the condemned one on the vertical beam of the cross. John's gospel tells us that the inscription on Jesus' cross was provided by Pilate himself, and it was written in Hebrew, Greek, and Latin so that as many people as possible could read it (19:19–20). We have no evidence that Pilate believed the veracity of the inscription he wrote, and yet, he refused to alter it when the Jewish religious leaders asked him to change it to say, "He said, 'I am the King of the Jews'" (vv. 21–22).

Jesus was not the only man crucified that morning: **With Him they also crucified two robbers, one on His right and the other on His left. So the Scripture was fulfilled which says, "And He was numbered with the transgressors"** (vv. 27–28). Here, Mark points out how another aspect of the crucifixion fulfilled prophecy, specifically Isaiah 53:12.

Mark then tells us: **And those who passed by blasphemed Him, wagging their heads and saying, "Aha! You who destroy the temple and build it in three days, save Yourself, and come down from the cross!" Likewise the chief priests also, mocking among themselves with the scribes, said, "He saved others; Himself He cannot save. Let the Christ, the King of Israel, descend now from the cross, that we may see and believe." Even those who were crucified with Him reviled Him** (vv. 29–32).

Jesus had already endured the mockery of the soldiers. As He hung on the cross in agony, He had to endure taunts from others. First, various passers-by reviled Him over His statement, "Destroy this temple, and in three days I will raise it up" (John 2:19). They did not understand that He was talking not about the temple but about His body, and therefore was foretelling His resurrection after three days in the grave (vv. 21–22). Then the chief priests mocked Him for His apparent inability to save Himself from execution. But Jesus was not about saving Himself. He was about saving His people, which required that He stay on that cross until the bitter end. The priests urged Jesus to descend from the cross as a definitive sign of His identity. They had seen sign after sign, miracle after miracle, but they had not believed. Finally, Mark tells us that even the two robbers who were crucified with Him reviled Him. Thankfully we know from Luke's gospel that one of the robbers came to faith before he died that day (23:39–43).

Mark goes on, **Now when the sixth hour had come, there was darkness over the whole land until the ninth hour** (v. 33). From noon until 3 p.m., the heart of the day, the light of the sun was blotted out and darkness came over the land. In antiquity, people were often terrified when a solar eclipse occurred because they did not understand the reason for it. However, an eclipse lasted only for minutes, and the darkness was not deep. But when God brought darkness over Jerusalem, it lasted for hours, and it was thick and oppressive. We can only imagine how fearful the people were.

It was in this time that God turned away the light of His countenance, refusing for the first time to gaze on His Son as He carried the full measure of the pollution of our wickedness, an obscenity God is too holy to behold. At the climax of that period of darkness, Jesus cried in agony—not the agony of the scourging or the agony of the thorns and nails, but the agony of forsakenness.

This, then, is the terrible abuse and torment our Lord endured. Thankfully, God the Father delivered His beloved Son from His suffering when the moment was right.

56

JESUS' DEATH
AND BURIAL

Mark 15:34–47

～

And at the ninth hour Jesus cried out with a loud voice, saying, "Eloi, Eloi, lama sabachthani?" which is translated, "My God, My God, why have You forsaken Me?" Some of those who stood by, when they heard that, said, "Look, He is calling for Elijah!" Then someone ran and filled a sponge full of sour wine, put it on a reed, and offered it to Him to drink, saying, "Let Him alone; let us see if Elijah will come to take Him down." And Jesus cried out with a loud voice, and breathed His last. Then the veil of the temple was torn in two from top to bottom. So when the centurion, who stood opposite Him, saw that He cried out like this and breathed His last, he said, "Truly this Man was the Son of God!" There were also women looking on from afar, among whom were Mary Magdalene, Mary the mother of James the Less and of Joses, and Salome, who also followed Him and ministered to Him when He was in Galilee, and many other women who came up with Him to Jerusalem. Now when evening had come, because it was the Preparation Day, that is, the day before the Sabbath, Joseph of Arimathea, a prominent council member, who was himself waiting for the kingdom of God, coming and taking courage, went in to Pilate and asked for the body of Jesus. Pilate marveled that He was already dead; and summoning the centurion, he asked him if He had been dead for some time. So when he found out from the centurion, he granted the body to Joseph. Then he bought fine linen, took Him down, and wrapped Him in the linen. And he laid Him in a tomb which had been hewn out of the rock, and rolled a stone against the door of the tomb. And Mary Magdalene and Mary the mother of Joses observed where He was laid.

We come now in our study of Mark to the hour of Jesus' death, the moment for which He came into the world and for which He had set His face like flint so that He might obey the will of His Father. It is a terrible thing about which to read, and yet, it is the source of the great salvation enjoyed by those who put their faith in Him. On Good Friday, God wrought great good through the sin and evil of men.

Mark writes, **And at the ninth hour Jesus cried out with a loud voice, saying, "Eloi, Eloi, lama sabachthani?" which is translated, "My God, My God, why have You forsaken Me?"** (v. 34).

The eyewitnesses were not sure what Jesus had said. Mark tells us: **Some of those who stood by, when they heard that, said, "Look, He is calling for Elijah!" Then someone ran and filled a sponge full of sour wine, put it on a reed, and offered it to Him to drink, saying, "Let Him alone; let us see if Elijah will come to take Him down"** (vv. 35–36). So they waited, but no one came. **And Jesus cried out with a loud voice, and breathed His last** (v. 37).

The site of the crucifixion is traditionally associated with Mount Moriah, the place where Abraham was commanded to sacrifice his son Isaac. When Abraham obediently bound his son and raised the knife to plunge it into the heart of his son, an angel of God called to him at the last second, saying, "Do not lay your hand on the lad, or do anything to him; for now I know that you fear God, since you have not withheld your son, your only son, from Me" (Gen. 22:12). Then Abraham saw a ram caught in a thicket, and he offered the ram on the altar as a substitute for his son (v. 13). Hundreds of years later, on that same hill, God sacrificed His own Son, but no angel came to stop it. Jesus was sacrificed on the cross as the Substitute for the people of God.

Mark also reports two immediate outcomes of the death of Jesus: **Then the veil of the temple was torn in two from top to bottom** (v. 38). The veil separated fallen humanity from the sacred Holy of Holies in the temple. In effect, it separated men from God. It was a thick woven veil, but all three of the Synoptic Gospels report that at the moment Jesus died, it was suddenly torn from top to bottom, and that wall of separation was pierced.

Also, **when the centurion, who stood opposite Him, saw that He cried out like this and breathed His last, he said, "Truly this Man was the Son of God!"** (v. 39). The Romans customarily assigned four soldiers to guard prisoners during executions. These four were under the command of a centurion.

The centurion who was overseeing the men guarding Jesus saw something in the manner of Jesus' death that caused him to confess that Jesus was the Son of God. He appears to have been the first to realize that something of cosmic significance was happening that afternoon outside Jerusalem.

The Meaning of the Cross

With the possible exception of the centurion, I am convinced that those who witnessed the execution of Jesus did not understand what was going on. I simply do not believe that it was immediately transparent to any of the bystanders that what was taking place on Golgotha that day was anything more than an everyday occurrence. They only knew they were watching the execution of a human being at the hands of the Romans. Yet what was happening in that place at that time was nothing less than the most momentous cosmic event imaginable. The epistles of the New Testament, written under divine inspiration, give us the theological significance of this event—it was an atonement by which the wrath and justice of God were satisfied by a Substitute.

An atonement is "a reconciliation of alienated parties, the restoration of a broken relationship. It is accomplished by making amends, blotting out offenses, and giving satisfaction for wrongs done."[1] In short, man, because of his sin, is alienated from God and therefore under His judgment. But man is unable to make satisfaction for his sins. He needs someone to act as His Substitute, to suffer the wrath of God in his place.

Anselm of Canterbury (ca. 1033–1109) wrote a little book titled *Cur Deus Homo?* (*Why the God-Man?*) that explained why man could not make atonement for himself and why God had to come to earth in human form to stand in man's place under His own wrath. Only a man who was morally perfect, Anselm showed, was fit to be the Substitute. That is why Jesus was born and lived as a man before He went to the cross. He was the Lamb without blemish because He kept the law of God perfectly.

Orthodox Christianity has always taught that the atoning death of Jesus was absolutely necessary, that sinners could not be saved apart from it. Of course, those who are lost in their sins refuse to believe they need a Savior or an atonement. Sadly, many in the church have questioned the necessity of the atonement, too. In the early years of the church, the Pelagians taught that Jesus' death and atonement were not necessary at all, that God could have redeemed His people by waving His wand of mercy and grace, pronouncing pardon on sinners without putting His Son through a grisly execution. Others said that the cross was only

[1] "The Atonement," in *The Reformation Study Bible* (Lake Mary, Fla.: Ligonier Ministries, 2005), 1772.

hypothetically necessary; God could have saved man in numerous ways, but from all eternity He chose to reconcile the world to Himself by way of an atoning death. It was necessary only because an agreement had been reached between the Father and the Son; once that covenant was made, it had to be carried out.

I encountered this antipathy to the atonement in my first year of seminary. One day in my preaching class, a student gave a moving and eloquent sermon on the substitutionary satisfaction view of the atonement. In that class, when a student gave a sermon, it was customary for the professor to critique it. The expectation was that he would give constructive criticism, but that day the professor was furious. He glared at the student and said, "How dare you preach the substitutionary satisfaction view of the atonement in this day and age." That professor despised the idea that Jesus died as a Substitute, satisfying the wrath of God that was due to others.

I believe this attitude is possible only when man loses sight of the character of God. We tend to see Him as a celestial grandfather or a cosmic bellhop who is on duty twenty-four hours a day to supply all our needs and wants. We allow the love of God to swallow up His justice, His righteousness, and His holiness. We think not only that God will forgive all of our sins without an atonement, but that He must do it if He really is good and loving. That is our propensity. We exchange the God of heaven and earth for an idol. We fashion for ourselves a God who requires no satisfaction, who requires no payment for sin.

Let me simply remind you of the words of the Apostle Paul: "I determined not to know anything among you except Jesus Christ and Him crucified" (1 Cor. 2:2). Paul focused on the cross. All that he knew and all that he taught converged in the central message of what took place that day on the cross.

In a day and age when many preach that God loves all people unconditionally, who in the world needs an atonement? You do and I do. The justice of God had to be satisfied. By God's grace, when Jesus cried out, "It is finished!" (John 19:30), the atonement was complete and divine justice was satisfied.

The Women at the Cross

Mark also notes: **There were also women looking on from afar, among whom were Mary Magdalene, Mary the mother of James the Less and of Joses, and Salome, who also followed Him and ministered to Him when He was in Galilee, and many other women who came up with Him to Jerusalem** (vv. 40–41). I maintain that a person cannot be a loyal follower of Jesus from a distance, but I have to commend these women because they were there at Golgotha. The disciples had fled for their lives, but these women, who had been in Jesus' entourage during His earthly ministry, at least stayed close enough to be observers of His death. They had followed Jesus and ministered to Him during His ministry in Galilee, and they made the journey to Jerusalem with Him.

Mary Magdalene was one from whom Jesus cast out seven demons (Luke 8:2). Some believe she was a prostitute, but there is no biblical evidence for that notion. Even more gratuitous is the blasphemous idea that Jesus was married to Mary Magdalene or had some kind of love affair with her, the idea that is propagated in the novel *The Da Vinci Code* and the film of the same name. The Scriptures show she was a faithful follower of Christ, she was at the cross, and she was the first or one of the first to see Him in His resurrection. Mark also mentions another Mary, whom he identifies as "the mother of James the Less and of Joses." Mark has already informed us that Jesus had brothers named James and Joses (6:3), so many believe that this Mary was the mother of Jesus. It is not clear, however, why Mark does not identify her as such. We cannot be sure precisely who Salome was; this passage and Matthew 27:56 both mention Mary Magdalene and Mary the mother of James and Joses, but whereas Mark then mentions Salome, Matthew identifies the third woman as "the mother of Zebedee's sons." Thus, it is possible that Salome was the mother of James and John. Mark also tells us that there were many other women who had come from Galilee looking on with these three.

The Courage of Joseph

Mark writes: **Now when evening had come, because it was the Preparation Day, that is, the day before the Sabbath, Joseph of Arimathea, a prominent council member, who was himself waiting for the kingdom of God, coming and taking courage, went in to Pilate and asked for the body of Jesus** (vv. 42–43). We know that Jesus died at 3 p.m. on Friday. The Jewish Sabbath day begins at sundown on Friday; presumably, then, it was late afternoon when Joseph of Arimathea went to Pilate seeking permission to have the body of Jesus released into his care for burial. There was little time for His body to be removed from the cross and then to be given a proper burial.

Mark identifies Joseph as a prominent council member. The council of which Mark speaks could only be the Sanhedrin, the very council of the Jews that had turned Jesus over to Pilate and sought His execution. That indicates that not everyone who was on the council of Jewish leadership was opposed to Jesus; indeed, Luke tells us that Joseph "had not consented" to the council's decision on Jesus' fate (23:51). We also know that Nicodemus at one point questioned the Sanhedrin's procedures against Jesus (John 7:50) and that he helped Joseph prepare Jesus' body for burial (John 19:39). Joseph, Mark writes, was waiting for the coming of the kingdom of God, a strong indication that he was a believer in Jesus.

"Taking courage," he went to Pilate and asked for the body. It required courage to go to the man who had ordered the execution of Jesus as a criminal to ask permission for the body because the Romans usually did not release executed prisoners' bodies in that way. The bodies were not given to the families or even given perfunctory burials. Instead, they were deposited in Gehenna, the garbage dump outside Jerusalem, which Jesus used as a metaphor for hell (see chap. 31). Throwing a body into the dump was an indication of contempt. Sometimes, however, the Romans left the bodies on the crosses for a significant period of time, even until the bodies began to decay and decompose, as a warning to others who might be contemplating committing the same crimes. This was the way the Romans handled the bodies of those condemned to death.

The Hasty Burial

Mark goes on to say, **Pilate marveled that He was already dead; and summoning the centurion, he asked him if He had been dead for some time** (v. 44). When Joseph asked for Jesus' body, Pilate was very surprised to hear that He had died. It was not unusual for a crucified criminal to live for two or three days as he hung on the cross. Death was ultimately the cumulative effect of blood loss, dehydration, exposure, and hunger. Sometimes, to hasten the process, the Romans would break the legs of one they had crucified. When the victim could no longer push his hanging body up in order to breathe more freely, death came quickly by asphyxiation. Jesus was spared this indignity because He died before the Romans began to break the legs of the crucifixion victims that day (John 19:31–33).

Pilate, therefore, summoned the centurion who had been in charge of the detachment guarding Jesus, who confirmed that Jesus was dead. Mark writes, **when he found out from the centurion, he granted the body to Joseph** (v. 45).

Joseph, Mark tells us, **bought fine linen, took Him down, and wrapped Him in the linen. And he laid Him in a tomb which had been hewn out of the rock, and rolled a stone against the door of the tomb** (v. 46). He took great pains to give Jesus a proper burial. He wrapped Jesus' body in fine linen, then put it in a magnificent tomb that was carved into the rock. John tells us this tomb was in a garden close to Golgotha and that it was brand new (19:41). Matthew tells us the tomb belonged to Joseph himself (27:60).

The one thing Joseph was not able to do was to anoint the body properly with spices; he did not have time before sunset. That is what the women came to do on the morning after the Sabbath, as we will see in the next chapter. To this end, **Mary Magdalene and Mary the mother of Joses observed where He was laid** (v. 47).

57

THE RESURRECTION

Mark 16:1–8

❧

Now when the Sabbath was past, Mary Magdalene, Mary the mother of James, and Salome bought spices, that they might come and anoint Him. Very early in the morning, on the first day of the week, they came to the tomb when the sun had risen. And they said among themselves, "Who will roll away the stone from the door of the tomb for us?" But when they looked up, they saw that the stone had been rolled away—for it was very large. And entering the tomb, they saw a young man clothed in a long white robe sitting on the right side; and they were alarmed. But he said to them, "Do not be alarmed. You seek Jesus of Nazareth, who was crucified. He is risen! He is not here. See the place where they laid Him. But go, tell His disciples—and Peter—that He is going before you into Galilee; there you will see Him, as He said to you." So they went out quickly and fled from the tomb, for they trembled and were amazed. And they said nothing to anyone, for they were afraid.

In the day and age in which we live, the death of Jesus Christ on the cross is proclaimed from the pulpits of evangelical churches regularly. That is as it should be. However, it seems that Jesus' resurrection from the death He died on the cross is rarely addressed other than on Easter Sunday. This is strange given the fact that evangelicals gather for corporate worship on the first day of each week rather than the seventh because Jesus rose on Sunday, and so the Sabbath became the Lord's Day in Christian categories. Every Sunday is an implicit celebration of the resurrection of Christ, and we would do well to celebrate it more explicitly.

Mark begins his characteristically brief account of the resurrection with these words: **Now when the Sabbath was past, Mary Magdalene, Mary the mother of James, and Salome bought spices, that they might come and anoint Him. Very early in the morning, on the first day of the week, they came to the tomb when the sun had risen** (vv. 1–2). The weekly Sabbath of the Jews ended at sundown on Saturday. At that time, Mary Magdalene, Mary the mother of James and Joses, and Salome went to the market and purchased spices so that they might anoint Jesus' body. As we saw in the previous chapter, they did not have time to do that on Friday because the Sabbath observance was about to begin. It was important to them to anoint Jesus' body with myrrh, aloe, and other precious spices, for this custom was practiced not to preserve the corpse but to show respect and devotion to the departed loved one. These women, who had witnessed the crucifixion and burial of Jesus, were eager to show that devotion to their Lord.

In chapter 49, we looked at Mark's narrative of the anointing of Jesus at Bethany. We saw that a woman brought a flask of oil of spikenard and poured it on Jesus' head. When some criticized her for wasting the expensive oil, Jesus told them to be silent, saying, "She has come beforehand to anoint My body for burial" (14:3–9). That anointing was premature, but it was to be the only anointing His body would receive. Mary Magdalene, Mary, and Salome wanted to see His body properly anointed, but they were not to find a body in the tomb to anoint.

The Tomb Opened by God

Very early on Sunday morning, as soon as it was light, they set out for the tomb. As they made their way there, **they said among themselves, "Who will roll away the stone from the door of the tomb for us?"** (v. 3). As we have seen, Jesus was buried in a tomb that was hewn into a wall of rock. It was basically a cave. Such tombs were the customary form of burial among the Jews. They did not place bodies in coffins, then bury the coffins in the ground. Rather, they hollowed out caves in porous rock, with shelves or pedestals on which to lay the bodies. The entrances to most of these caves were covered by square stones to protect the tombs from graverobbers. However, a tomb of a wealthy family, such as that of Joseph of Arimathea, had a circular stone that stood against the entrance. The stone stood in a rut across the front of the tomb, so, with great effort, it could be rolled aside. The women, knowing they were not strong enough to roll the stone away from Jesus' tomb, were wondering who they could call on to help them. After all, it seems all the male disciples were still in hiding.

However, their problem was solved when they reached the tomb. Mark writes: **But when they looked up, they saw that the stone had been rolled away—for it was very large** (v. 4). They unexpectedly found the tomb open. Matthew tells us how it happened: "Behold, there was a great earthquake; for an angel of the Lord descended from heaven, and came and rolled back the stone from the door, and sat on it" (28:2). God Himself opened the tomb.

Mark then tells us, **And entering the tomb, they saw a young man clothed in a long white robe sitting on the right side; and they were alarmed** (v. 5). This language is clearly describing an angel. Mark mentions only that he was wearing a long white robe, but the other gospel writers are more descriptive. Matthew says, "His countenance was like lightning, and his clothing as white as snow" (28:3), while Luke speaks of "shining garments" (24:4). It was obvious to the women that this was a supernatural being.

Not surprisingly, they were frightened. The word that is translated as "alarmed" indicates profound fear and distress. It is the same word that is used to describe the inner conflict our Lord experienced in the garden of Gethsemane. Of course, any time an angel appears to someone in the biblical records, the initial response is terror at being in the presence of a being from the supernatural realm.

I have heard people argue that the New Testament cannot possibly be inspired or inerrant because the resurrection accounts disagree, and one of the chief disagreements that is cited is the number of angels who were present at the tomb. Matthew and Mark each mention one angel, while Luke and John speak of two. This is alleged to be a contradiction. I try to remind people of the elementary principles of logic. If two angels were present, and someone says there was an angel there, that is not a contradiction, because manifestly if there were two angels there, there had to be one angel there. If Mark had said, "There was one angel and only one angel," and the other biblical writers had said, "There were two angels," we would have a contradiction. But Mark only mentions what the women saw on the right side of the tomb, where they saw a young man in a flowing white robe.

Jesus Raised by God

Mark tells us: **But he said to them, "Do not be alarmed. You seek Jesus of Nazareth, who was crucified. He is risen! He is not here. See the place where they laid Him"** (v. 6). The angel told the women not to be afraid. Then came the most unexpected yet most fantastic announcement in the history of the world: "He is risen!" The angel was very clear that he was speaking of Jesus, for he identified Him as "Jesus of Nazareth, who was crucified." He was equally clear that the women were in the place where Jesus' body was placed, for he encouraged them to look at the very shelf where His body had lain.

I do have one quibble with the way many of our Bibles translate the angel's announcement, but I think it is an important quibble. In the original language, the text does not say, "He is risen!" In the Greek, the verb is in the passive form, and the text actually says, "He has been raised!" Saying "He is risen" suggests that Jesus came back to life on His own, but the biblical testimony is not that Jesus was able supernaturally to defeat the jaws of death and come out of the tomb; rather, it is that God raised Him from the dead. Just as God rolled away the stone, He raised Jesus from death. The resurrection is God's work through and through.

The angel continued: **"But go, tell His disciples—and Peter—that He is going before you into Galilee; there you will see Him, as He said to you"** (v. 7). The angel sent the women away with the happy news. They were to go to the disciples and tell them Jesus was alive and would meet them in Galilee, just as He had promised them (14:28).

It is very significant that Mark records the angel's particular instruction for the women to tell Peter. Peter was Mark's patron and source, and by mentioning him in this way, the angel showed definitively that Peter had not been rejected from future service in Christ's church because of his denial of Christ.

We know that Jesus appeared to the disciples before they left Jerusalem. Luke 24:36–49 tells of His surprise visit to them in the upper room. However, the Gospels also show us that He was with them for several weeks in Galilee. The last chapter of John includes poignant narratives about His appearance to them by the Sea of Galilee (21:1–14) and Peter's subsequent restoration (vv. 15–19).

Not surprisingly, the women **went out quickly and fled from the tomb, for they trembled and were amazed. And they said nothing to anyone, for they were afraid** (v. 8). What a mixture of emotions must have gripped them: fear, joy, shock, hope, astonishment, and more probably were all present. The other gospels tell us they went quickly to find the disciples, and when they found them, they told them what they had seen and heard. Thus, when Mark says "they said nothing to anyone," he apparently means they said nothing as they made their way to Peter and the others.

So the first word of the resurrection came to the disciples from these women, and our biblical records of what happened that morning are based on their reports. I think this is very significant. In the time of Jesus and the years immediately afterward, the Jews gave little credibility to the testimony of women in courts of law. They ranked the testimony of women with the testimony of

slaves and criminals. They did not think women could be trustworthy witnesses. In light of this bias, it is striking that the New Testament record of the
resurrection of Christ is heavily dependent on the testimony of women. It is
a certainty that if someone wanted to falsify the testimony of the resurrection
of Jesus, the last thing he would have done would have been to put the first
reports of the resurrection on the lips of women. But Mark is not interested in
the law courts. He is interested in truth and conveying exactly what happened,
and so he reports the testimony of the women down to the detail of where the
angel was standing.

It is crucial that we believe and trust these accounts, for Scripture says that
Jesus "was delivered up for our trespasses and raised for our justification" (Rom.
4:25, ESV). We have seen that on the cross our Savior satisfied the demands of
the righteousness of God. He remitted a payment for us vicariously. God did
not have to accept that payment, but when He raised Christ from the dead,
God declared to the whole world that our justification had been secured, for He
had accepted completely the atonement that Jesus had offered for His people.
The Father who sent Jesus to the cross also brought Him out of the grave for
our justification. By the power of God, Jesus is alive. By the grace of God in
Christ, so are we.

58

JESUS' FAREWELL

Mark 16:9–20

⸺◦⸺

Now when He rose early on the first day of the week, He appeared first to Mary Magdalene, out of whom He had cast seven demons. She went and told those who had been with Him, as they mourned and wept. And when they heard that He was alive and had been seen by her, they did not believe. After that, He appeared in another form to two of them as they walked and went into the country. And they went and told it to the rest, but they did not believe them either. Later He appeared to the eleven as they sat at the table; and He rebuked their unbelief and hardness of heart, because they did not believe those who had seen Him after He had risen. And He said to them, "Go into all the world and preach the gospel to every creature. He who believes and is baptized will be saved; but he who does not believe will be condemned. And these signs will follow those who believe: In My name they will cast out demons; they will speak with new tongues; they will take up serpents; and if they drink anything deadly, it will by no means hurt them; they will lay hands on the sick, and they will recover." So then, after the Lord had spoken to them, He was received up into heaven, and sat down at the right hand of God. And they went out and preached everywhere, the Lord working with them and confirming the word through the accompanying signs. Amen.

The late Dr. Roger Nicole was one of the great theologians of the twentieth century. He was a dedicated defender of the inspiration and inerrancy of the Bible. On one occasion, in the midst of a controversy over the reliability of the books of the Bible, he asked a searching question: If the building that houses the National Institute of Standards and Technology in Washington, D.C., were to burn down and the standard yardstick, the official measurement of a yard, were to be destroyed, would our understanding of the yard as a measurement of distance be lost? His answer was "no," for we would be able to use the myriad copies of the official yardstick that we have to reconstruct the official yard to within a tiny fraction of an inch of accuracy.

Through the centuries, the church has confessed her confidence that the Bible is inspired, inerrant, and infallible. However, that confession has always carried the qualifier that it was the *autographa*, the original manuscripts, that were inspired, inerrant, and infallible. The Protestant church has never argued for the inspiration of copies. The manuscripts of the biblical books were copied thousands of times, often by monks and scribes whose sole task was to carefully, assiduously, precisely copy the texts word for word. Even so, from time to time we find variations between copies. So, if we do not have the original manuscripts, only copies, and those copies do not all agree, why do we still speak of having an infallible Bible?

That is where Dr. Nicole's analogy of the yardstick comes in. The science of textual criticism, which is concerned with the reconstruction of the original documents, is one of the most exact, impressive sciences in the field of biblical studies. By closely examining the thousands of manuscripts that have been copied from the first century onward, textual critics have been able to reconstruct the original documents with a high degree of accuracy. Dr. Nicole's point was that even though the Bible we have today does not contain the original manuscripts that were written by the prophets, the Apostles, and other recipients of revelation, we can have confidence that what we have is very, very close to what the original authors wrote.

I provide all this background because one of the most difficult portions of all the New Testament in which to reconstruct the original content is the final chapter of Mark. The problem is the text we are considering in this chapter, which is known as the "long ending" of Mark (as opposed to the "short ending" that is included in some other early manuscripts).

When biblical scholars try to determine what was in the original manuscripts, they look at external information, such as quotations of the original text by first- and second-century church fathers, and then they consider internal matters, such as abrupt changes in style. It is the latter issue that leads to the questions about this passage. Specifically, verses 9–11 seem rather odd in light of verses 1–8. It seems Mark begins his resurrection morning narrative all over again, this time with only one woman present—Mary Magdalene.

So, this internal analysis, as well as manuscript evidence, leads scholars to conclude that the long ending of Mark was not in the original manuscript but was added to this gospel later in time by someone other than Mark. I agree with that conclusion.

If that is the case, why are these verses in our Bibles? The translators believe that even though the authenticity of this section is disputed, it provides a suitable conclusion to the gospel of Mark. If it were not part of the book, Mark's gospel would end with verse 8, which says: "So they went out quickly and fled from the tomb, for they trembled and were amazed. And they said nothing to anyone, for they were afraid." That terse conclusion would leave out information about the disciples' encounters with the risen Christ and about His ascension. It is believed that early in the second century, the Christian church wanted to give an appropriate conclusion to the abrupt ending of Mark, so this section was added based on what the Apostles recalled and the other gospel writers had said. In any case, the doctrines that are found in this passage are consistent with what is taught throughout the New Testament. Thus, we can read and study it with confidence and profit.

Resurrection Disbelief

In verses 9–13, Mark writes: **Now when He rose early on the first day of the week, He appeared first to Mary Magdalene, out of whom He had cast seven demons. She went and told those who had been with Him, as they mourned and wept. And when they heard that He was alive and had been seen by her, they did not believe. After that, He appeared in another form to two of them as they walked and went into the country. And they went and told it to the rest, but they did not believe them either.**

Mary Magdalene, Mark tells us, encountered Jesus (just as John says, 20:11–18), then went straight to the disciples, who were still mourning and weeping. However, the disciples did not believe her. Later, Jesus appeared to two disciples who were traveling to the country, a clear parallel to the account of the two men who met the risen Jesus on the road to Emmaus (Luke 24:13–35); they, too, reported Jesus' resurrection to the disciples, but still they did not believe.

Not surprisingly, Mark tells us, **He appeared to the eleven as they sat at the table; and He rebuked their unbelief and hardness of heart, because they did not believe those who had seen Him after He had risen** (v. 14). Jesus rebuked the disciples for not accepting the reports of His resurrection. Luke tells us that Jesus appeared to them in the evening of the day He rose (24:36–43). Even when He stood in their presence, they struggled to believe. At one point, Luke notes that "they still did not believe for joy" (v. 41). Aside from the fact that men simply do not come back to life, it was hard for the disciples to believe Jesus was alive because it was so wonderful.

This was the first of many interactions between Jesus and the disciples over several weeks. As we saw in the previous chapter, Jesus and His disciples traveled to Galilee. The Bible tells us that during this time He was seen alive by literally hundreds of people (1 Cor. 15:6).

Gospel Commission

Mark then writes: **And He said to them, "Go into all the world and preach the gospel to every creature. He who believes and is baptized will be saved; but he who does not believe will be condemned"** (vv. 15–16). Here we find Mark's version of the Great Commission, which is better known from Matthew 28:18–20. This is the mission Christ gave to His church. We are to preach the gospel. This good news has definite content, as we see from the apostolic record. The gospel is not that God loves us and has a wonderful plan for our lives. The gospel is not that if we come to Christ, we will have purpose in our lives. The gospel is not my personal testimony or yours. It has to do with the announcement of the person and the ministry of Jesus, and of how the benefits of His life and death can be appropriated by faith. According to our Lord's directive, this gospel is to be preached to every creature in all the world.

On the day you read these words, a new record will be set. More people will die on this day without hearing the gospel than on any previous day. This new record will break the record that was set one day ago. It will stand for only one day, for a new record will be set tomorrow. The population explosion of the world has made it more and more likely that someone will be born, live, and die without ever hearing of Jesus. It seems the church cannot keep up, but there is no choice but to continue to strive to get the message out. This was Jesus' last mandate. We must heed Him.

Jesus' statement that "He who believes and is baptized will be saved" is somewhat confusing. Some people conclude from it that baptism is necessary for salvation. Therefore, they infer that just as faith is a necessary condition for salvation, so is baptism. However, the rest of the New Testament makes it very clear that the only absolutely necessary condition for our salvation is faith, and that condition is sufficient. Anyone who truly puts his trust in Christ will be justified at that very second. Furthermore, we see examples in Scripture of people who were saved without being baptized, such as the thief on the cross (Luke 23:39–43).

Jesus added, "he who does not believe will be condemned." Notice the absence of the term *baptism* in that part of Jesus' statement. He did not say, in a parallel fashion, that anyone who is not baptized is condemned. However, faith *is* essential for salvation; therefore, the lack of it results in condemnation. Most Christians are familiar with John 3:16: "For God so loved the world that He gave His only begotten Son, that whoever believes in Him should not perish but have everlasting life." However, John 3:18 makes the opposite point: "He who believes in [Jesus] is not condemned; but he who does not believe is condemned already, because he has not believed in the name of the only begotten Son of God."

I stress this for this reason: Jesus did not come into a world of innocent people but a world in which every person was under the condemnation of God. Many people believe and teach that those who never hear of Jesus are not condemned because they cannot reject a Savior of whom they do not hear. But Jesus taught that all people, even those who never hear of Him, are in a state of condemnation because they have universally rejected the general revelation of God the Father, who has made Himself known to every creature (Rom. 1:18–21). Every human being has exchanged the knowledge of God for idols, exchanged the truth for a lie, and worships and serves created things rather than the Creator (vv. 22–25), for which reason all people are under God's righteous condemnation.

Accompanying Signs

Jesus concluded His final words to His disciples by saying: **"And these signs will follow those who believe: In My name they will cast out demons; they will speak with new tongues; they will take up serpents; and if they drink anything deadly, it will by no means hurt them; they will lay hands on the sick, and they will recover"** (vv. 17–18). Jesus here listed a number of signs that He said would "follow" (that is, be characteristic of) those who have faith in Him. Let us consider these one by one. First, "they will cast out demons." The Apostles certainly delivered people from demonic possession, as we see in the book of Acts (5:16; 8:7; 16:18; 19:12). Second, "they will speak with new tongues." This sign also appeared during the apostolic era (Acts 2:4, 11; 10:46; 19:6). Third, "they will take up serpents." Paul was bitten by a viper but was not affected (Acts 28:3–5).

Of course, this verse is used as the proof text for snake-handling cults. These groups believe it is a crucial article of the Christian faith to prove one's faith by handling poisonous snakes. The idea is that if they have the proper amount of faith, they will be able to handle such snakes and will not be fatally wounded. Some of them become very proficient at handling snakes without irritating them, so they can successfully pick up deadly snakes without harm. Yet, we regularly read of people in snake-handling cults being bitten and suffering the effects of the venom. These words from the lips of Jesus were not intended to establish a test of faith.

Fourth, "if they drink anything deadly, it will by no means hurt them." We have no biblical record of anyone drinking poison and surviving. However, there is a testimony from early church history of one Christian who, during a time of persecution, was forced to drink poison and survived the experience without becoming ill. Fifth, "they will lay hands on the sick, and they will recover." This sign was common in the apostolic era (Acts 3:1–8; 5:16; 8:7; 9:32–34; 14:8–10; 19:12).

So, we can conclude that these signs were present during the era of the Apostles, but it is not clear that these things should be considered normative for the church of all ages.

Ascension and Session

Mark then writes, **So then, after the Lord had spoken to them, He was received up into heaven, and sat down at the right hand of God** (v. 19). Two of the most important events in the ministry of our Lord are covered in this short sentence. First, Mark recounts the ascension of Jesus. After several weeks of interactions with His disciples, Jesus was taken up to heaven for His coronation, fulfilling a prophecy of Daniel:

> "I was watching in the night visions, and behold, One like the Son of Man, coming with the clouds of heaven! He came to the Ancient of Days, and they brought Him near before Him. Then to Him was given dominion and glory and a kingdom, that all peoples, nations, and languages should serve Him. His dominion is an everlasting dominion, which shall not pass away, and His kingdom the one which shall not be destroyed." (Dan. 7:13–14)

Second, we see the session of Jesus, His reign in power at the right hand of the Father, which we examined in some detail in chapter 44. This ministry flows out of His ascension and coronation. He is reigning as King of kings and Lord of lords, governing every event in this world, so that there are no maverick molecules.

Finally, Mark relates: **And they went out and preached everywhere, the Lord working with them and confirming the word through the accompanying signs. Amen** (v. 20). As soon as Jesus left this world, the Apostles took up their assigned ministry, preaching the gospel everywhere. Yet, Mark declares that Jesus worked with them. When our Lord announced His imminent departure to His disciples, He said, "A little while longer and the world will see Me no more" (John 14:19a). However, He also said, "I am with you always, even to the end of the age" (Matt. 28:20b). Concerning His human nature, Jesus is no longer present with us. Concerning His divine nature, He is never absent from us. So, the task Jesus gave to the church is not a task the church must accomplish by its effort alone. It is carried out with the help of the Lord who works with His people, who goes before His people. We go out, only to find that He is already there. He does not follow the ministry of the church. He leads the ministry of the church.

When Mark speaks of Jesus "confirming the word through the accompanying signs," he is speaking of miracles and the purpose of miracles. Miracles were given to the apostolic church essentially to confirm the truth proclaimed by the apostolic testimony. This followed the pattern of the Old Testament, when agents of revelation were demonstrated to be messengers from God by the miracles they performed. People sometimes say, "I will believe in God if I see a miracle." However, no one can define a miracle as a miracle until he first acknowledges there is a God, because a miracle by definition is something that only God can do.

Finally, Mark ends with a single word: "Amen." As we saw in chapter 10, this little word simply means "this is the truth." Luke says he writes so that Theophilus might know "the certainty of those things in which you were instructed" (1:4). John says, "This is the disciple who testifies of these things, and wrote these things; and we know that his testimony is true" (21:24). Mark takes a simpler approach, simply saying, "Amen," but equally affirming that the things he has written of Jesus are true. We do well to believe his testimony.

INDEX OF NAMES

ABOUT THE AUTHOR

Dr. R.C. Sproul was founder of Ligonier Ministries, founding pastor of Saint Andrew's Chapel in Sanford, Fla., first president of Reformation Bible College, and executive editor of *Tabletalk* magazine. His radio program, *Renewing Your Mind,* is still broadcast daily on hundreds of radio stations around the world and can also be heard online. He was author of more than one hundred books, including *The Holiness of God, Chosen by God,* and *Everyone's a Theologian.* He was recognized throughout the world for his articulate defense of the inerrancy of Scripture and the need for God's people to stand with conviction upon His Word.